The fire that drips from fangs does not fade
The blade burns away the field
Revealing my hidden friend

BLEACH 73 | BATTLE FIELD BURNING

ALL STARS ★ AND

アスキン・
ナックルヴァール

ASKIN
NAKK LE VAAR

KISUKE
URAHARA

浦原喜助
ウラハラキスケ

黒崎一護
クロサキイチゴ

ICHIGO
KUROSAKI

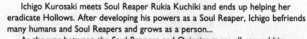

★ **plot**

Ichigo Kurosaki meets Soul Reaper Rukia Kuchiki and ends up helping her eradicate Hollows. After developing his powers as a Soul Reaper, Ichigo befriends many humans and Soul Reapers and grows as a person...

As the war between the Soul Reapers and Quincies rages all around him, Ichigo reaches the enemy base, Wahrwelt. There he runs into Uryu, who reveals he has a plan to destroy the Quincy castle all by himself. Ichigo is reassured by his friend's intentions, but Haschwalth soon appears. Uryu then stays behind to fight while Ichigo heads to the top of the castle. Meanwhile, Urahara finds himself in a tough battle against Nakk Le Vaar.

BLEACH

YHWACH

ユーハバッハ

ジェラルド・ヴァルキリー

GERARD VALKYRIE

TOSHIRO HITSUGAYA

日番谷冬獅郎
ヒツガヤトウシロウ

STORIES

BLEACH 73

BATTLEFIELD BURNING

CONTENTS

664. THE GIFT —————————————7
665. THE PRINCESS DISSECTION ——————25
666. EMPTY, PUPPET, TEMPLE ——————43
667. BIGGER, LOUDER, STRONGER ————61
668. BIGGER, FASTER, STRONGER ————79
669. BLADE II ——————————————97
670. THE PERFECT CRIMSON ——————115
671. THE PERFECT CRIMSON 2 —————133
672. SON OF DARKNESS ————————151
673. FATHER ————————————169
674. FATHER 2 ————————————187

664. THE GIFT

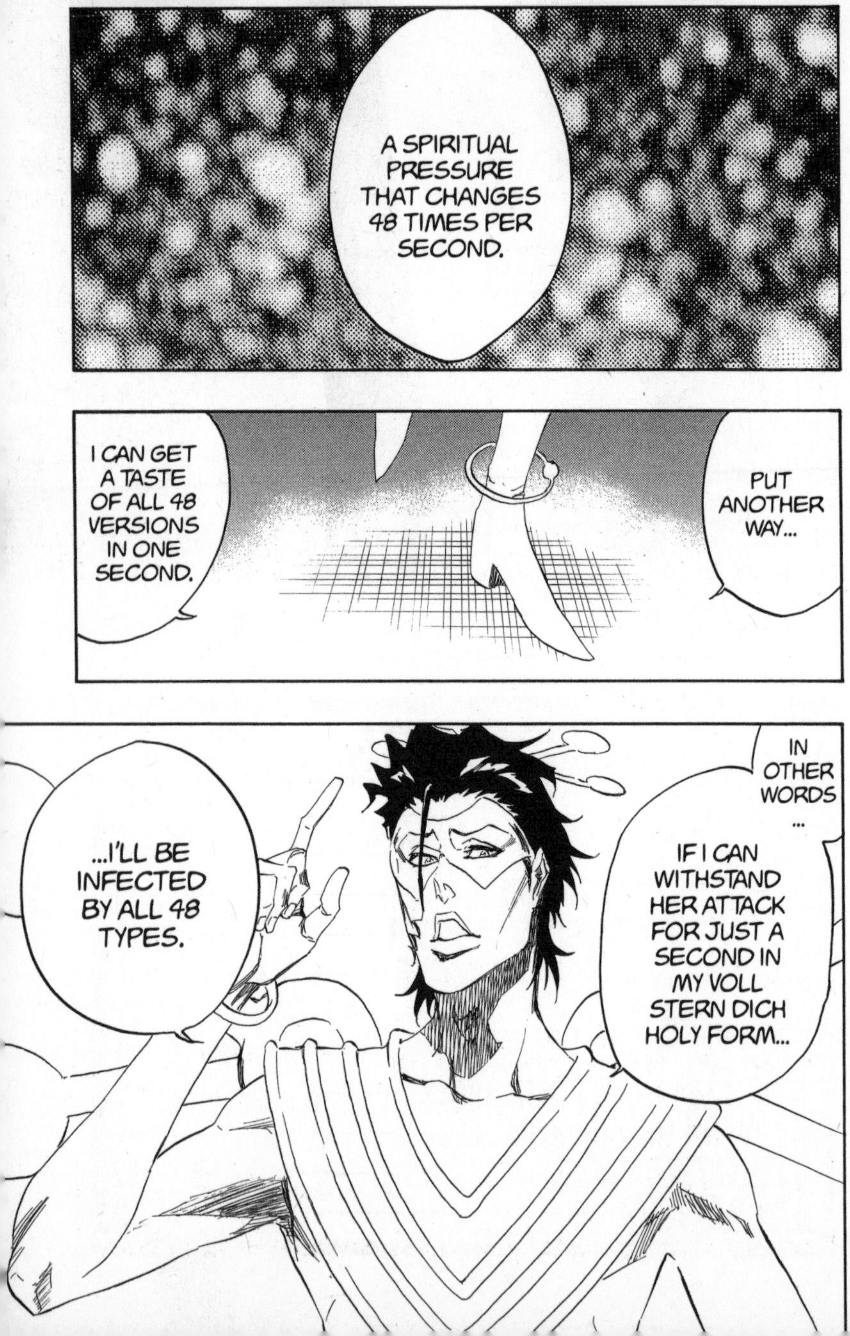
A SPIRITUAL PRESSURE THAT CHANGES 48 TIMES PER SECOND.
PUT ANOTHER WAY...
I CAN GET A TASTE OF ALL 48 VERSIONS IN ONE SECOND.
IN OTHER WORDS...
IF I CAN WITHSTAND HER ATTACK FOR JUST A SECOND IN MY VOLL STERN DICH HOLY FORM...
...I'LL BE INFECTED BY ALL 48 TYPES.

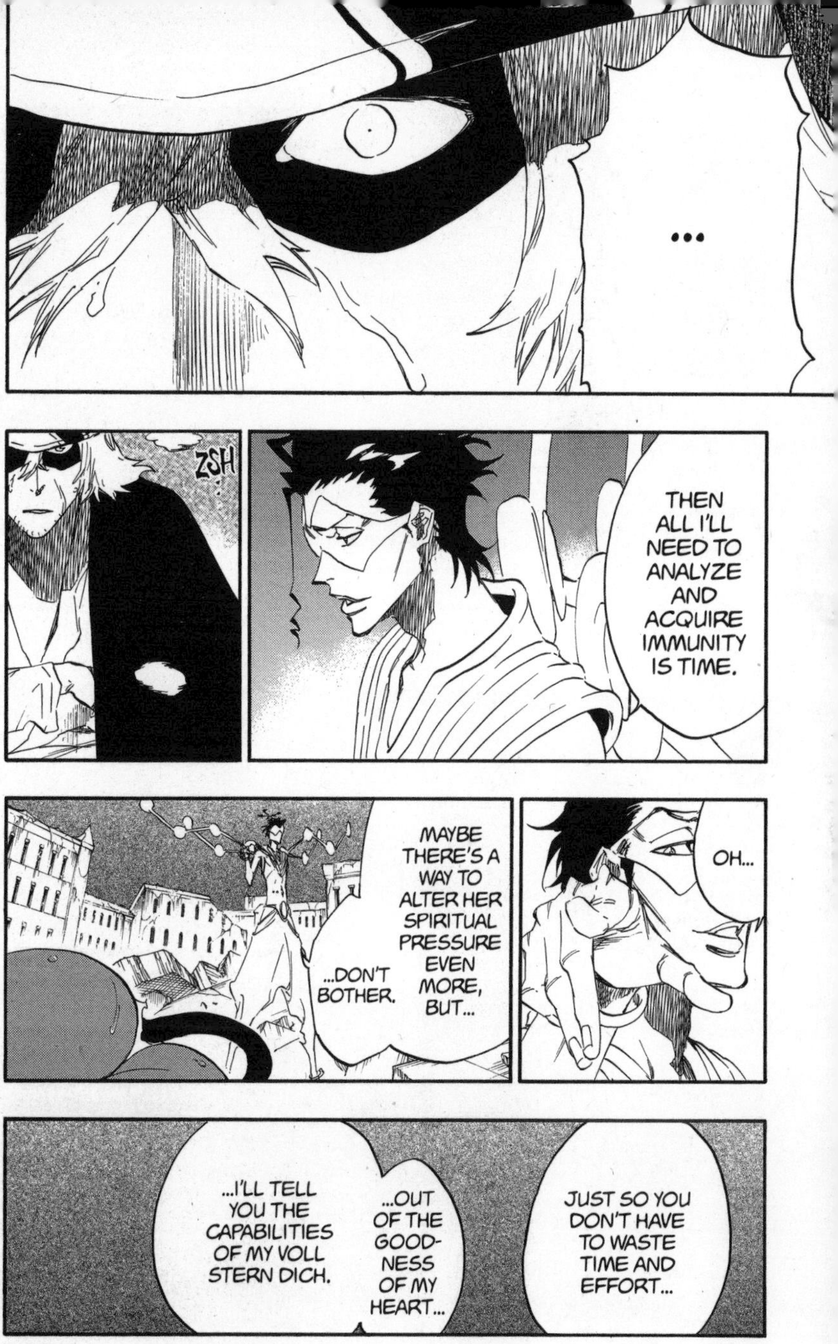
...
THEN ALL I'LL NEED TO ANALYZE AND ACQUIRE IMMUNITY IS TIME.
ZSH
OH...
MAYBE THERE'S A WAY TO ALTER HER SPIRITUAL PRESSURE EVEN MORE, BUT...
...DON'T BOTHER.
JUST SO YOU DON'T HAVE TO WASTE TIME AND EFFORT...
...OUT OF THE GOODNESS OF MY HEART...
...I'LL TELL YOU THE CAPABILITIES OF MY VOLL STERN DICH.

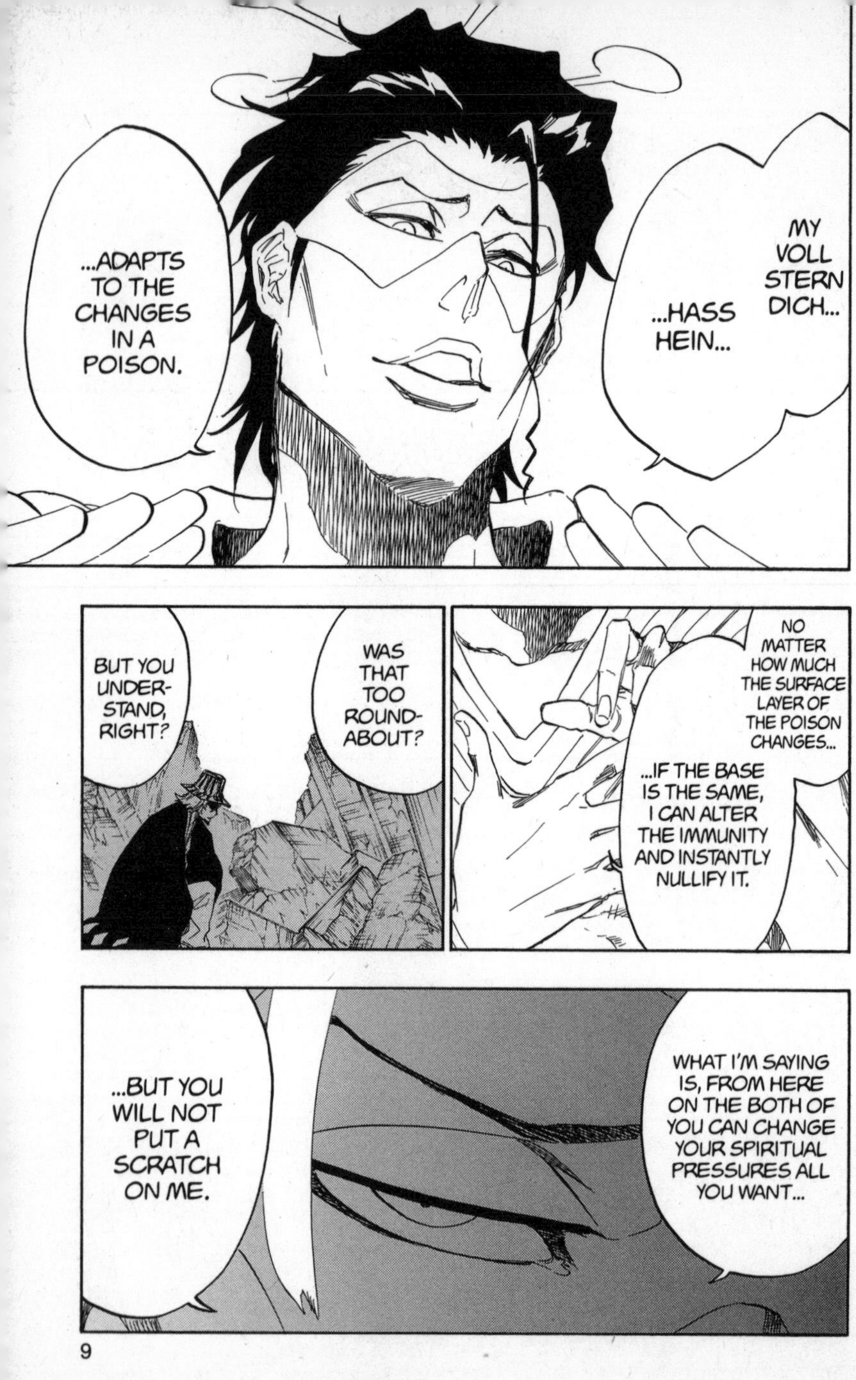
MY VOLL STERN DICH...
...HASS HEIN...
...ADAPTS TO THE CHANGES IN A POISON.
NO MATTER HOW MUCH THE SURFACE LAYER OF THE POISON CHANGES...
...IF THE BASE IS THE SAME, I CAN ALTER THE IMMUNITY AND INSTANTLY NULLIFY IT.
WAS THAT TOO ROUND-ABOUT?
BUT YOU UNDER-STAND, RIGHT?
WHAT I'M SAYING IS, FROM HERE ON THE BOTH OF YOU CAN CHANGE YOUR SPIRITUAL PRESSURES ALL YOU WANT...
...BUT YOU WILL NOT PUT A SCRATCH ON ME.

WHAT'RE YOU GONNA DO, KISUKE URAHARA?

SO?

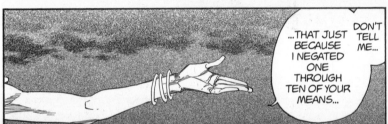

...THAT JUST BECAUSE I NEGATED ONE THROUGH TEN OF YOUR MEANS...

DON'T TELL ME...

664.

BLEACH

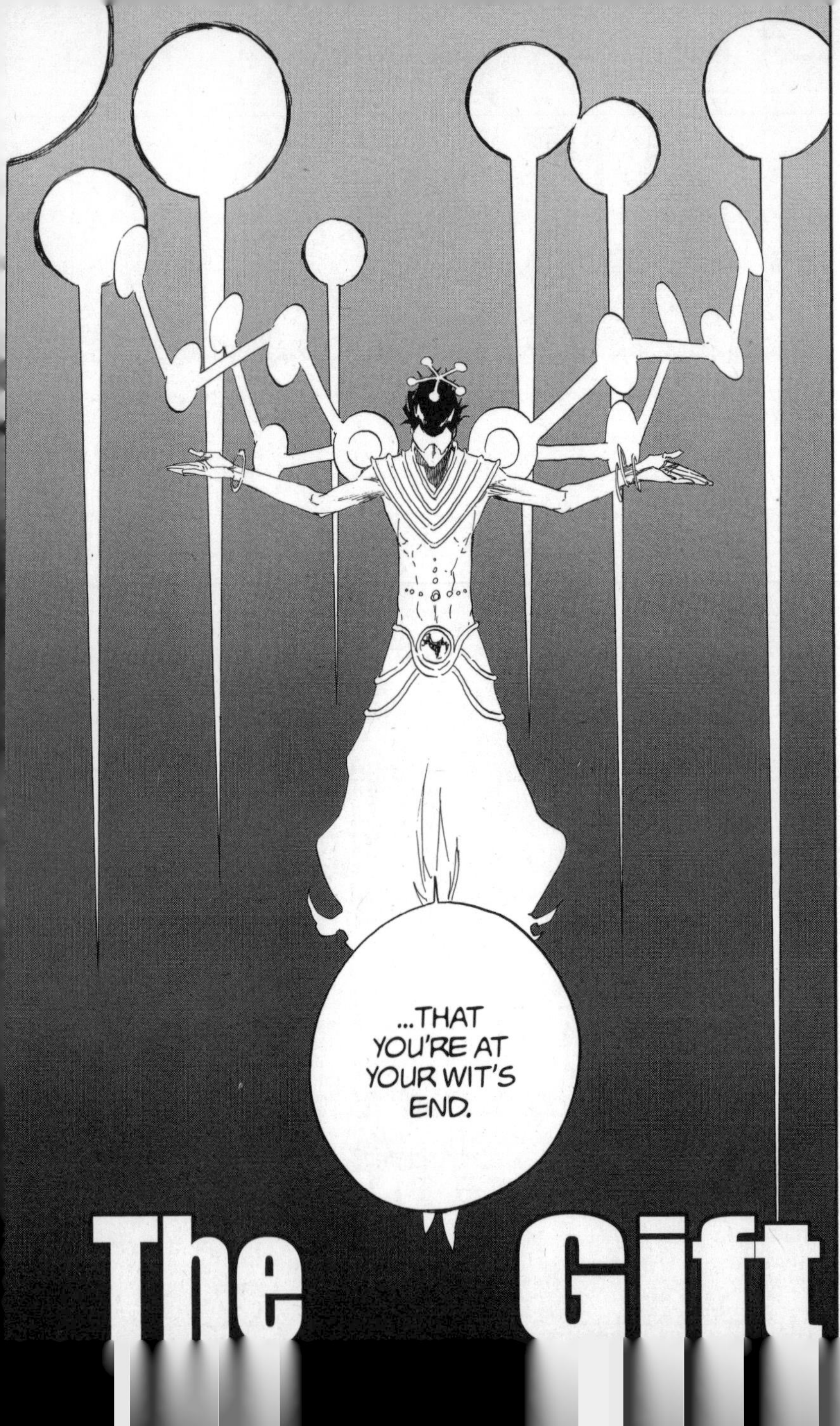
...THAT YOU'RE AT YOUR WIT'S END.
The Gift

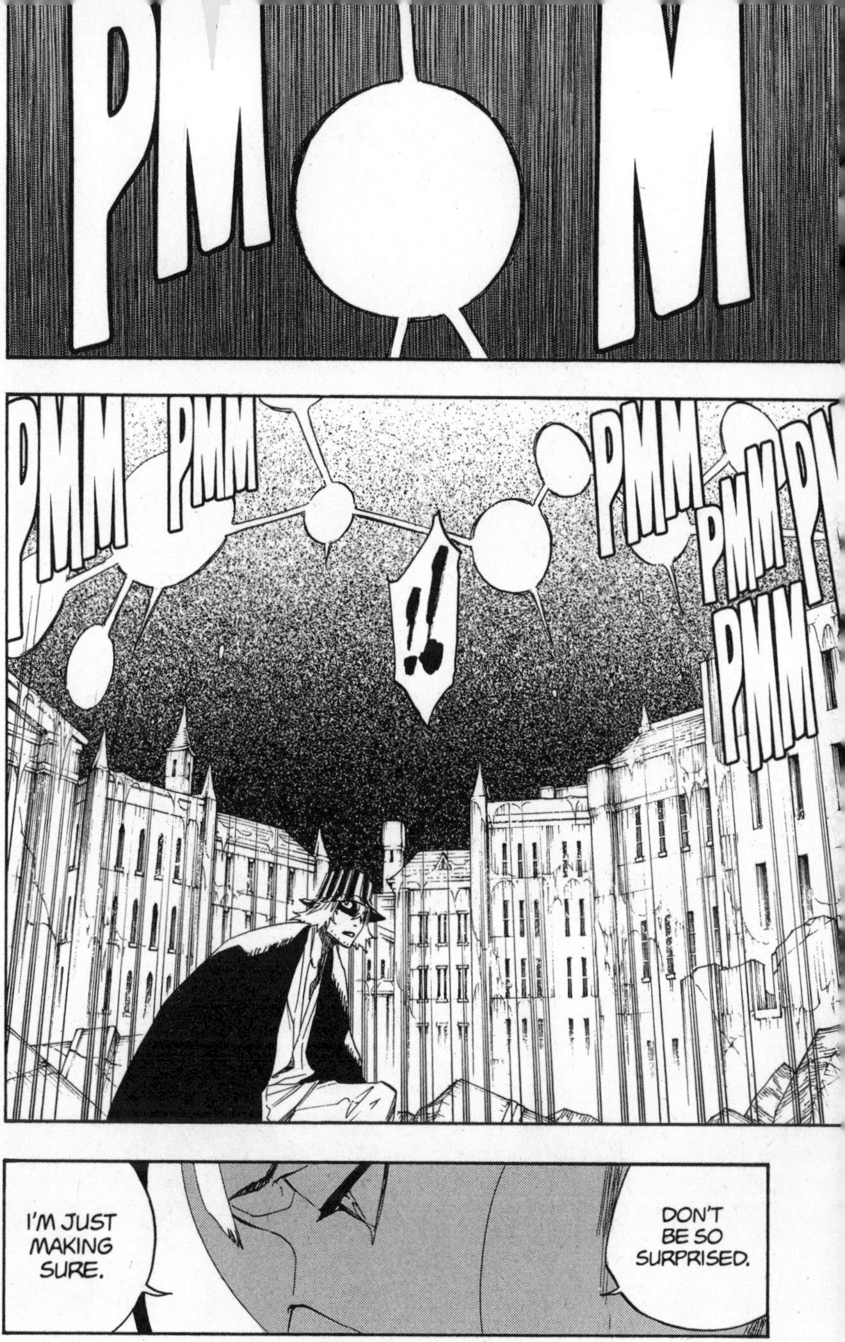
PMM
PMM
PMM
PMM
PMM
PMM
PMM
!!
DON'T BE SO SURPRISED.
I'M JUST MAKING SURE.

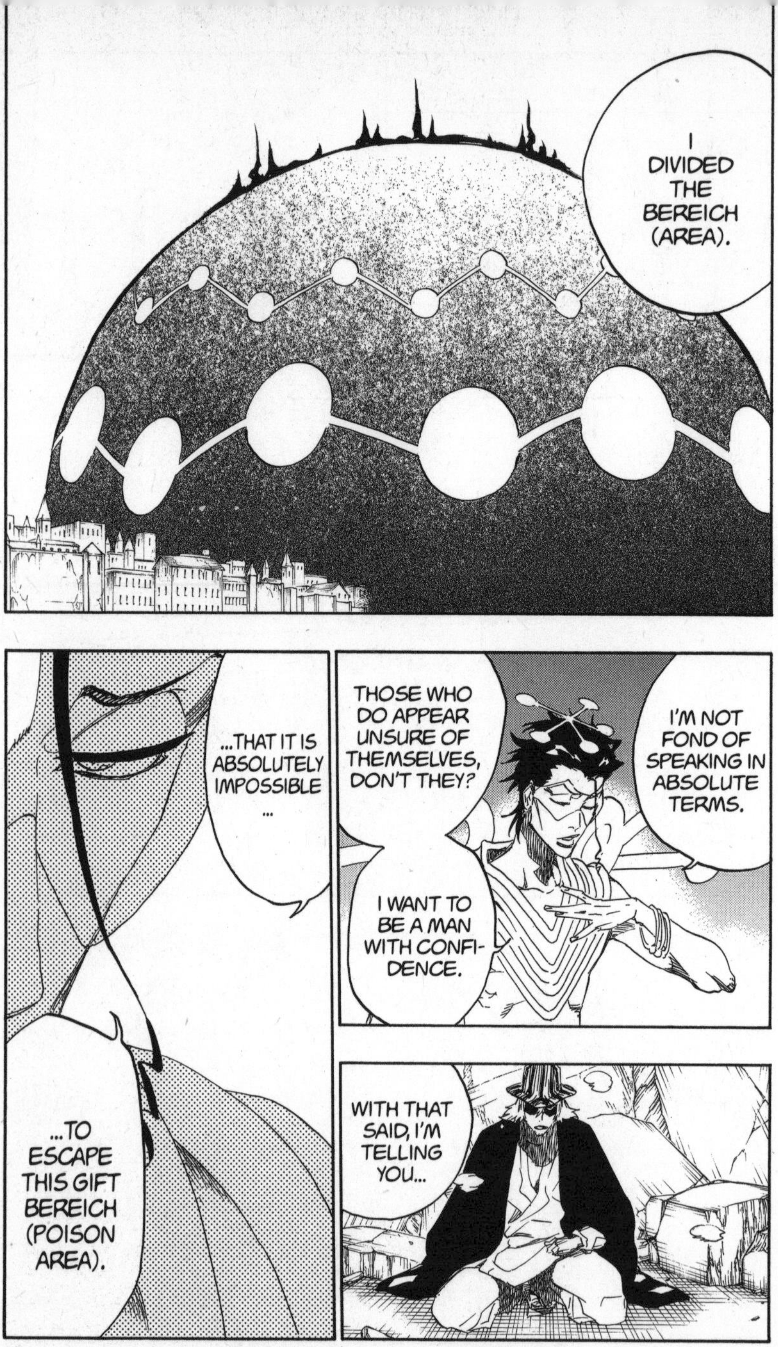
I DIVIDED THE BEREICH (AREA).
I'M NOT FOND OF SPEAKING IN ABSOLUTE TERMS.
THOSE WHO DO APPEAR UNSURE OF THEMSELVES, DON'T THEY?
I WANT TO BE A MAN WITH CONFI-DENCE.
WITH THAT SAID, I'M TELLING YOU...
...THAT IT IS ABSOLUTELY IMPOSSIBLE...
...TO ESCAPE THIS GIFT BEREICH (POISON AREA).

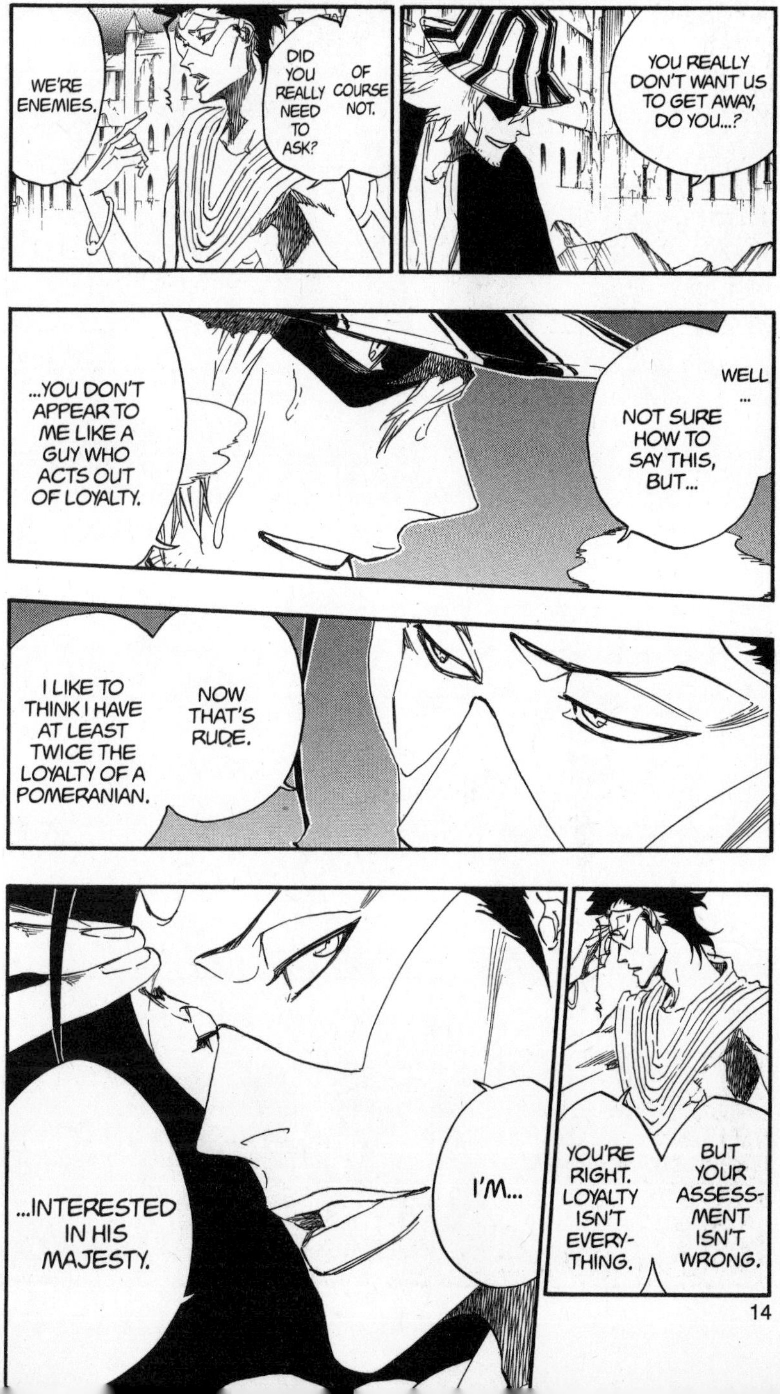
YOU REALLY DON'T WANT US TO GET AWAY, DO YOU...?
OF COURSE NOT.
DID YOU REALLY NEED TO ASK?
WE'RE ENEMIES.
WELL...
NOT SURE HOW TO SAY THIS, BUT...
...YOU DON'T APPEAR TO ME LIKE A GUY WHO ACTS OUT OF LOYALTY.
NOW THAT'S RUDE.
I LIKE TO THINK I HAVE AT LEAST TWICE THE LOYALTY OF A POMERANIAN.
BUT YOUR ASSESSMENT ISN'T WRONG.
YOU'RE RIGHT. LOYALTY ISN'T EVERYTHING.
I'M...
...INTERESTED IN HIS MAJESTY.

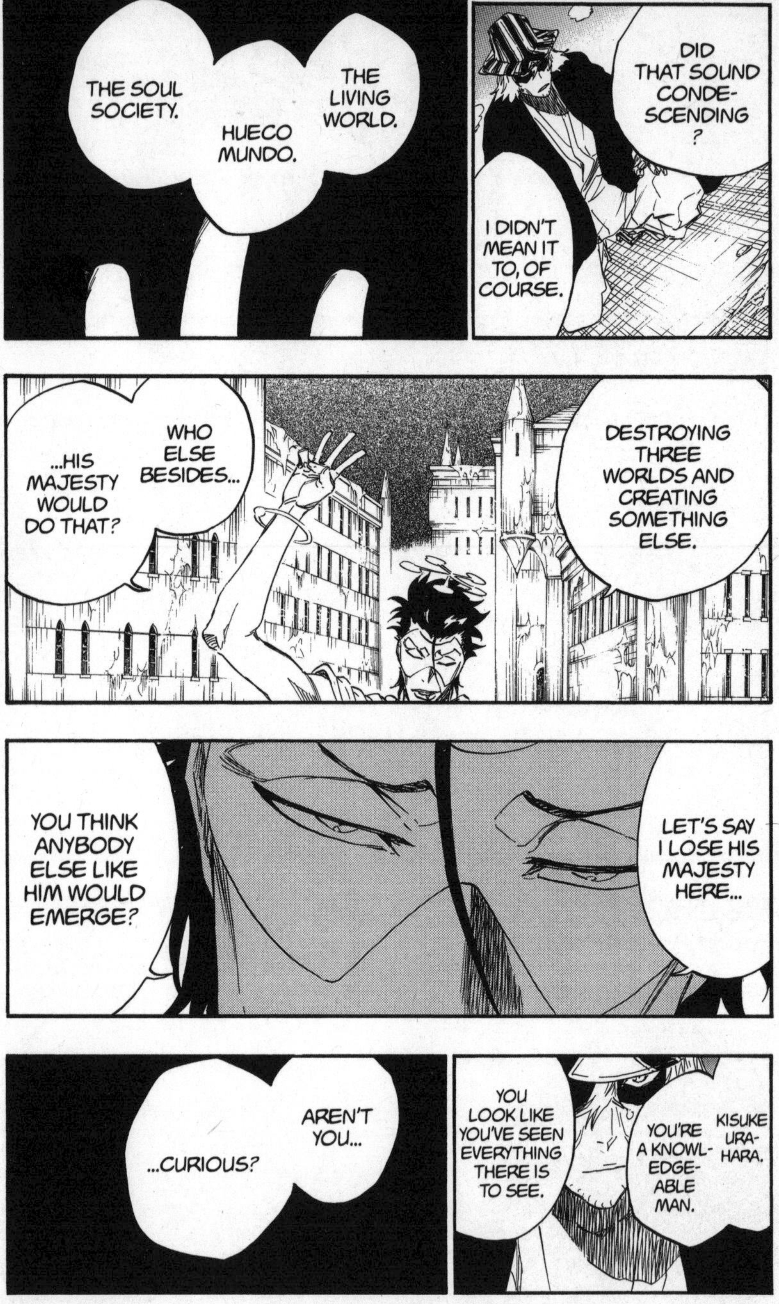
DID THAT SOUND CONDESCENDING?
I DIDN'T MEAN IT TO, OF COURSE.
THE LIVING WORLD.
HUECO MUNDO.
THE SOUL SOCIETY.
DESTROYING THREE WORLDS AND CREATING SOMETHING ELSE.
WHO ELSE BESIDES...
...HIS MAJESTY WOULD DO THAT?
LET'S SAY I LOSE HIS MAJESTY HERE...
YOU THINK ANYBODY ELSE LIKE HIM WOULD EMERGE?
KISUKE URAHARA.
YOU'RE A KNOWLEDGEABLE MAN.
YOU LOOK LIKE YOU'VE SEEN EVERYTHING THERE IS TO SEE.
AREN'T YOU...
...CURIOUS?

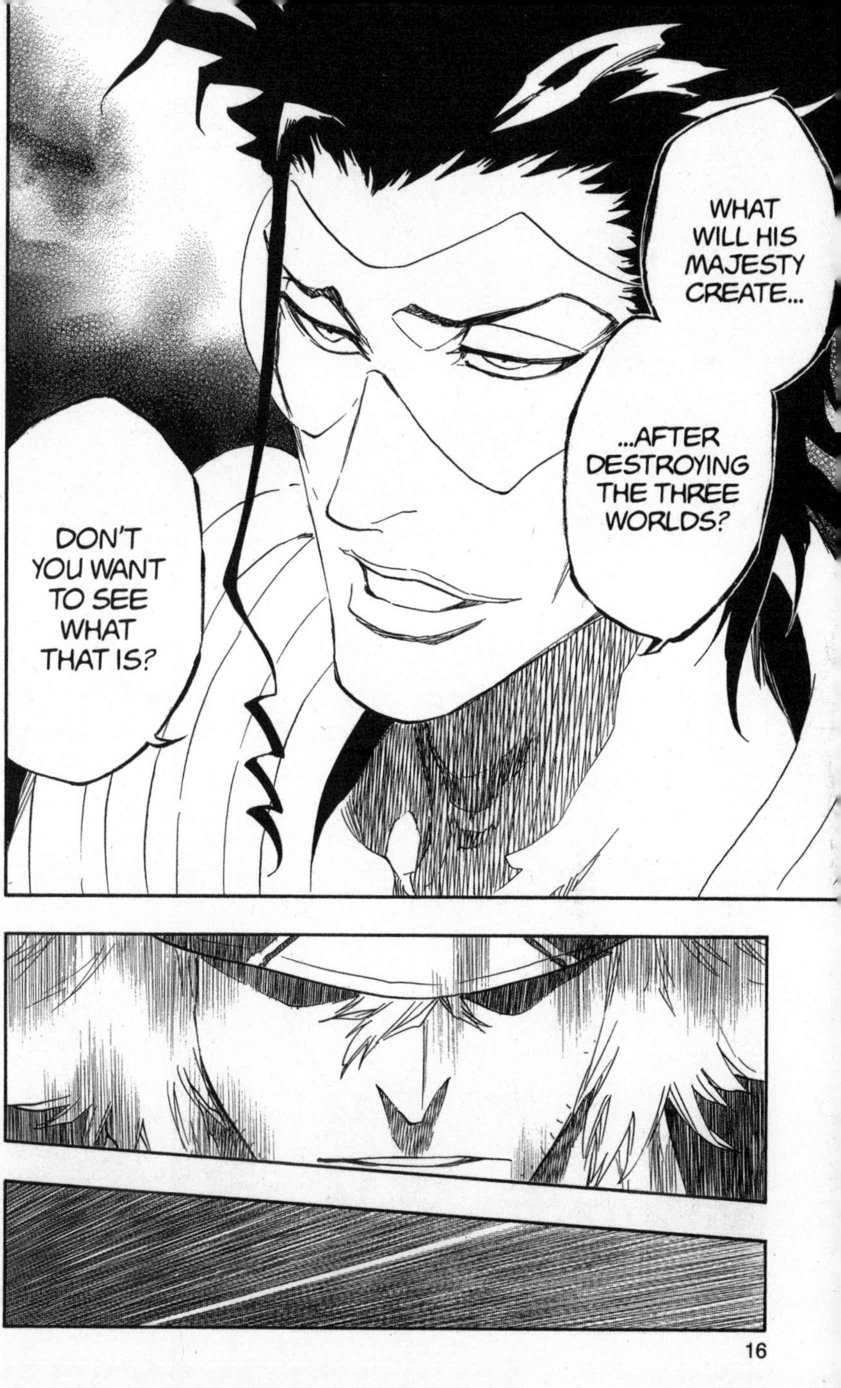
WHAT WILL HIS MAJESTY CREATE...
...AFTER DESTROYING THE THREE WORLDS?
DON'T YOU WANT TO SEE WHAT THAT IS?

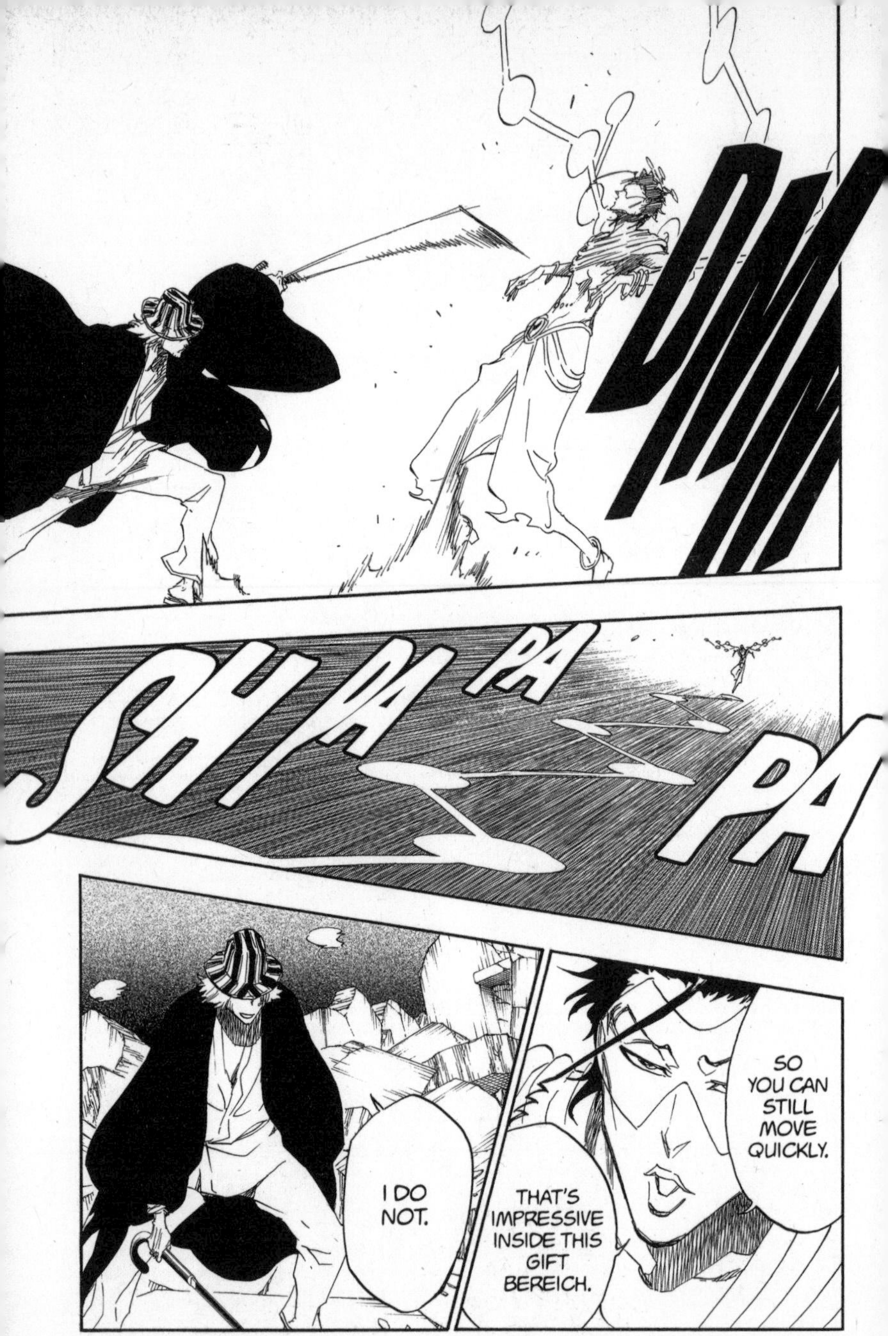
DWN
SHIPA PA PA
SO YOU CAN STILL MOVE QUICKLY.
THAT'S IMPRESSIVE INSIDE THIS GIFT BEREICH.
I DO NOT.

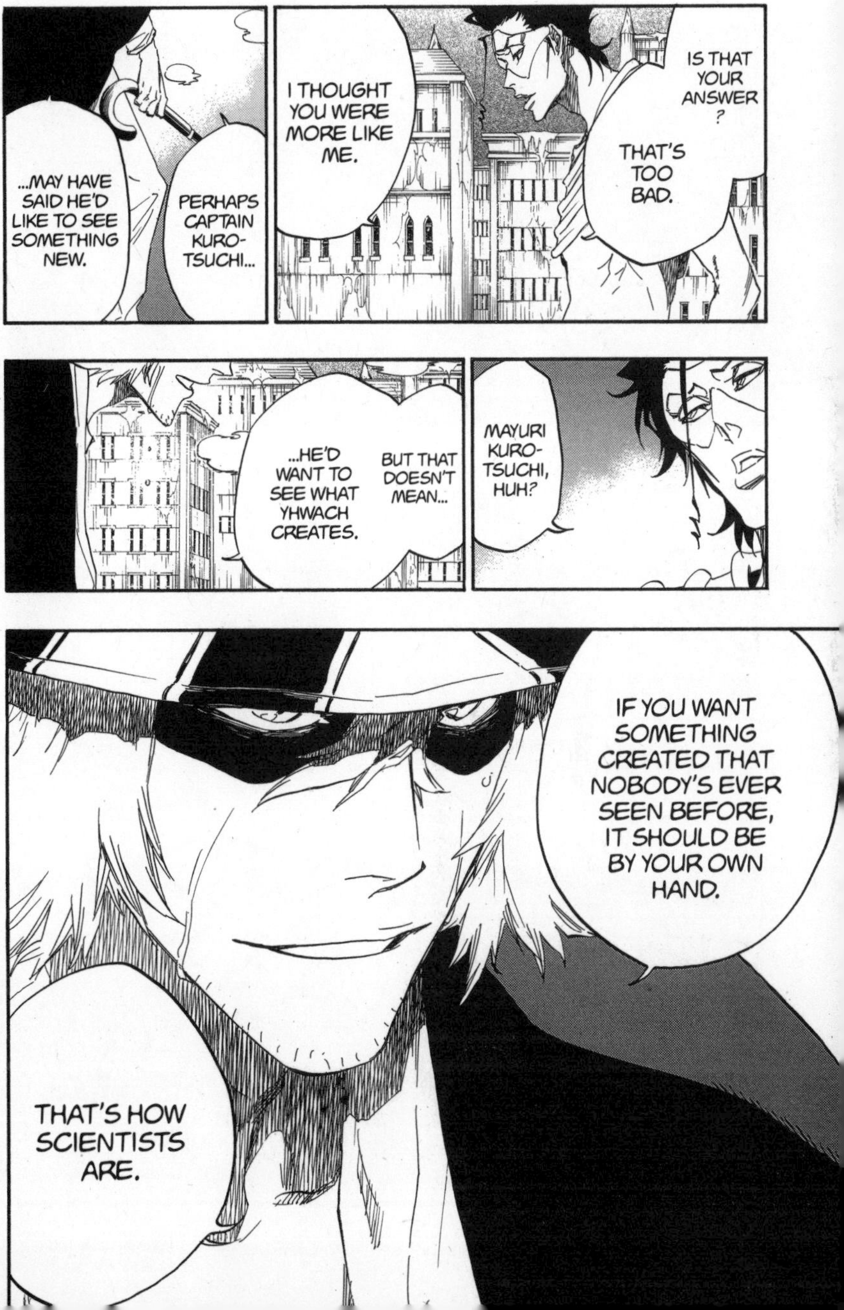
IS THAT YOUR ANSWER?
THAT'S TOO BAD.
I THOUGHT YOU WERE MORE LIKE ME.
PERHAPS CAPTAIN KURO-TSUCHI...
...MAY HAVE SAID HE'D LIKE TO SEE SOMETHING NEW.
MAYURI KURO-TSUCHI, HUH?
BUT THAT DOESN'T MEAN...
...HE'D WANT TO SEE WHAT YHWACH CREATES.
IF YOU WANT SOMETHING CREATED THAT NOBODY'S EVER SEEN BEFORE, IT SHOULD BE BY YOUR OWN HAND.
THAT'S HOW SCIENTISTS ARE.

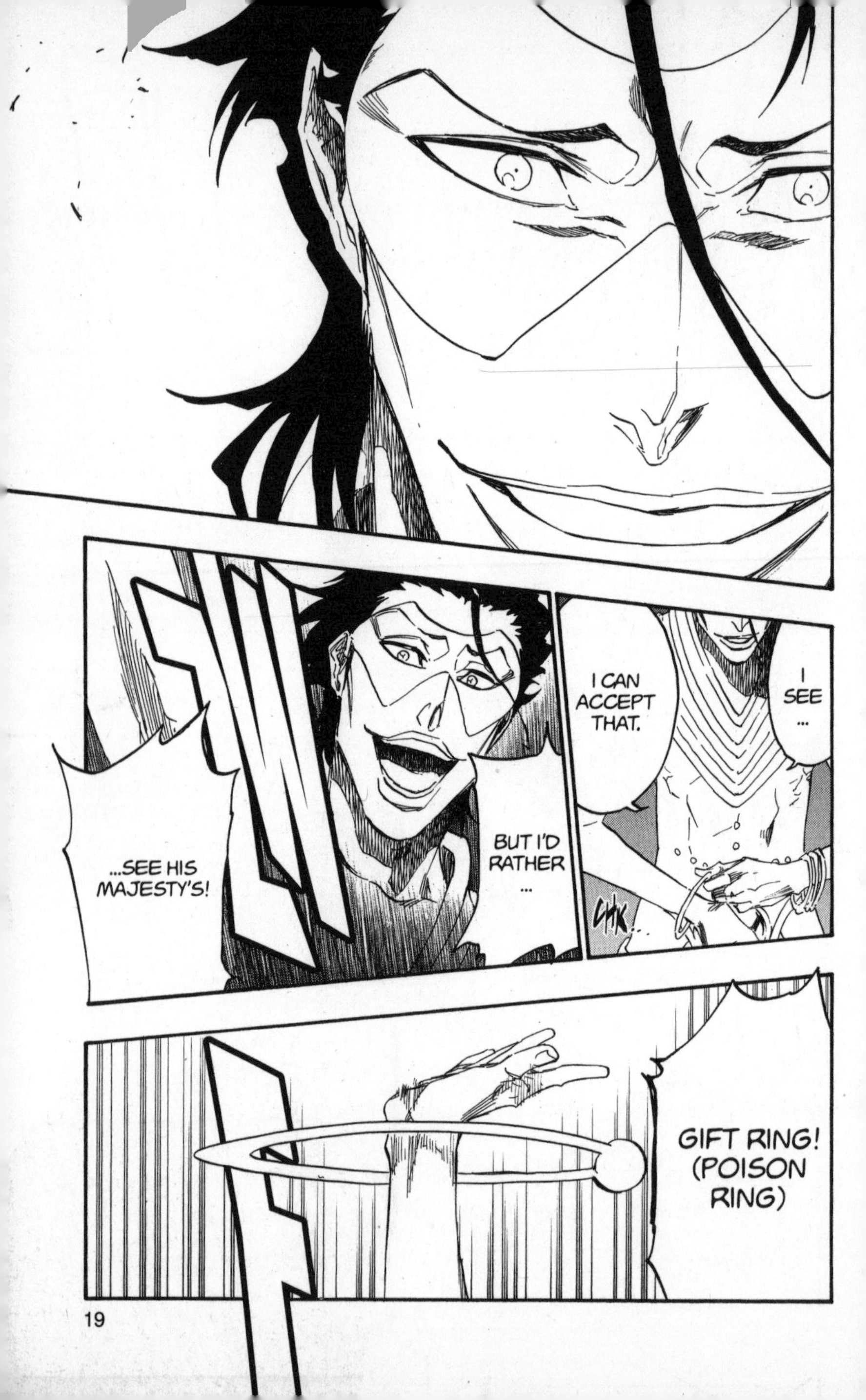
I SEE...
I CAN ACCEPT THAT.
CHK...
BUT I'D RATHER...
...SEE HIS MAJESTY'S!
GIFT RING! (POISON RING)

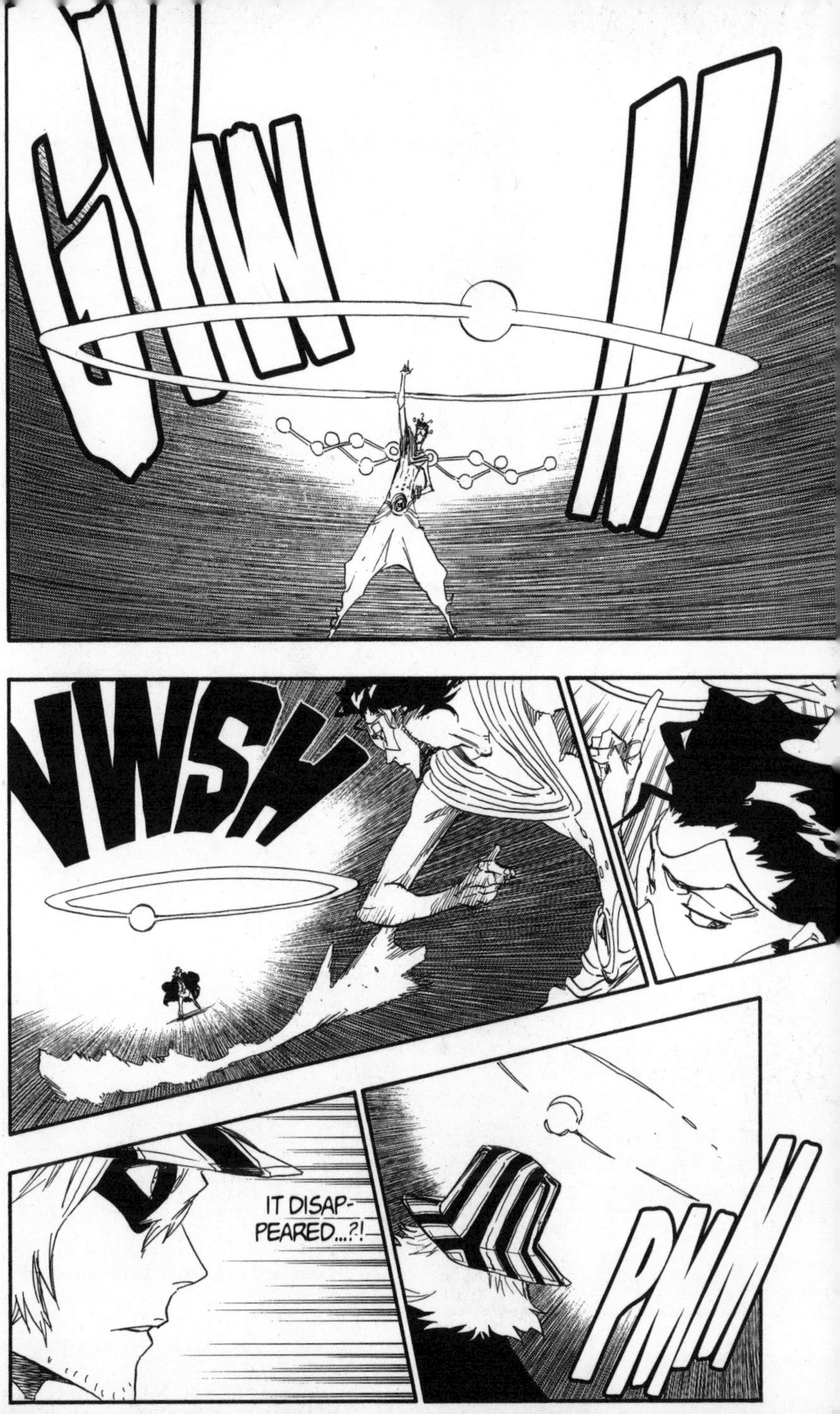
VWSH
IT DISAP-
PEARED...?!

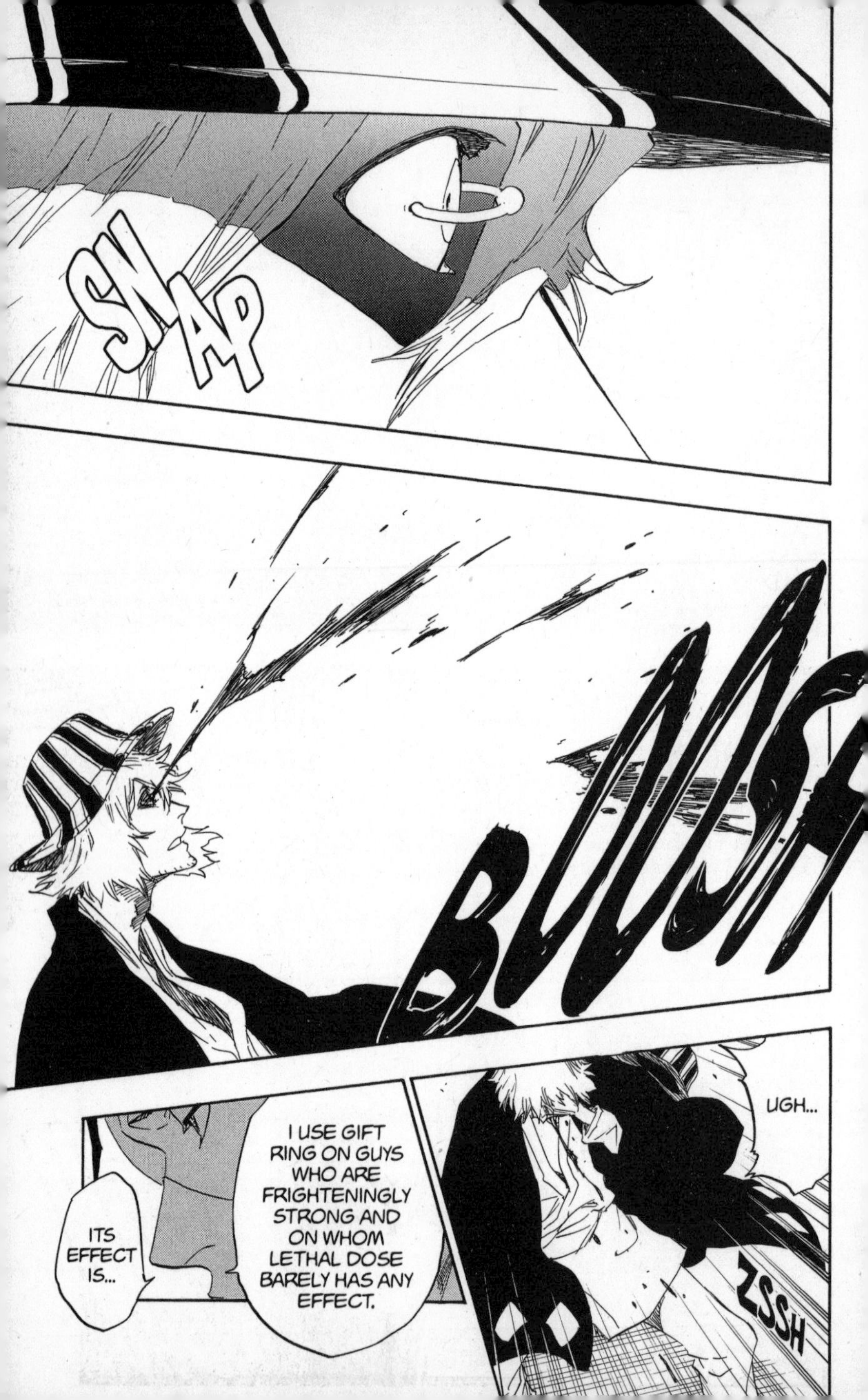
SNAP
BUOSH
UGH...
ZSSH
I USE GIFT RING ON GUYS WHO ARE FRIGHTENINGLY STRONG AND ON WHOM LETHAL DOSE BARELY HAS ANY EFFECT.
ITS EFFECT IS...

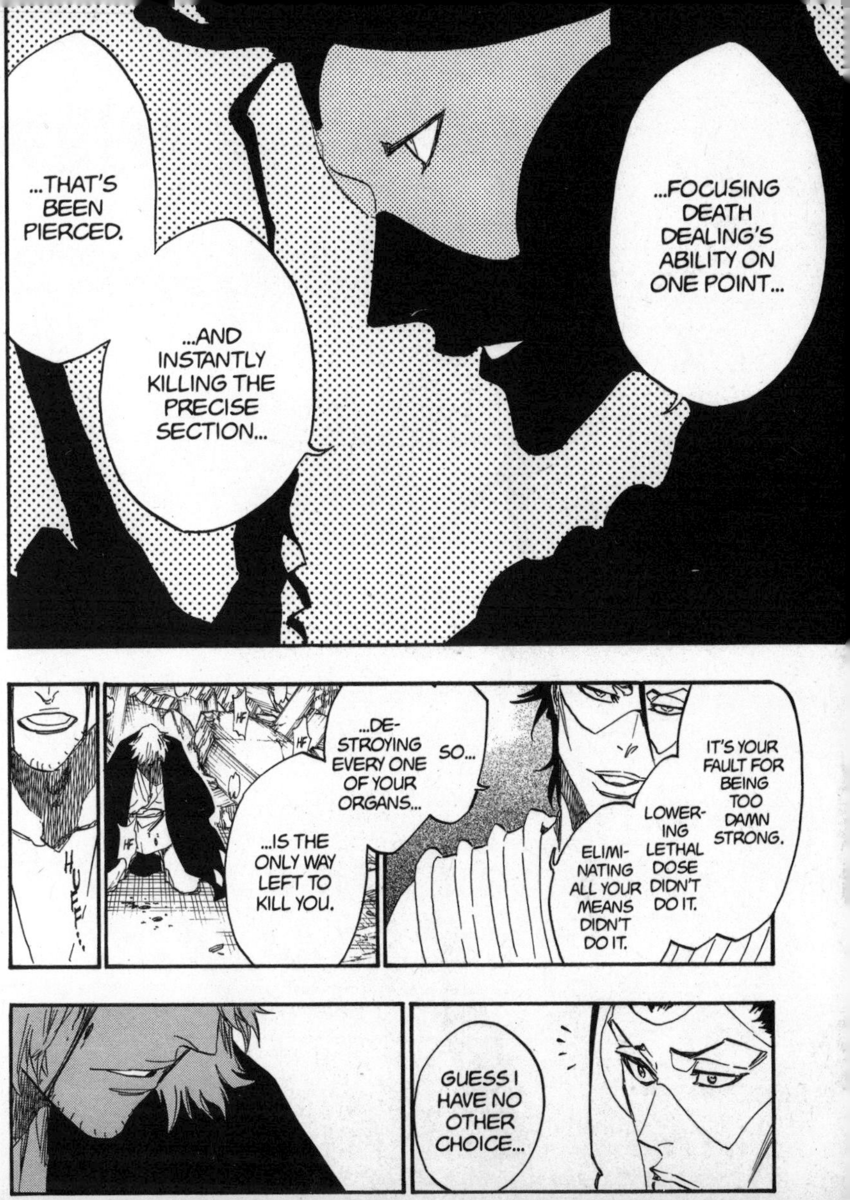
...FOCUSING DEATH DEALING'S ABILITY ON ONE POINT...
...THAT'S BEEN PIERCED.
...AND INSTANTLY KILLING THE PRECISE SECTION...
IT'S YOUR FAULT FOR BEING TOO DAMN STRONG.
LOWER-ING LETHAL DOSE DIDN'T DO IT.
ELIMI-NATING ALL YOUR MEANS DIDN'T DO IT.
SO...
...DE-STROYING EVERY ONE OF YOUR ORGANS...
...IS THE ONLY WAY LEFT TO KILL YOU.
HF
HF
HF
HUFF...
GUESS I HAVE NO OTHER CHOICE...

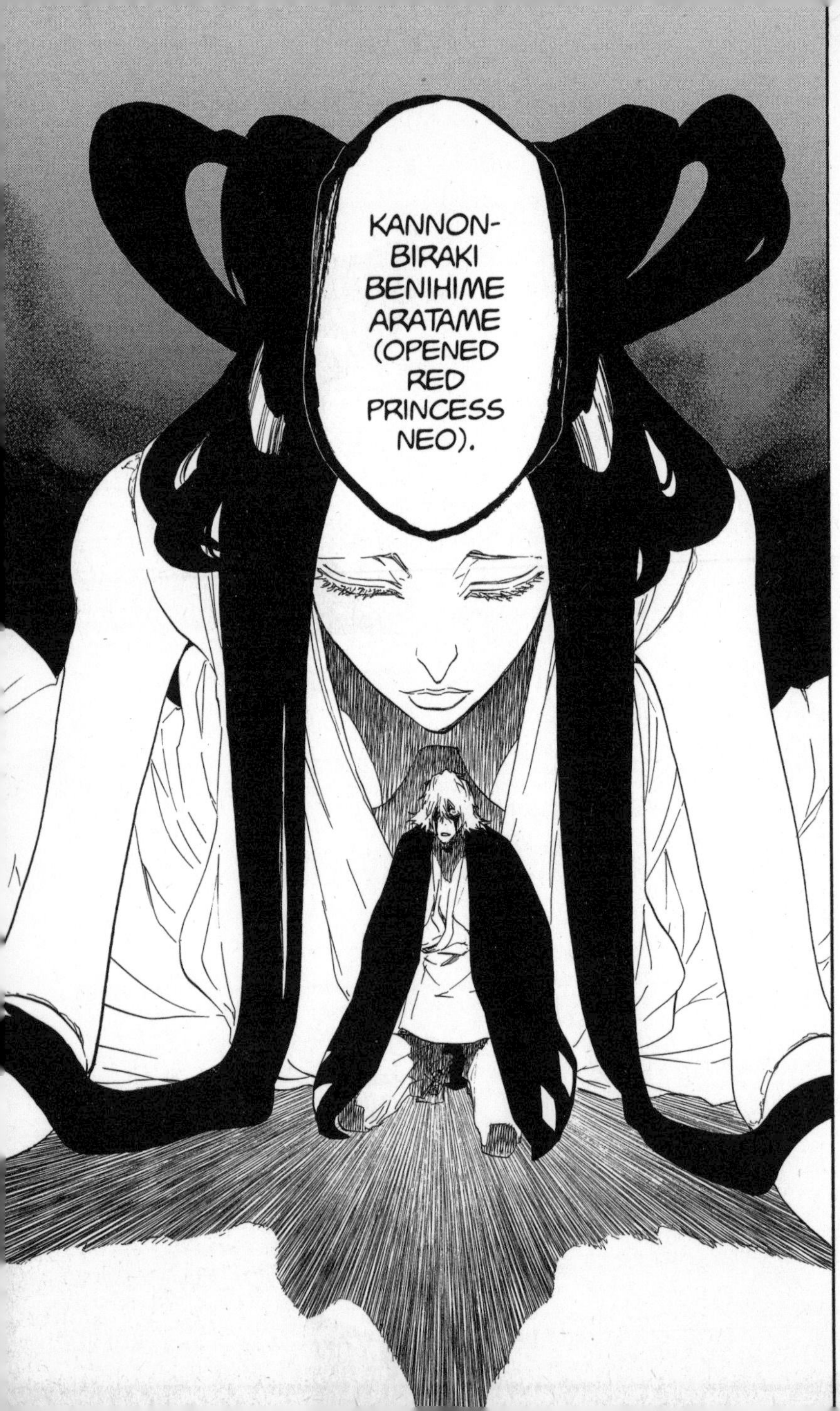
KANNON-BIRAKI BENIHIME ARATAME (OPENED RED PRINCESS NEO).

665.THE PRINCESS DISSECTION

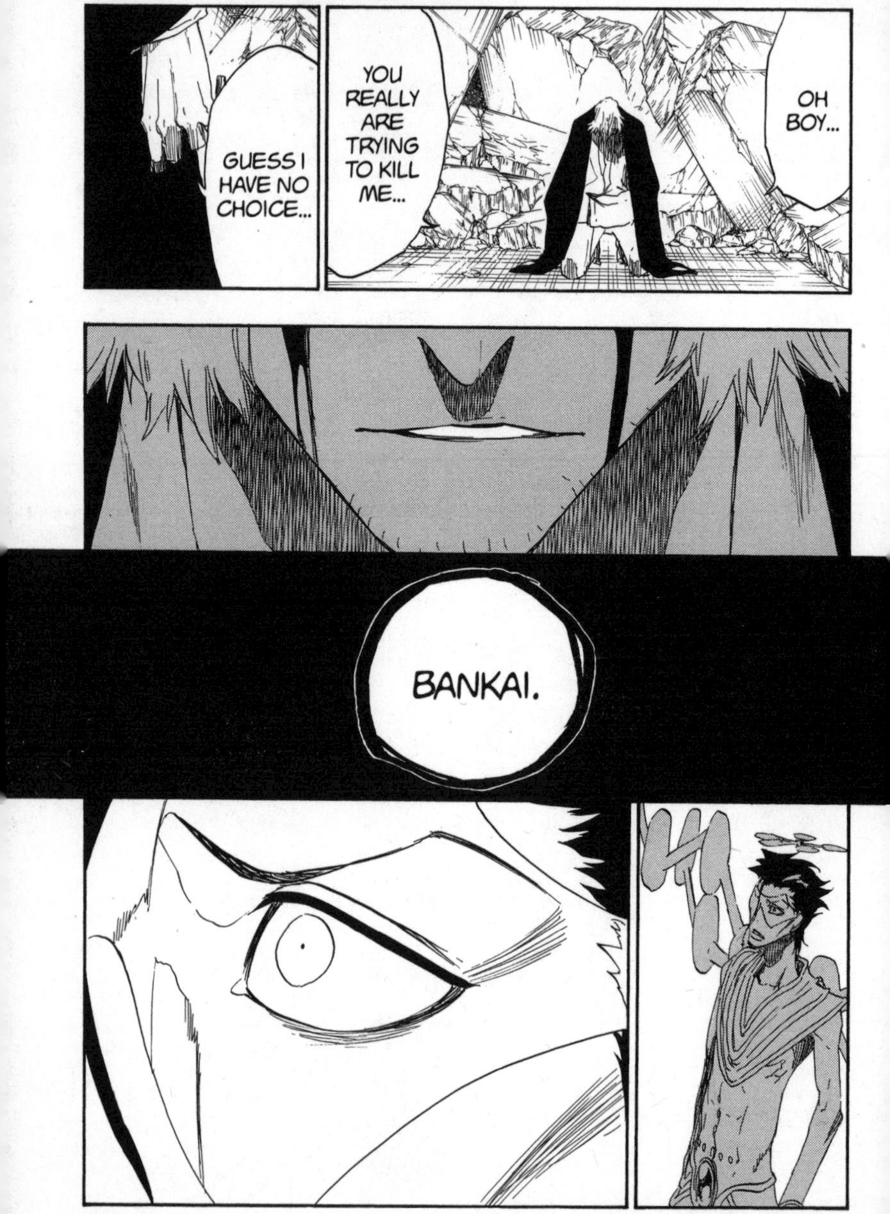
OH BOY...
YOU REALLY ARE TRYING TO KILL ME...
GUESS I HAVE NO CHOICE...
BANKAI.

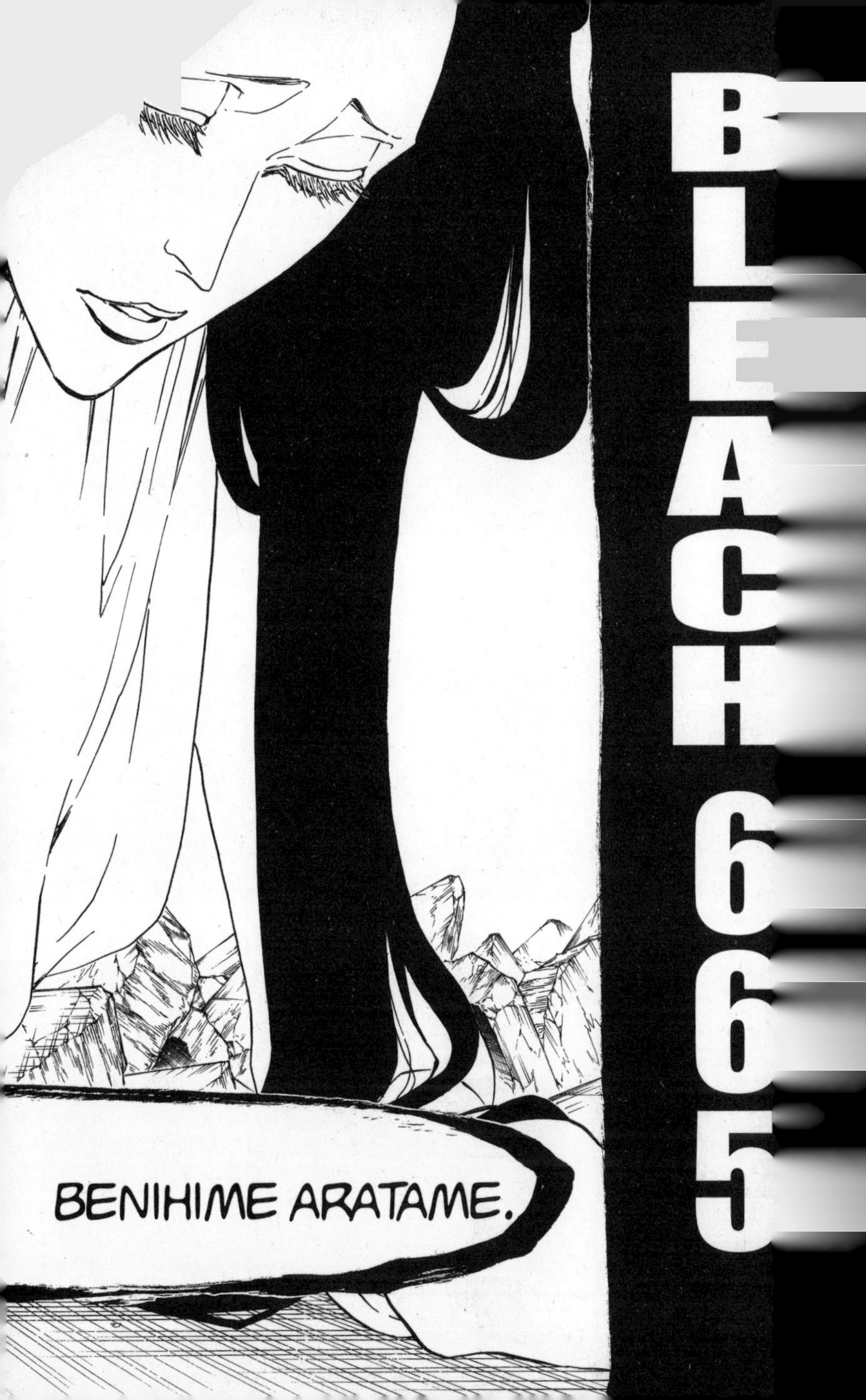
BLEACH 65
BENIHIME ARATAME.

The Princess Dissection

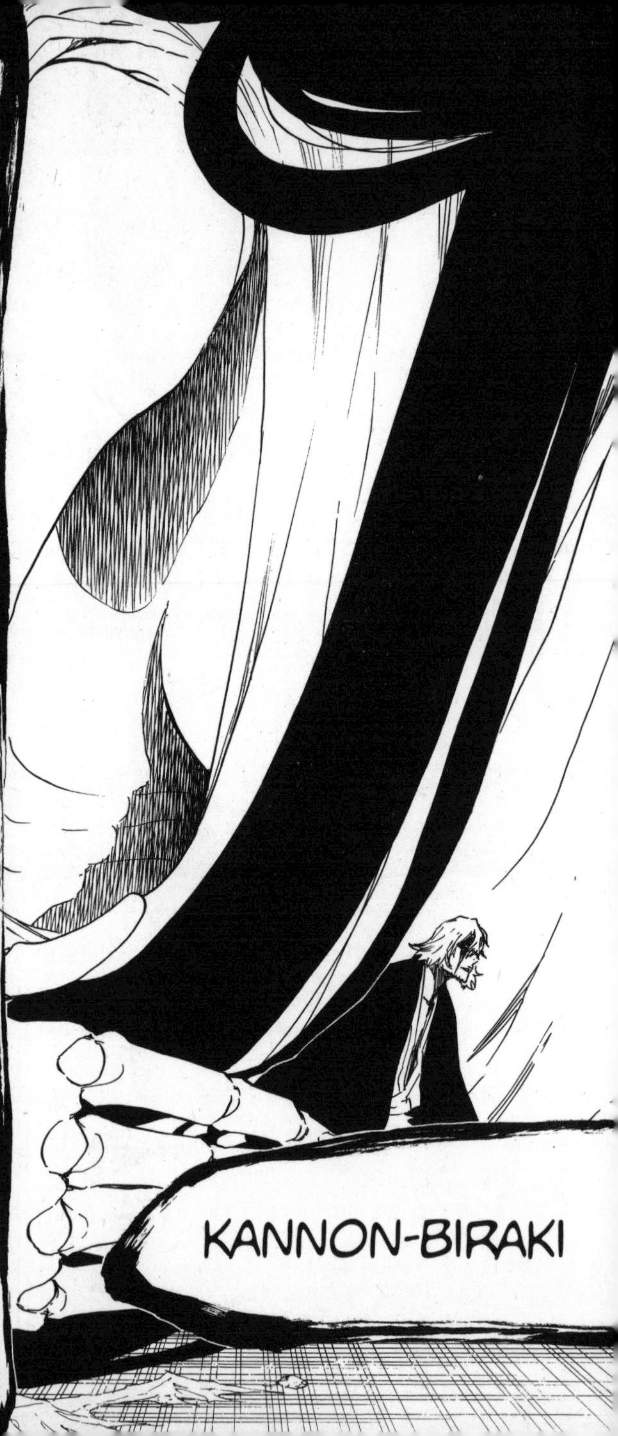
KANNON-BIRAKI

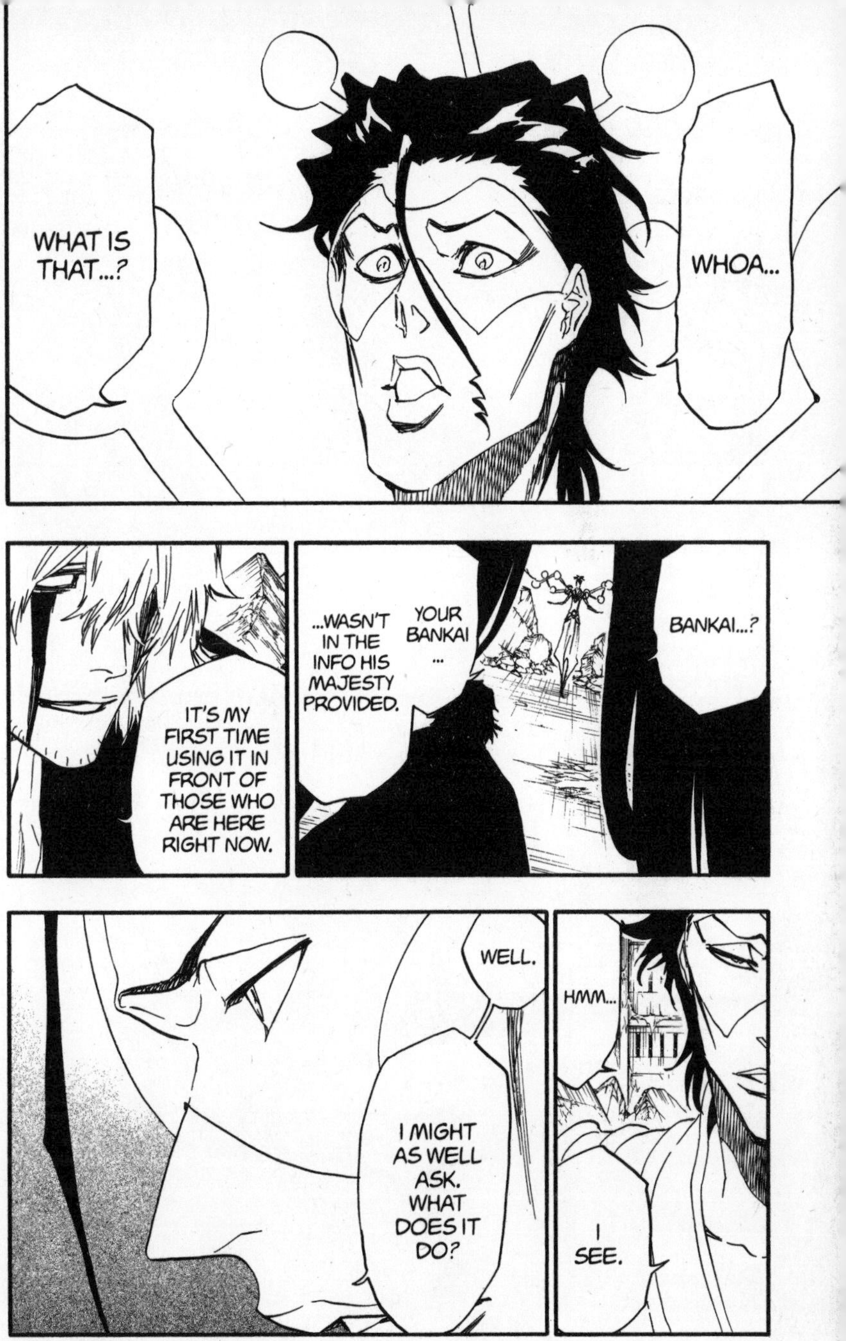
WHOA...
WHAT IS THAT...?
BANKAI...?
YOUR BANKAI ...
...WASN'T IN THE INFO HIS MAJESTY PROVIDED.
IT'S MY FIRST TIME USING IT IN FRONT OF THOSE WHO ARE HERE RIGHT NOW.
HMM...
I SEE.
WELL.
I MIGHT AS WELL ASK. WHAT DOES IT DO?

READ THIS WAY

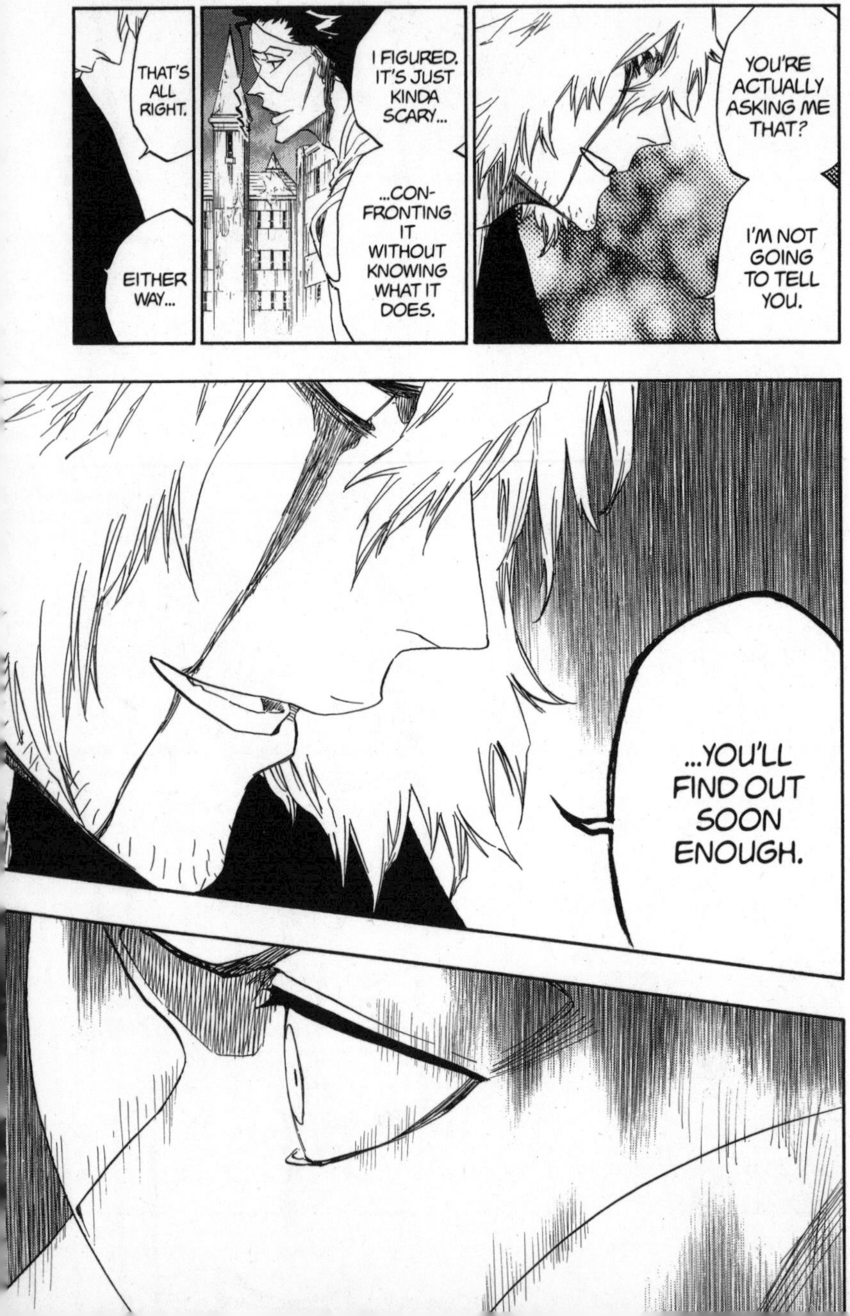
YOU'RE ACTUALLY ASKING ME THAT?
I'M NOT GOING TO TELL YOU.
I FIGURED. IT'S JUST KINDA SCARY...
...CON-FRONTING IT WITHOUT KNOWING WHAT IT DOES.
THAT'S ALL RIGHT.
EITHER WAY...
...YOU'LL FIND OUT SOON ENOUGH.

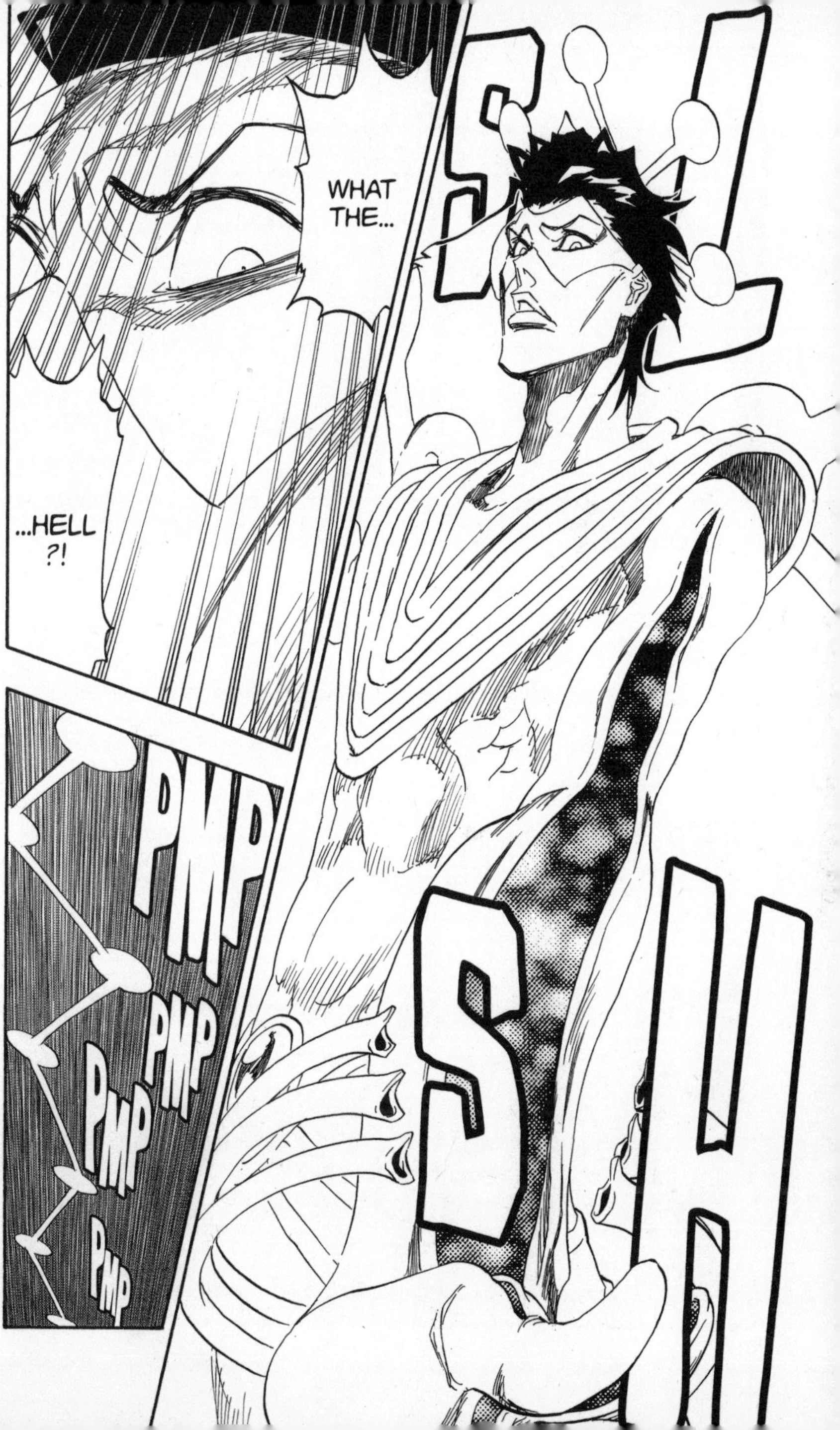

SH
SH
WHAT THE...
...HELL ?!
PMP
PMP
PMP
PMP

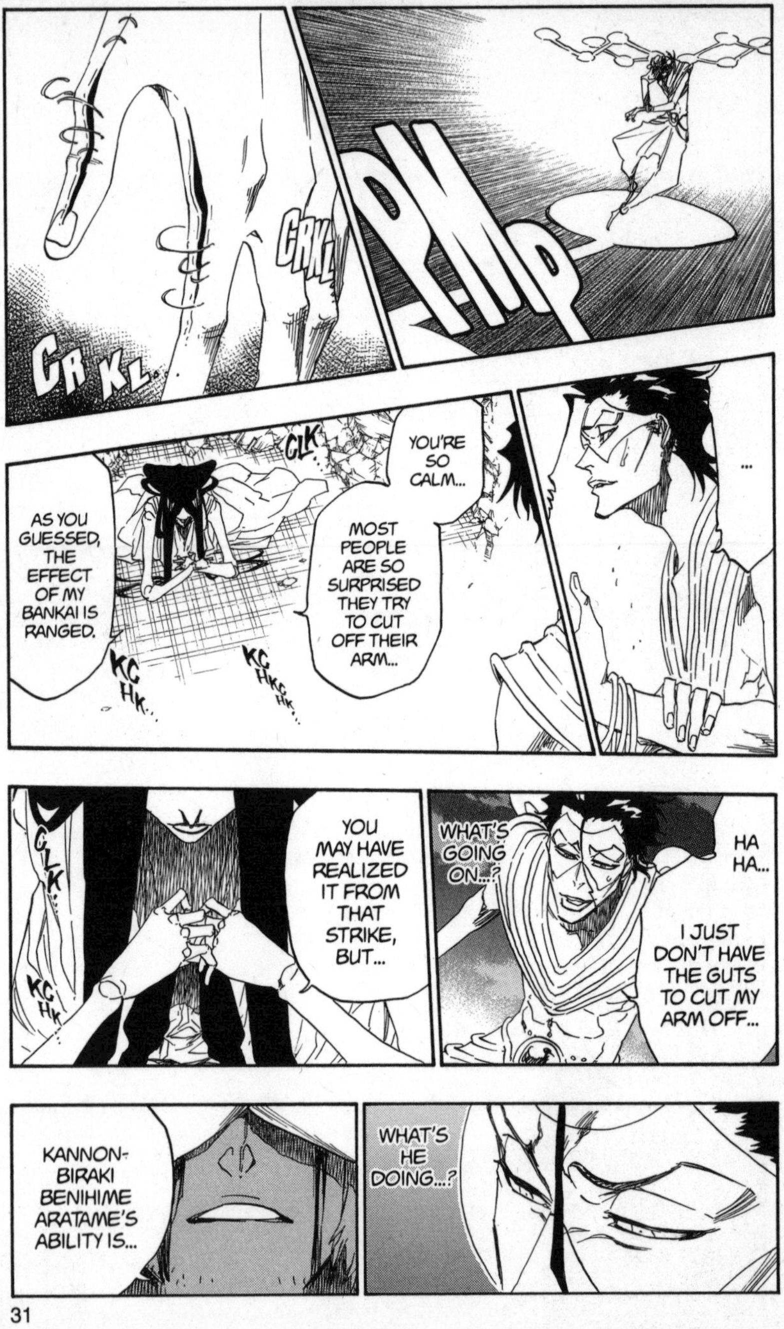

PMP
CRKL
CR KL
...
YOU'RE SO CALM...
MOST PEOPLE ARE SO SURPRISED THEY TRY TO CUT OFF THEIR ARM...
CLK
AS YOU GUESSED, THE EFFECT OF MY BANKAI IS RANGED.
KCHK...
KCHKCHK
HA HA...
I JUST DON'T HAVE THE GUTS TO CUT MY ARM OFF...
WHAT'S GOING ON...?
YOU MAY HAVE REALIZED IT FROM THAT STRIKE, BUT...
CLK...
KCHK...
WHAT'S HE DOING...?
KANNON-BIRAKI BENIHIME ARATAME'S ABILITY IS...

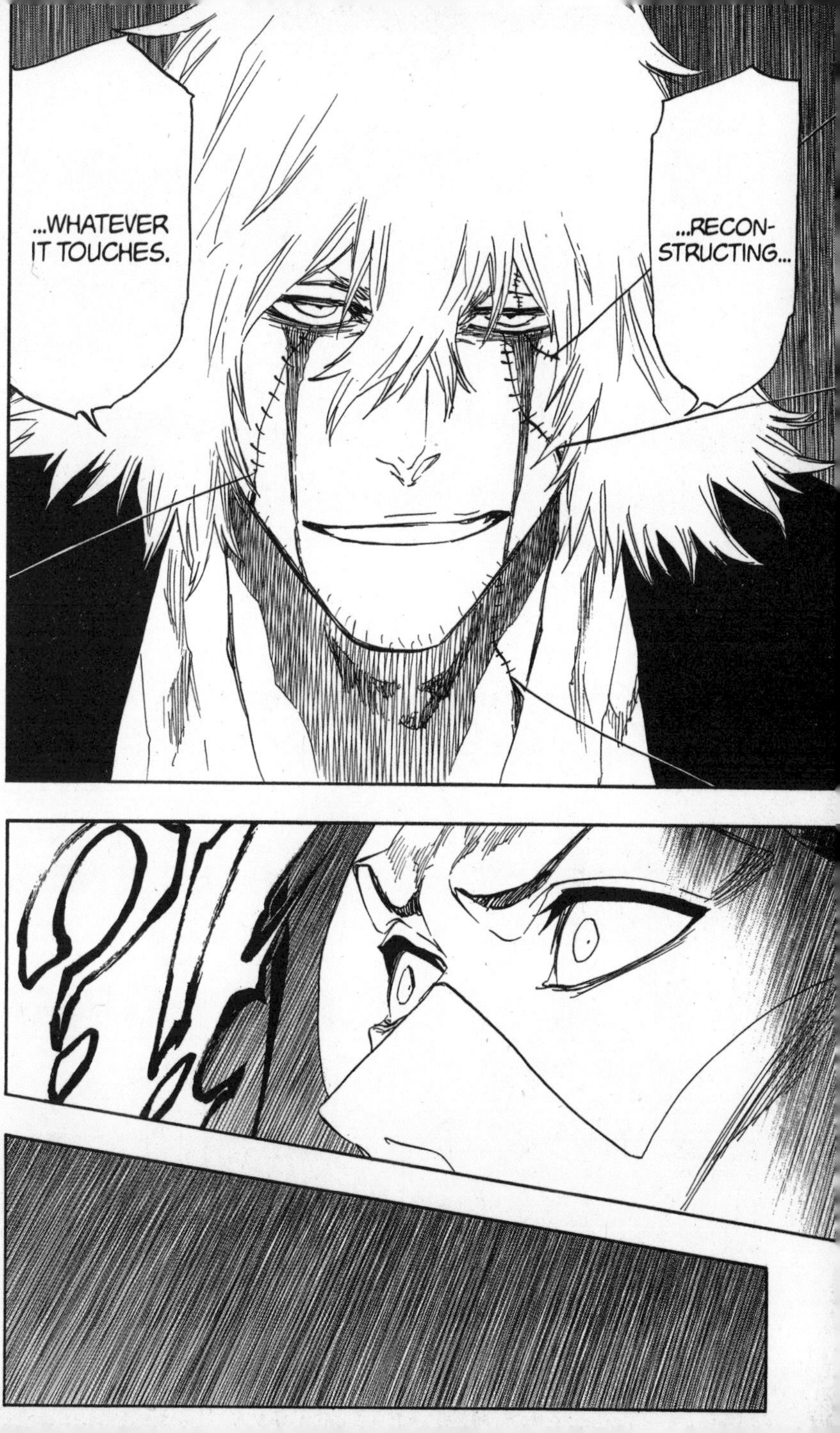
...RECON-
STRUCTING...
...WHATEVER
IT TOUCHES.

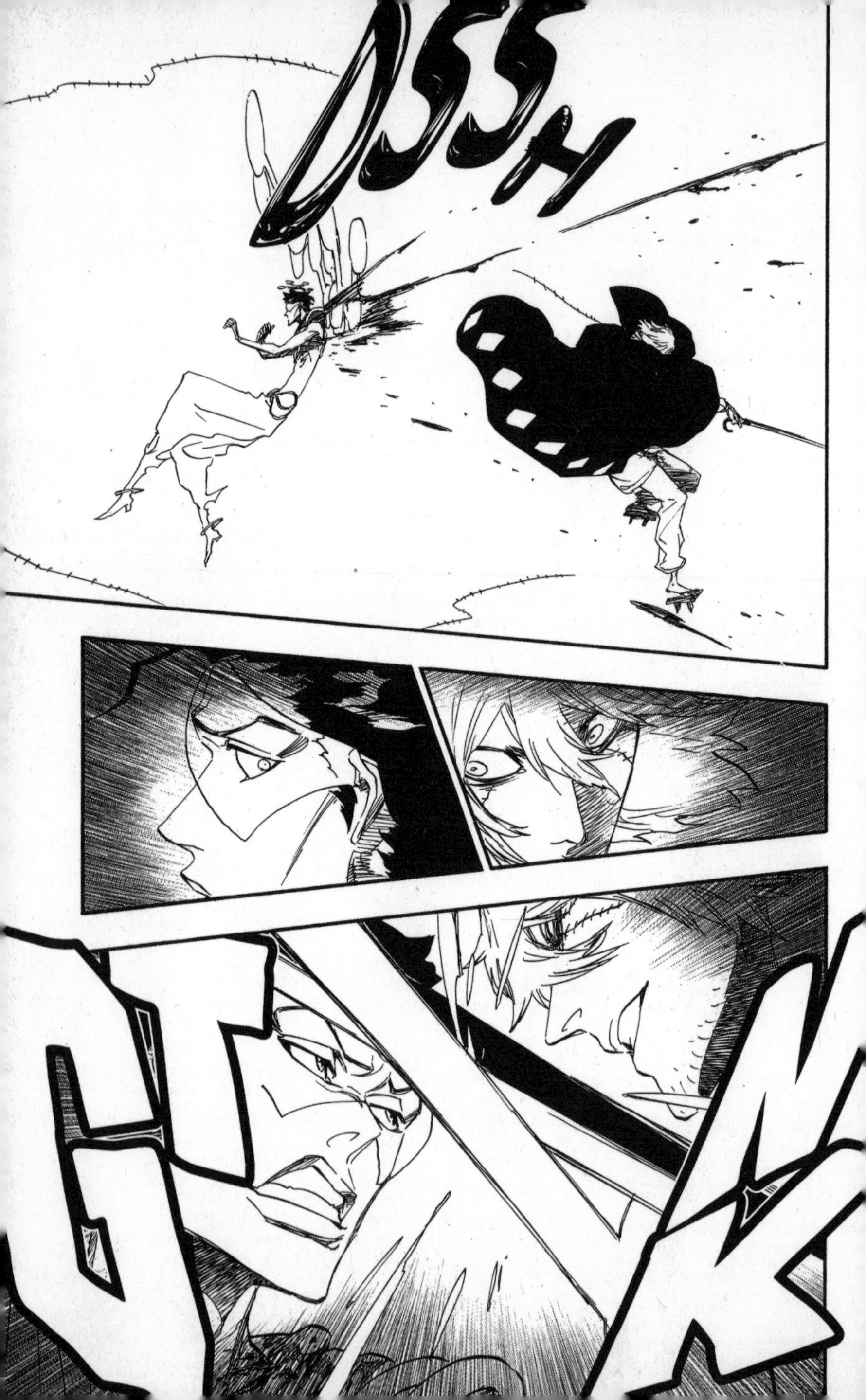
DSSH

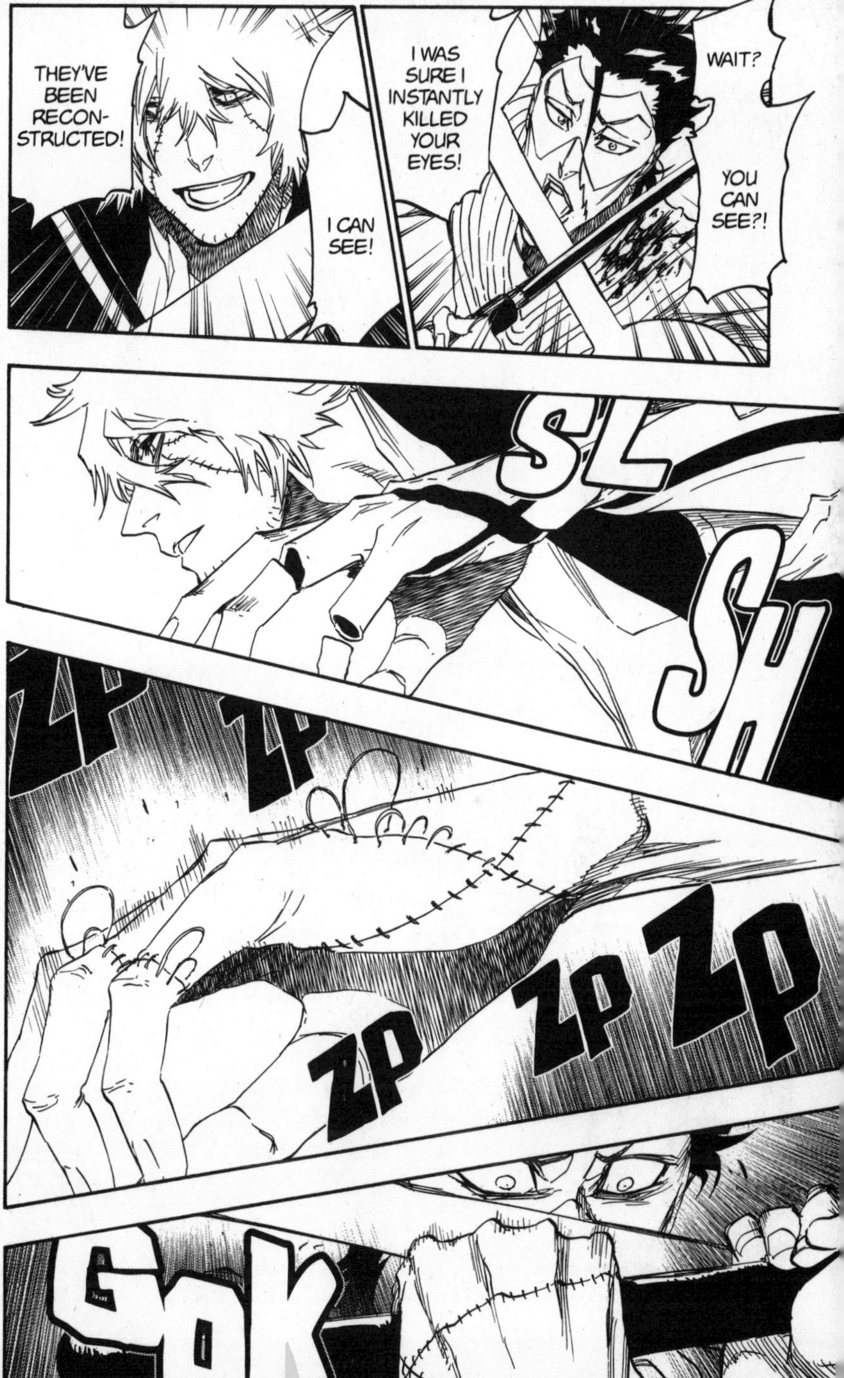
WAIT?
YOU CAN SEE?!
I WAS SURE I INSTANTLY KILLED YOUR EYES!
I CAN SEE!
THEY'VE BEEN RECON-STRUCTED!
SL
SH
ZP
ZP
ZP
ZP
ZP
ZP
GOK

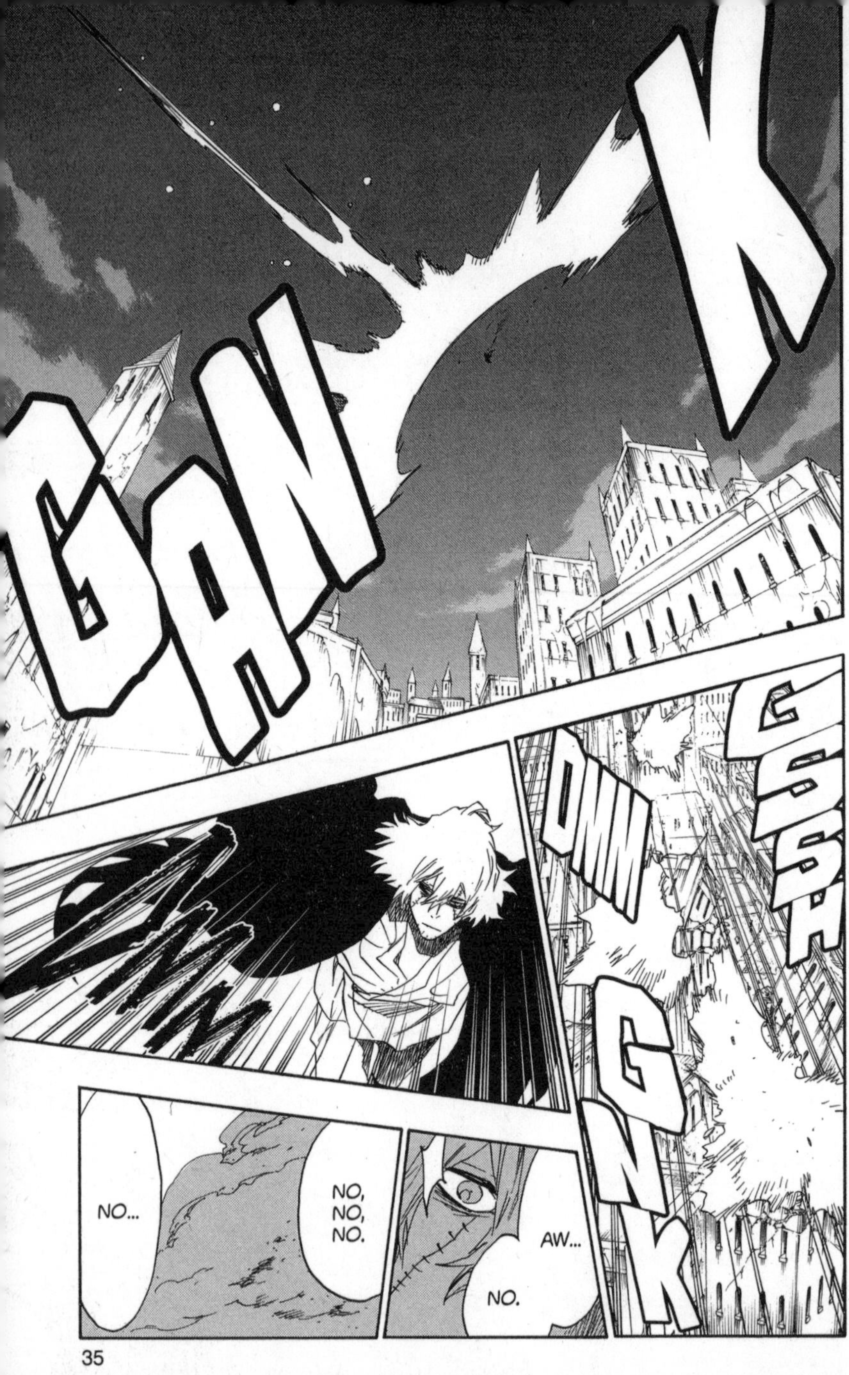
GANK
AW...
NO.
NO, NO, NO.
NO...

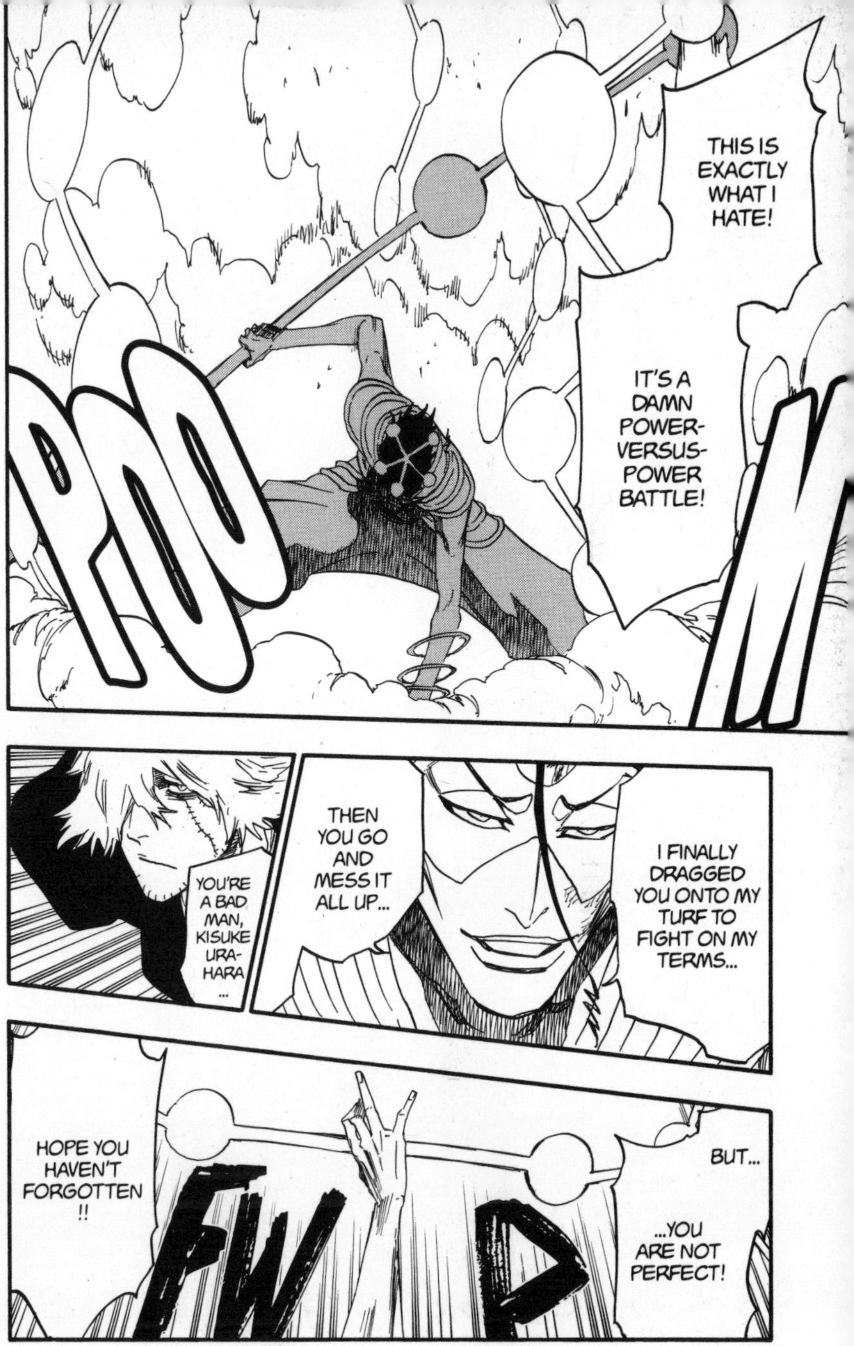
THIS IS EXACTLY WHAT I HATE!
IT'S A DAMN POWER-VERSUS-POWER BATTLE!
POOM
I FINALLY DRAGGED YOU ONTO MY TURF TO FIGHT ON MY TERMS...
THEN YOU GO AND MESS IT ALL UP...
YOU'RE A BAD MAN, KISUKE URA-HARA...
BUT...
...YOU ARE NOT PERFECT!
FWP
HOPE YOU HAVEN'T FORGOTTEN!!

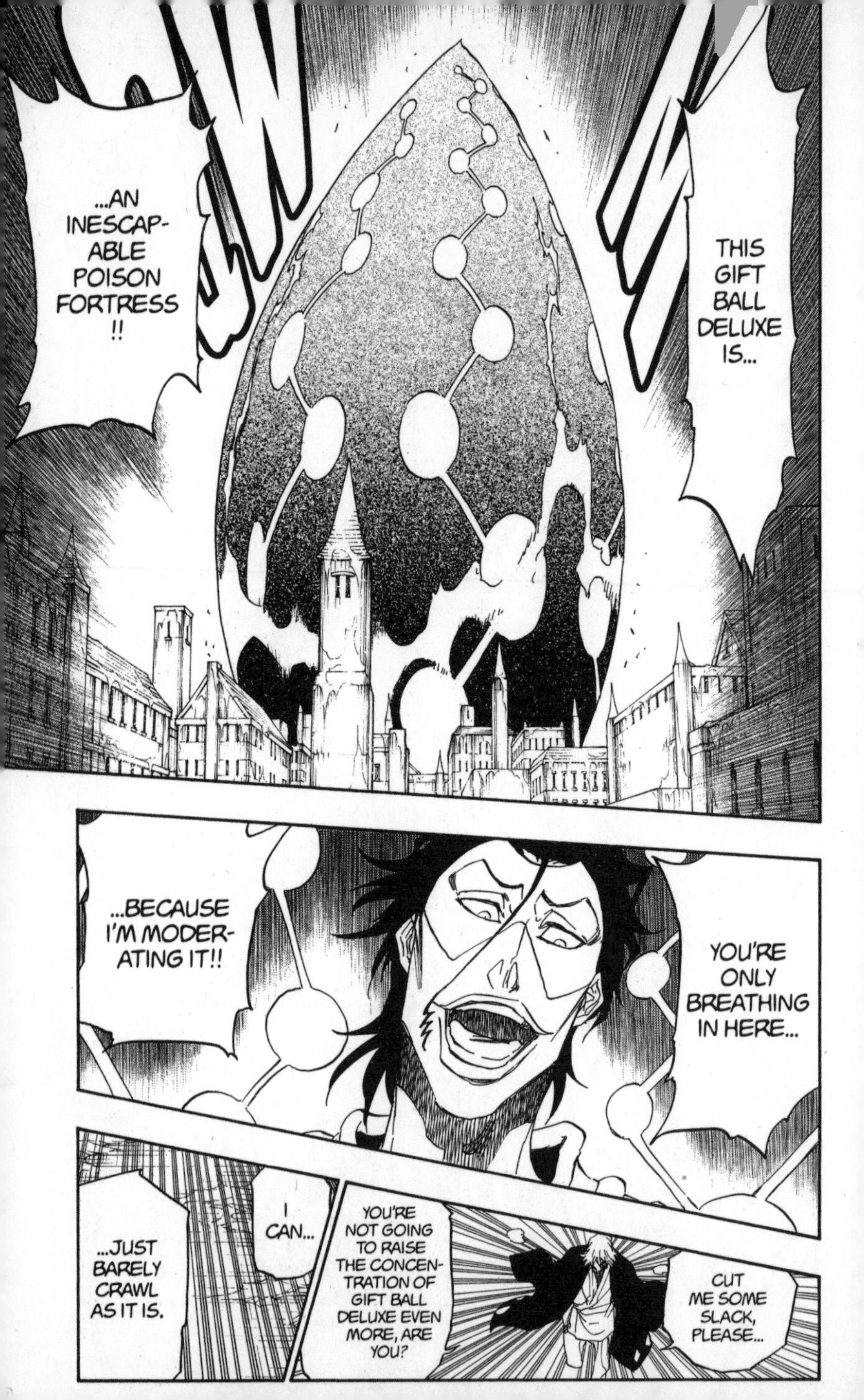
THIS GIFT BALL DELUXE IS...
...AN INESCAPABLE POISON FORTRESS!!
YOU'RE ONLY BREATHING IN HERE...
...BECAUSE I'M MODERATING IT!!
CUT ME SOME SLACK, PLEASE...
YOU'RE NOT GOING TO RAISE THE CONCENTRATION OF GIFT BALL DELUXE EVEN MORE, ARE YOU?
I CAN...
...JUST BARELY CRAWL AS IT IS.

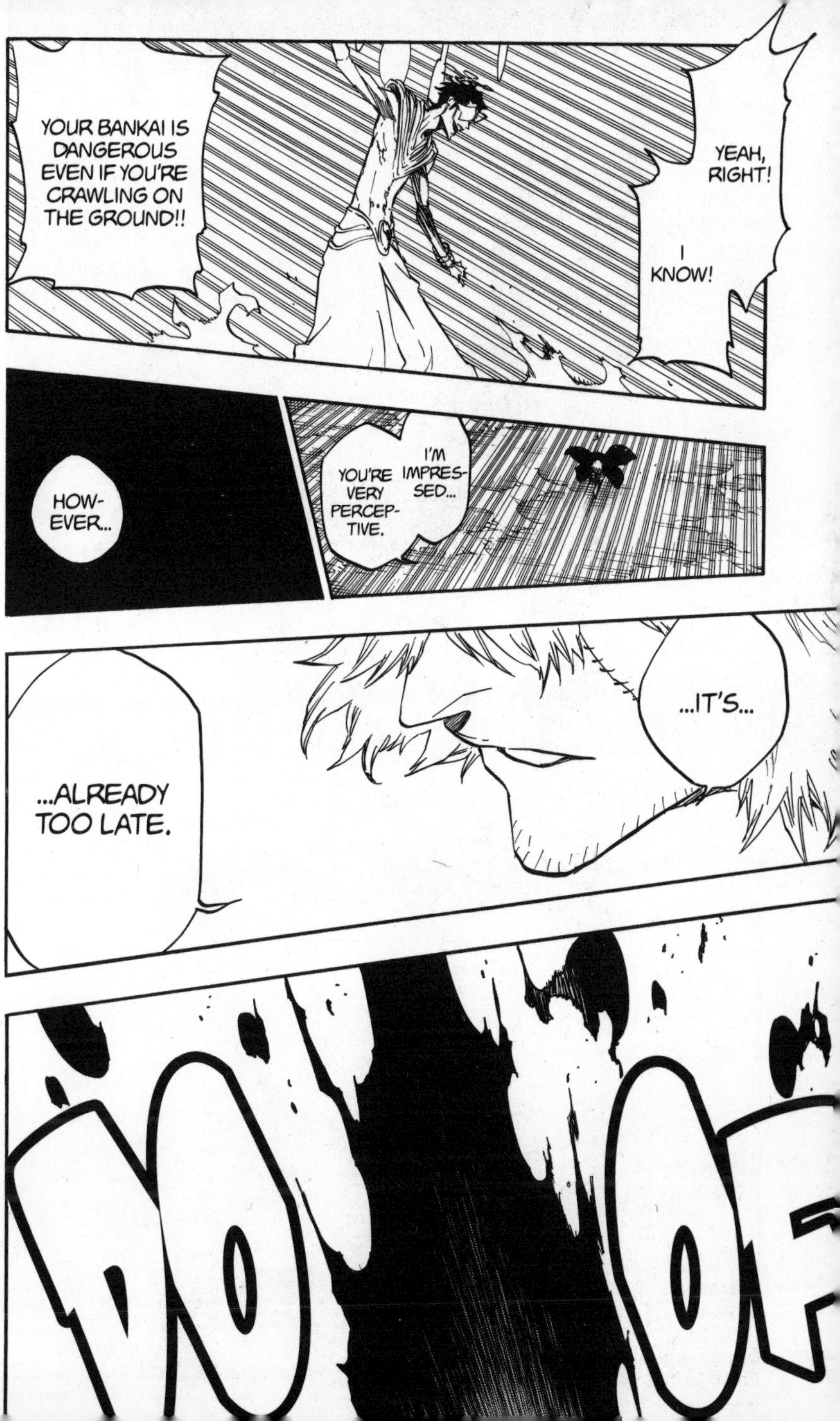
YEAH, RIGHT!
I KNOW!
YOUR BANKAI IS DANGEROUS EVEN IF YOU'RE CRAWLING ON THE GROUND!!
I'M IMPRESSED...
YOU'RE VERY PERCEPTIVE.
HOWEVER...
...IT'S...
...ALREADY TOO LATE.

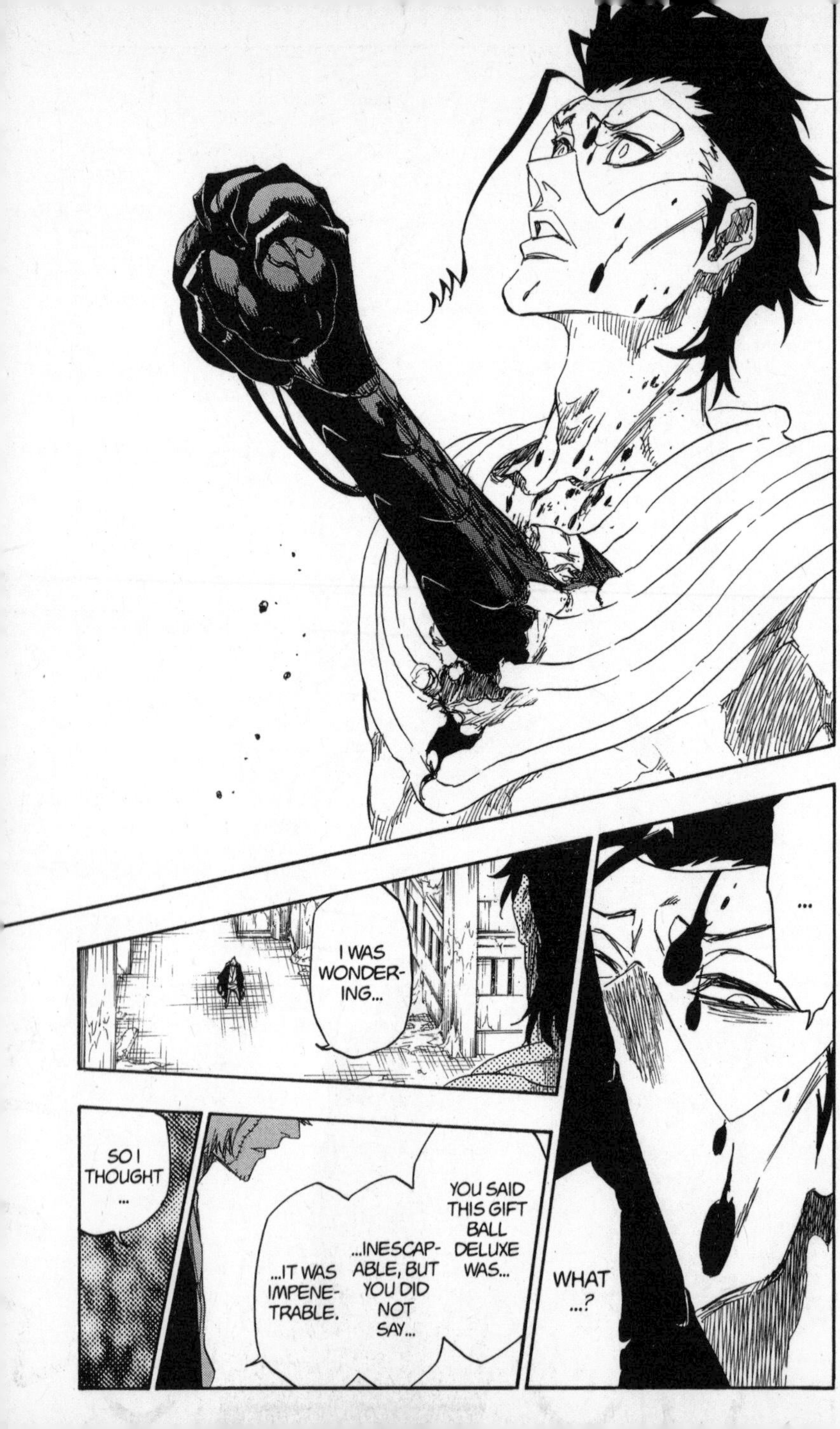
...
WHAT ...?
I WAS WONDERING...
YOU SAID THIS GIFT BALL DELUXE WAS...
...INESCAPABLE, BUT YOU DID NOT SAY...
...IT WAS IMPENETRABLE.
SO I THOUGHT ...

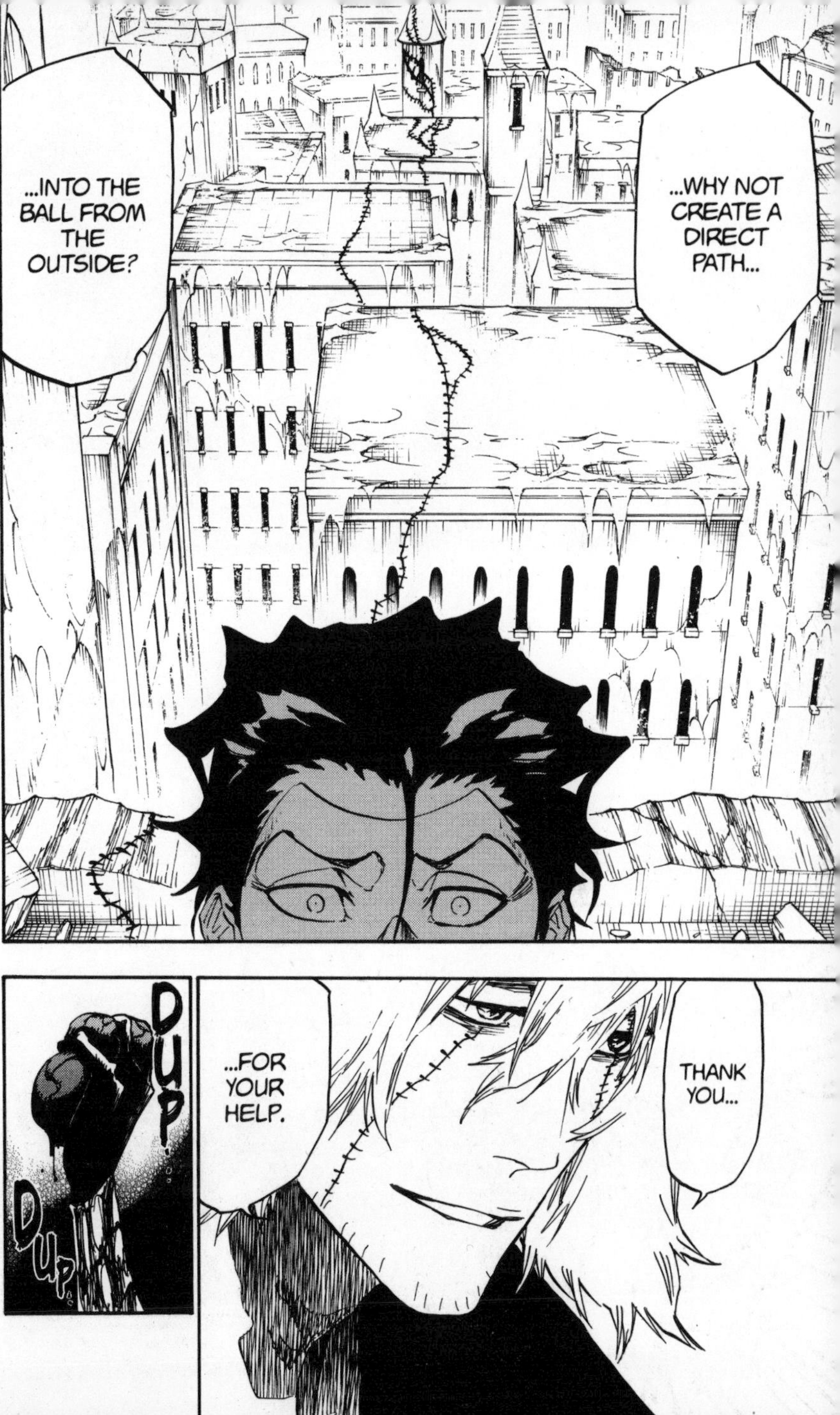
...WHY NOT CREATE A DIRECT PATH...
...INTO THE BALL FROM THE OUTSIDE?
THANK YOU...
...FOR YOUR HELP.
DUP
DUP

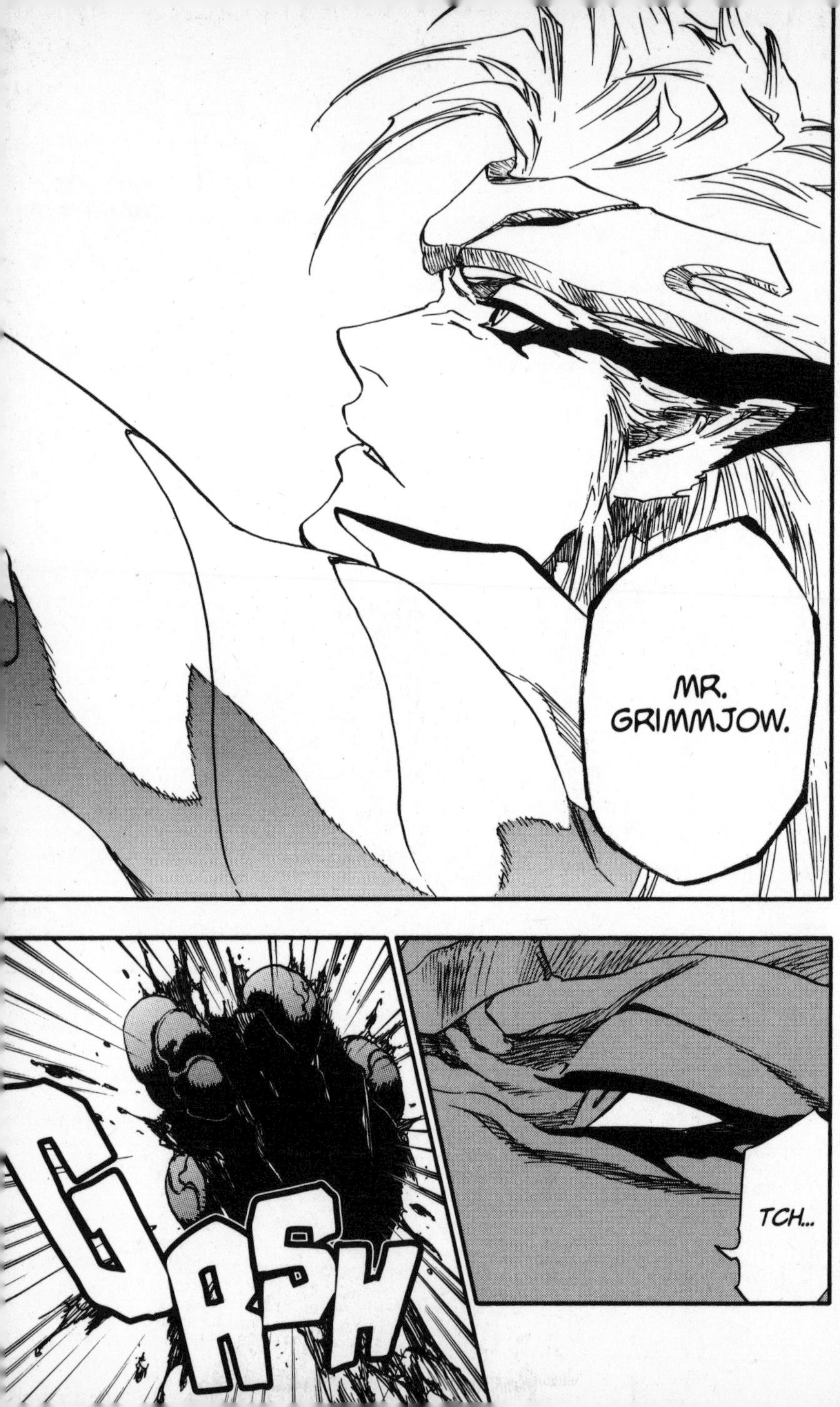
MR. GRIMMJOW.
TCH...

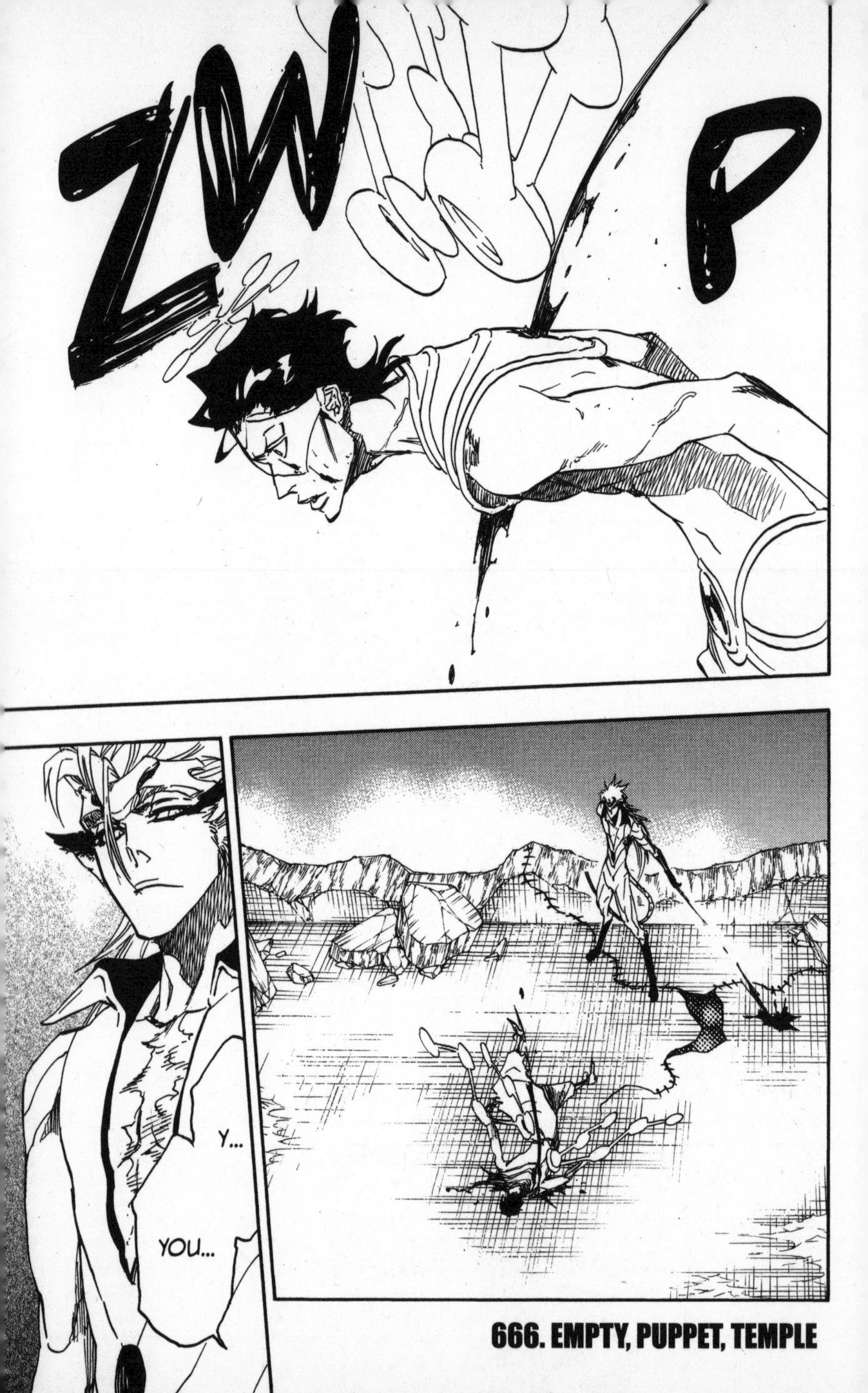
ZWIP
Y...
YOU...

666. EMPTY, PUPPET, TEMPLE

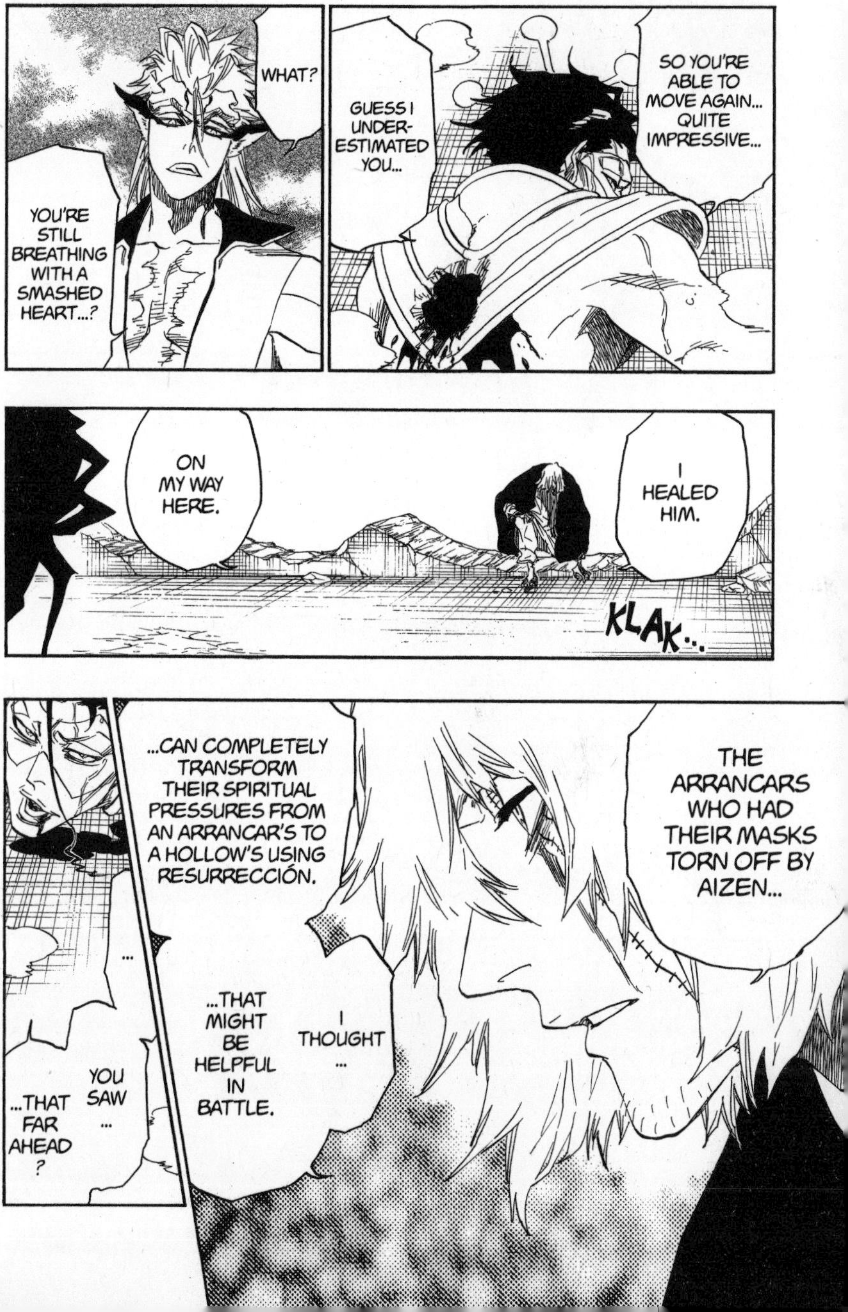
SO YOU'RE ABLE TO MOVE AGAIN... QUITE IMPRESSIVE...
GUESS I UNDER-ESTIMATED YOU...
WHAT?
YOU'RE STILL BREATHING WITH A SMASHED HEART...?
I HEALED HIM.
ON MY WAY HERE.
KLAK...
THE ARRANCARS WHO HAD THEIR MASKS TORN OFF BY AIZEN...
...CAN COMPLETELY TRANSFORM THEIR SPIRITUAL PRESSURES FROM AN ARRANCAR'S TO A HOLLOW'S USING RESURRECCIÓN.
I THOUGHT...
...THAT MIGHT BE HELPFUL IN BATTLE.
...
YOU SAW...
...THAT FAR AHEAD?

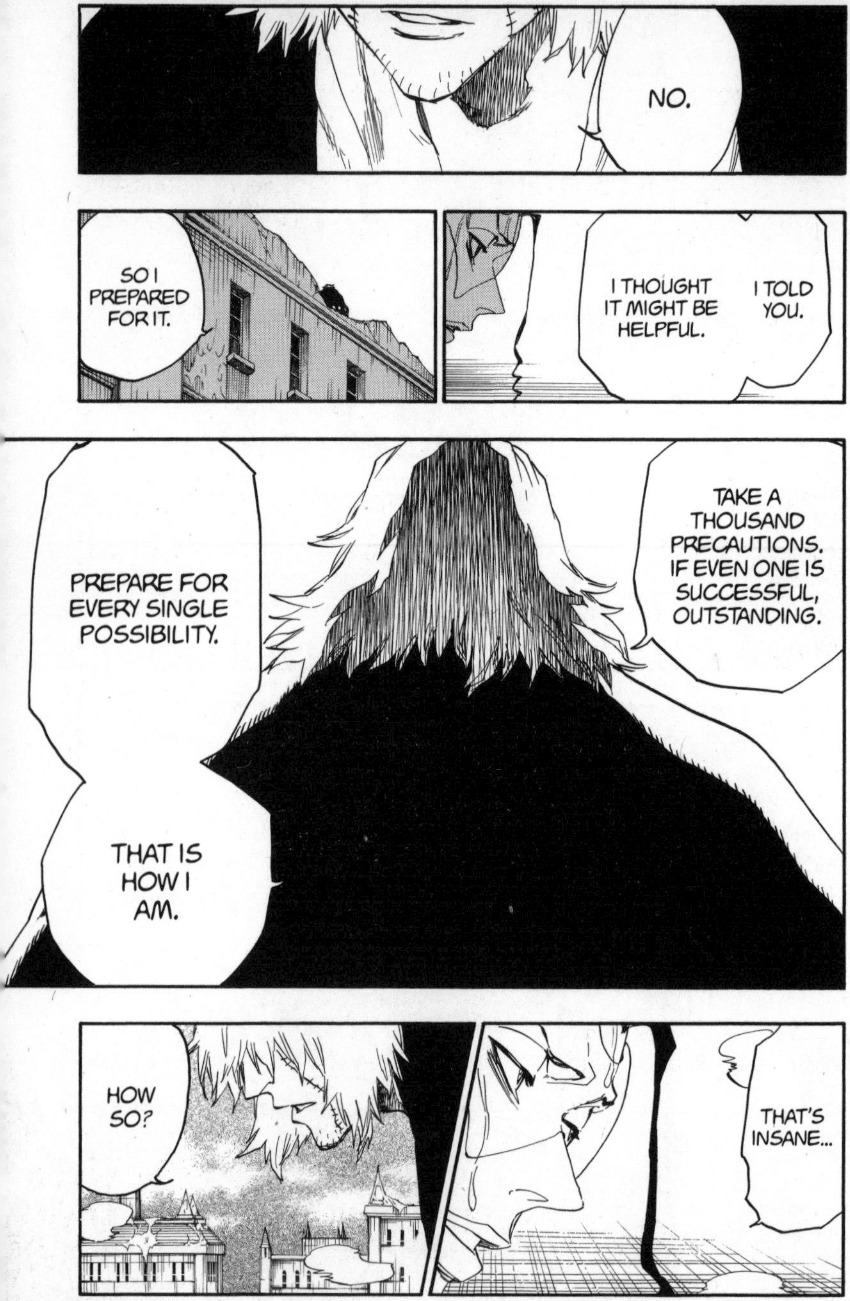
NO.
I TOLD YOU.
I THOUGHT IT MIGHT BE HELPFUL.
SO I PREPARED FOR IT.
TAKE A THOUSAND PRECAUTIONS. IF EVEN ONE IS SUCCESSFUL, OUTSTANDING.
PREPARE FOR EVERY SINGLE POSSIBILITY.
THAT IS HOW I AM.
THAT'S INSANE...
HOW SO?

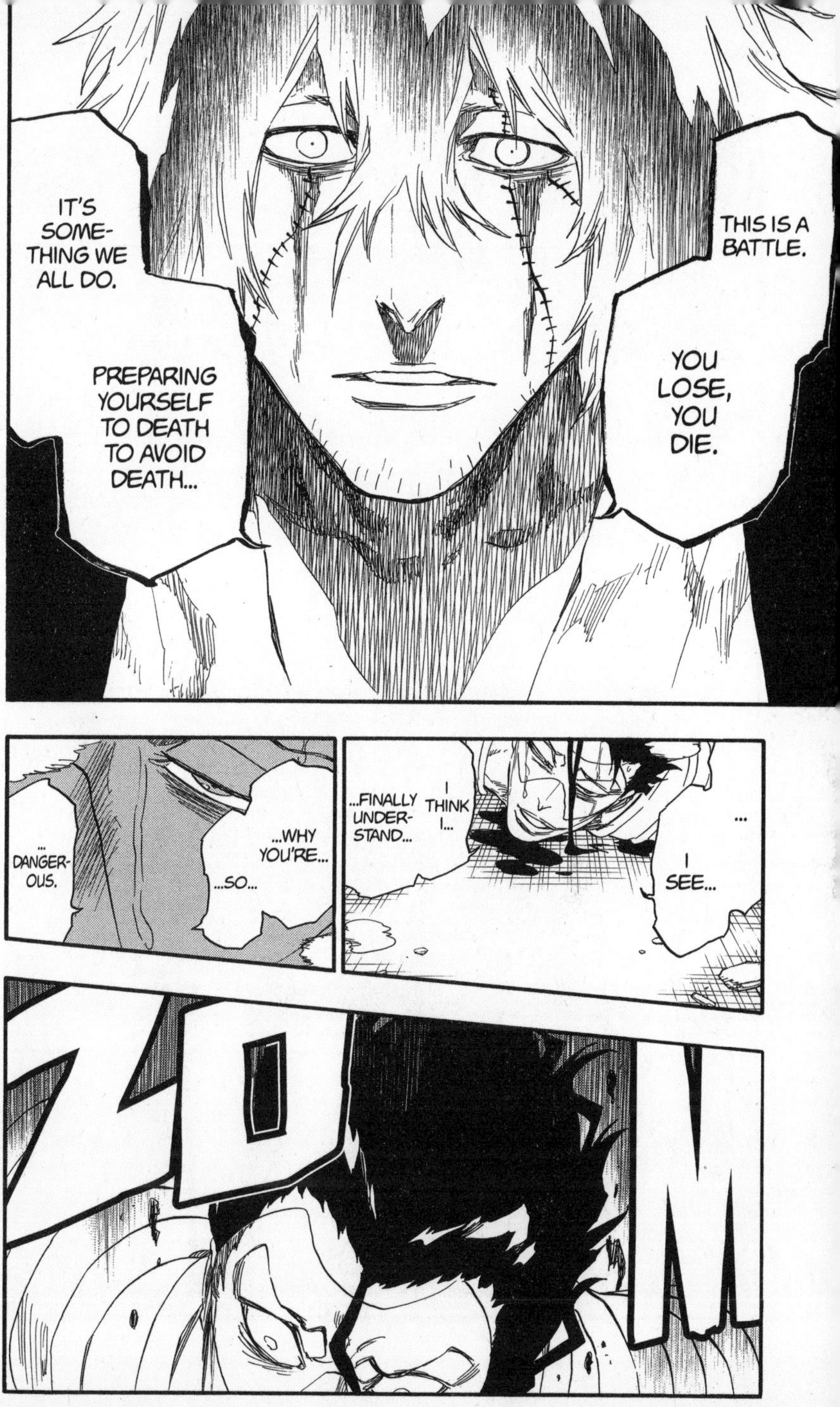
THIS IS A BATTLE.
YOU LOSE, YOU DIE.
IT'S SOME-THING WE ALL DO.
PREPARING YOURSELF TO DEATH TO AVOID DEATH...
...
I SEE...
I THINK I...
...FINALLY UNDER-STAND...
...WHY YOU'RE...
...SO...
...DANGER-OUS.
ZOOM

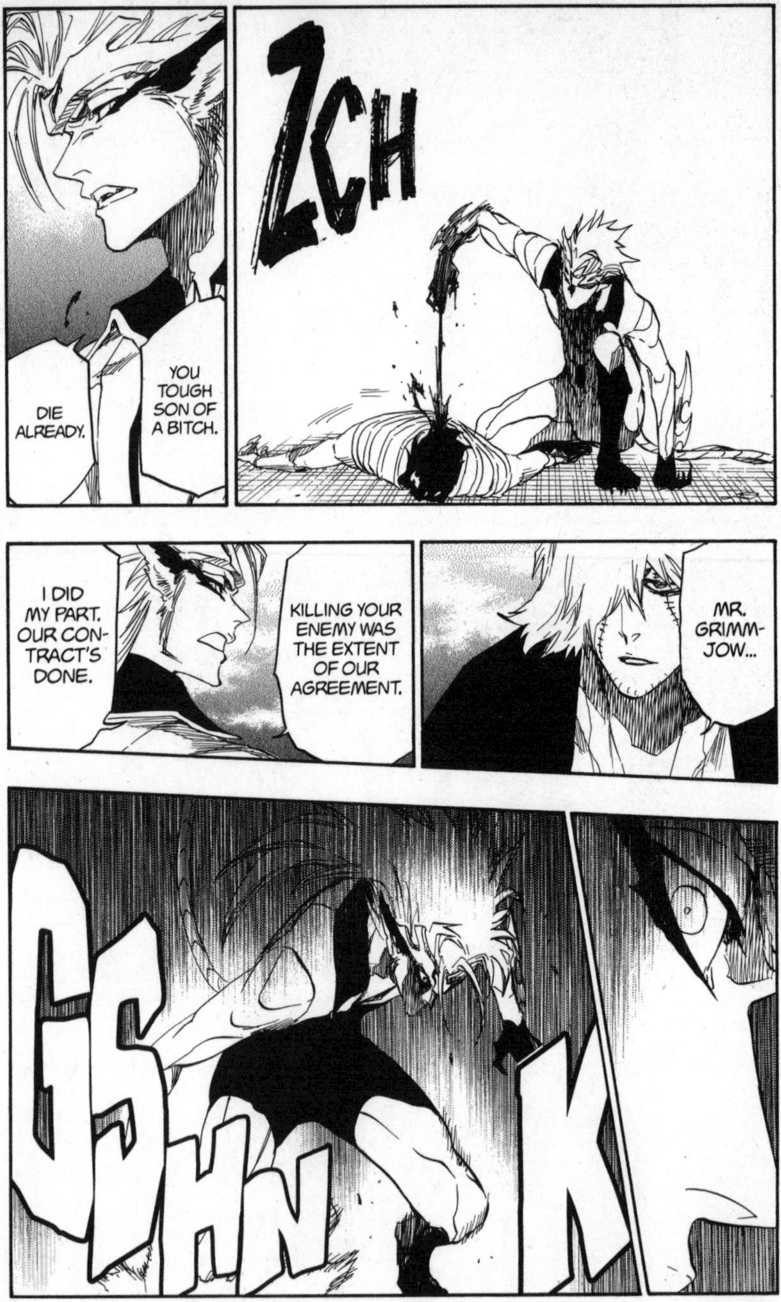
ZCH
YOU TOUGH SON OF A BITCH.
DIE ALREADY.
MR. GRIMMJOW...
KILLING YOUR ENEMY WAS THE EXTENT OF OUR AGREEMENT.
I DID MY PART. OUR CONTRACT'S DONE.
GSHNK

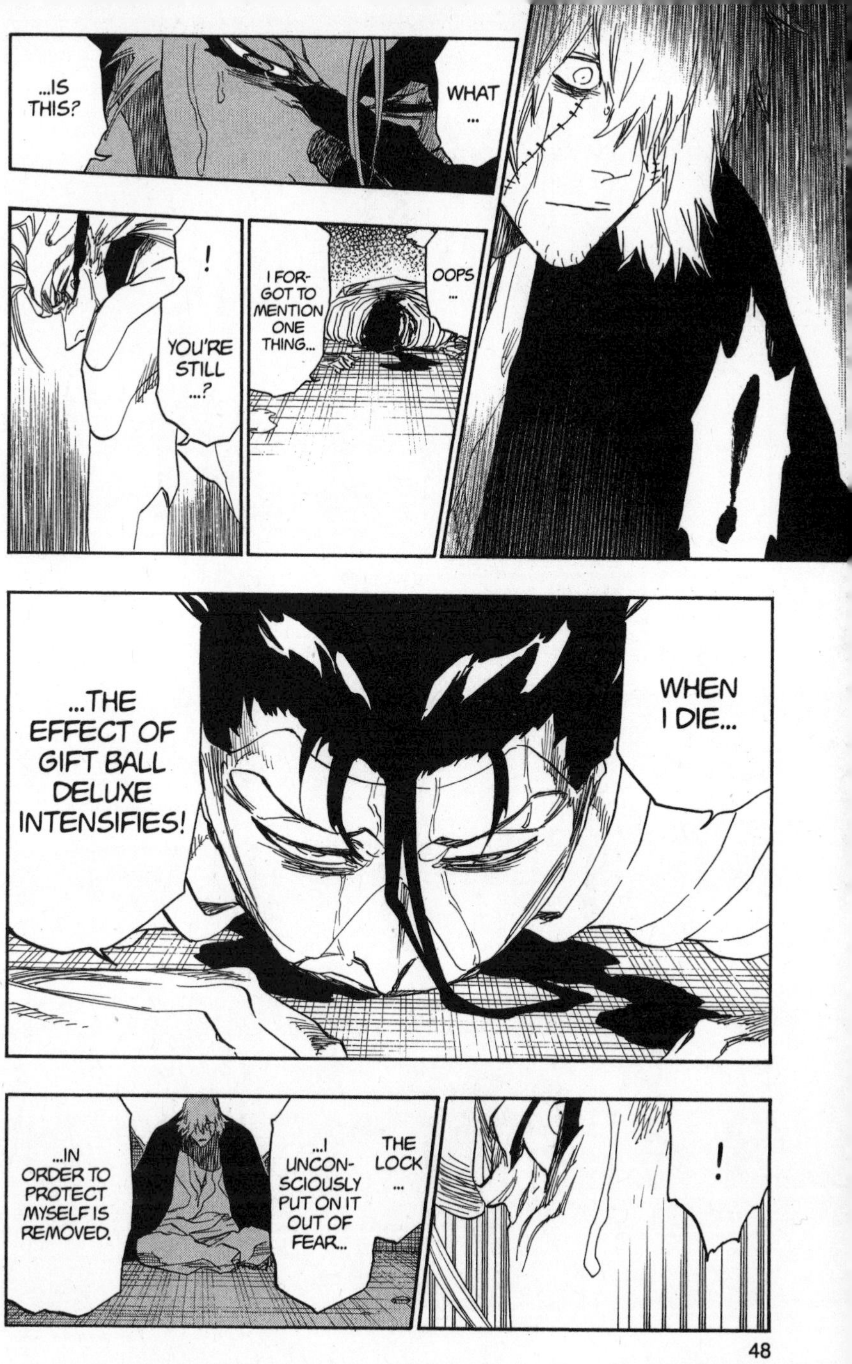
WHAT ...
...IS THIS?
OOPS ...
I FOR-GOT TO MENTION ONE THING...
!
YOU'RE STILL ...?
WHEN I DIE...
...THE EFFECT OF GIFT BALL DELUXE INTENSIFIES!
!
THE LOCK ...
...I UNCON-SCIOUSLY PUT ON IT OUT OF FEAR...
...IN ORDER TO PROTECT MYSELF IS REMOVED.

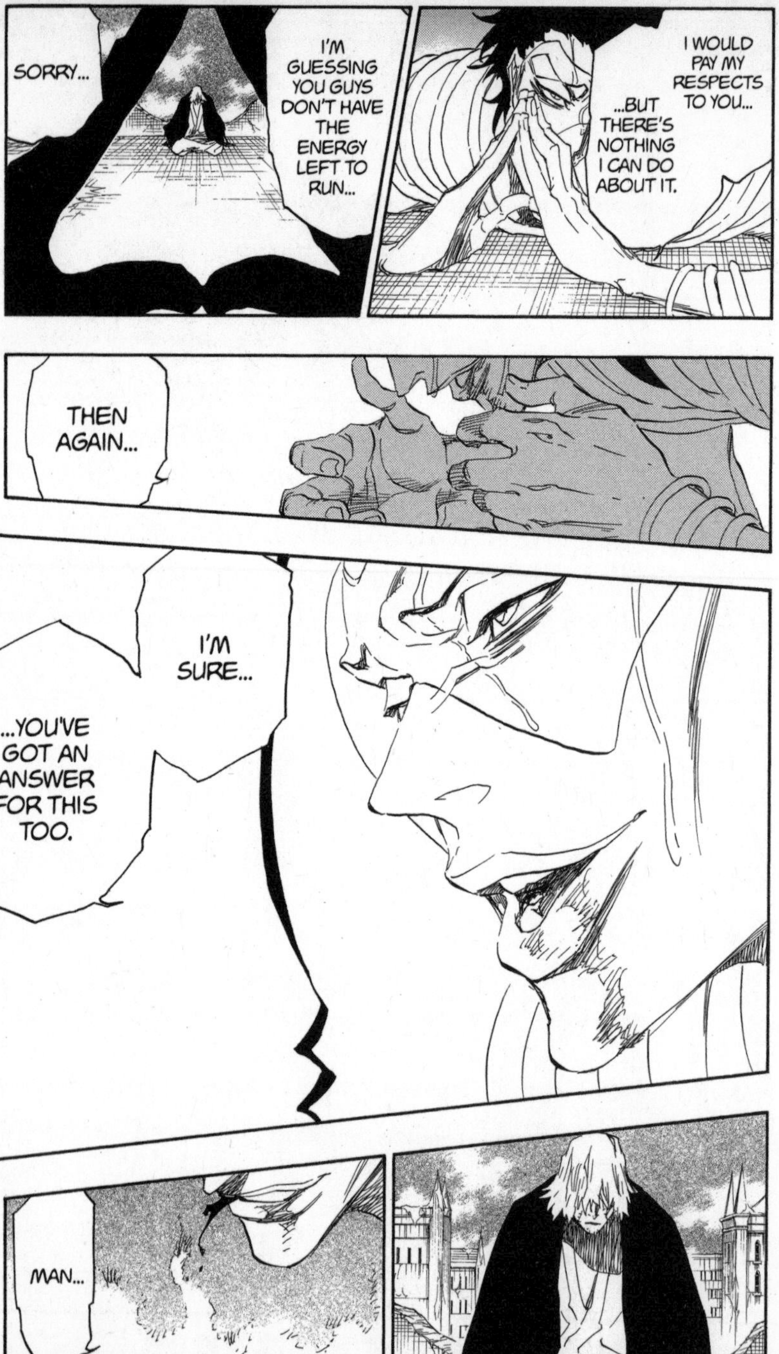
I WOULD PAY MY RESPECTS TO YOU...
...BUT THERE'S NOTHING I CAN DO ABOUT IT.
I'M GUESSING YOU GUYS DON'T HAVE THE ENERGY LEFT TO RUN...
SORRY...
THEN AGAIN...
I'M SURE...
...YOU'VE GOT AN ANSWER FOR THIS TOO.
MAN...

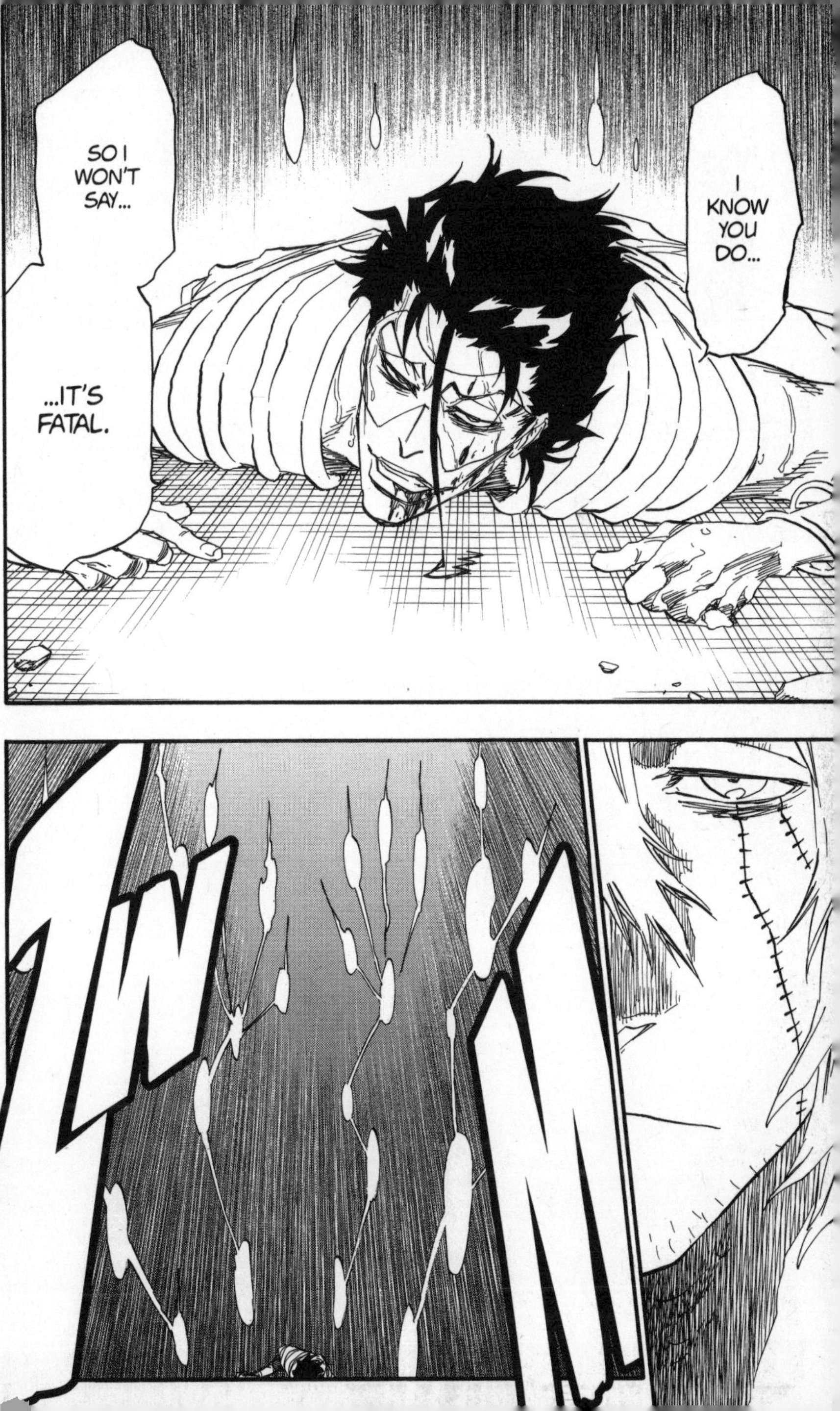
I KNOW YOU DO...
SO I WON'T SAY...
...IT'S FATAL.
ZWM

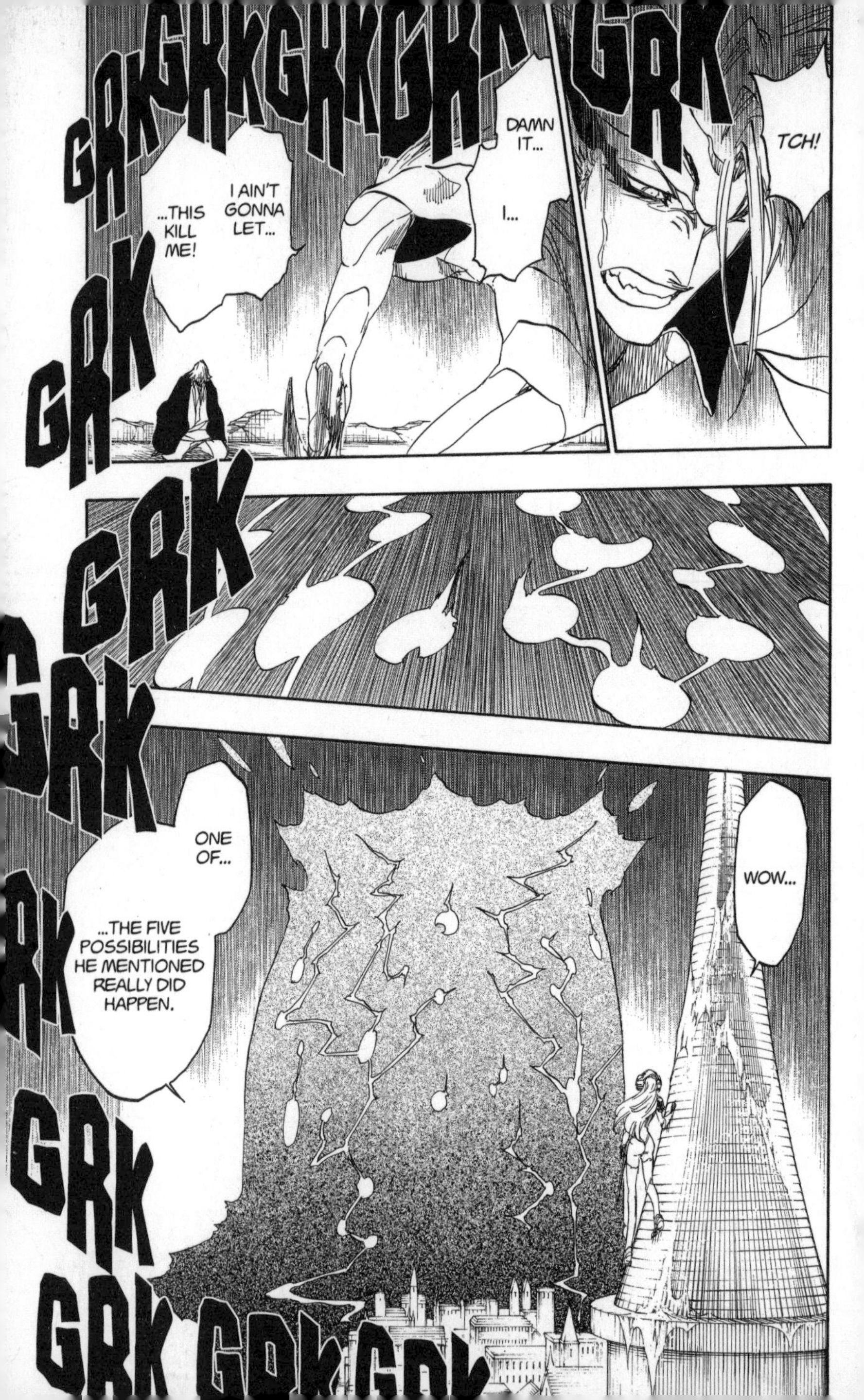
GRK
TCH!
DAMN IT...
I...
I AIN'T GONNA LET...
...THIS KILL ME!
GRK
GRK
GRK
WOW...
ONE OF...
...THE FIVE POSSIBILITIES HE MENTIONED REALLY DID HAPPEN.
GRK
GRK
GRK

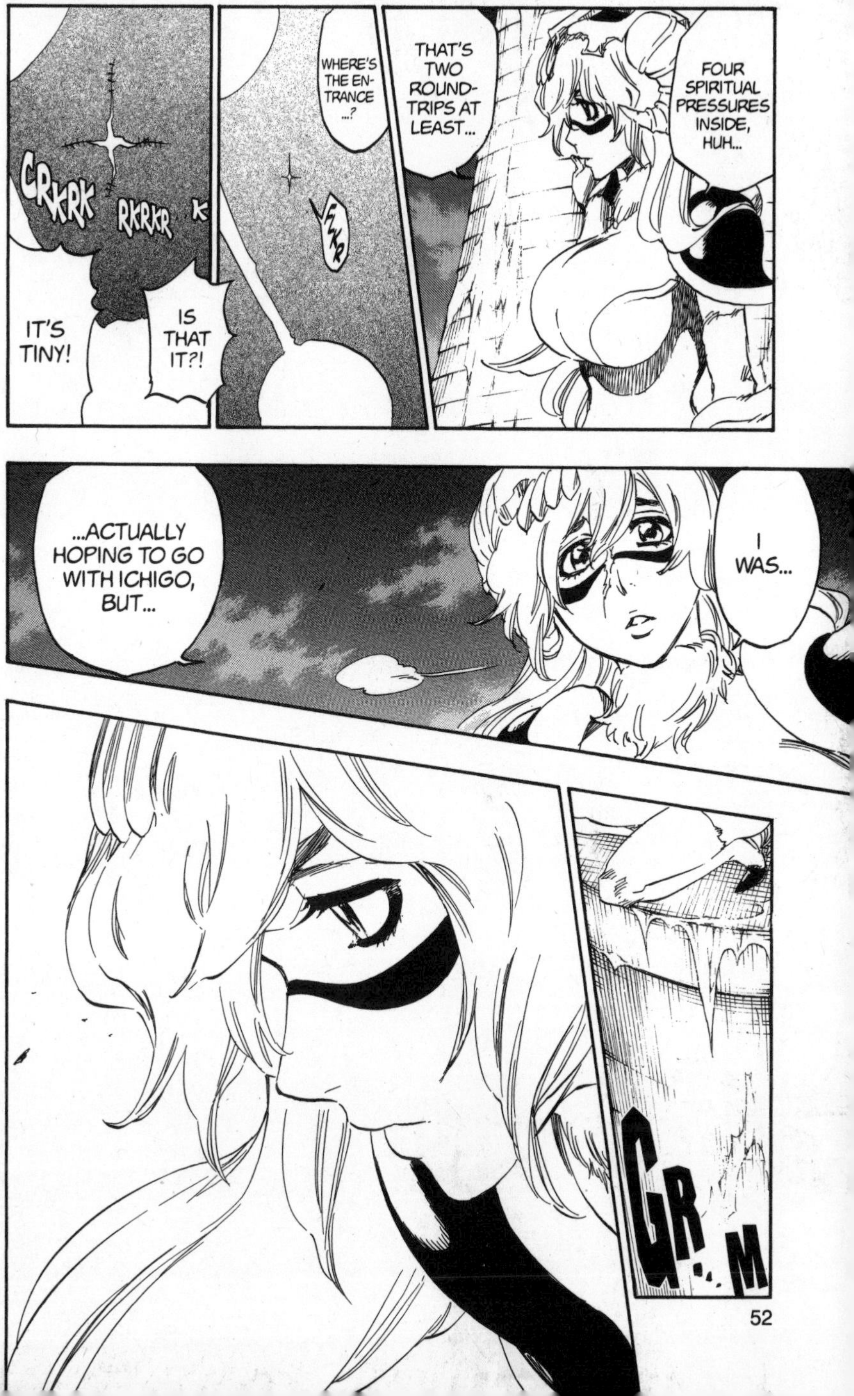
FOUR SPIRITUAL PRESSURES INSIDE, HUH...
THAT'S TWO ROUND-TRIPS AT LEAST...
WHERE'S THE EN-TRANCE ...?
FWKR
IS THAT IT?!
IT'S TINY!
CRKRK RKRKR K
I WAS...
...ACTUALLY HOPING TO GO WITH ICHIGO, BUT...
GR.. M

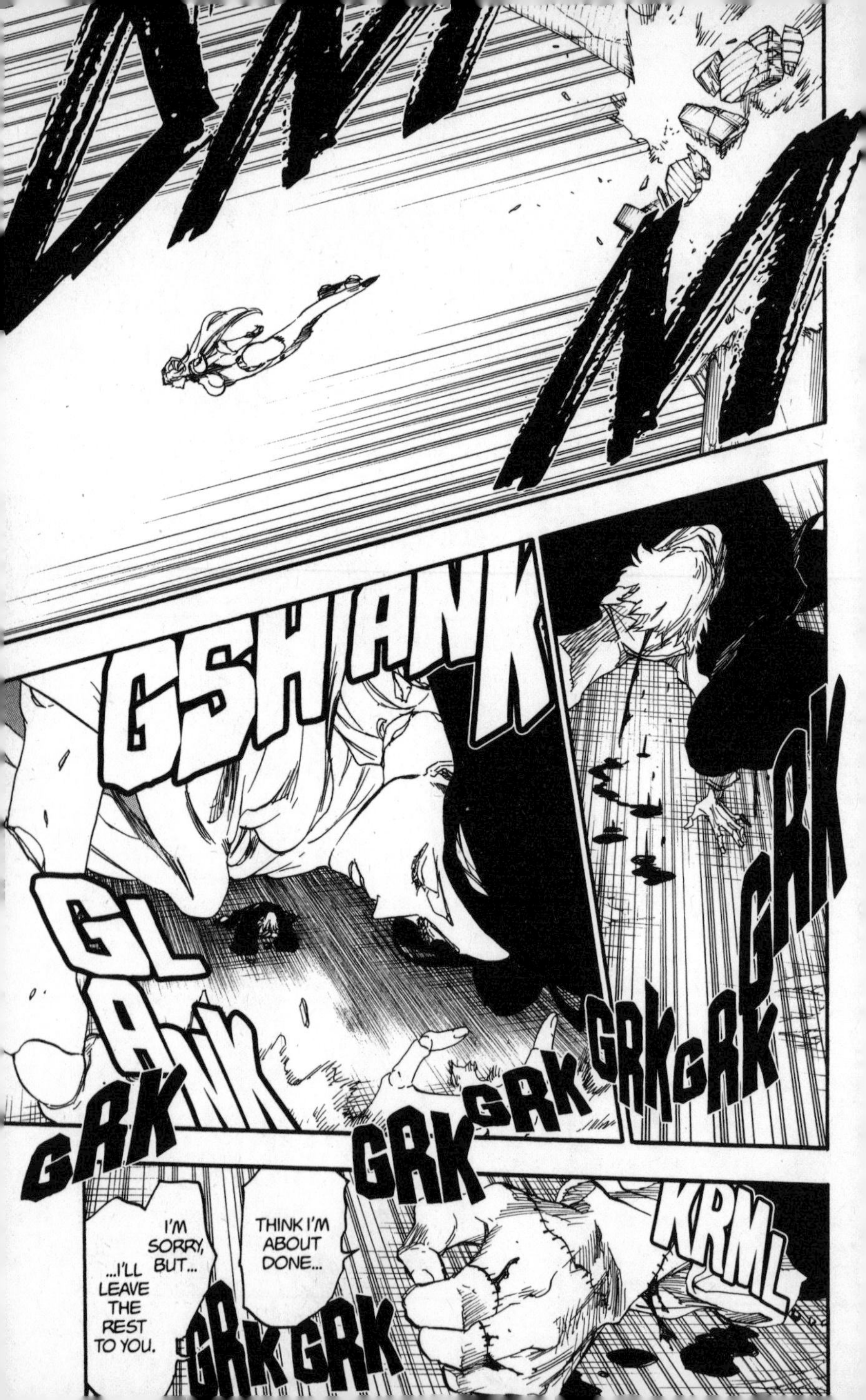
GRK GRK GRK GRK GRK GRK
GSHANK
GRK GRK
KRML
THINK I'M ABOUT DONE...
I'M SORRY, BUT...
...I'LL LEAVE THE REST TO YOU.
GRK GRK

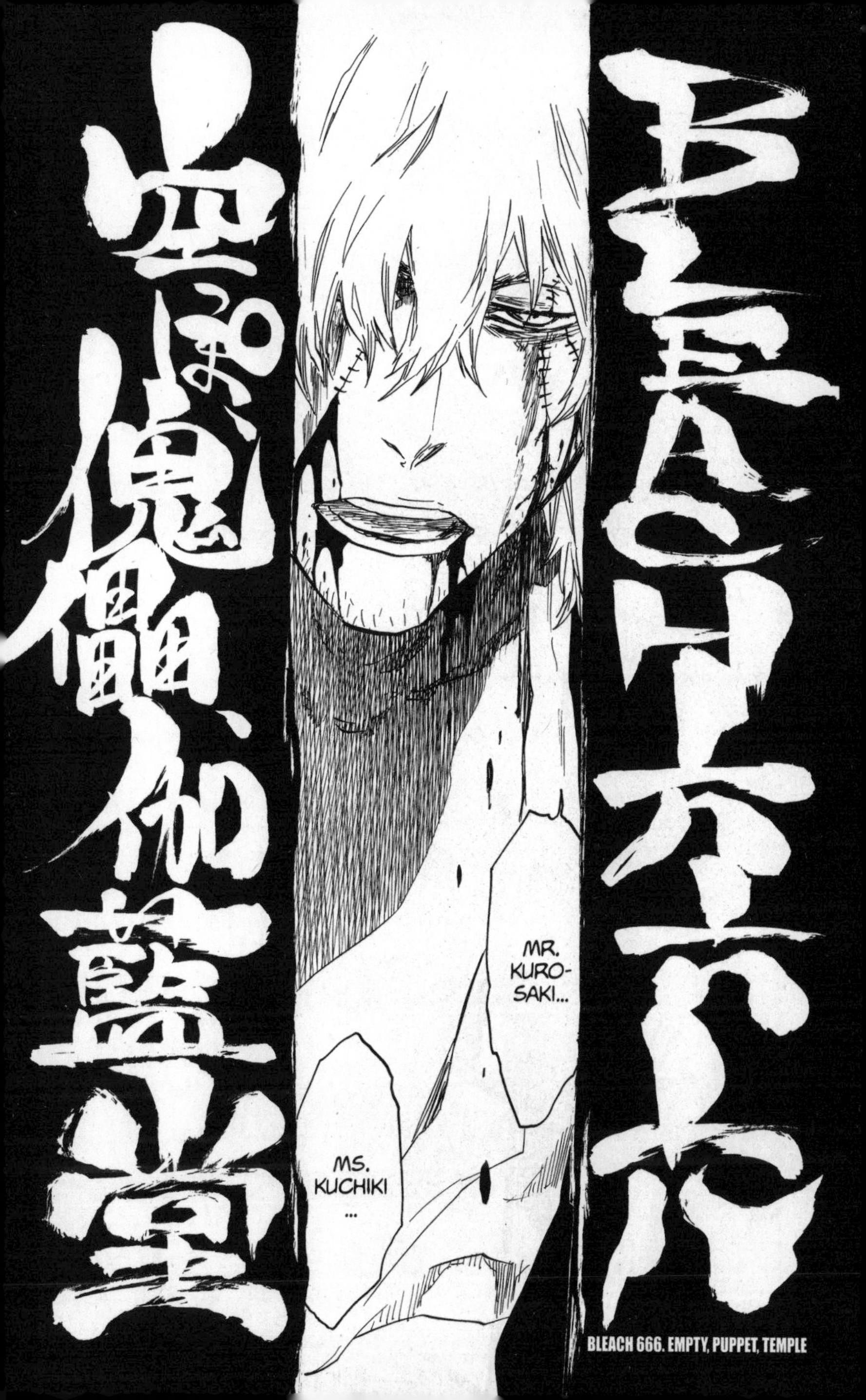
五百六十六
MR. KURO-SAKI...
MS. KUCHIKI ...
空っぽ傀儡伽藍堂
BLEACH 666. EMPTY, PUPPET, TEMPLE

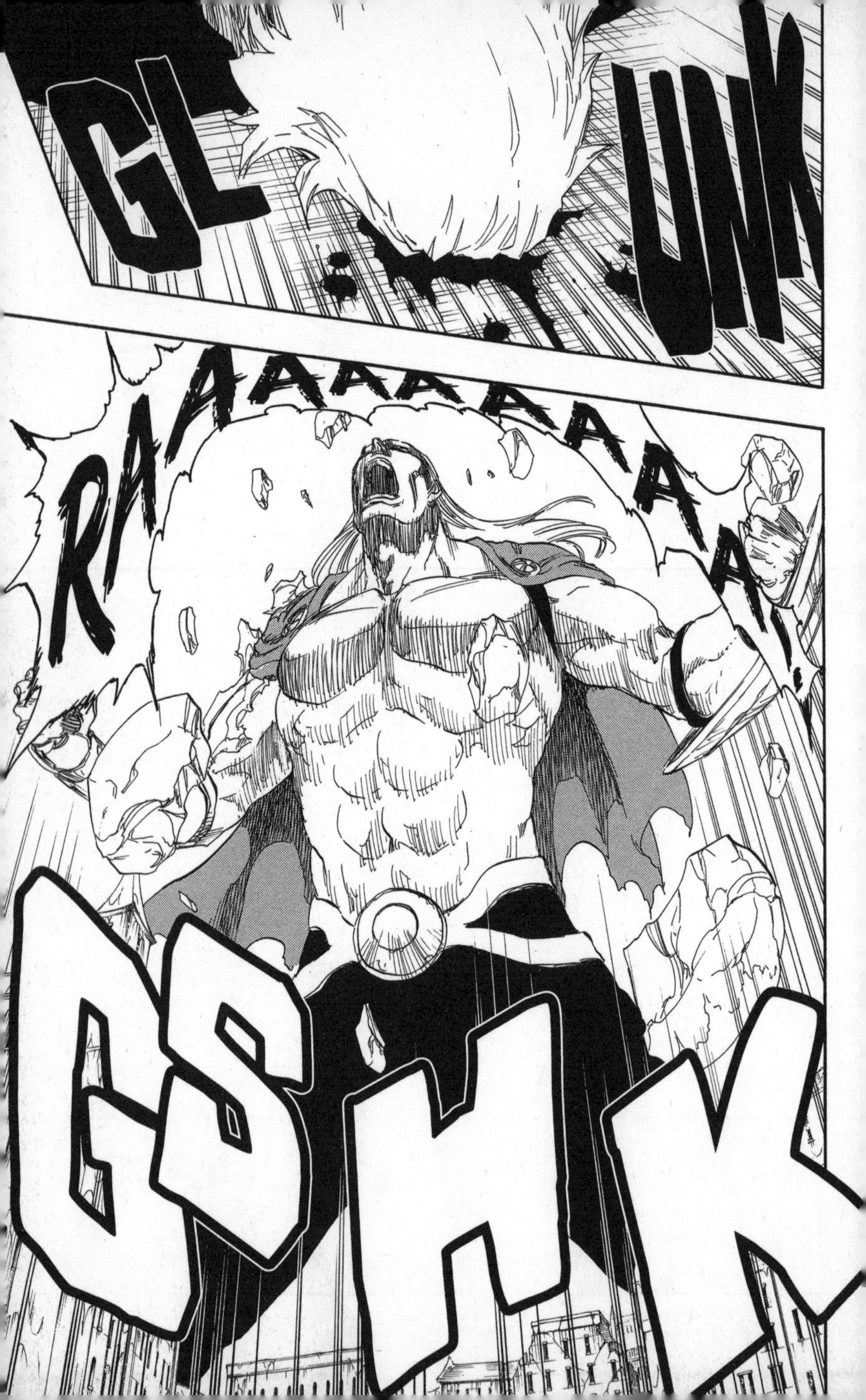
GLUNK
RAAAAAAAAAA!
GSHK

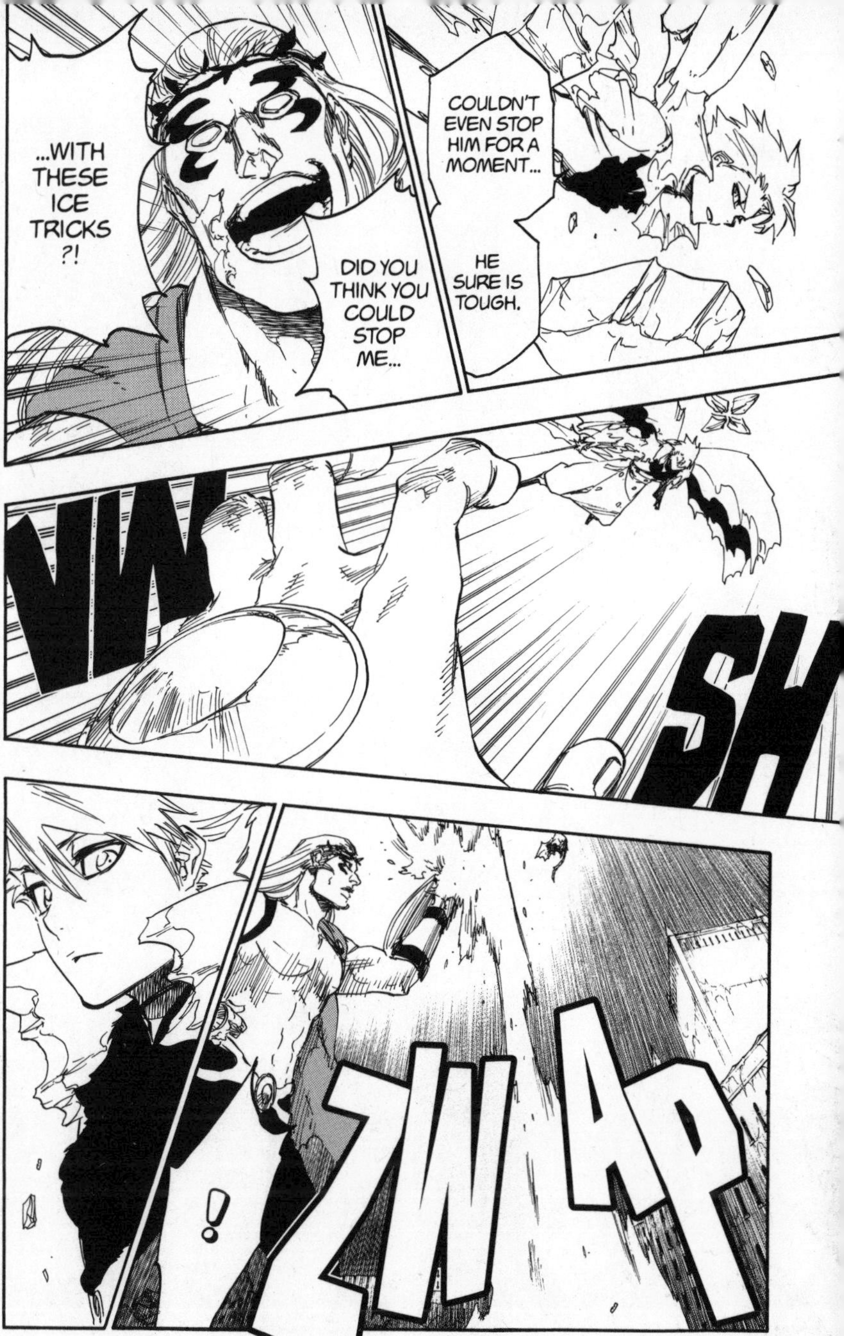
COULDN'T EVEN STOP HIM FOR A MOMENT...
HE SURE IS TOUGH.
DID YOU THINK YOU COULD STOP ME...
...WITH THESE ICE TRICKS ?!
SH
NW
ZW
AP
!

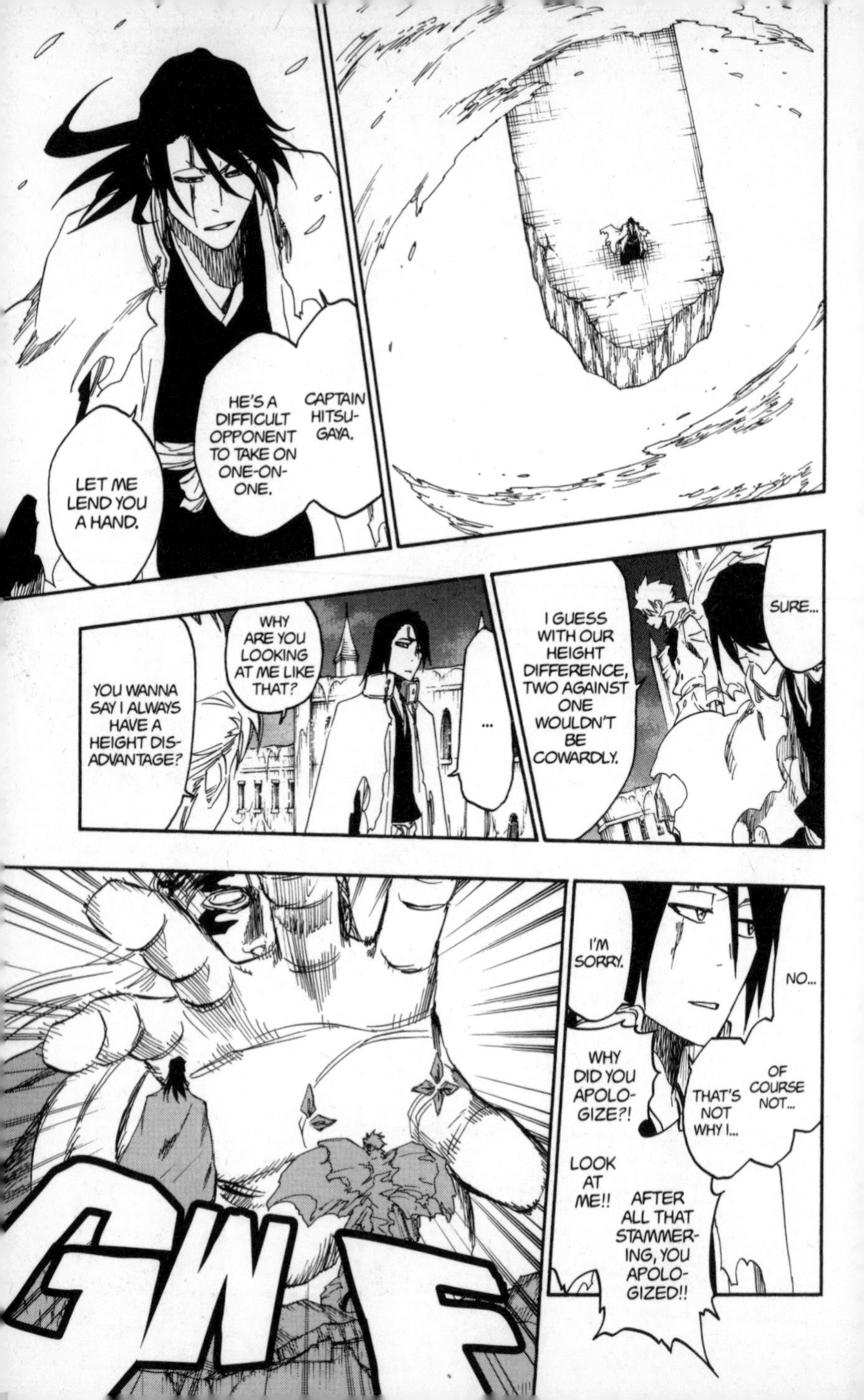

CAPTAIN HITSUGAYA.
HE'S A DIFFICULT OPPONENT TO TAKE ON ONE-ON-ONE.
LET ME LEND YOU A HAND.
SURE...
I GUESS WITH OUR HEIGHT DIFFERENCE, TWO AGAINST ONE WOULDN'T BE COWARDLY.
...
WHY ARE YOU LOOKING AT ME LIKE THAT?
YOU WANNA SAY I ALWAYS HAVE A HEIGHT DISADVANTAGE?
NO...
OF COURSE NOT...
THAT'S NOT WHY I...
I'M SORRY.
WHY DID YOU APOLOGIZE?!
LOOK AT ME!!
AFTER ALL THAT STAMMERING, YOU APOLOGIZED!!

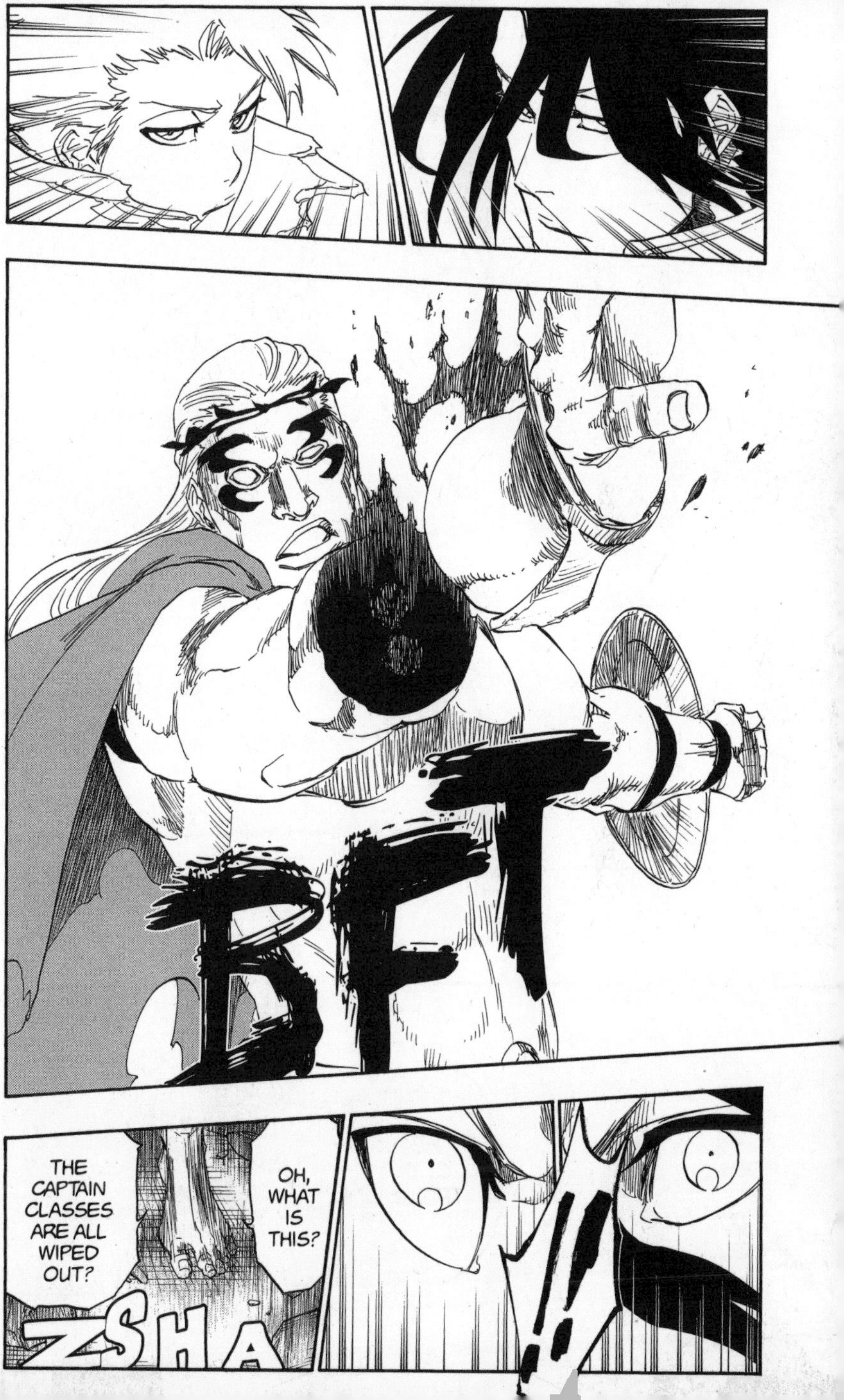
BFT
!!
OH, WHAT IS THIS?
THE CAPTAIN CLASSES ARE ALL WIPED OUT?
ZSHA

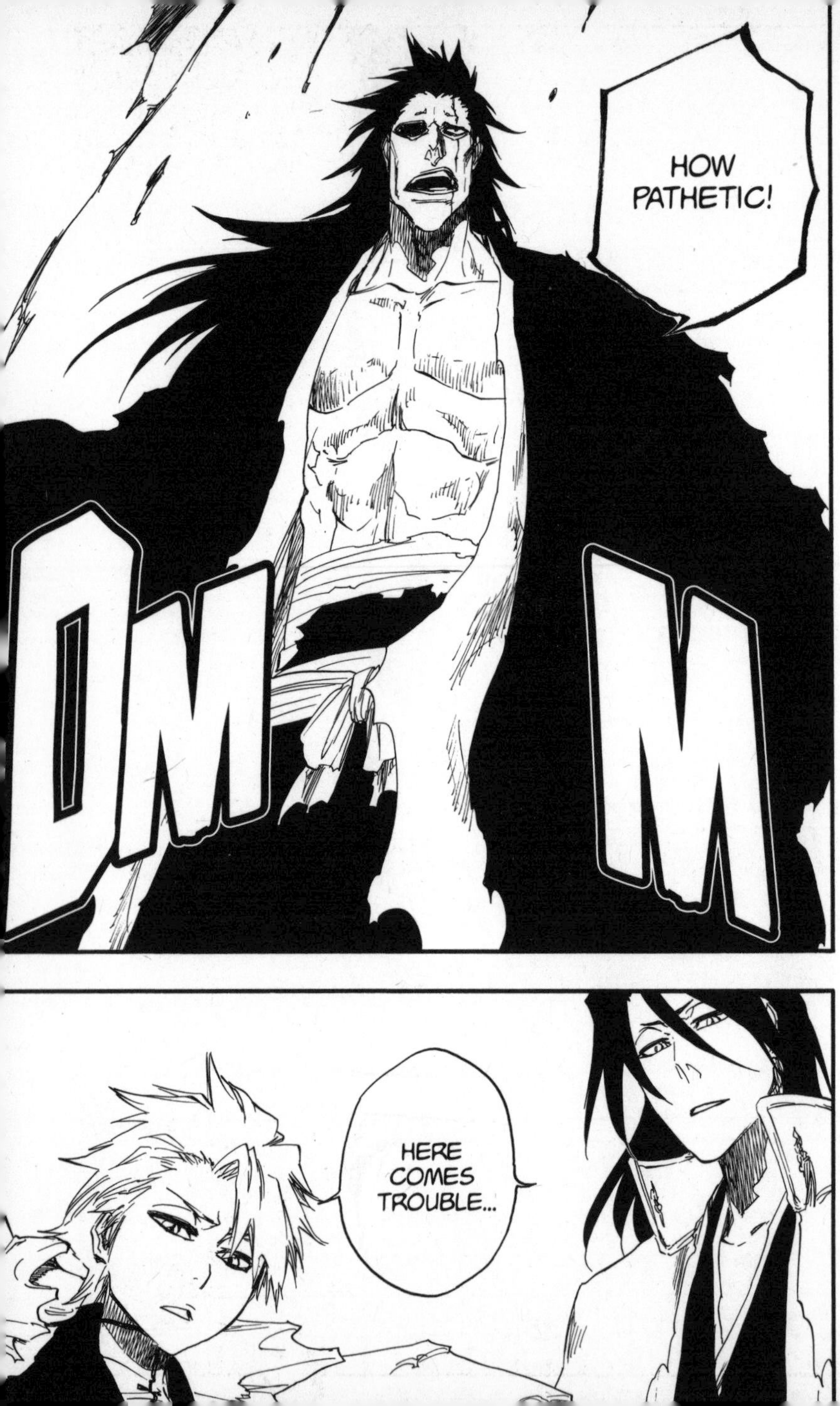
HOW PATHETIC!
HERE COMES TROUBLE...

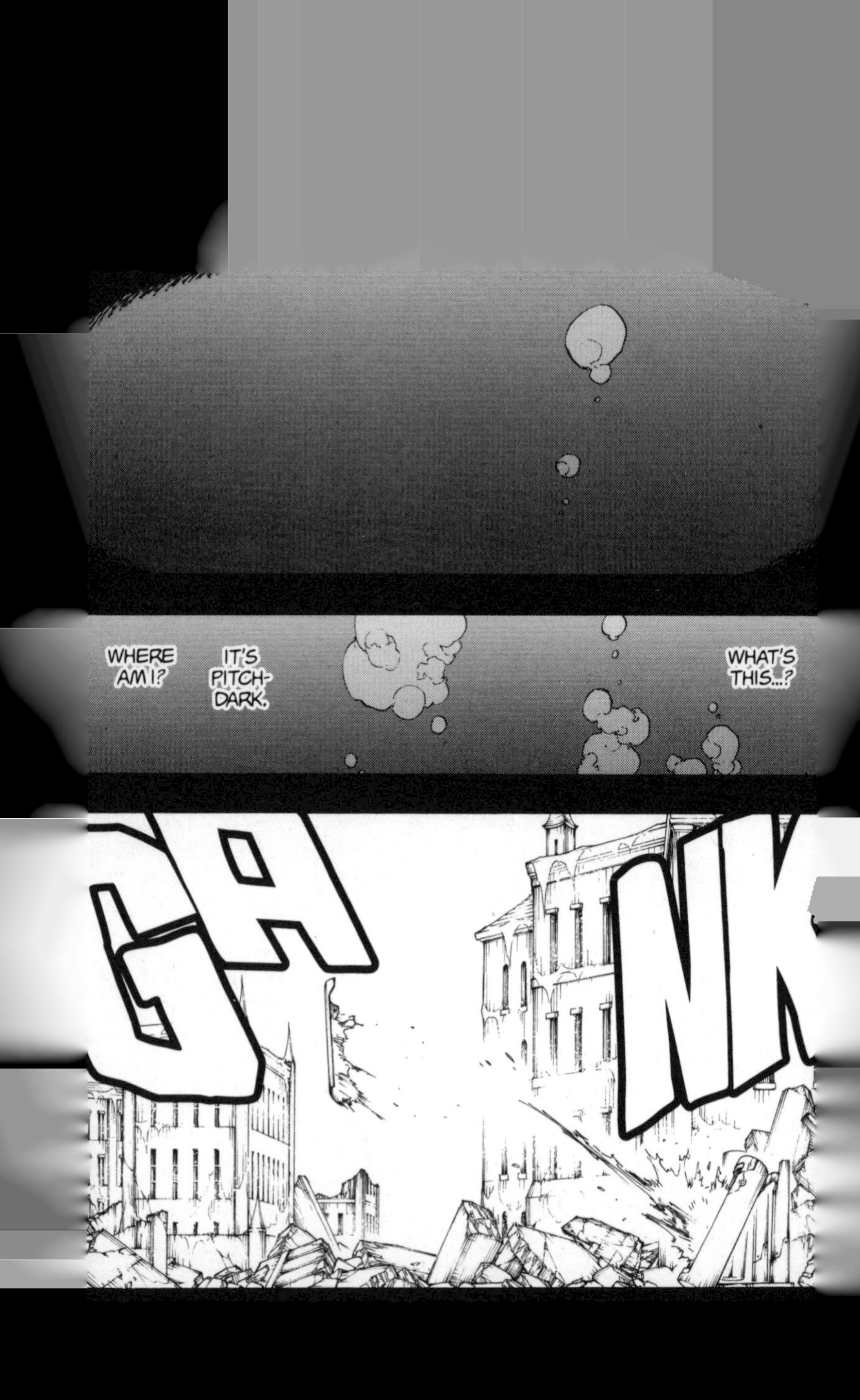
WHAT'S THIS...?
IT'S PITCH-DARK.
WHERE AM I?
GA
NK

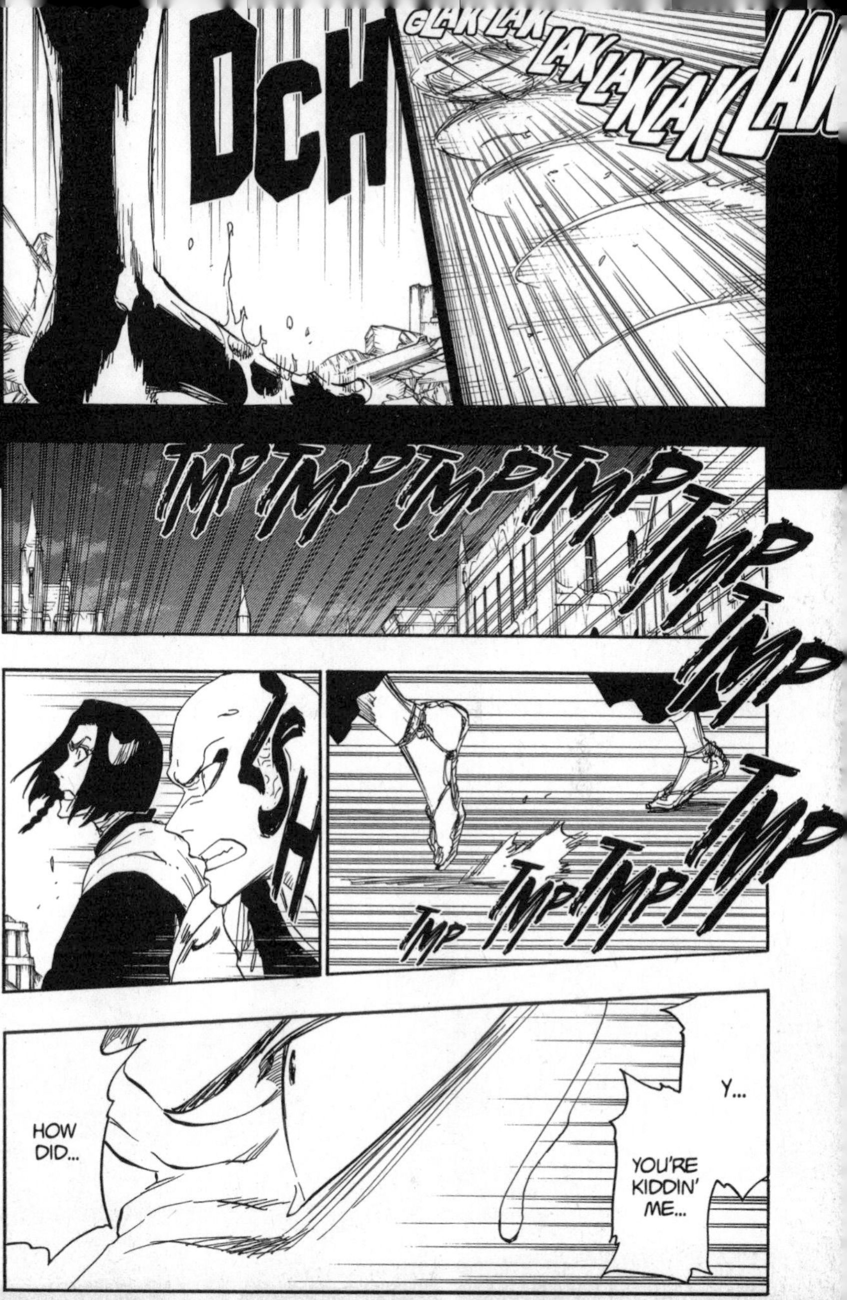
CLAK LAK
DCH
TMP TMP TMP TMP TMP TMP
TMP TMP TMP TMP TMP
TSH
Y...
YOU'RE KIDDIN' ME...
HOW DID...

BLEACH 667. BIGGER, LOUDER, STRONGER

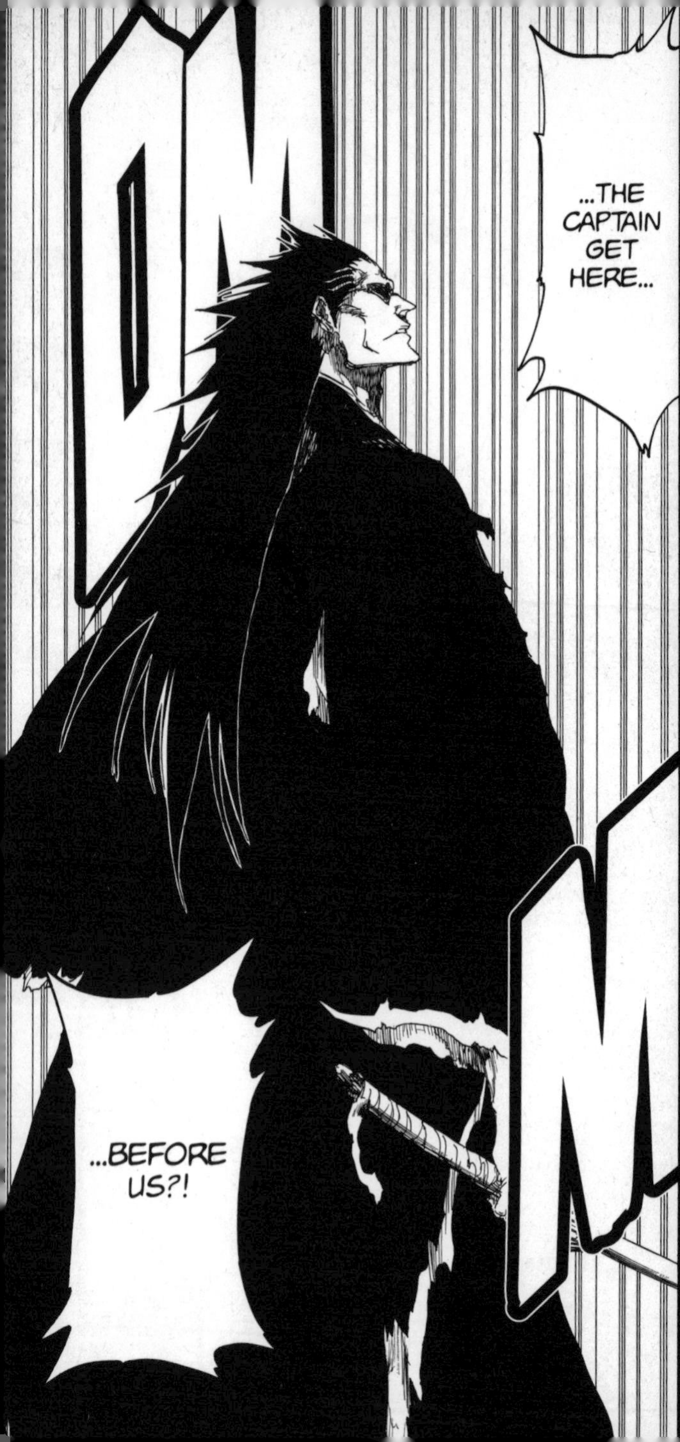
...THE CAPTAIN GET HERE...
...BEFORE US?!

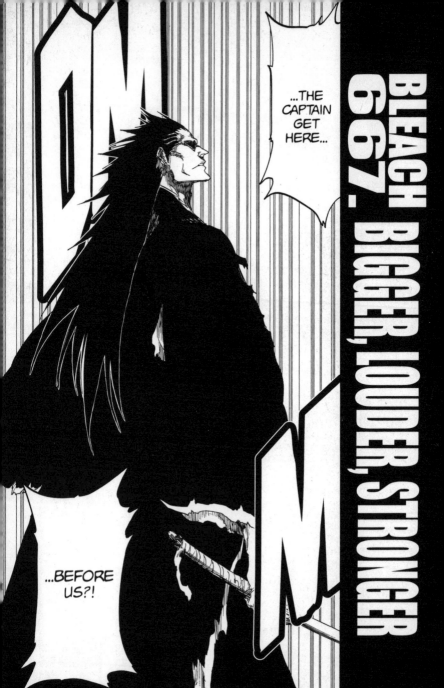

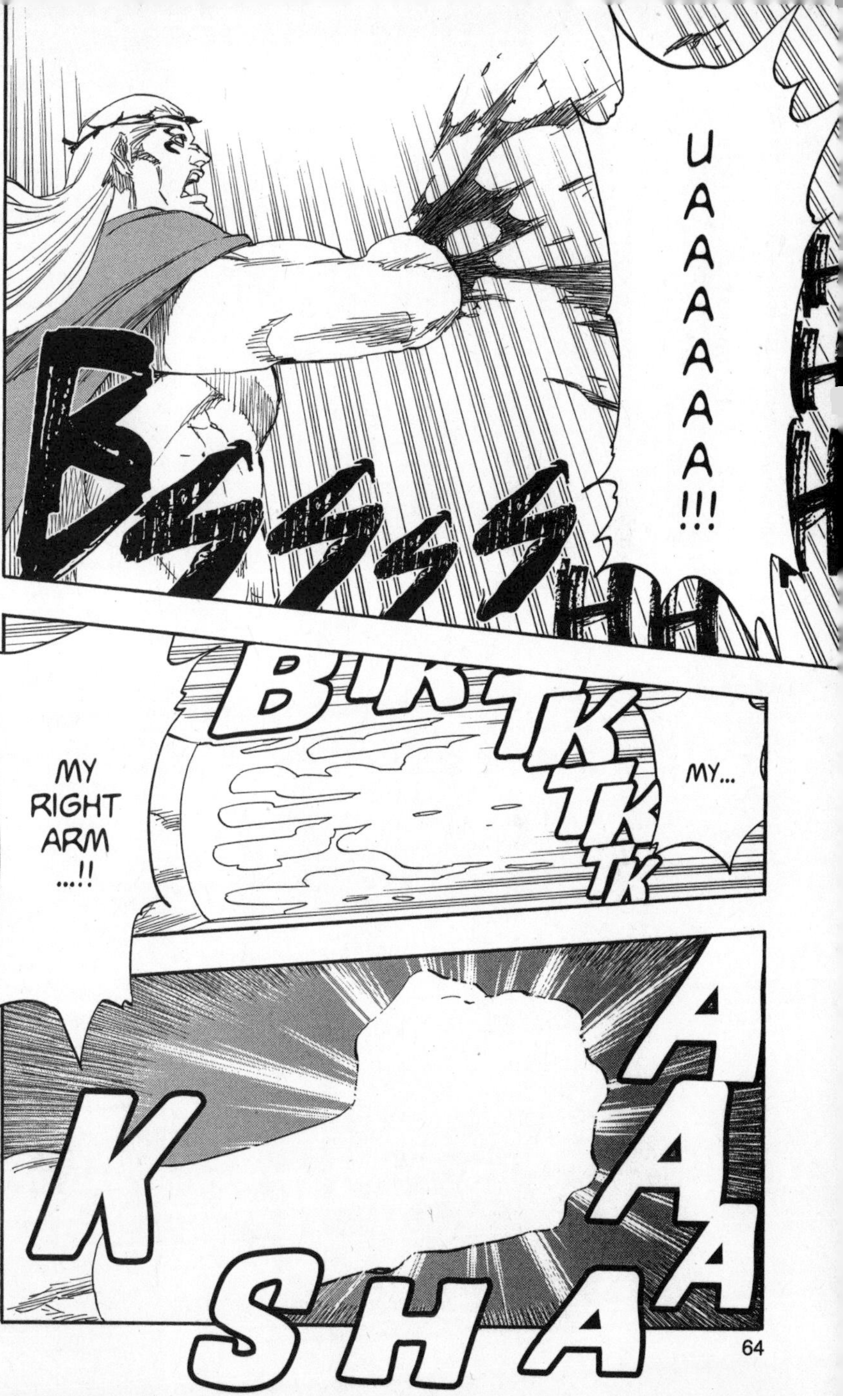
UAAAAAAA!!!
BSSSSHH
MY...
MY RIGHT ARM ...!!
BKTKTKTK
KSHAAAA

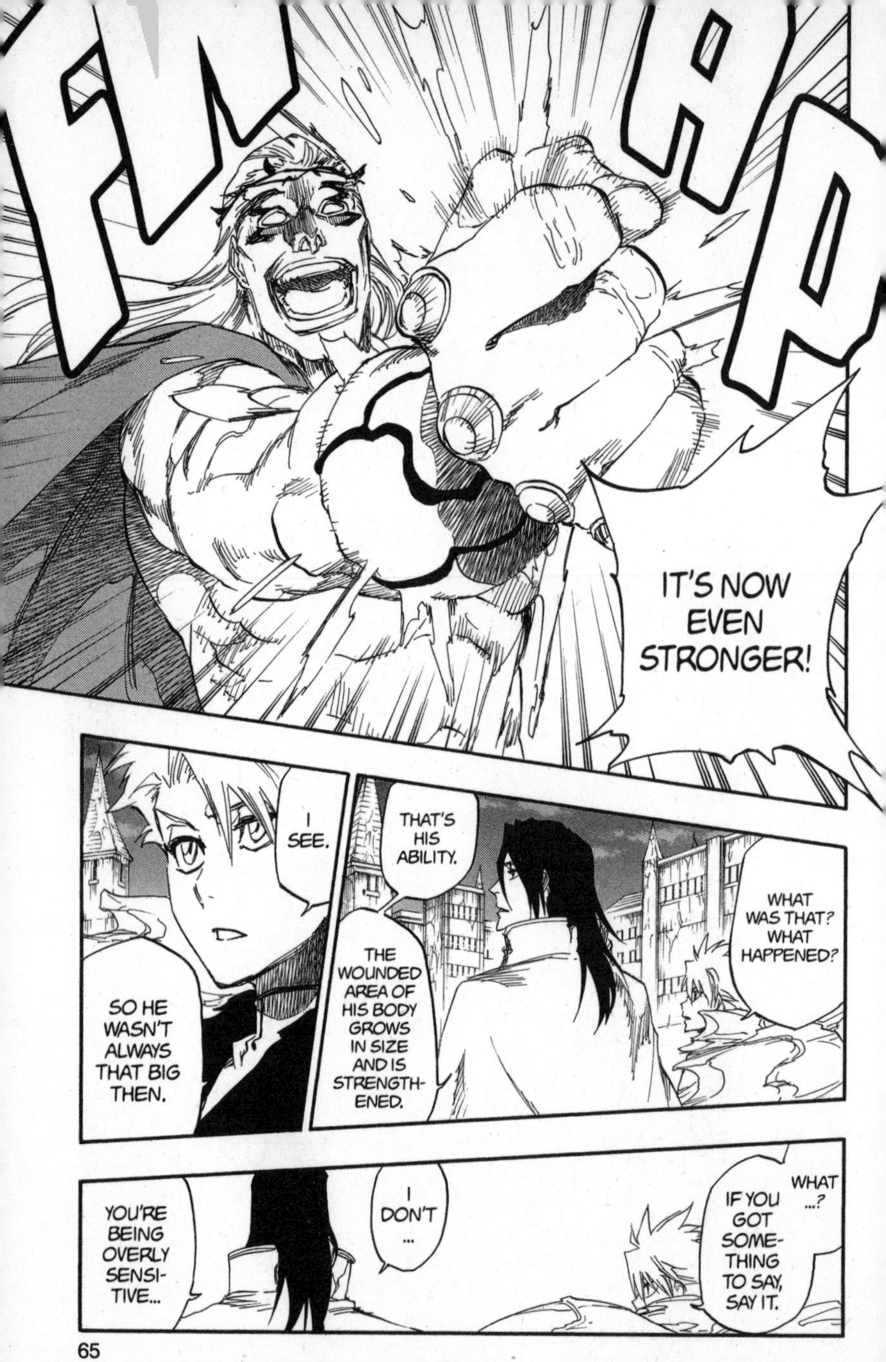
IT'S NOW EVEN STRONGER!
WHAT WAS THAT? WHAT HAPPENED?
THAT'S HIS ABILITY.
THE WOUNDED AREA OF HIS BODY GROWS IN SIZE AND IS STRENGTHENED.
I SEE.
SO HE WASN'T ALWAYS THAT BIG THEN.
WHAT ...?
IF YOU GOT SOMETHING TO SAY, SAY IT.
I DON'T ...
YOU'RE BEING OVERLY SENSITIVE...

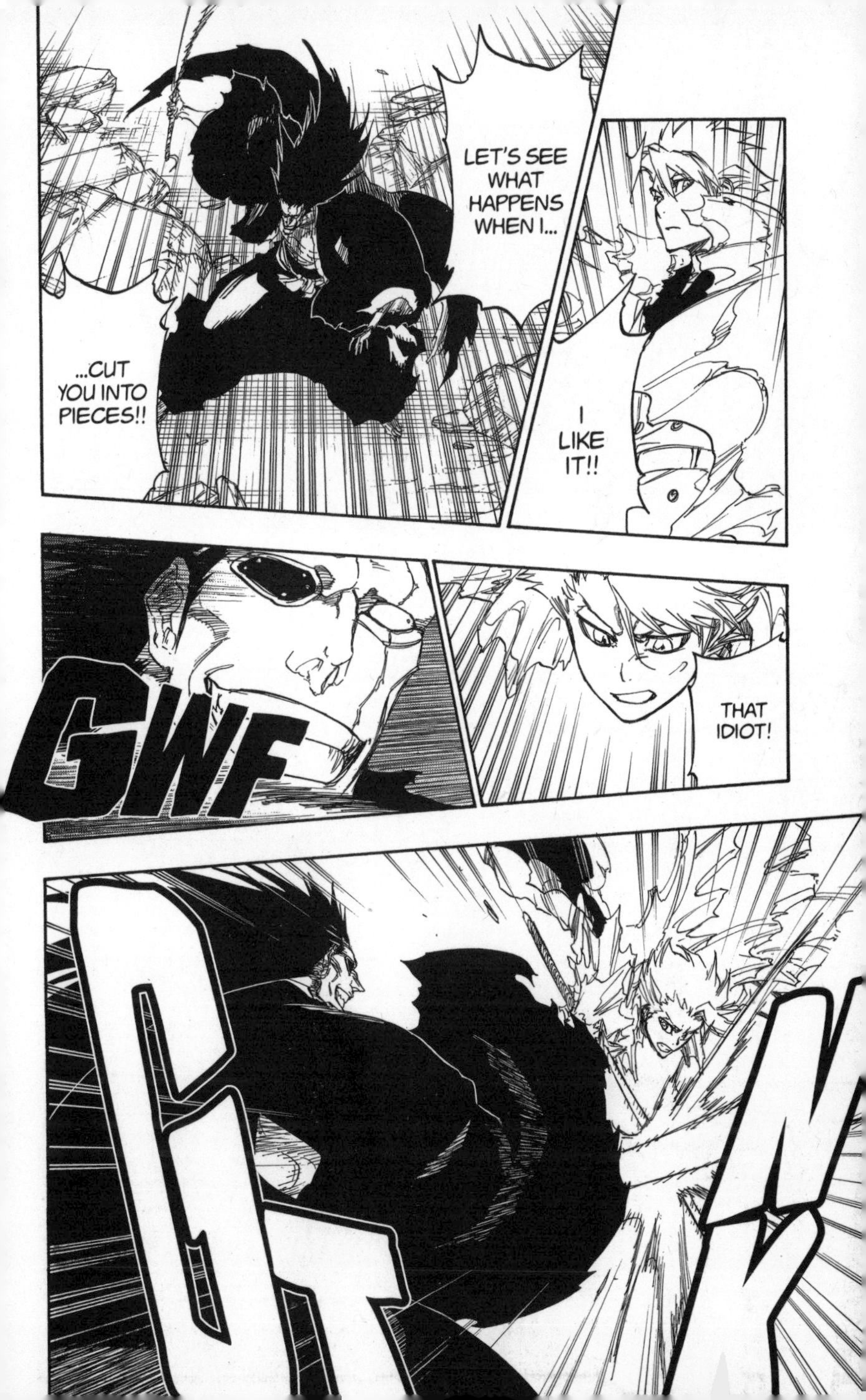
I LIKE IT!!
LET'S SEE WHAT HAPPENS WHEN I...
...CUT YOU INTO PIECES!!
THAT IDIOT!
GWF

READ THIS WAY

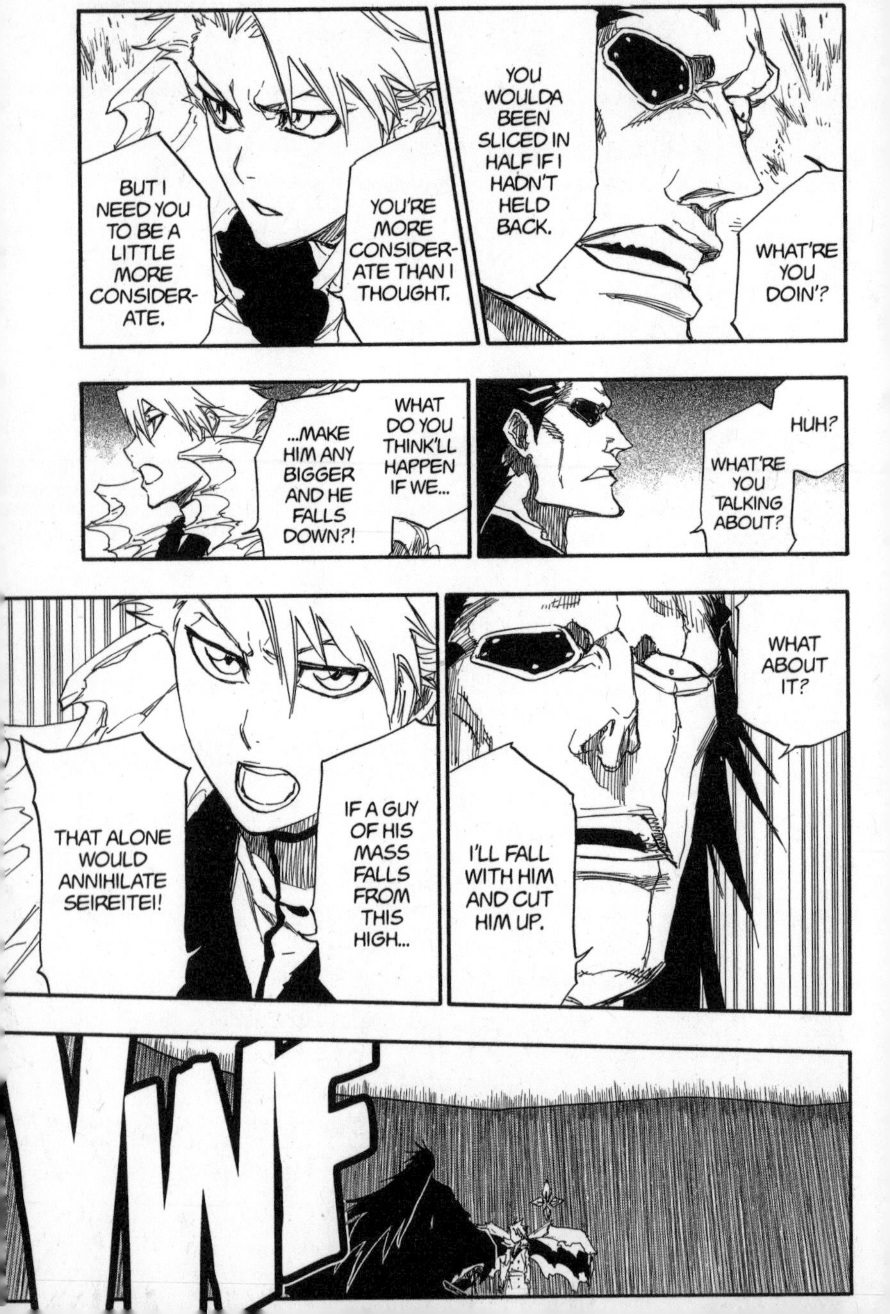

WHAT'RE YOU DOIN'?
YOU WOULDA BEEN SLICED IN HALF IF I HADN'T HELD BACK.
YOU'RE MORE CONSIDERATE THAN I THOUGHT.
BUT I NEED YOU TO BE A LITTLE MORE CONSIDERATE.
HUH?
WHAT'RE YOU TALKING ABOUT?
WHAT DO YOU THINK'LL HAPPEN IF WE...
...MAKE HIM ANY BIGGER AND HE FALLS DOWN?!
WHAT ABOUT IT?
I'LL FALL WITH HIM AND CUT HIM UP.
IF A GUY OF HIS MASS FALLS FROM THIS HIGH...
THAT ALONE WOULD ANNIHILATE SEIREITEI!

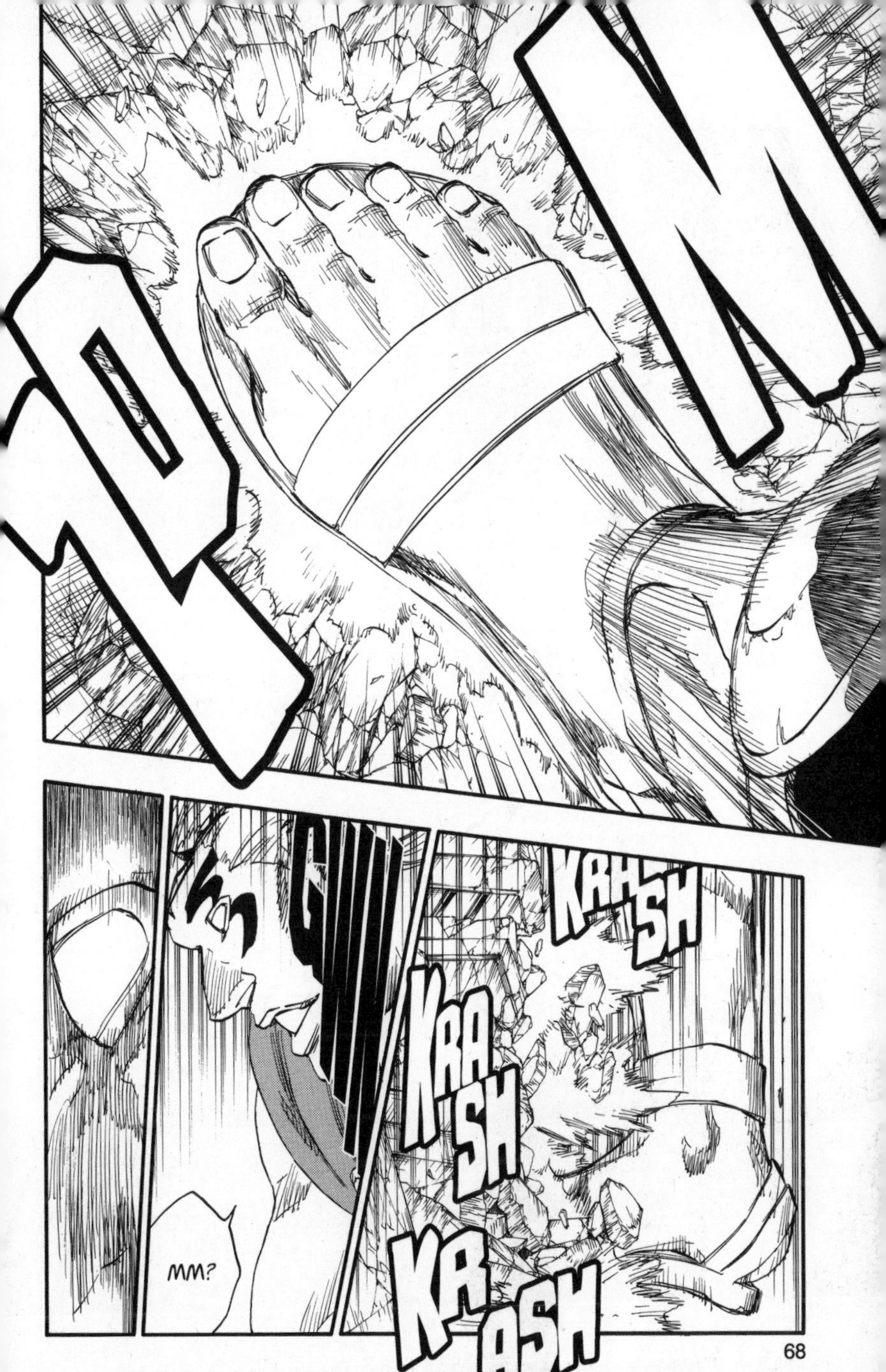
KRASH
KRASH
KRASH
MM?

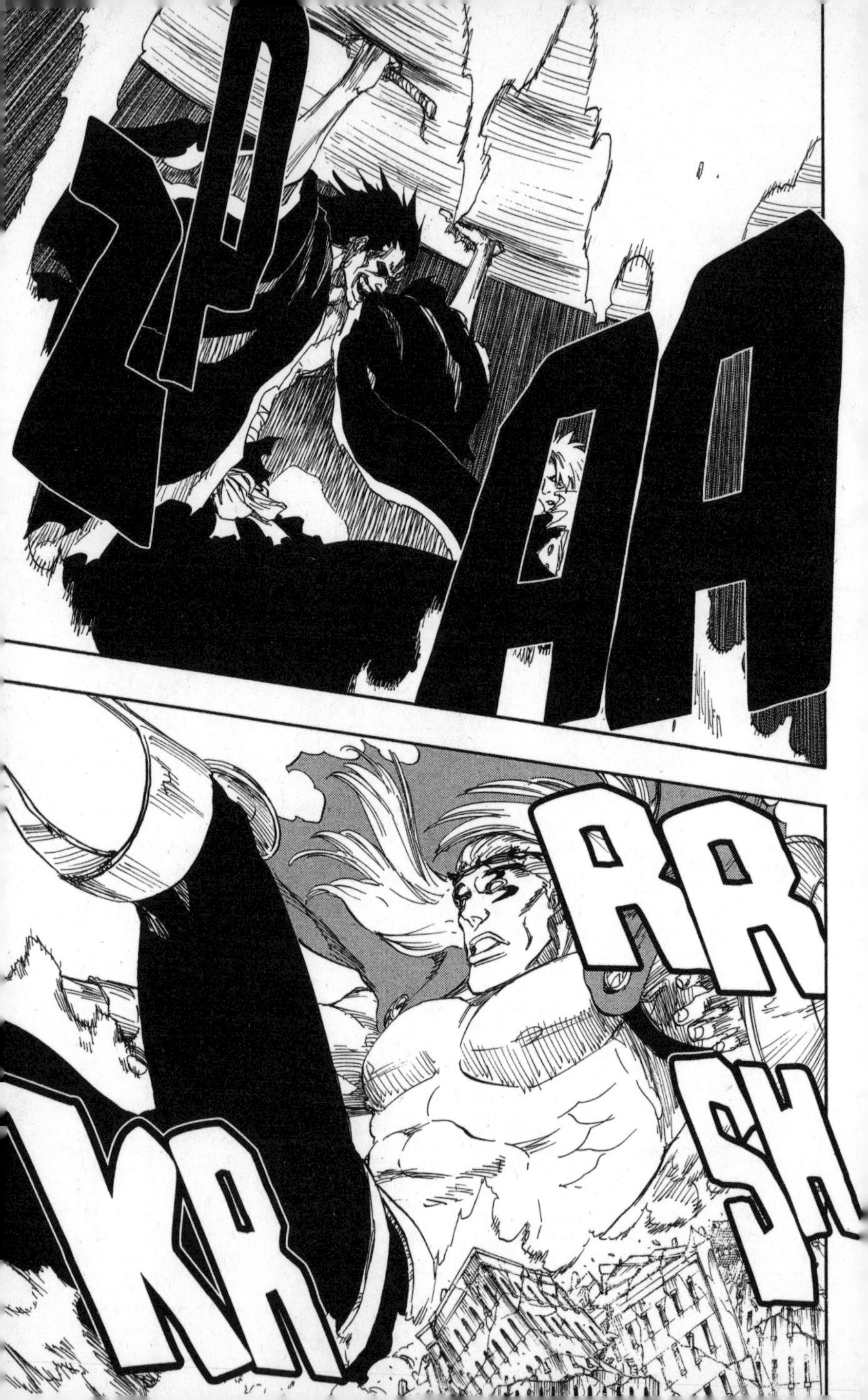
ZD
AA
RR
SH
KRA

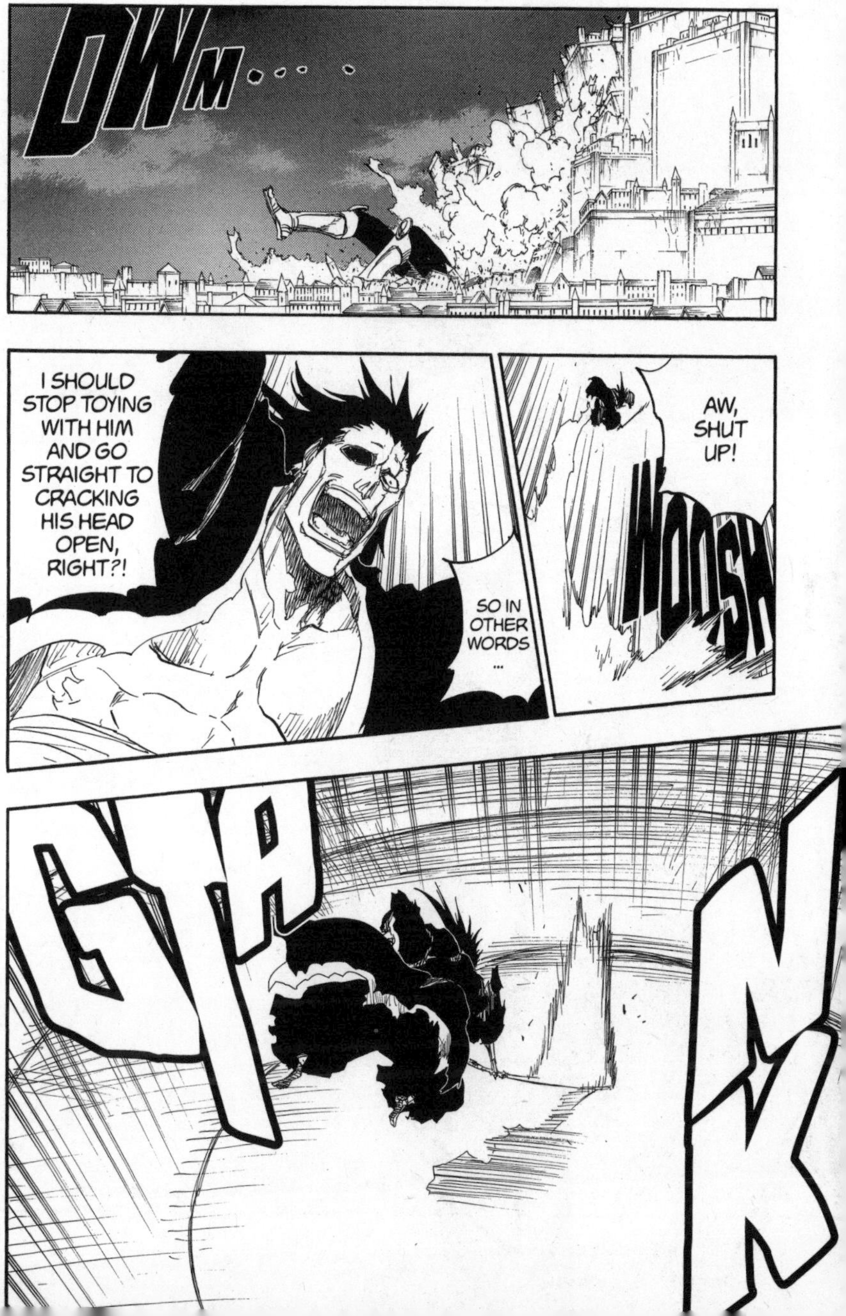
DWM...
AW, SHUT UP!
WOOSH
SO IN OTHER WORDS...
I SHOULD STOP TOYING WITH HIM AND GO STRAIGHT TO CRACKING HIS HEAD OPEN, RIGHT?!
GTANK

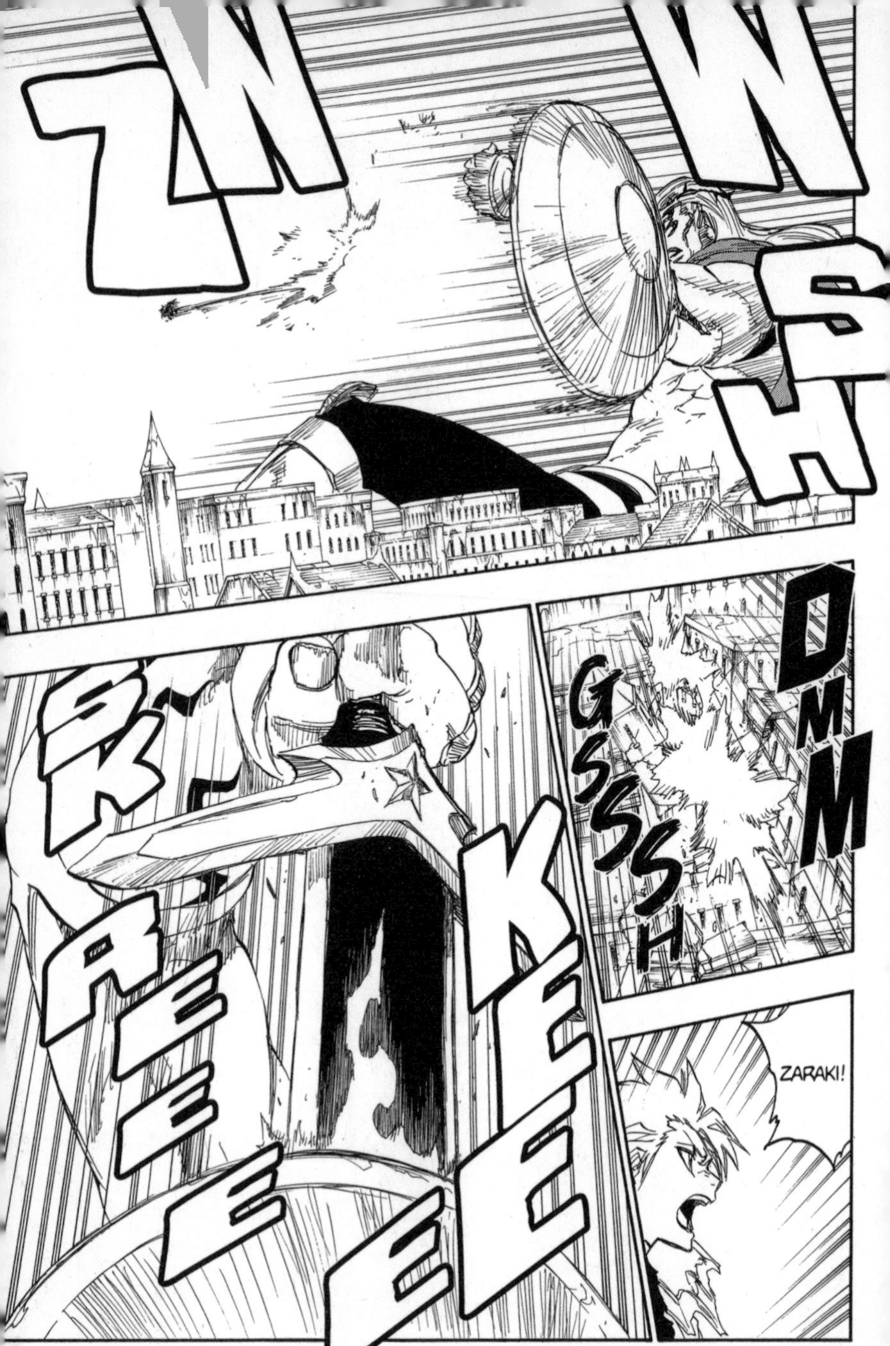
DMMM
GSSSH
ZARAKI!

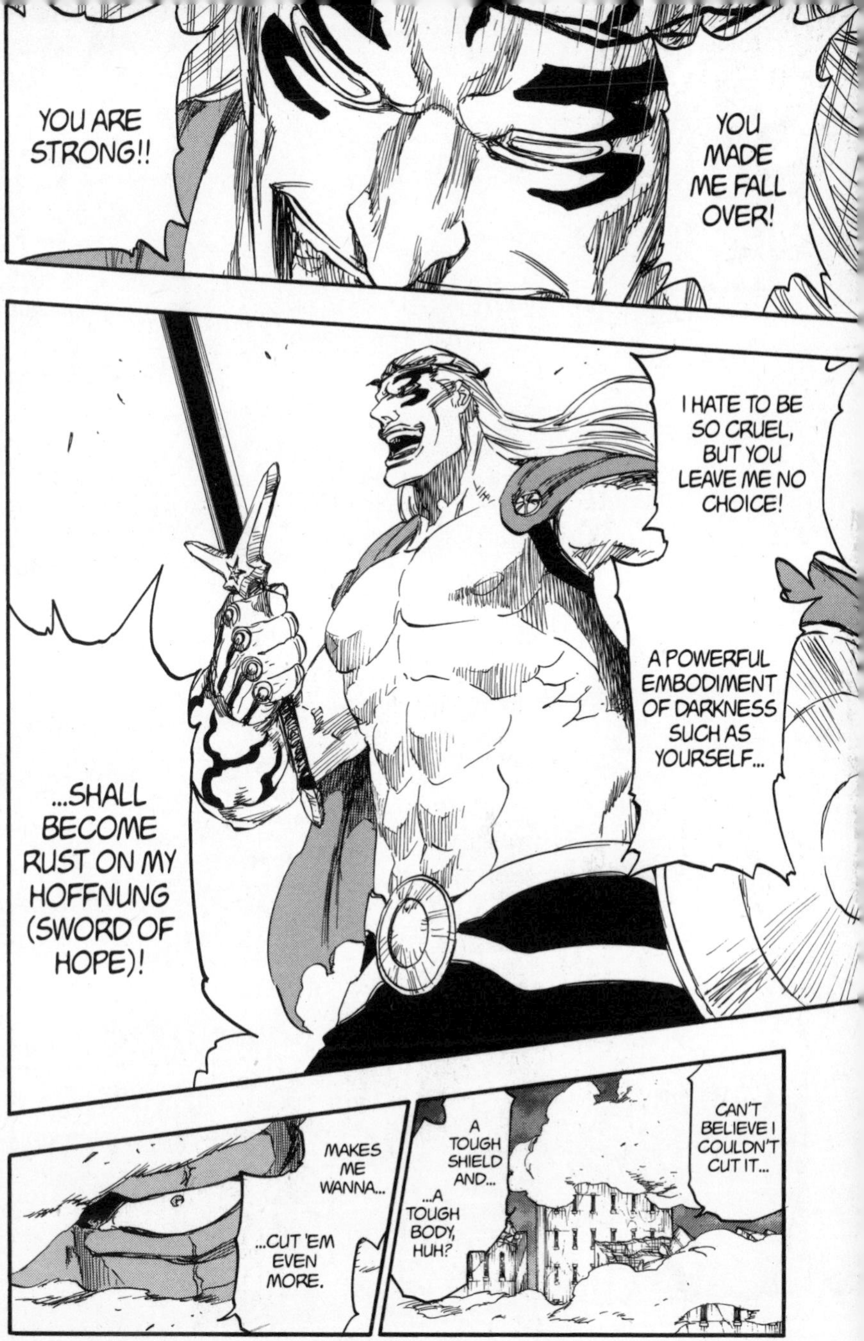
YOU MADE ME FALL OVER!
YOU ARE STRONG!!
I HATE TO BE SO CRUEL, BUT YOU LEAVE ME NO CHOICE!
A POWERFUL EMBODIMENT OF DARKNESS SUCH AS YOURSELF...
...SHALL BECOME RUST ON MY HOFFNUNG (SWORD OF HOPE)!
CAN'T BELIEVE I COULDN'T CUT IT...
A TOUGH SHIELD AND...
...A TOUGH BODY, HUH?
MAKES ME WANNA...
...CUT 'EM EVEN MORE.

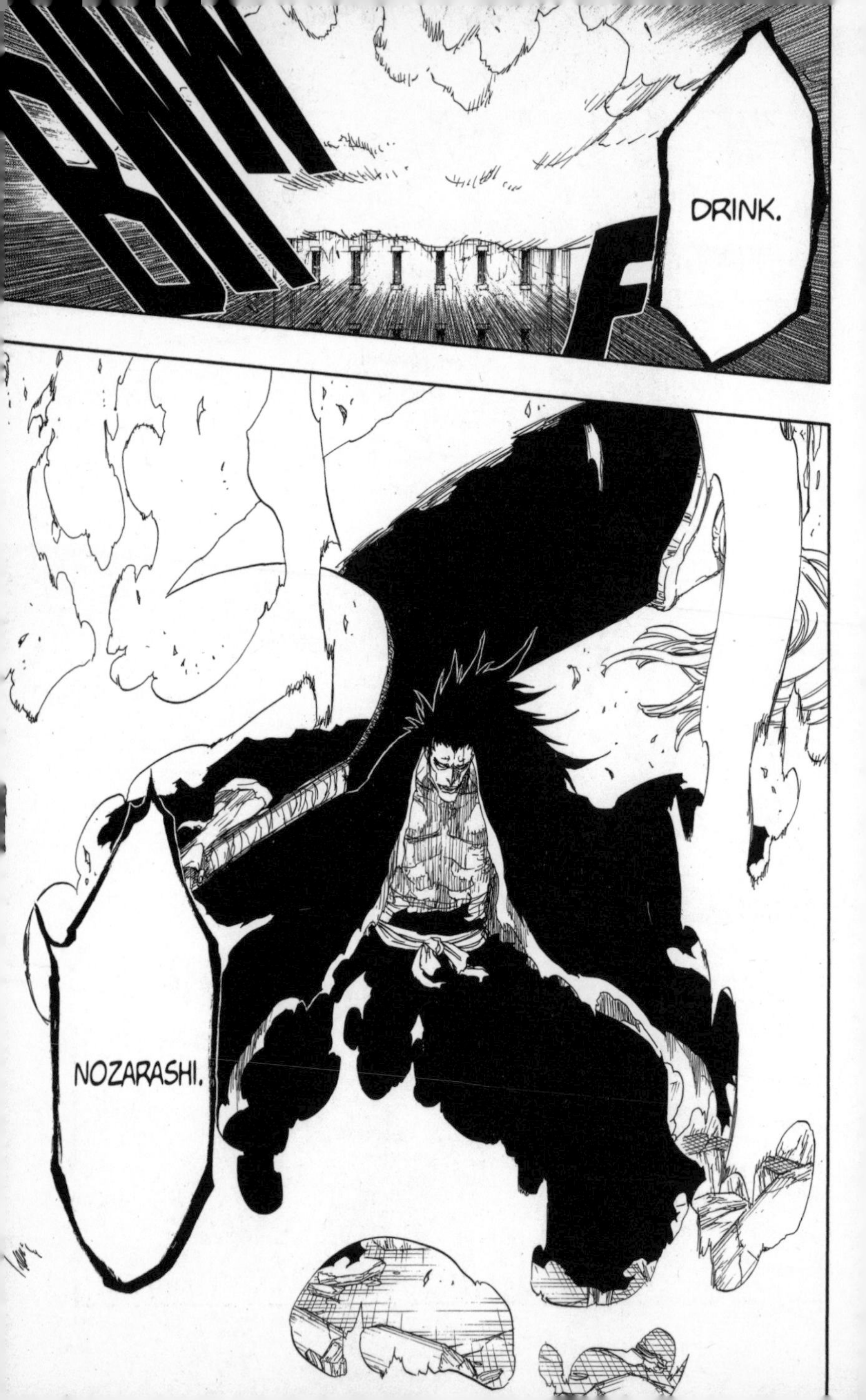
DRINK.
NOZARASHI.

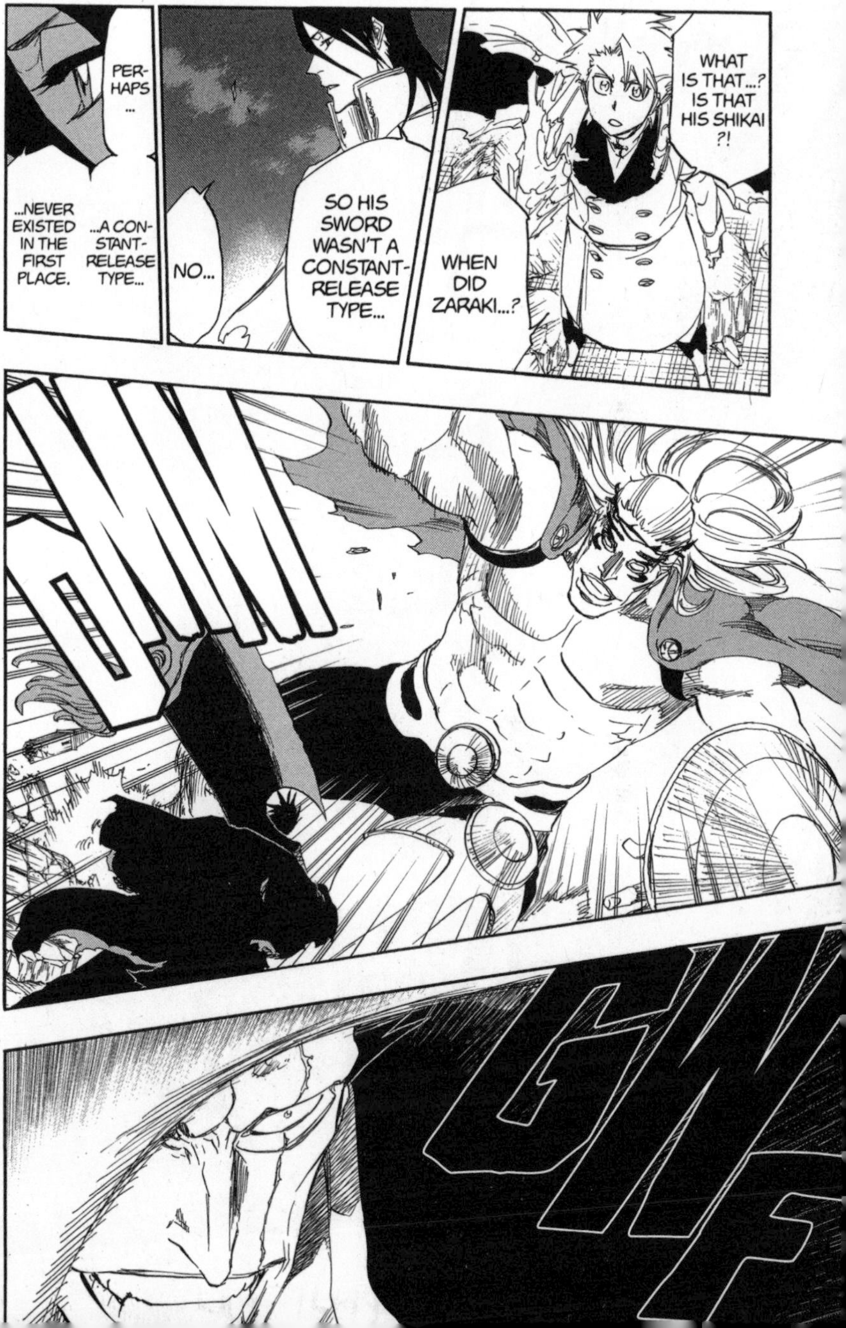
WHAT IS THAT...? IS THAT HIS SHIKAI ?!
WHEN DID ZARAKI...?
SO HIS SWORD WASN'T A CONSTANT-RELEASE TYPE...
NO...
PER-HAPS ...
...A CON-STANT-RELEASE TYPE...
...NEVER EXISTED IN THE FIRST PLACE.

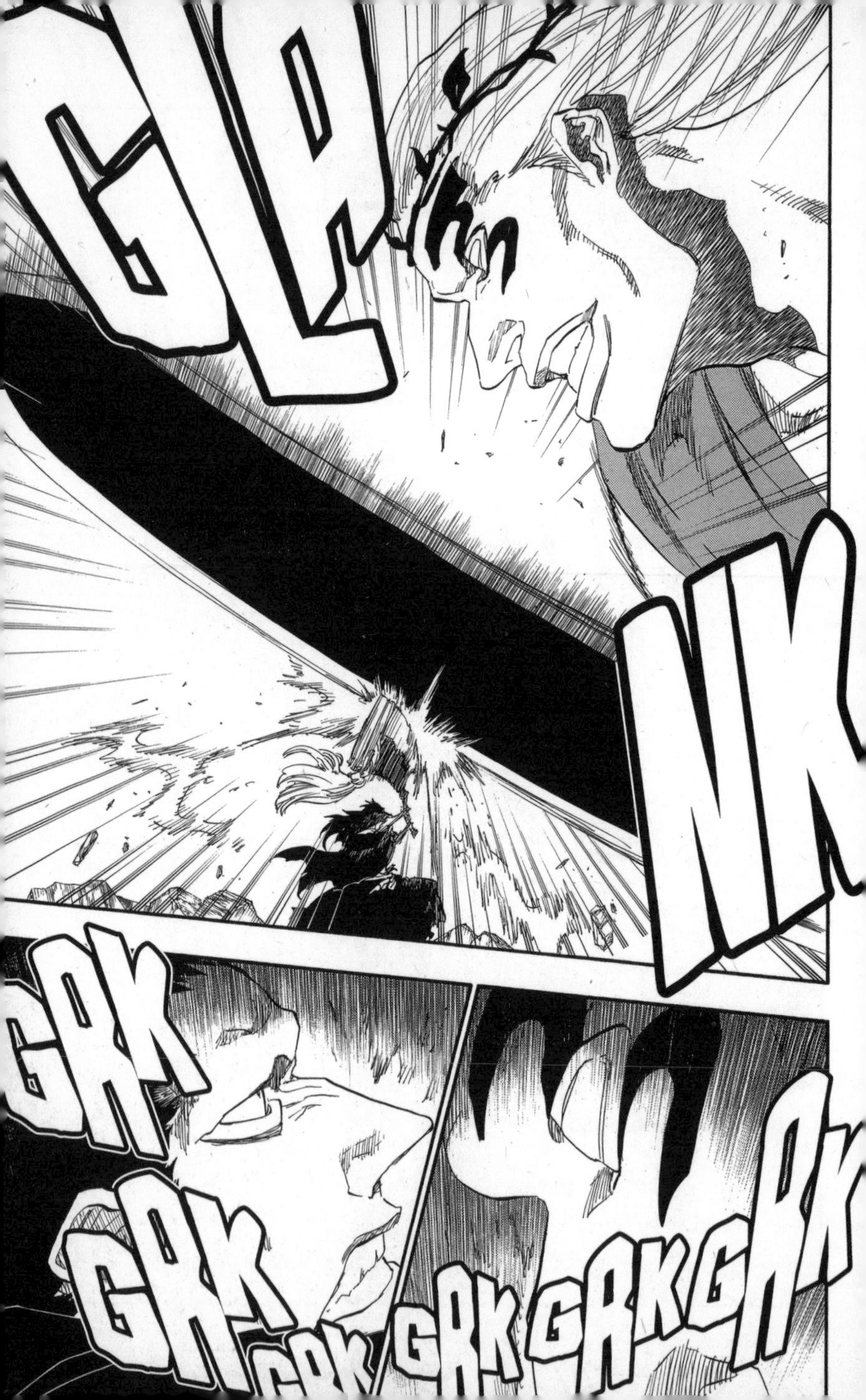
NK
GAK GAK GAK
GAK
GAK

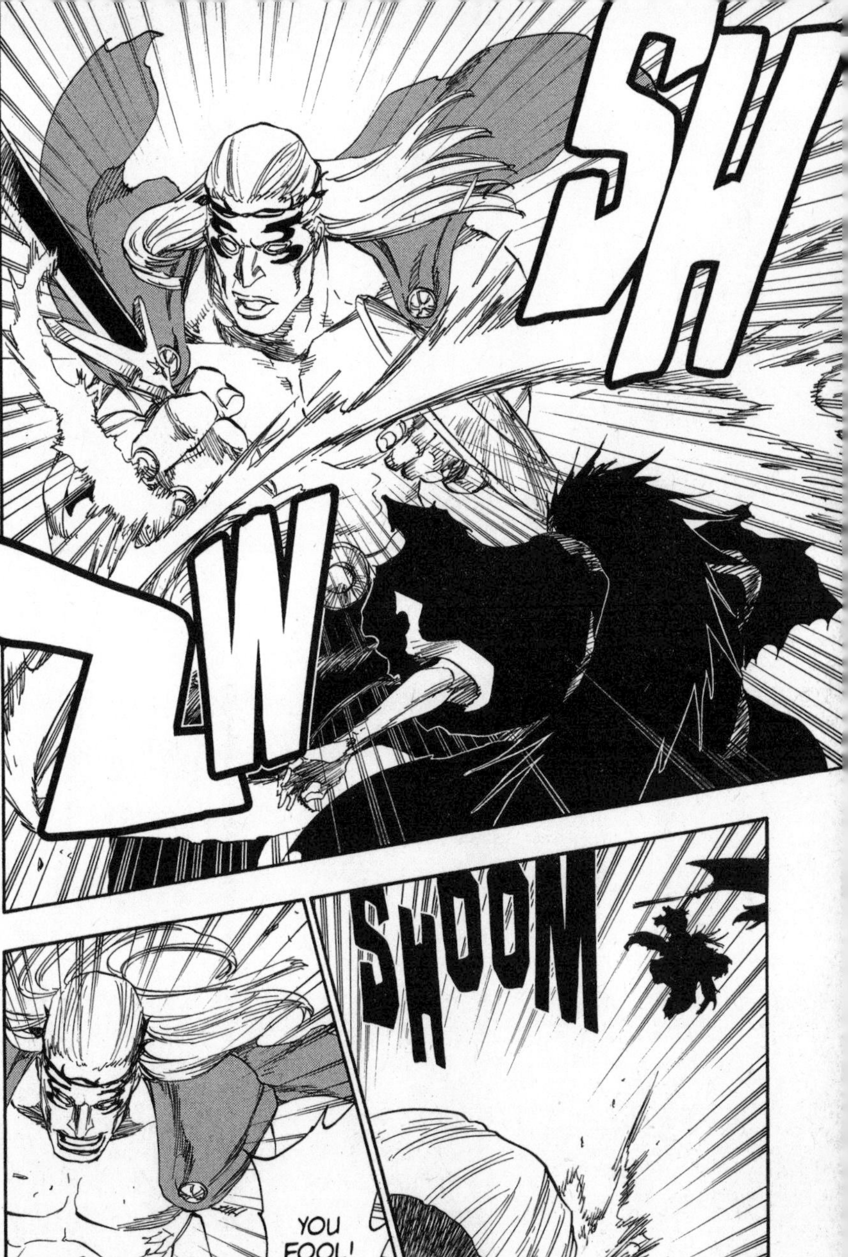
SH
ZW
SHOOM
YOU FOOL!

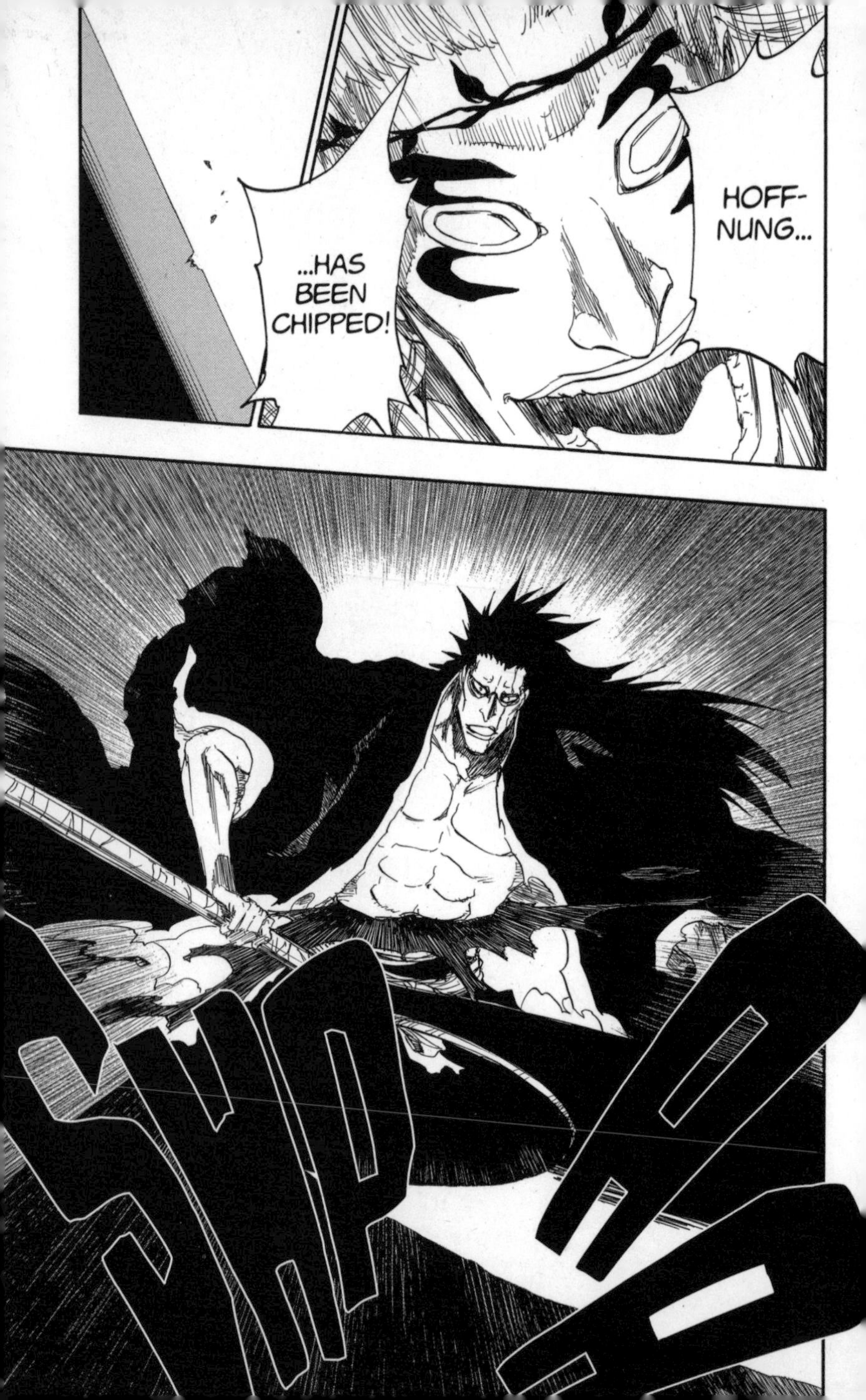
HOFF-
NUNG...
...HAS BEEN CHIPPED!

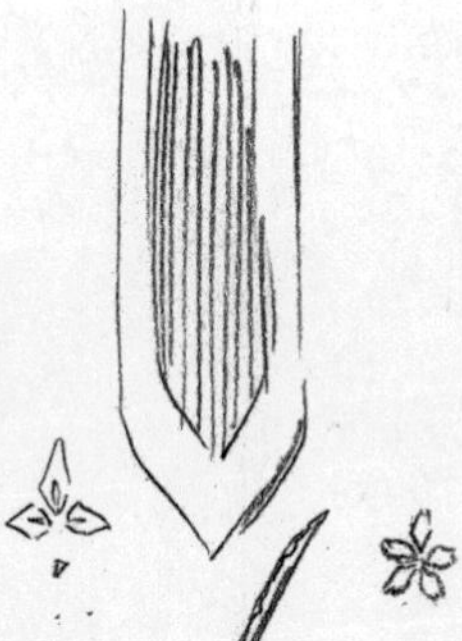

668. BIGGER, FASTER, STRONGER

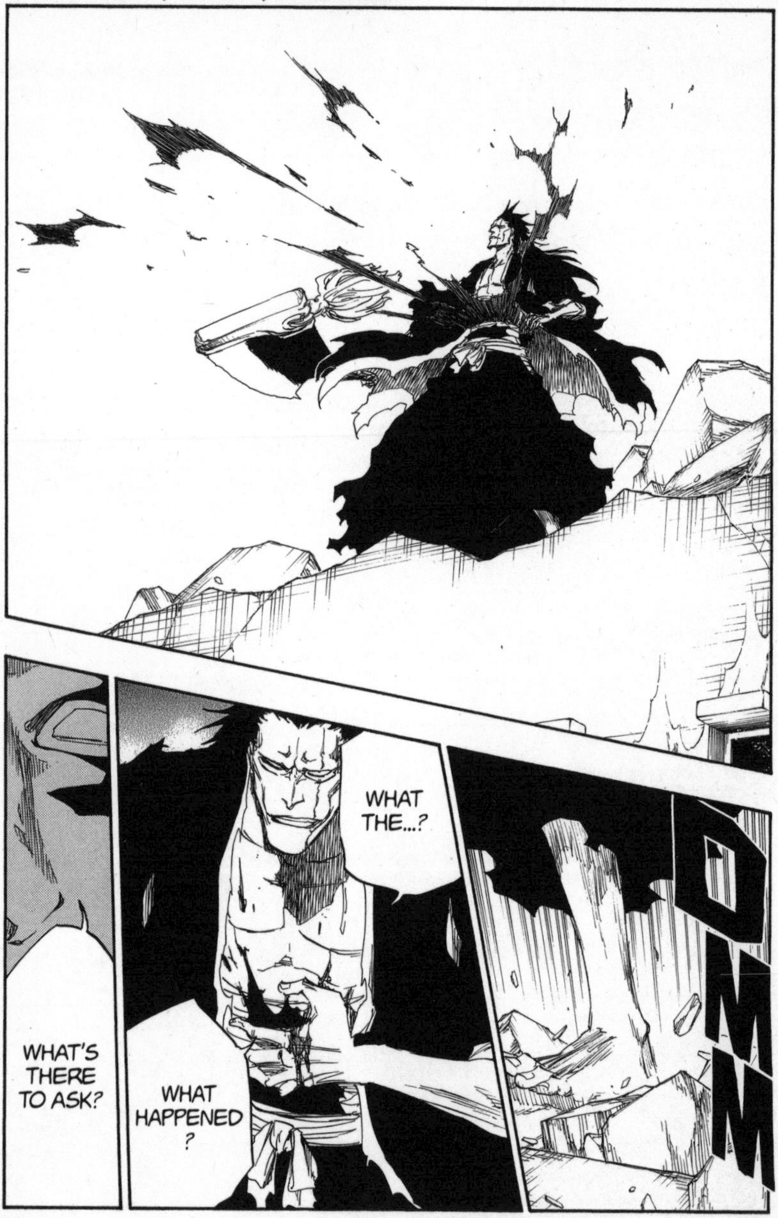

DOMM
WHAT THE...?
WHAT HAPPENED ?
WHAT'S THERE TO ASK?

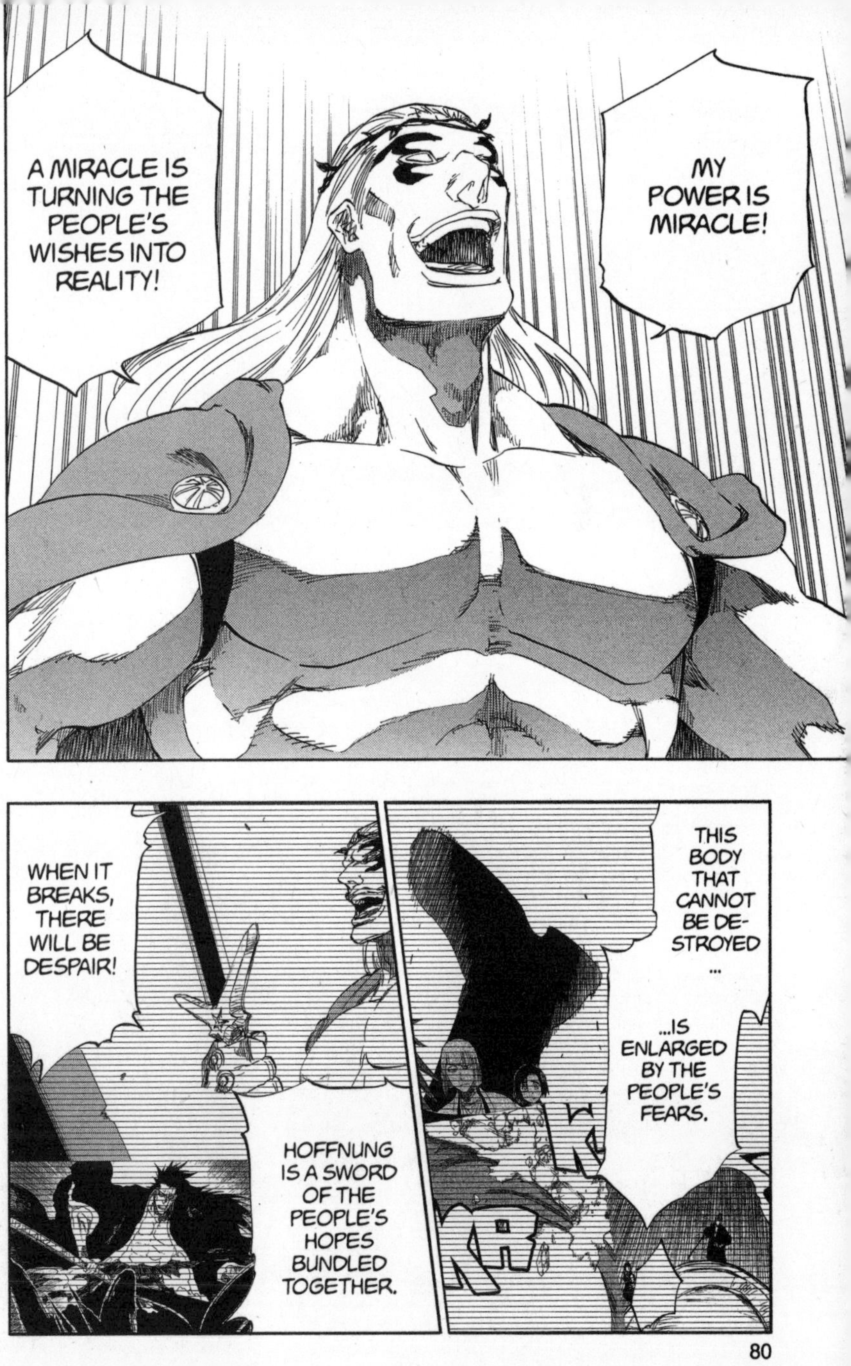
MY POWER IS MIRACLE!
A MIRACLE IS TURNING THE PEOPLE'S WISHES INTO REALITY!
THIS BODY THAT CANNOT BE DE- STROYED ...
...IS ENLARGED BY THE PEOPLE'S FEARS.
HOFFNUNG IS A SWORD OF THE PEOPLE'S HOPES BUNDLED TOGETHER.
WHEN IT BREAKS, THERE WILL BE DESPAIR!

READ THIS WAY

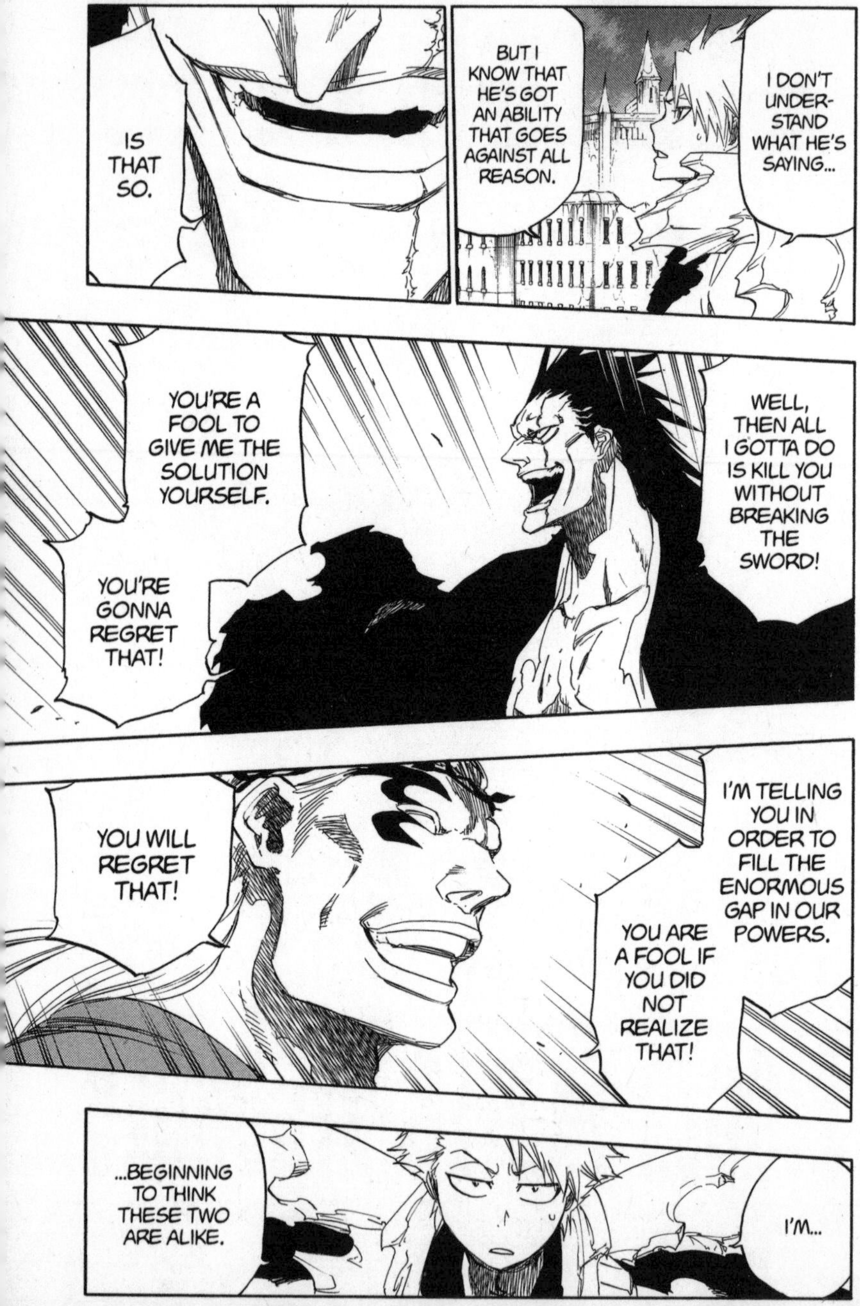
I DON'T UNDER-STAND WHAT HE'S SAYING...
BUT I KNOW THAT HE'S GOT AN ABILITY THAT GOES AGAINST ALL REASON.
IS THAT SO.
WELL, THEN ALL I GOTTA DO IS KILL YOU WITHOUT BREAKING THE SWORD!
YOU'RE A FOOL TO GIVE ME THE SOLUTION YOURSELF.
YOU'RE GONNA REGRET THAT!
I'M TELLING YOU IN ORDER TO FILL THE ENORMOUS GAP IN OUR POWERS.
YOU ARE A FOOL IF YOU DID NOT REALIZE THAT!
YOU WILL REGRET THAT!
I'M...
...BEGINNING TO THINK THESE TWO ARE ALIKE.

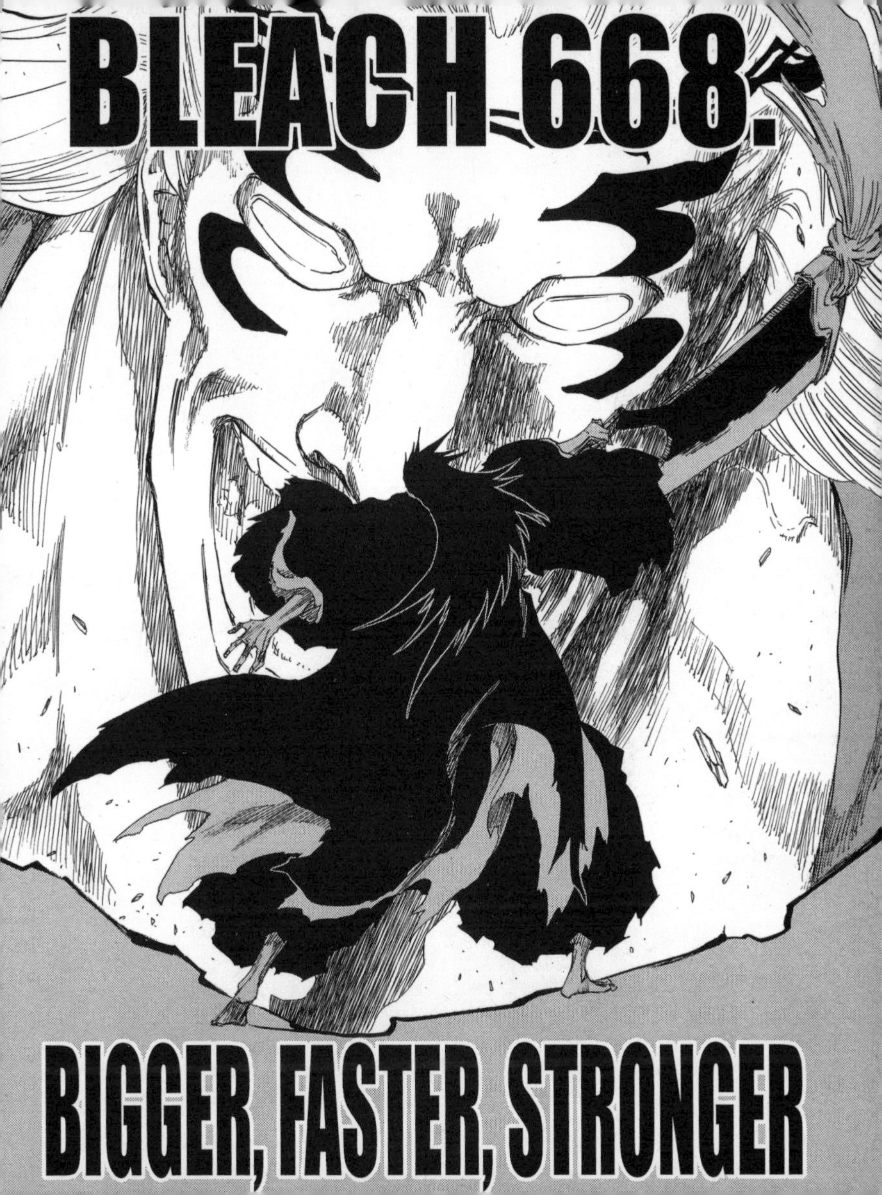
BLEACH 668.
BIGGER, FASTER, STRONGER

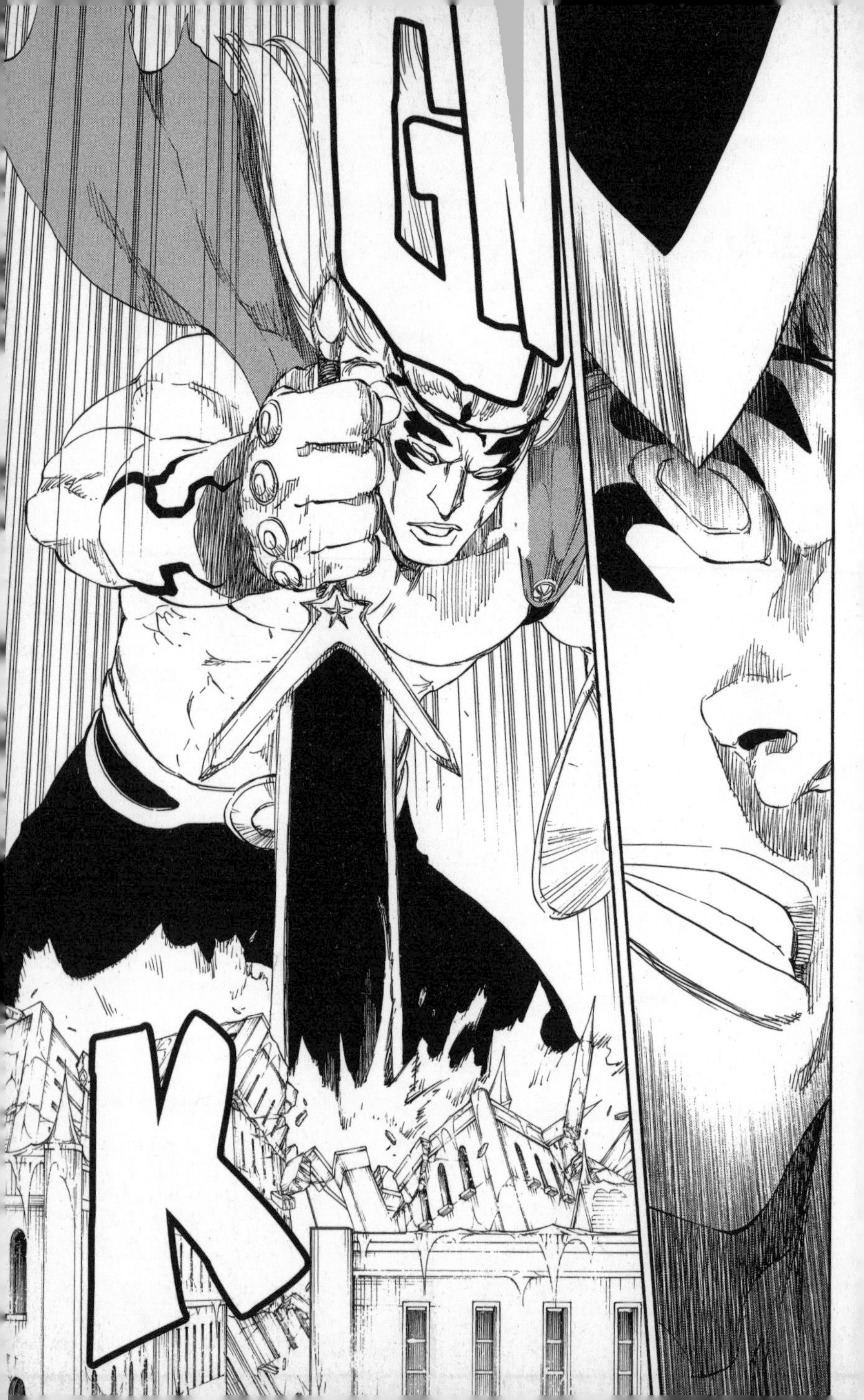
K

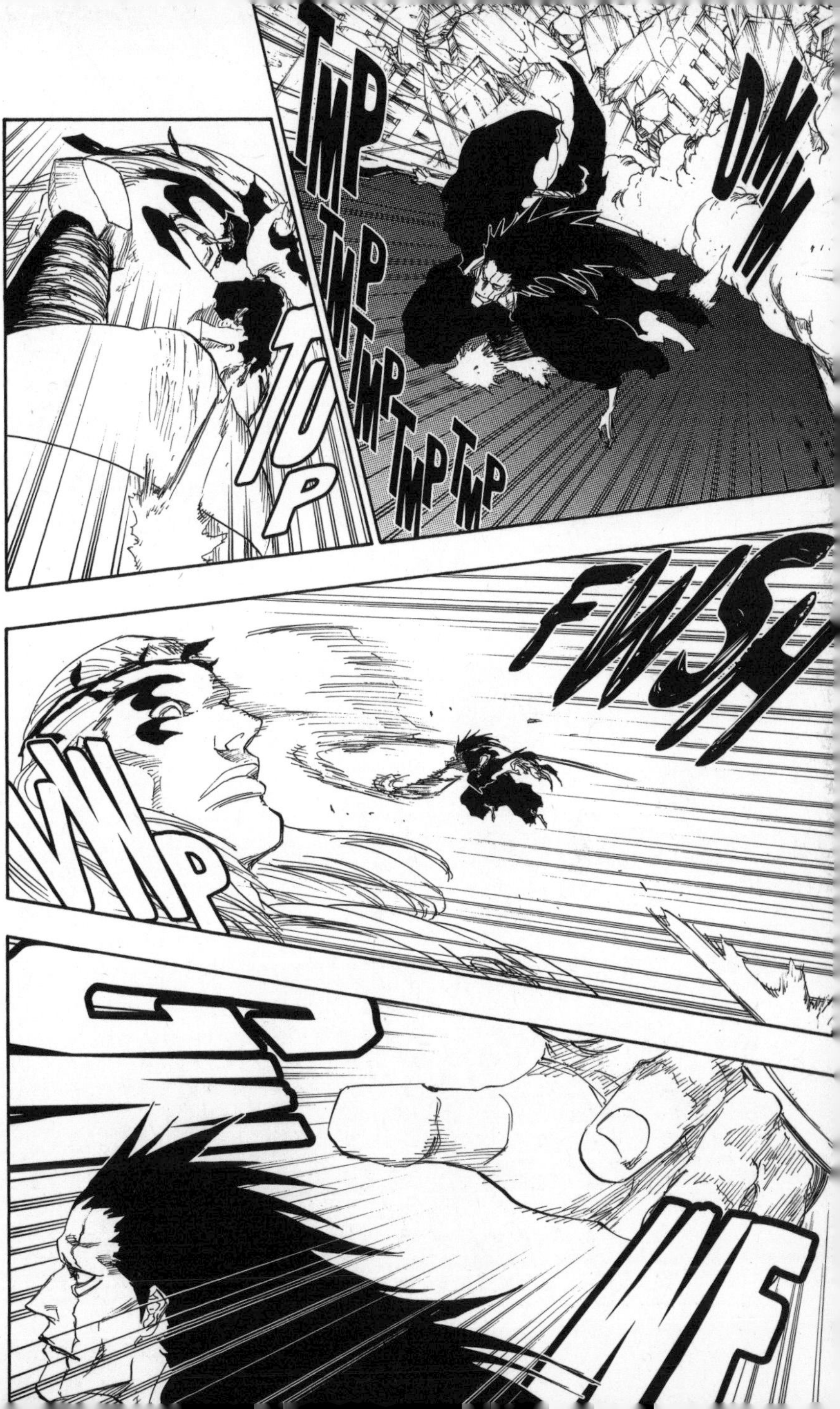
DMM
TMP TMP TMP TMP TMP TMP
TUP
FWSH

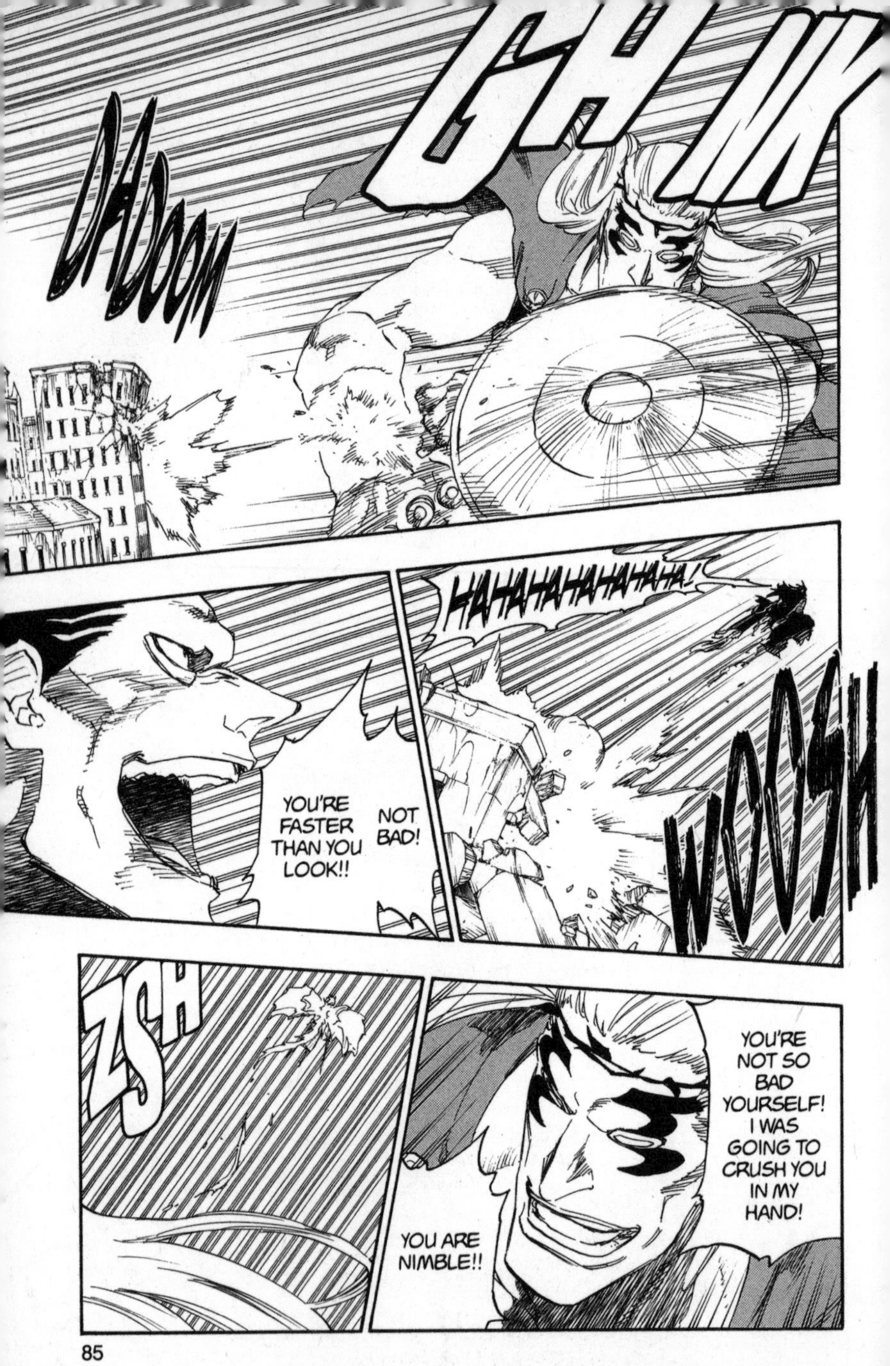

CHINK
DADOOM
HAHAHAHAHAHAHAHA!
WOOSH
NOT BAD!
YOU'RE FASTER THAN YOU LOOK!!
YOU'RE NOT SO BAD YOURSELF! I WAS GOING TO CRUSH YOU IN MY HAND!
YOU ARE NIMBLE!!
ZSH

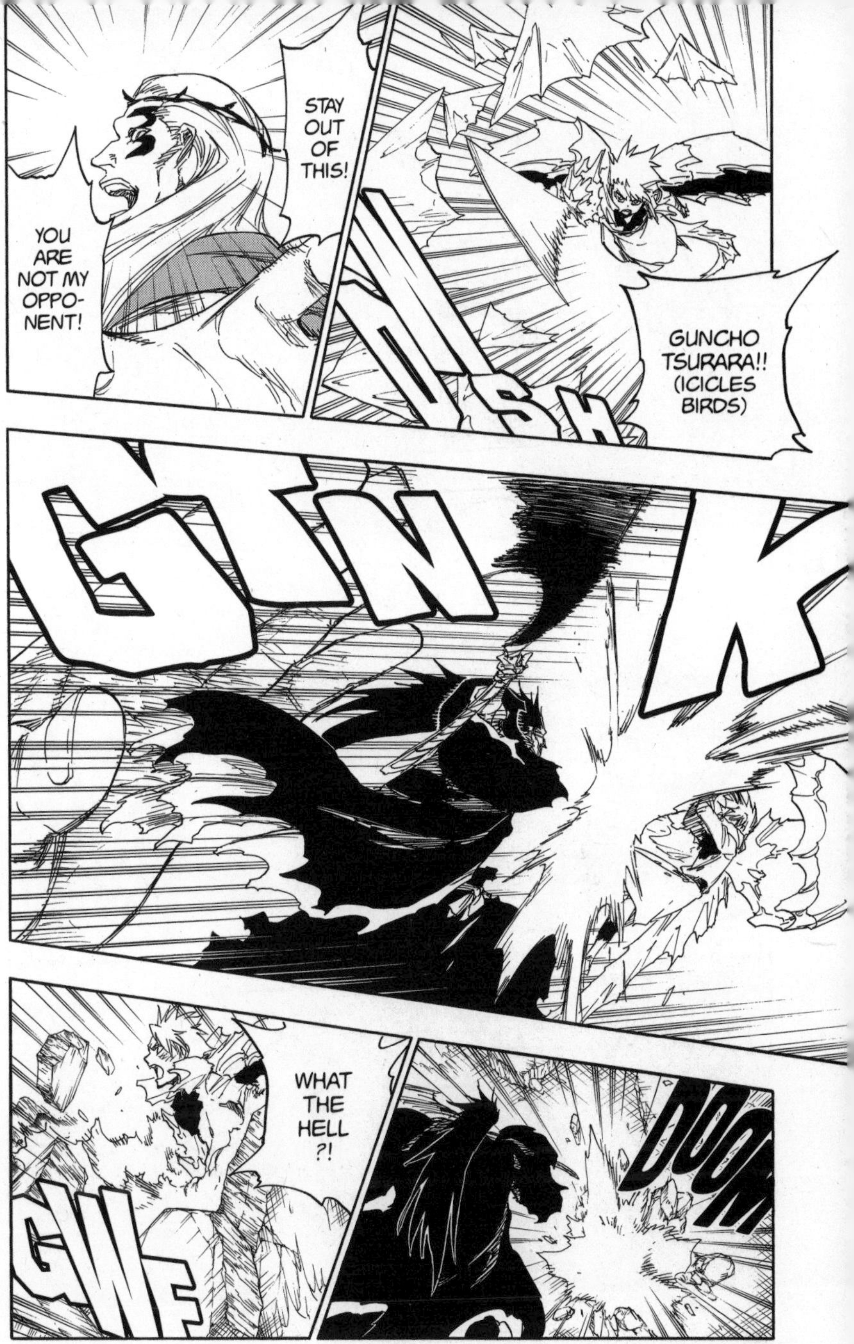
GUNCHO TSURARA!! (ICICLES BIRDS)
STAY OUT OF THIS!
YOU ARE NOT MY OPPONENT!
WHAT THE HELL ?!

READ THIS WAY

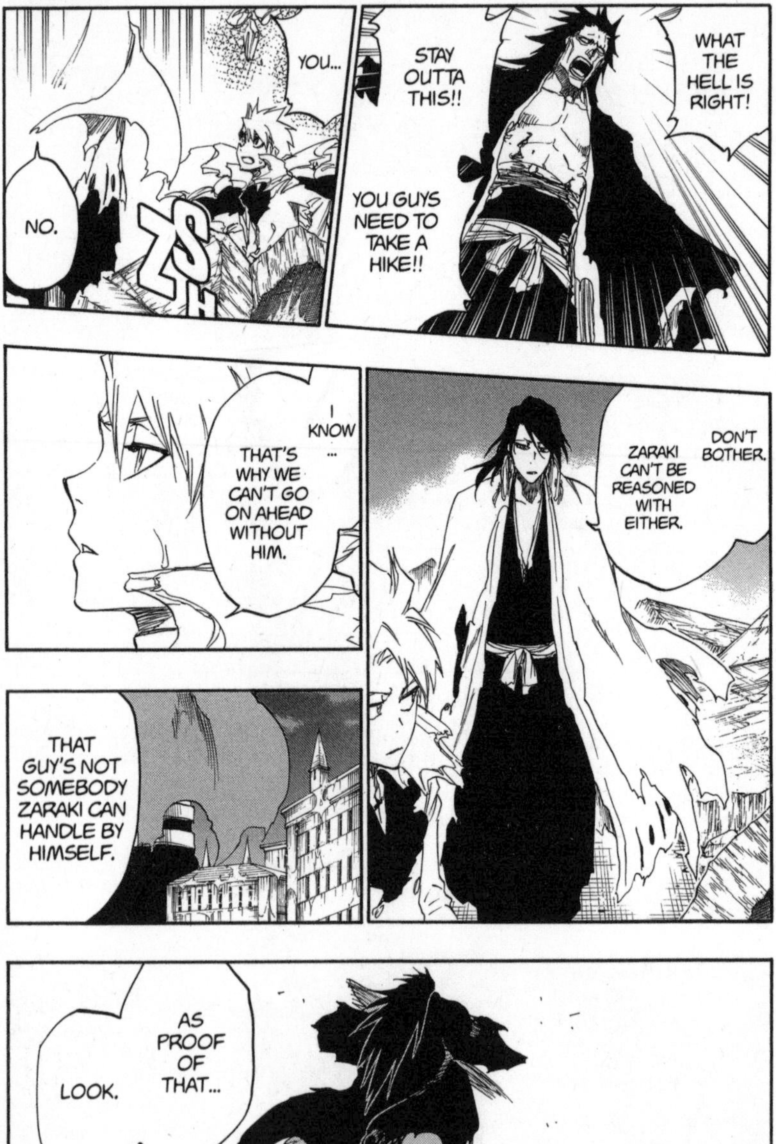
WHAT THE HELL IS RIGHT!
STAY OUTTA THIS!!
YOU GUYS NEED TO TAKE A HIKE!!
YOU...
NO.
ZSH
DON'T BOTHER.
ZARAKI CAN'T BE REASONED WITH EITHER.
I KNOW...
THAT'S WHY WE CAN'T GO ON AHEAD WITHOUT HIM.
THAT GUY'S NOT SOMEBODY ZARAKI CAN HANDLE BY HIMSELF.
AS PROOF OF THAT...
LOOK.

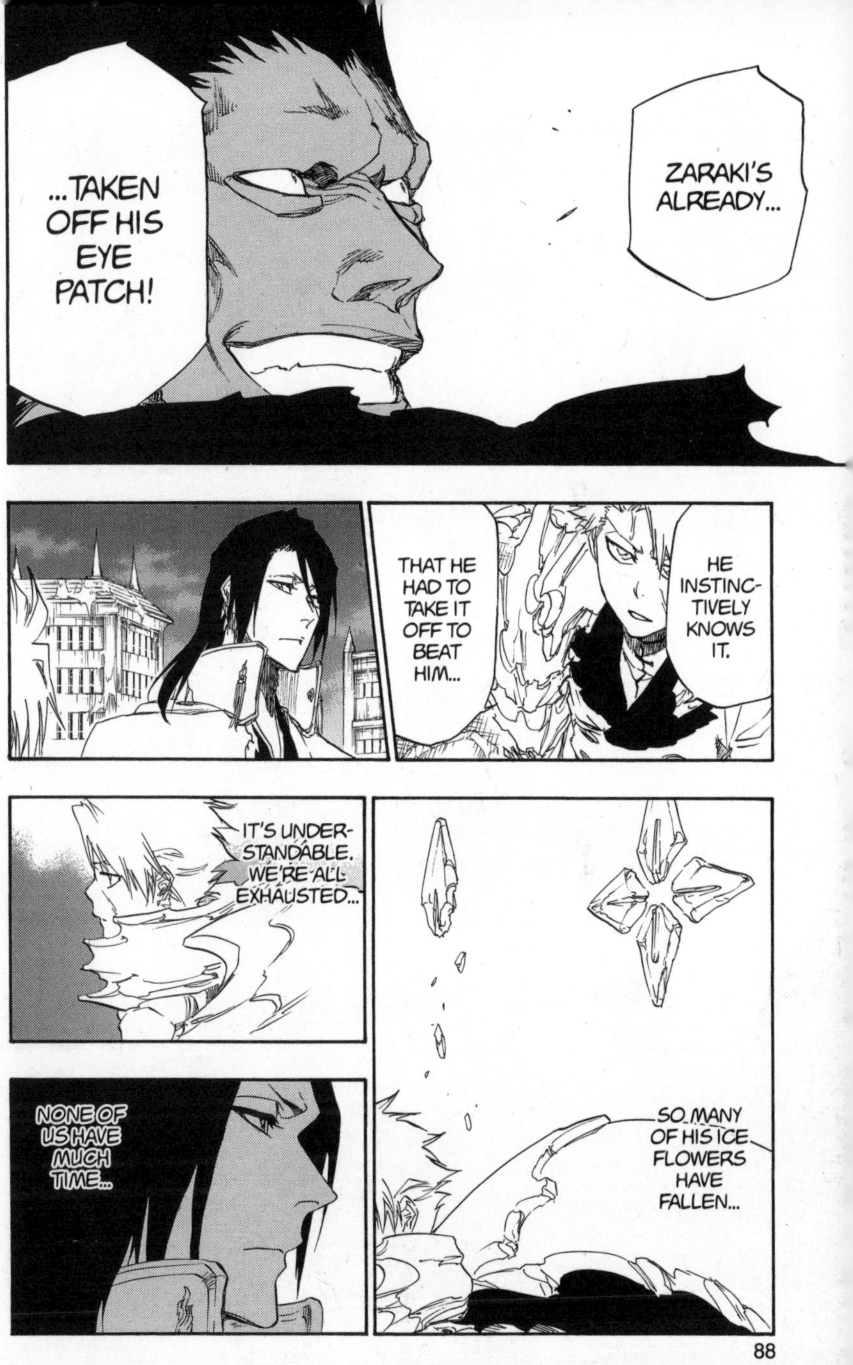
ZARAKI'S ALREADY...
...TAKEN OFF HIS EYE PATCH!
HE INSTINCTIVELY KNOWS IT.
THAT HE HAD TO TAKE IT OFF TO BEAT HIM...
SO MANY OF HIS ICE FLOWERS HAVE FALLEN...
IT'S UNDERSTANDABLE. WE'RE ALL EXHAUSTED...
NONE OF US HAVE MUCH TIME...

READ THIS WAY

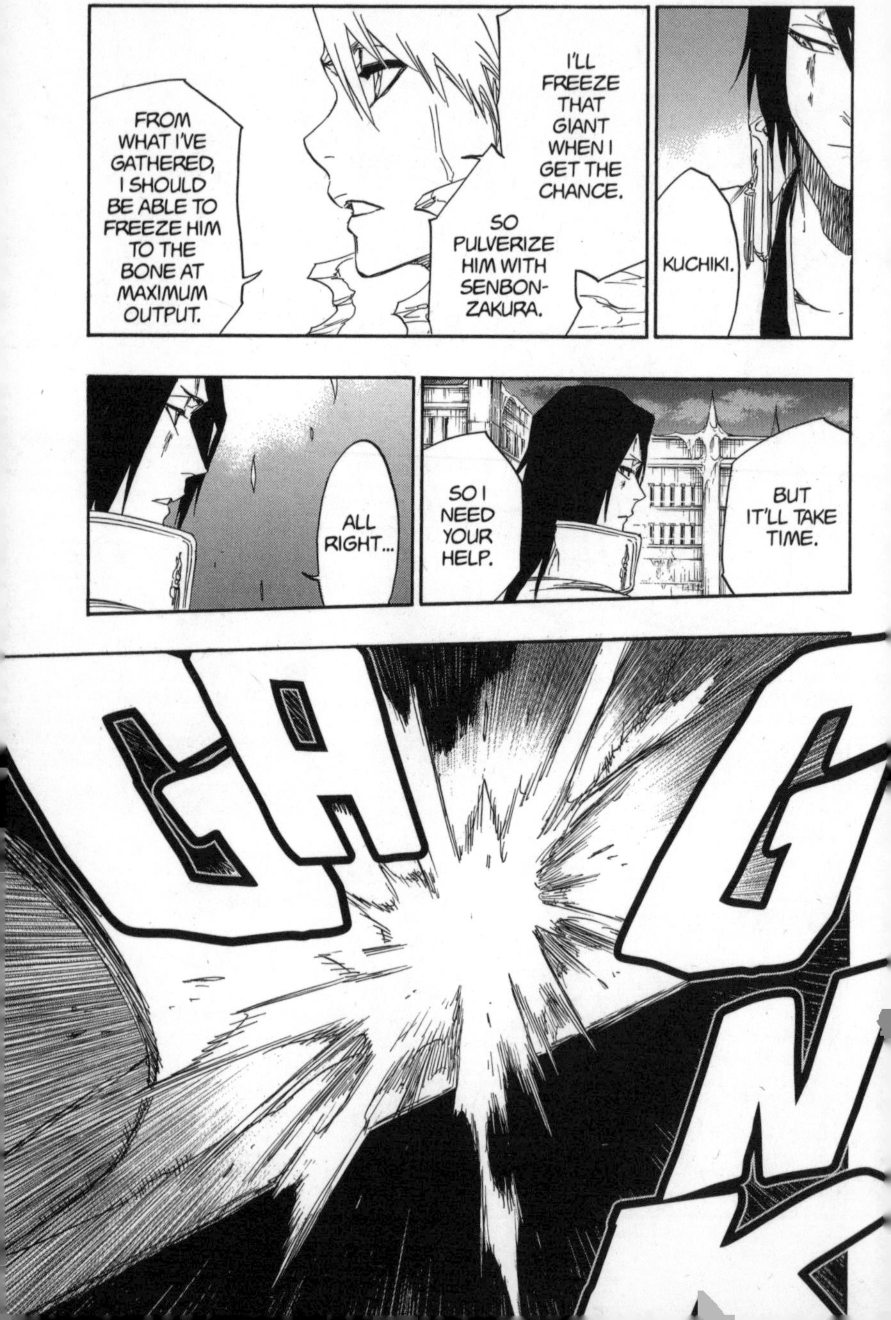
KUCHIKI.
I'LL FREEZE THAT GIANT WHEN I GET THE CHANCE.
SO PULVERIZE HIM WITH SENBON-ZAKURA.
FROM WHAT I'VE GATHERED, I SHOULD BE ABLE TO FREEZE HIM TO THE BONE AT MAXIMUM OUTPUT.
BUT IT'LL TAKE TIME.
SO I NEED YOUR HELP.
ALL RIGHT...
CHGNK

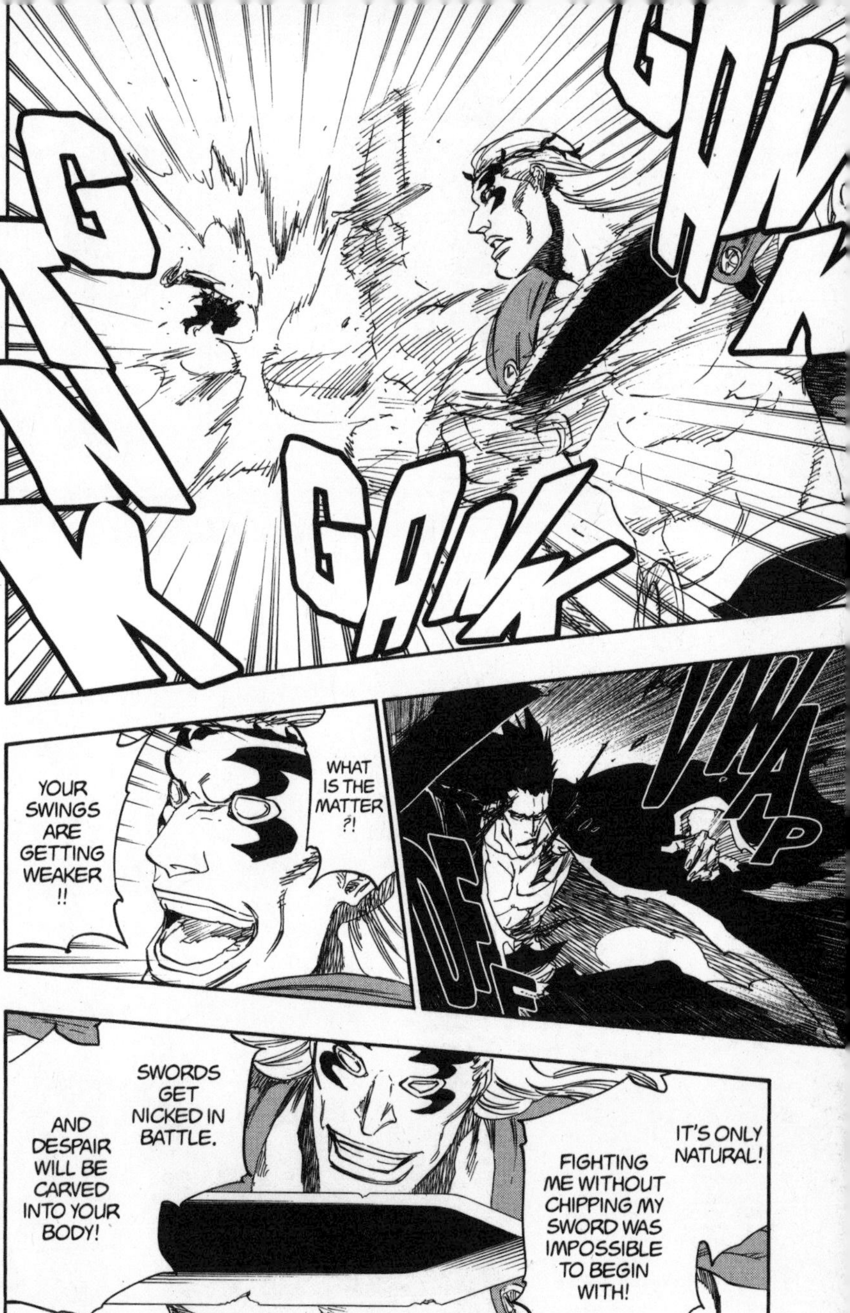
GANK
GANK
GANK
VWAP
WHAT IS THE MATTER?!
YOUR SWINGS ARE GETTING WEAKER!!
IT'S ONLY NATURAL!
FIGHTING ME WITHOUT CHIPPING MY SWORD WAS IMPOSSIBLE TO BEGIN WITH!
SWORDS GET NICKED IN BATTLE.
AND DESPAIR WILL BE CARVED INTO YOUR BODY!

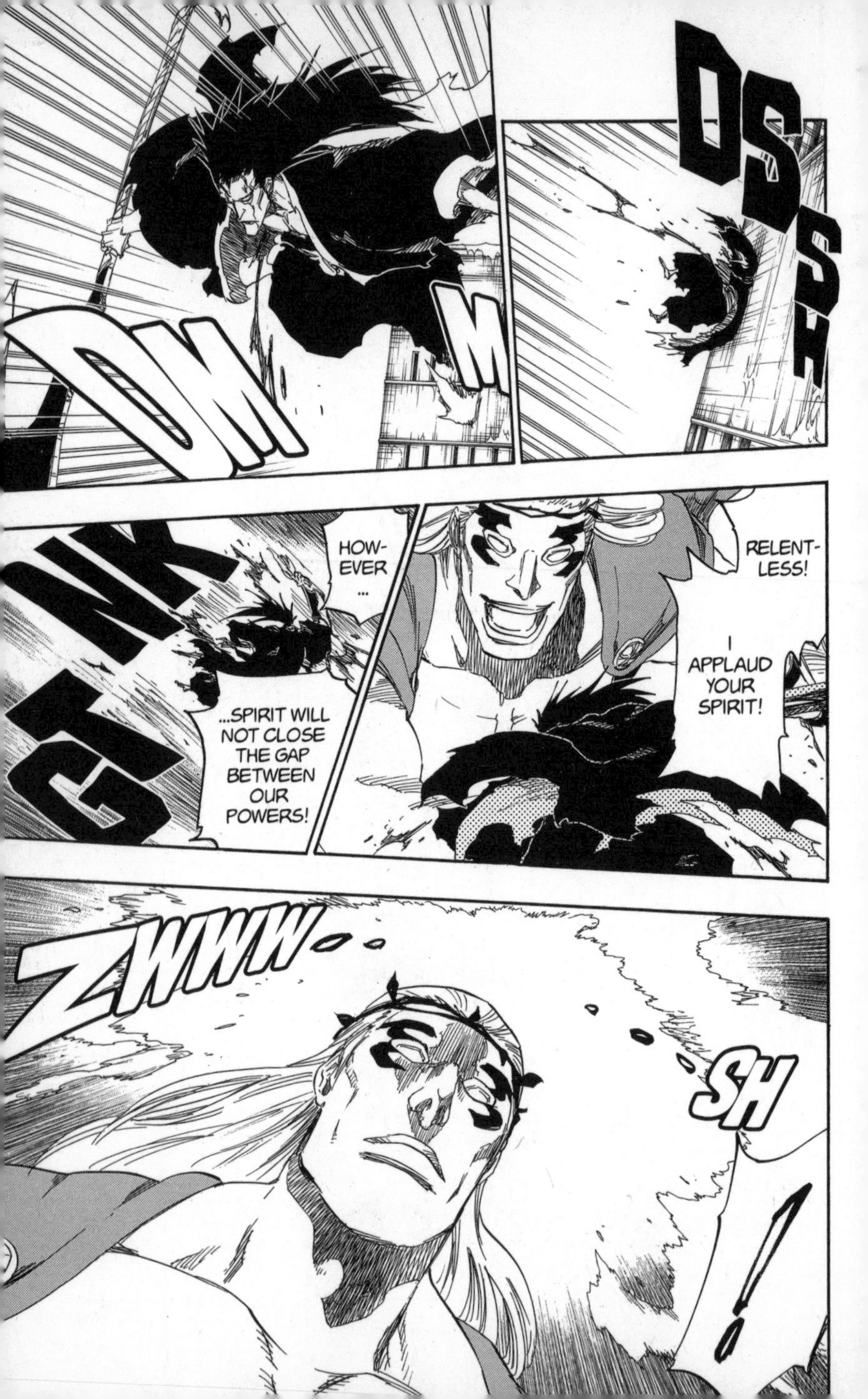
DSSH
DOMM
RELENT-LESS!
I APPLAUD YOUR SPIRIT!
HOW-EVER ...
...SPIRIT WILL NOT CLOSE THE GAP BETWEEN OUR POWERS!
GNK
ZWWW
SH

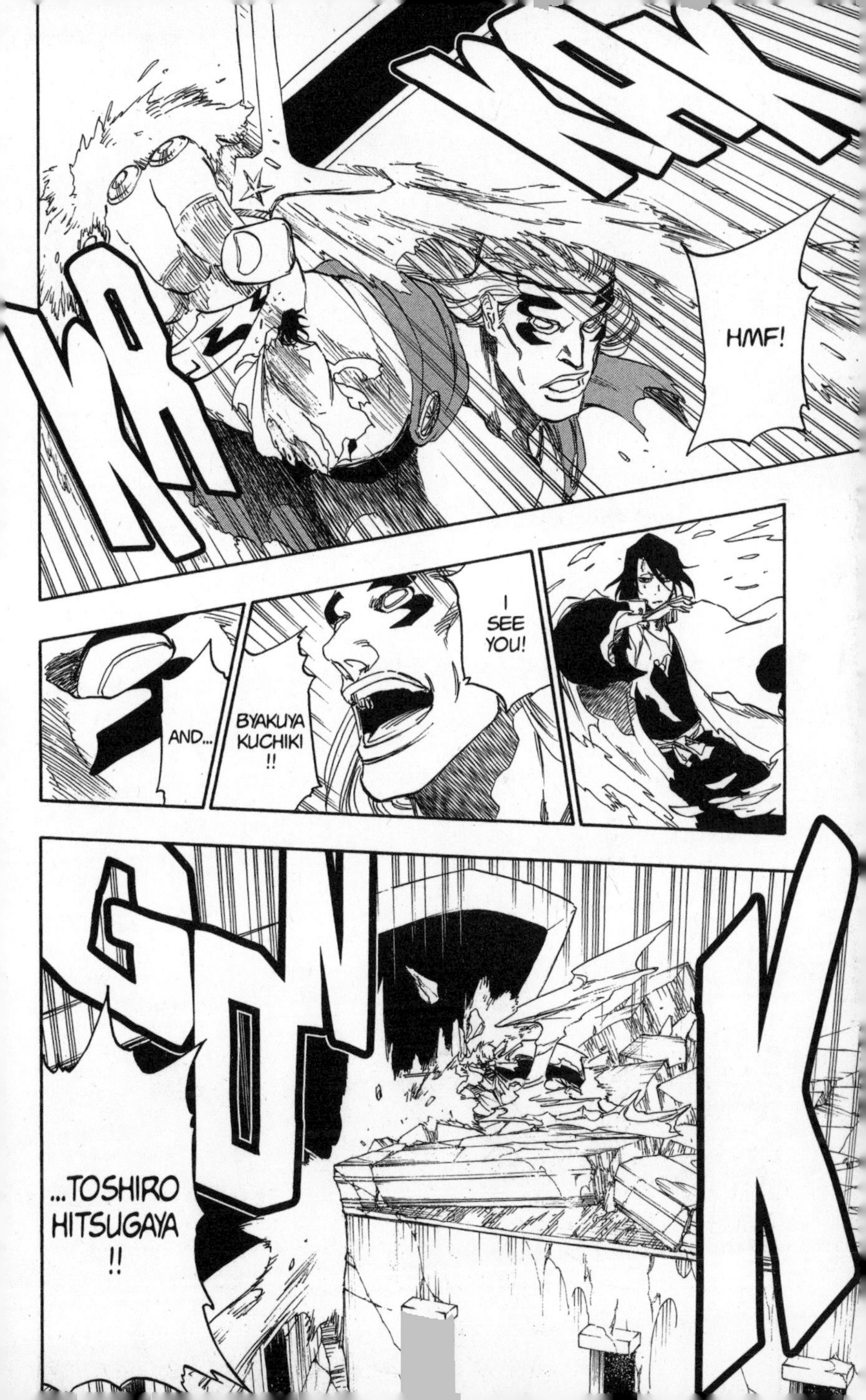
HMF!
I SEE YOU!
BYAKUYA KUCHIKI !!
AND...
...TOSHIRO HITSUGAYA !!

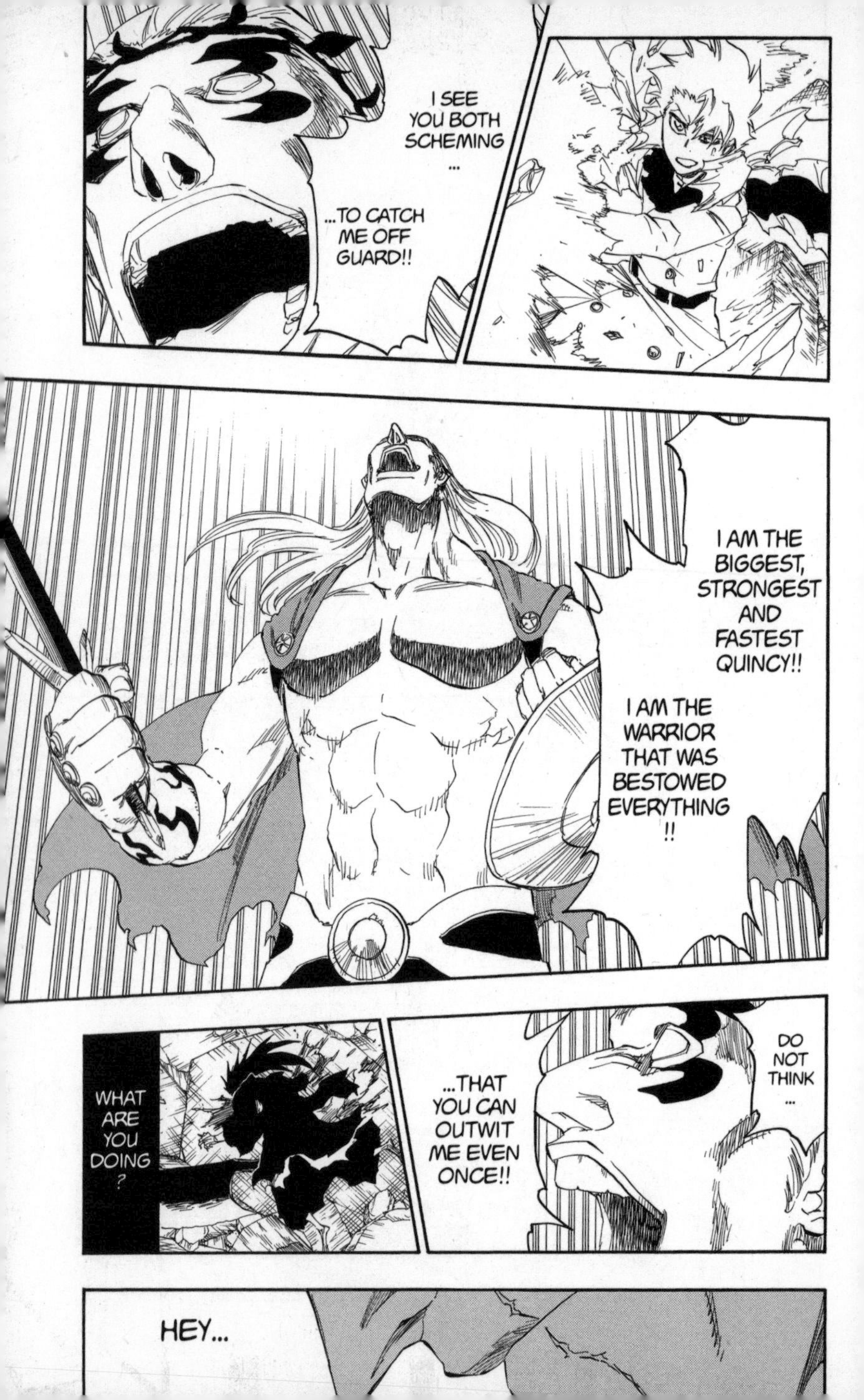
I SEE YOU BOTH SCHEMING ...
...TO CATCH ME OFF GUARD!!
I AM THE BIGGEST, STRONGEST AND FASTEST QUINCY!!
I AM THE WARRIOR THAT WAS BESTOWED EVERYTHING !!
DO NOT THINK ...
...THAT YOU CAN OUTWIT ME EVEN ONCE!!
WHAT ARE YOU DOING ?
HEY...

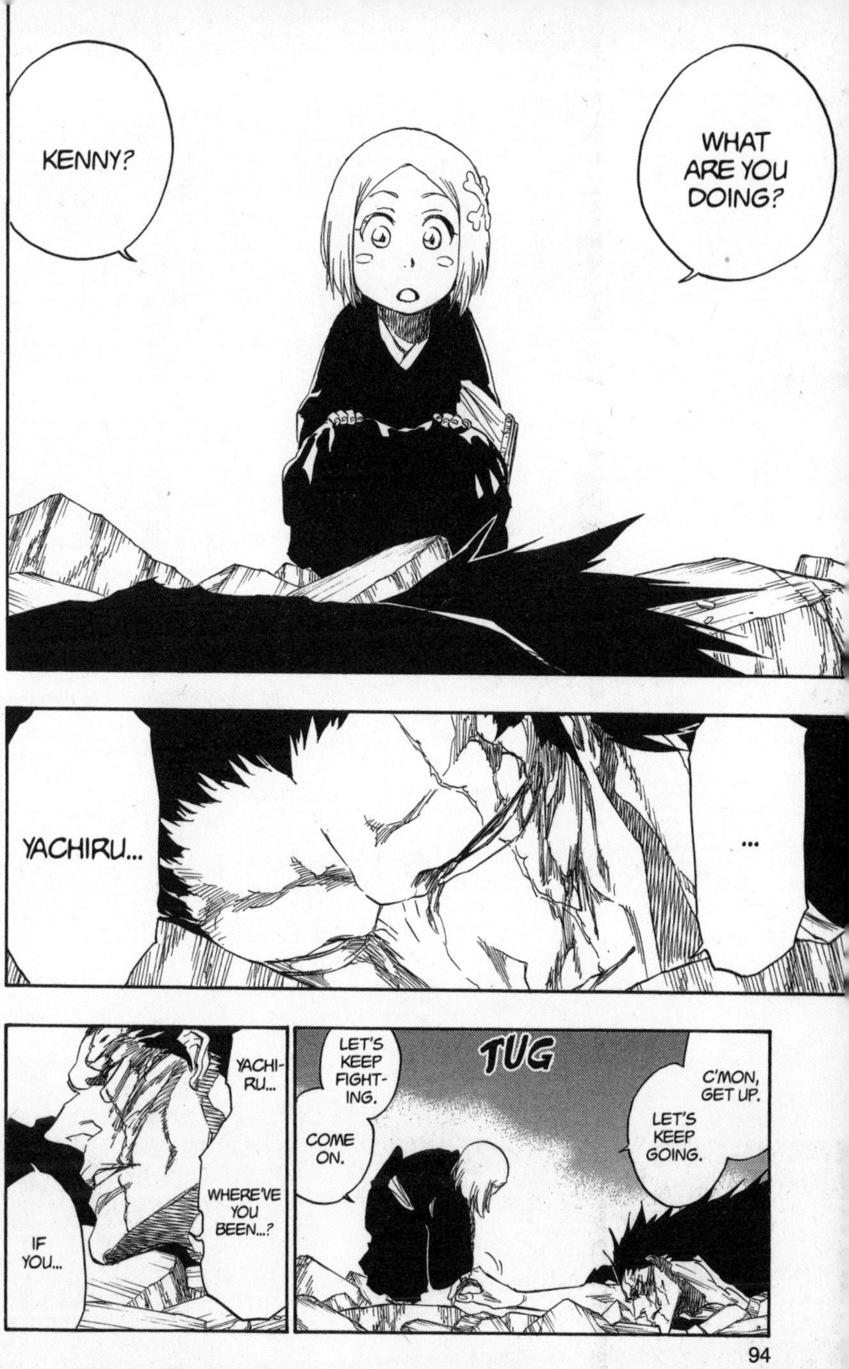
WHAT ARE YOU DOING?
KENNY?
...
YACHIRU...
C'MON, GET UP.
LET'S KEEP GOING.
TUG
LET'S KEEP FIGHT-ING.
COME ON.
YACHI-RU...
WHERE'VE YOU BEEN...?
IF YOU...

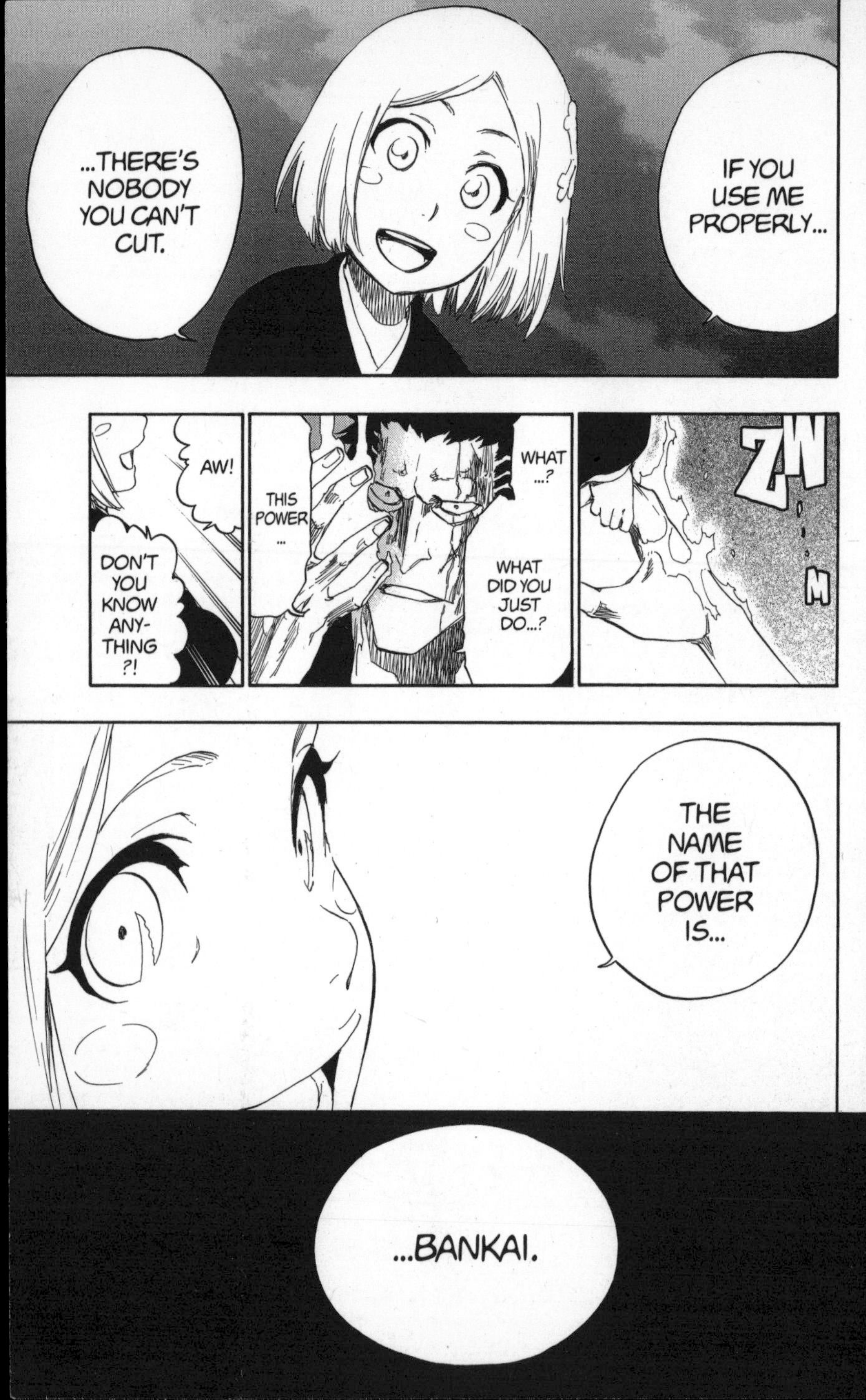
IF YOU USE ME PROPERLY...
...THERE'S NOBODY YOU CAN'T CUT.
ZWM
WHAT ...?
THIS POWER ...
WHAT DID YOU JUST DO...?
AW!
DON'T YOU KNOW ANYTHING ?!
THE NAME OF THAT POWER IS...
...BANKAI.

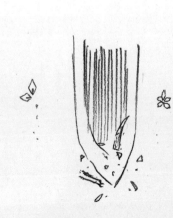

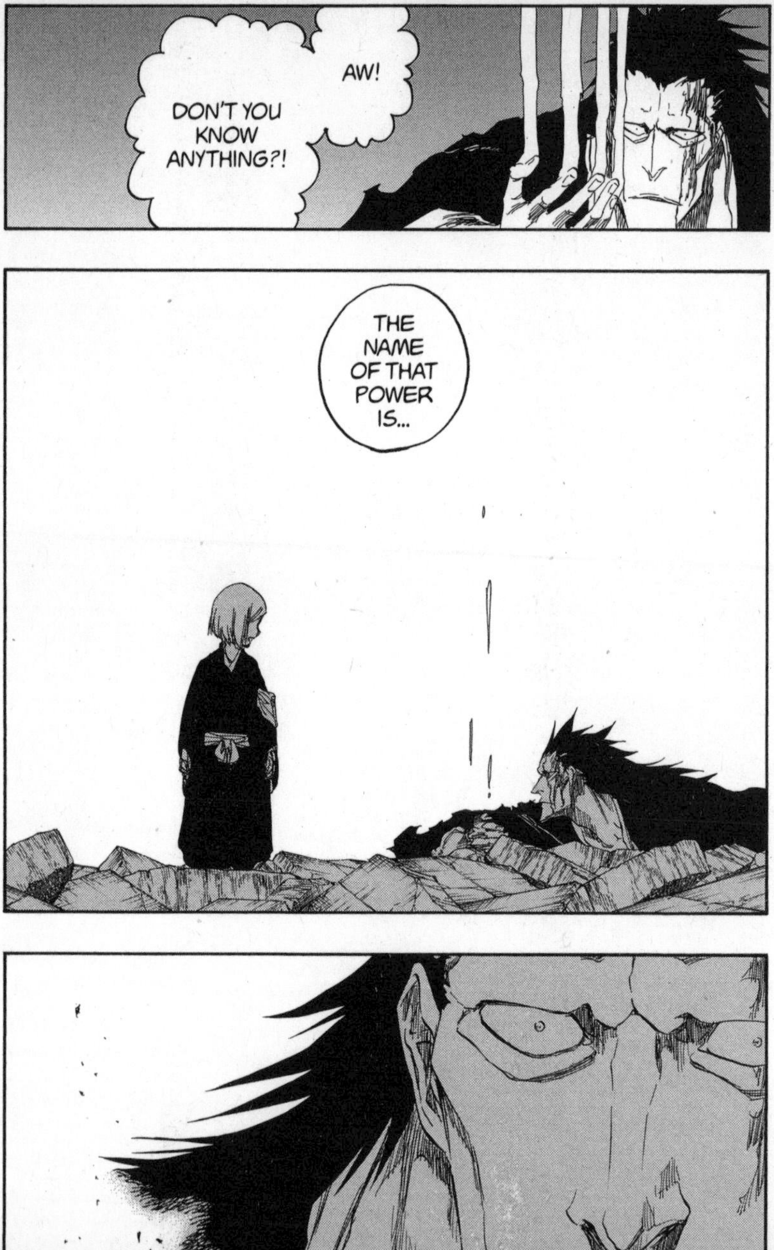
AW!
DON'T YOU KNOW ANYTHING?!
THE NAME OF THAT POWER IS...
!

BLEACH 669.

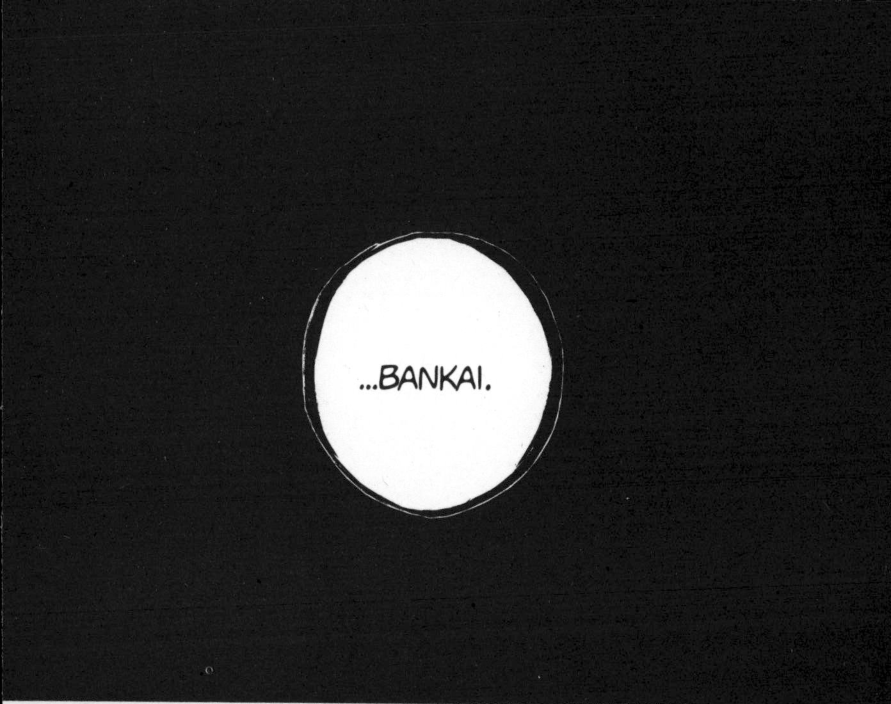
...BANKAI.

BLADE II

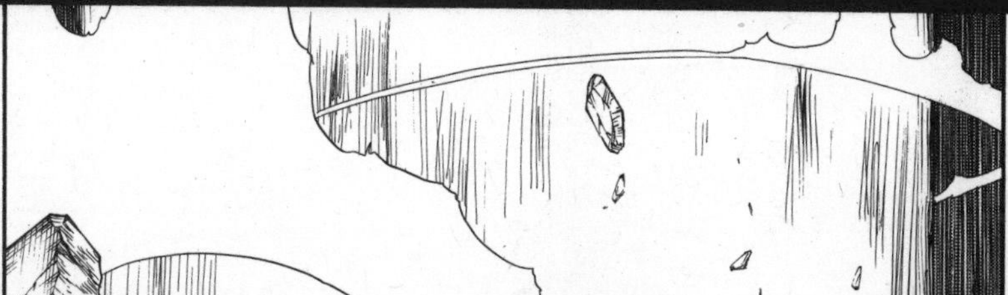

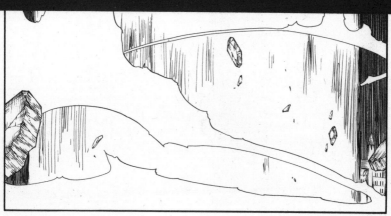

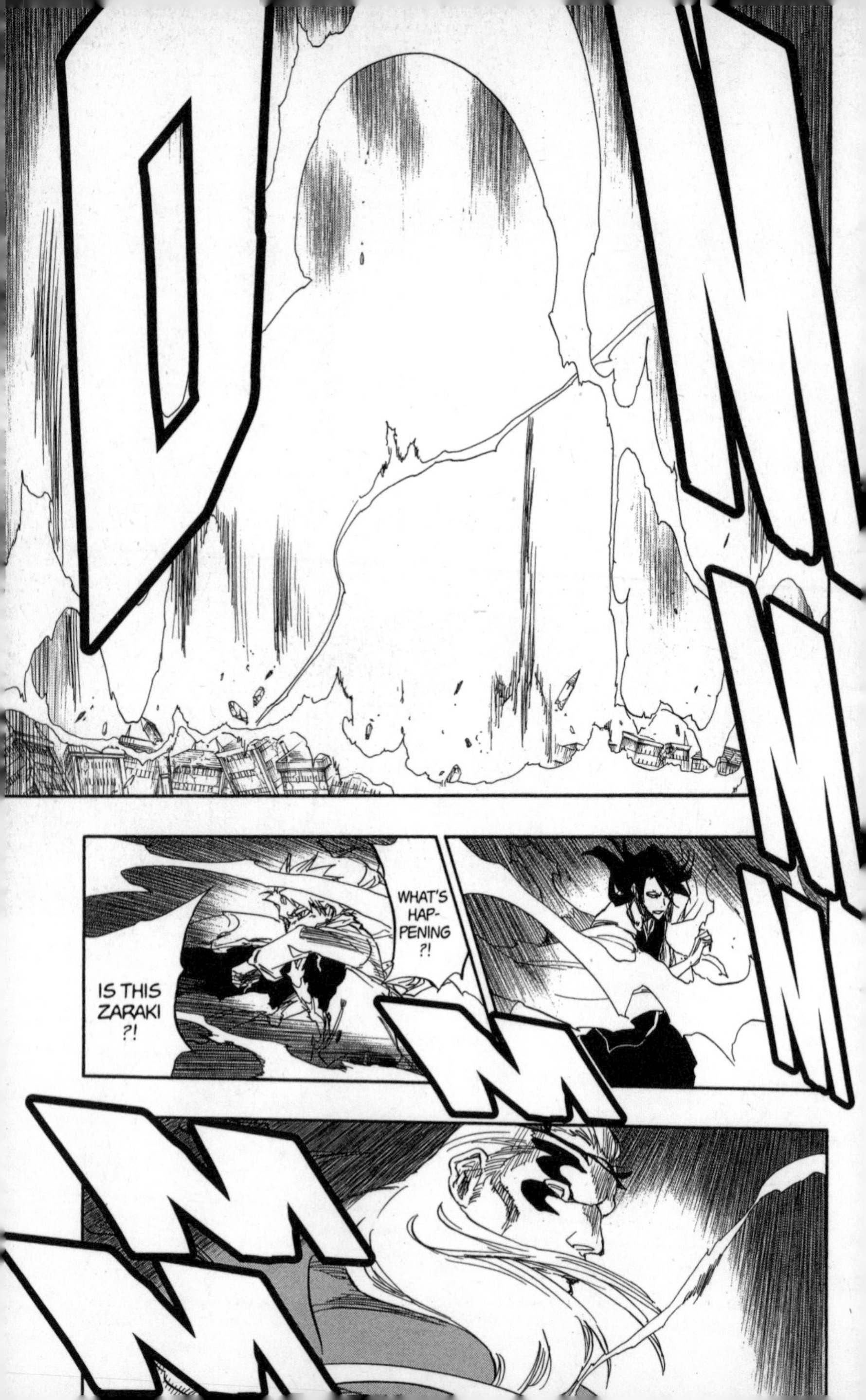
WHAT'S HAP-PENING ?!
IS THIS ZARAKI ?!

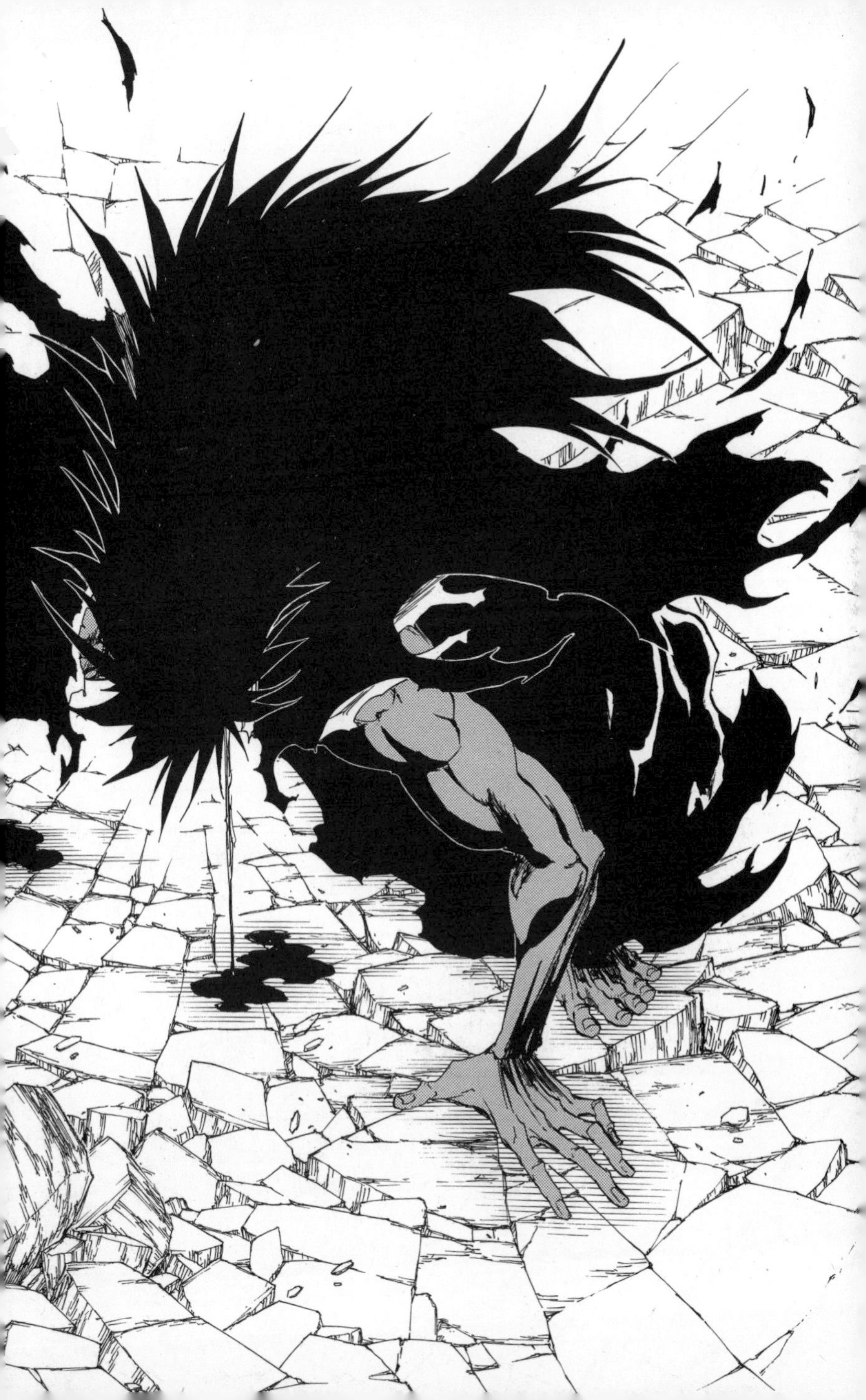

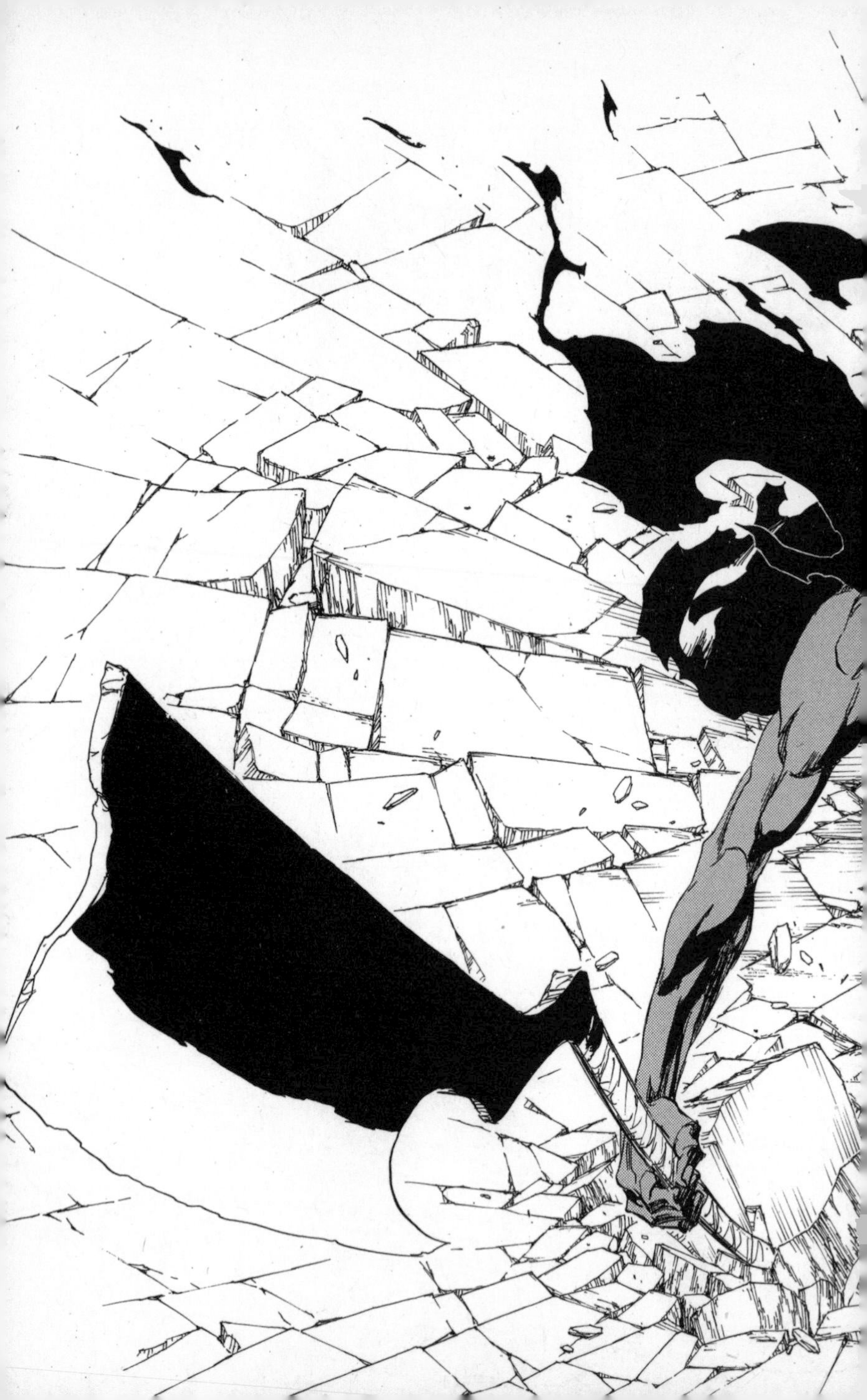

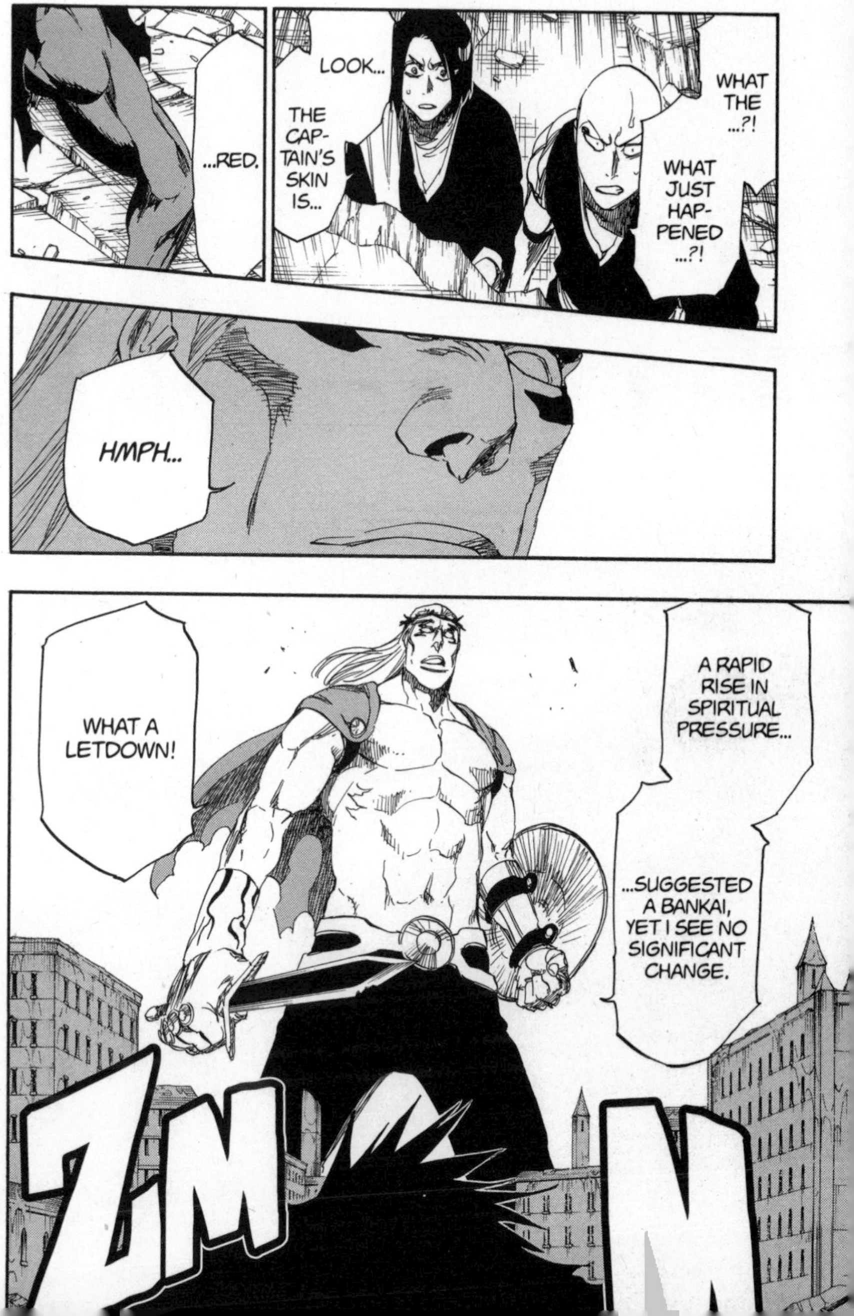
WHAT THE ...?!
WHAT JUST HAPPENED ...?!
LOOK...
THE CAPTAIN'S SKIN IS...
...RED.
HMPH...
A RAPID RISE IN SPIRITUAL PRESSURE...
...SUGGESTED A BANKAI, YET I SEE NO SIGNIFICANT CHANGE.
WHAT A LETDOWN!
ZM

READ THIS WAY

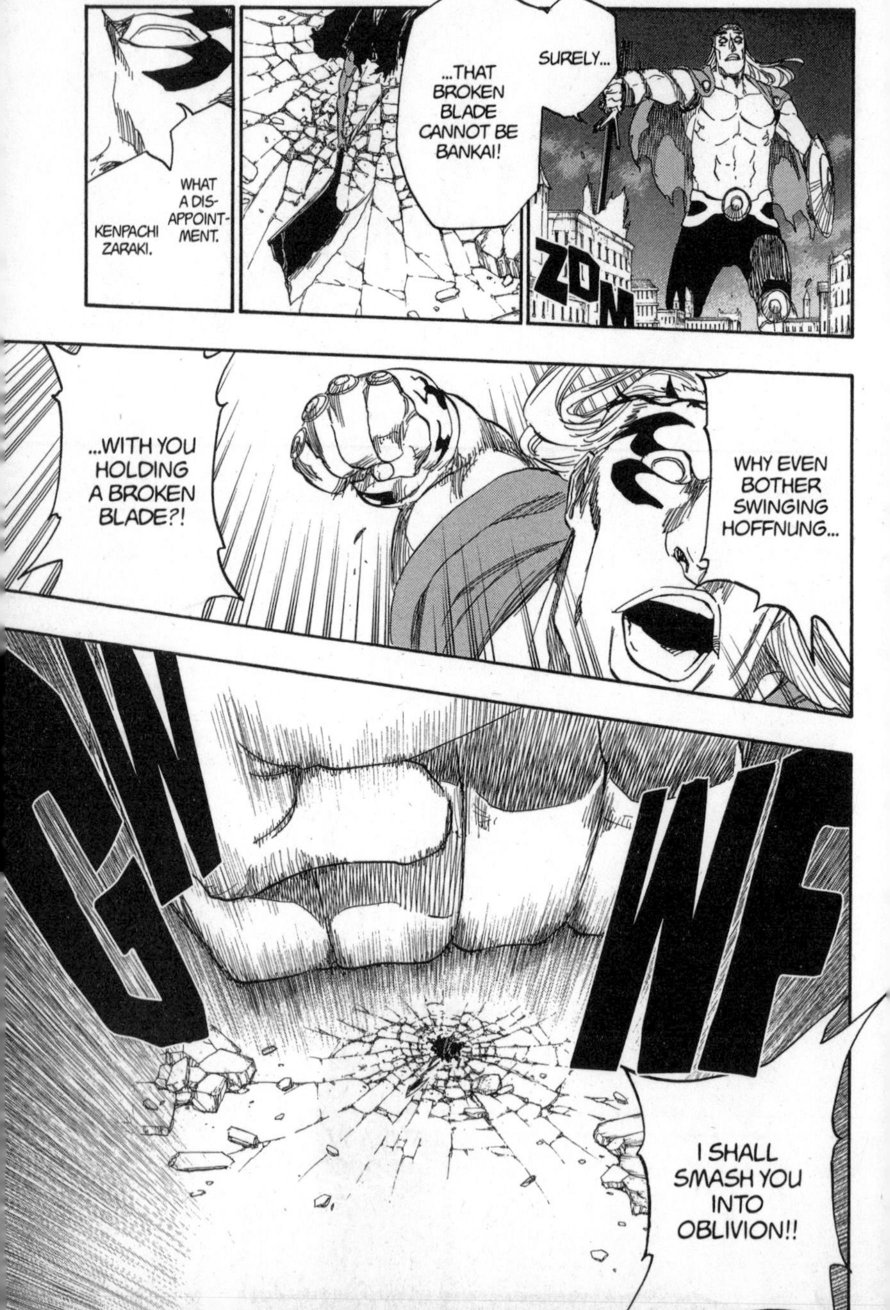
SURELY...
...THAT BROKEN BLADE CANNOT BE BANKAI!
ZOM
WHAT A DISAPPOINTMENT.
KENPACHI ZARAKI.
WHY EVEN BOTHER SWINGING HOFFNUNG...
...WITH YOU HOLDING A BROKEN BLADE?!
I SHALL SMASH YOU INTO OBLIVION!!

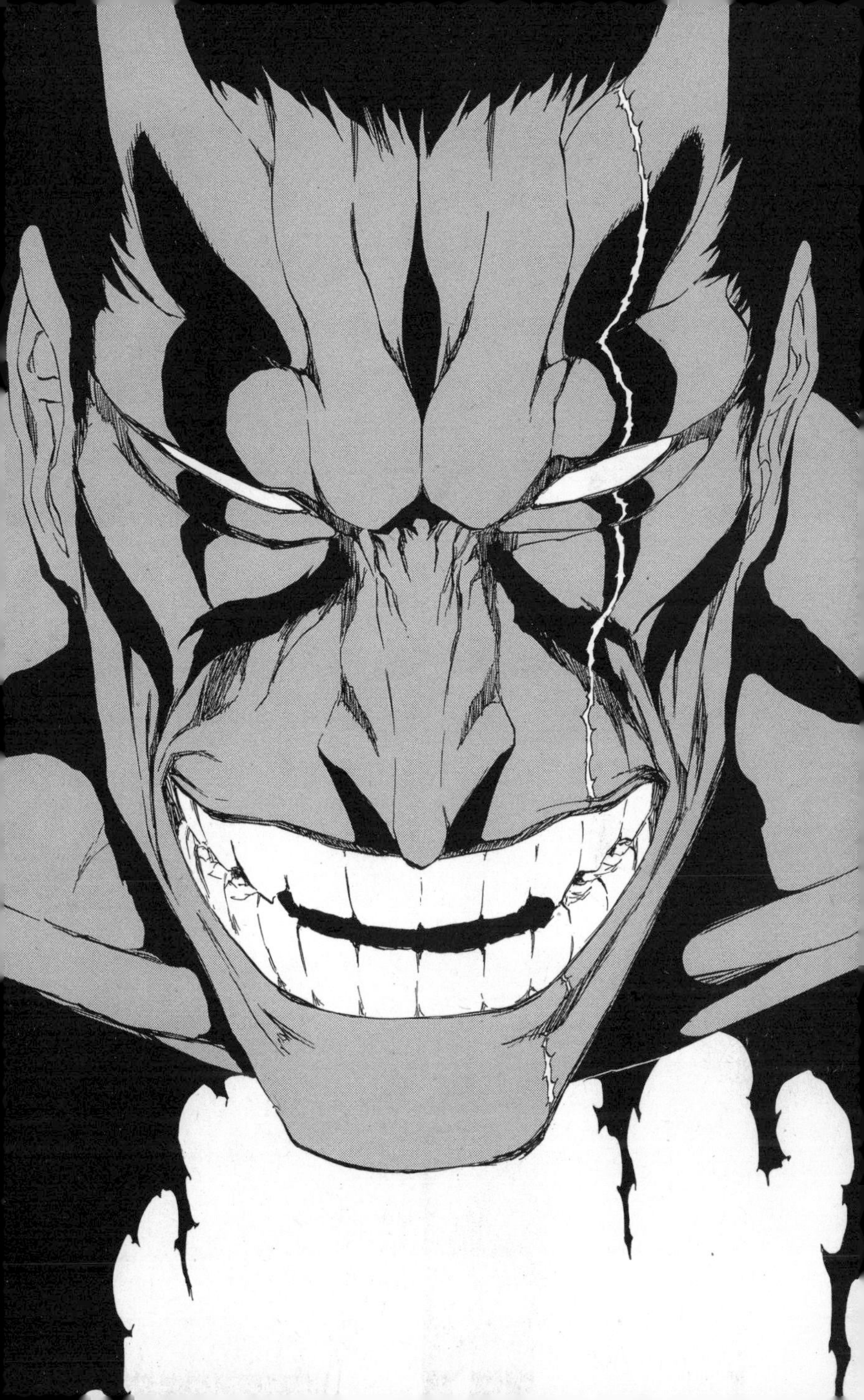

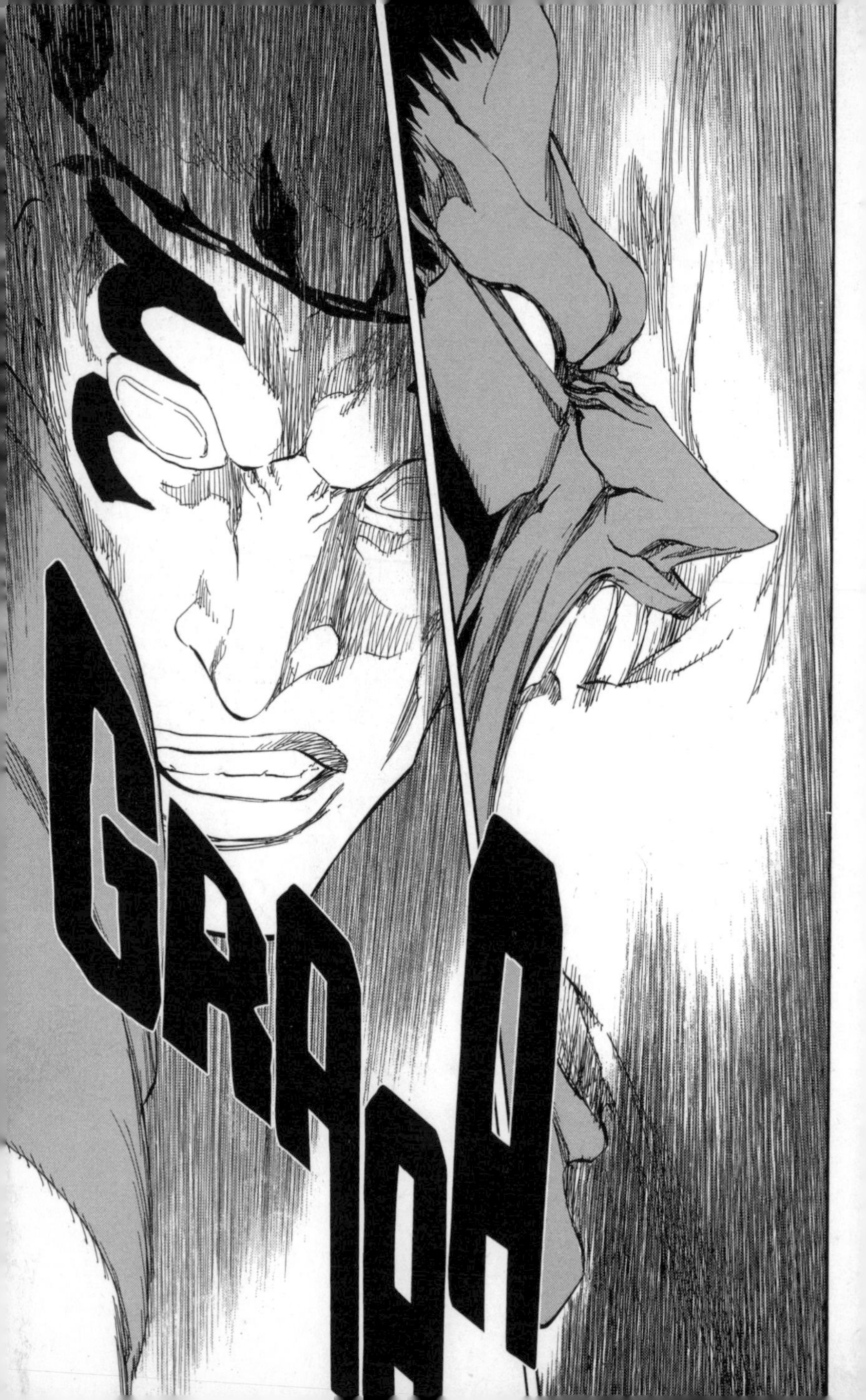
GRAAAA

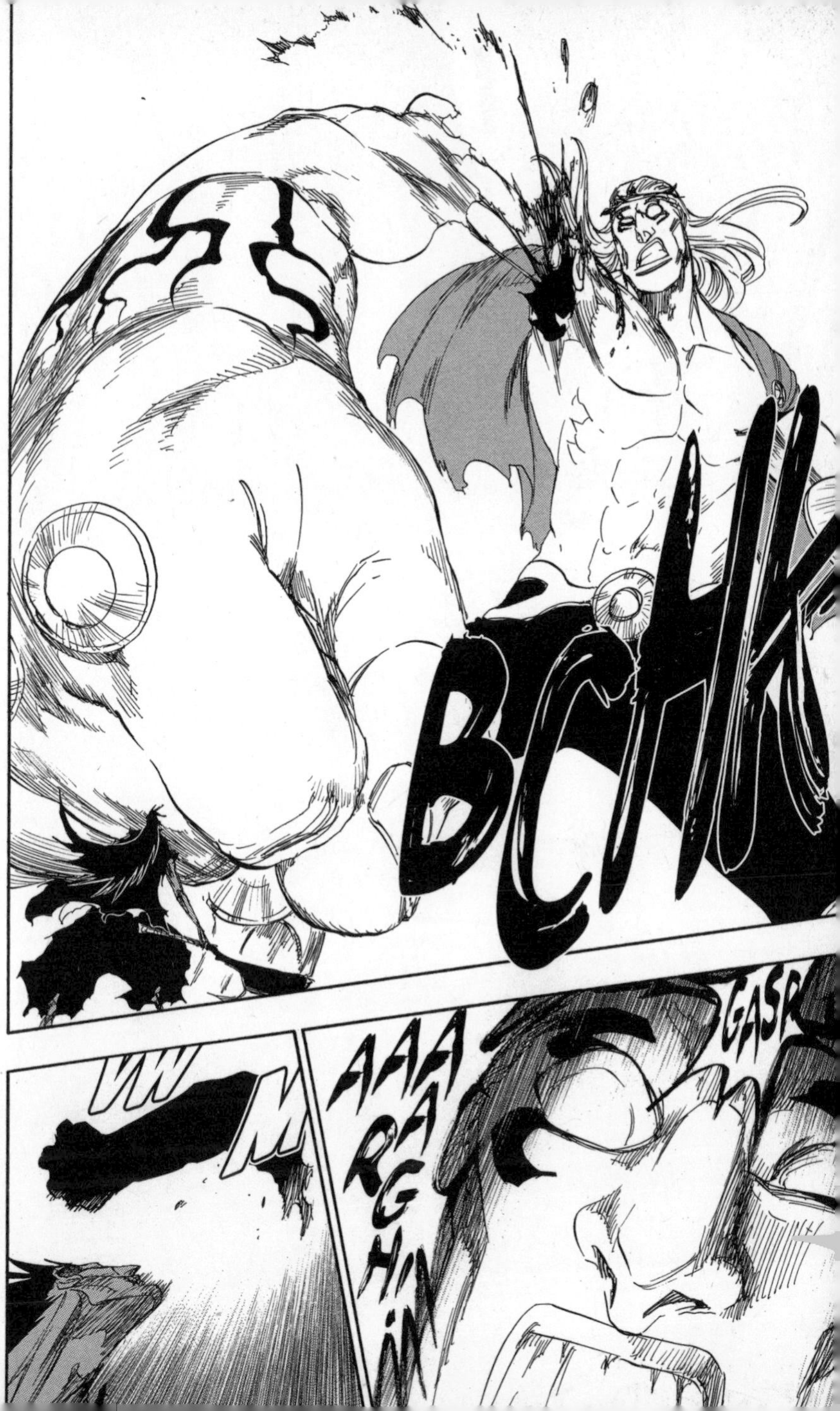
BCHK
GASP
AAARAARGHHH
VWM

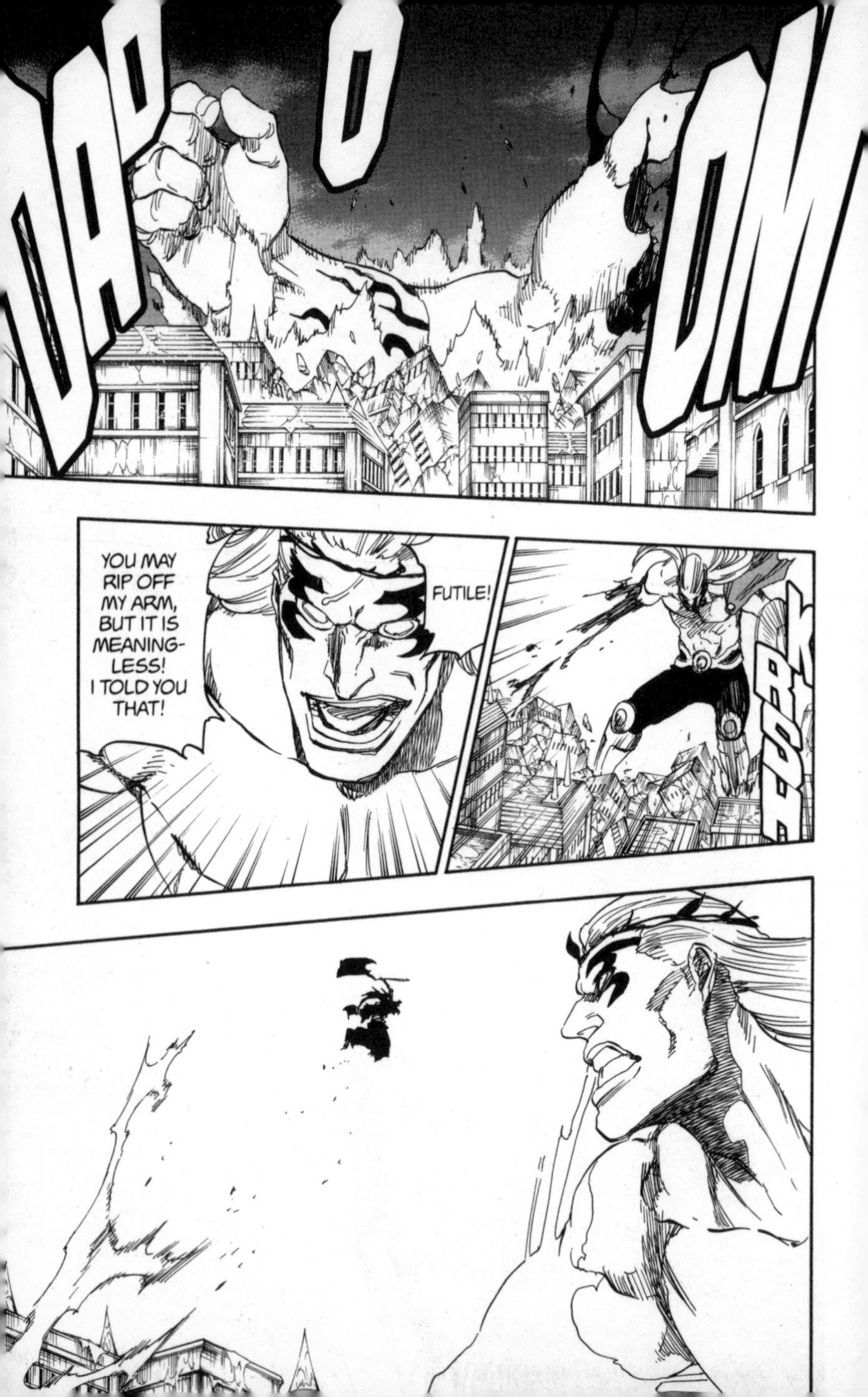
YOU MAY RIP OFF MY ARM, BUT IT IS MEANING-LESS! I TOLD YOU THAT!
FUTILE!

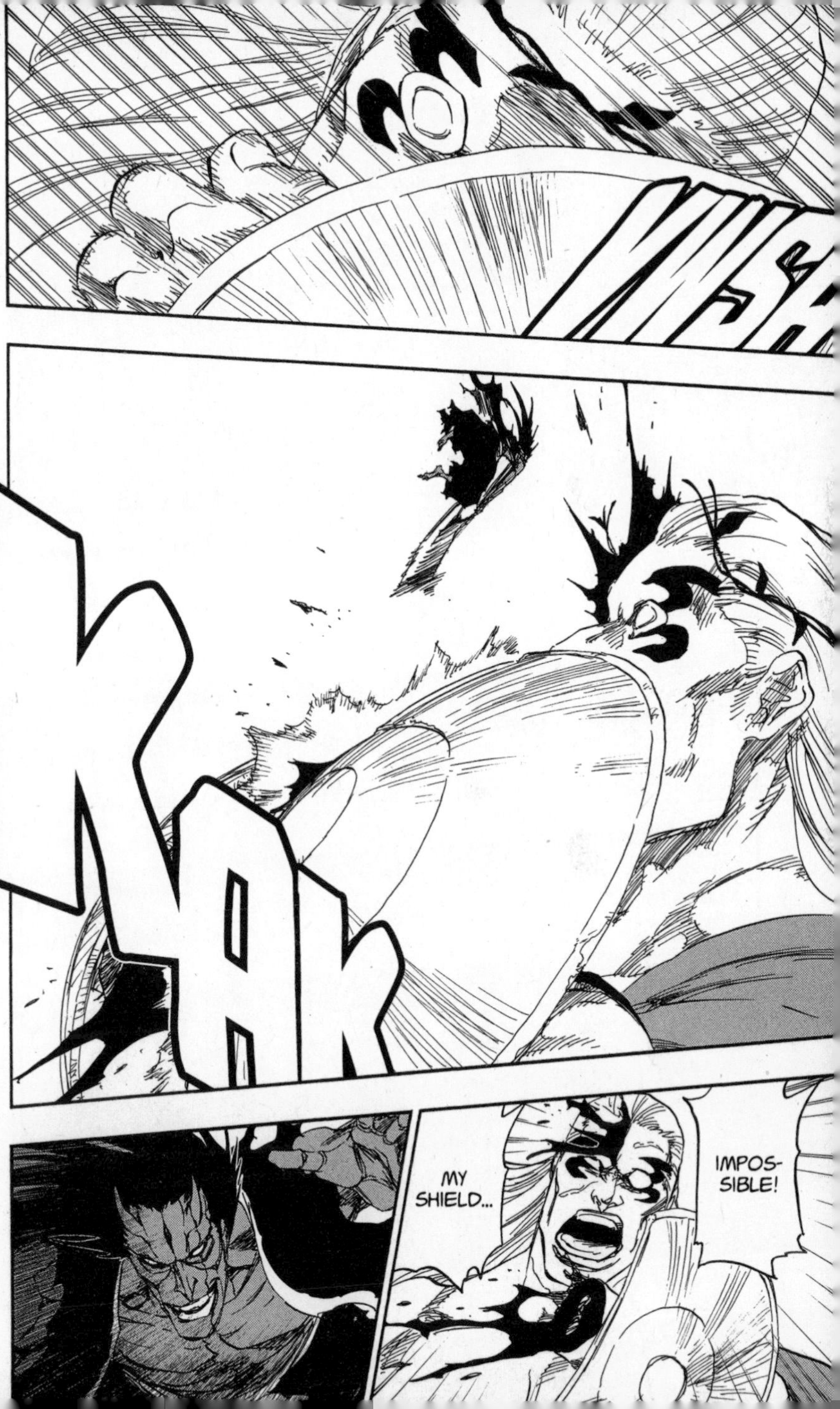
KRAK
IMPOS-SIBLE!
MY SHIELD...

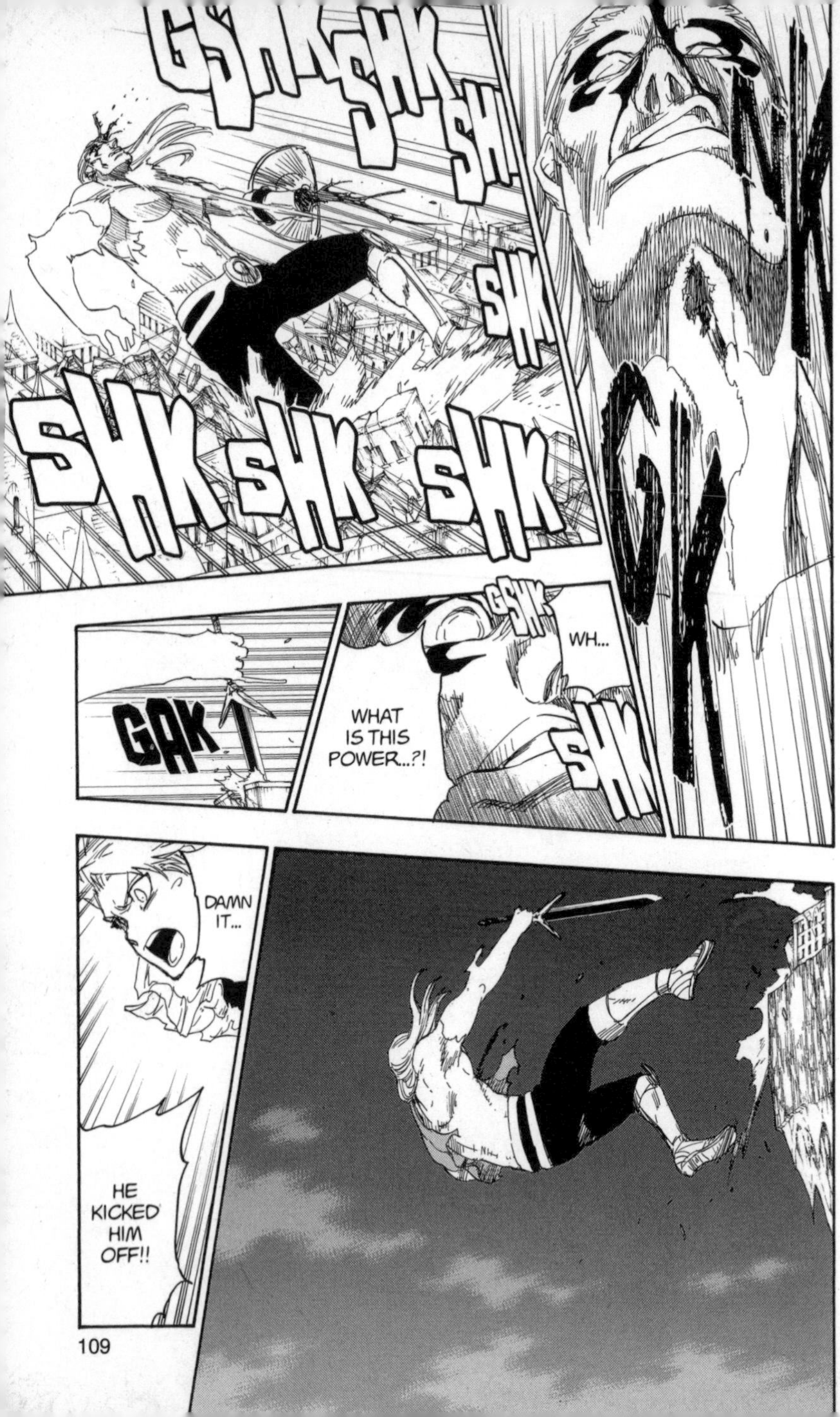
GSHK
SHK
SHK
SHK
SHK
SHK
SHK
GSHK
WH...
WHAT IS THIS POWER...?!
SHK
GAK
DAMN IT...
HE KICKED HIM OFF!!

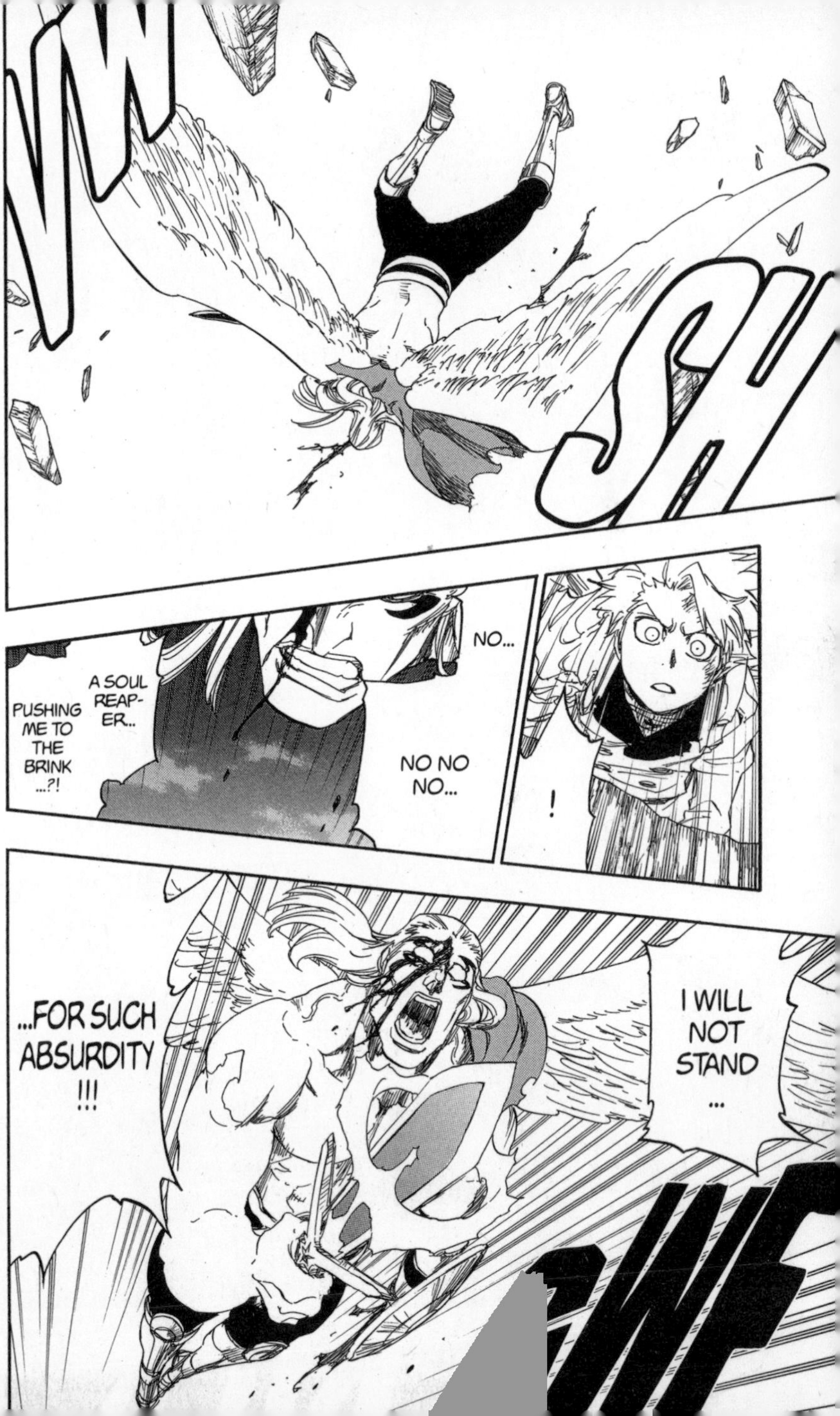
!
NO...
NO NO NO...
A SOUL REAPER...
PUSHING ME TO THE BRINK ...?!
I WILL NOT STAND ...
...FOR SUCH ABSURDITY !!!

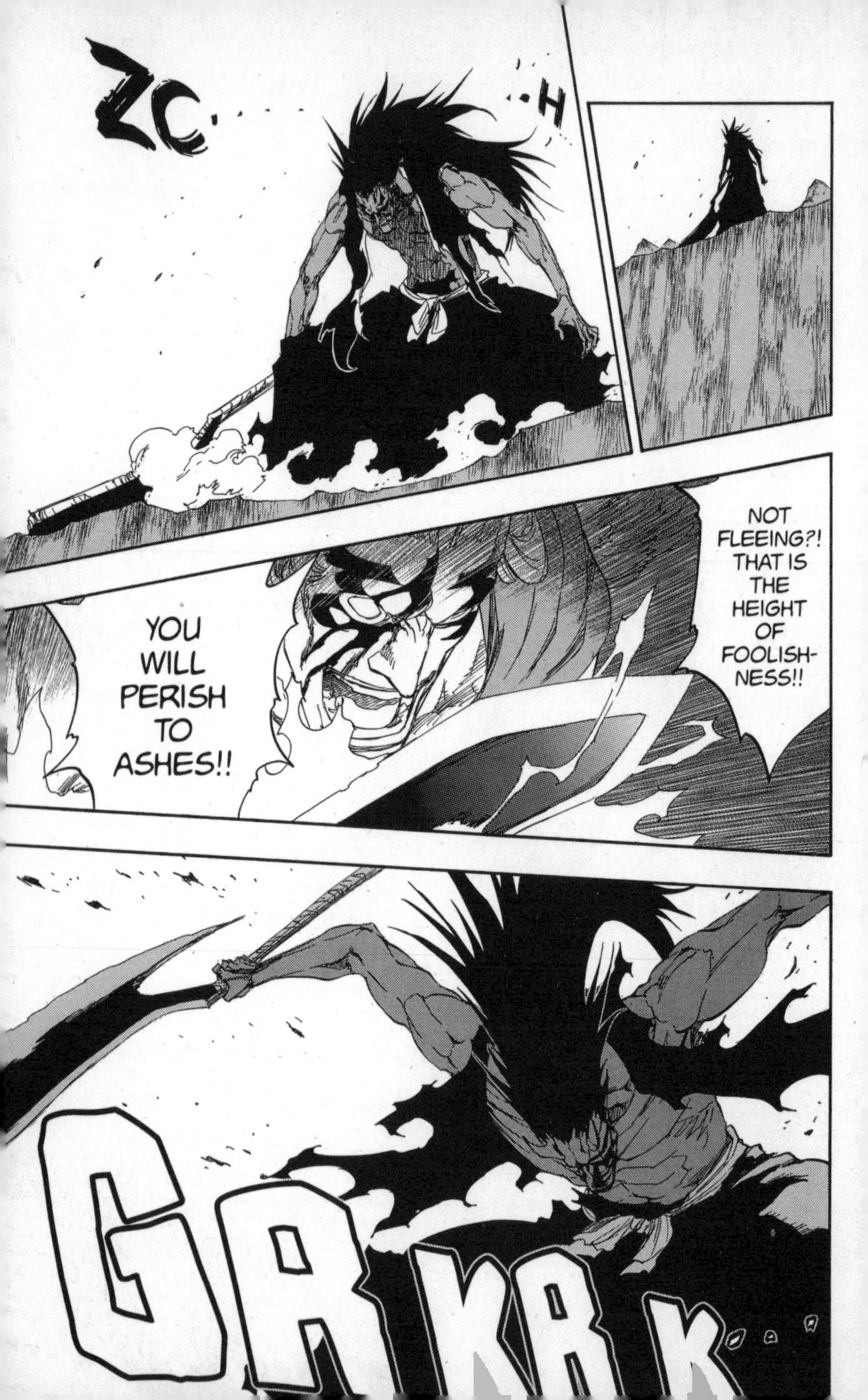
ZC...H
NOT FLEEING?! THAT IS THE HEIGHT OF FOOLISHNESS!!
YOU WILL PERISH TO ASHES!!
GRKAK

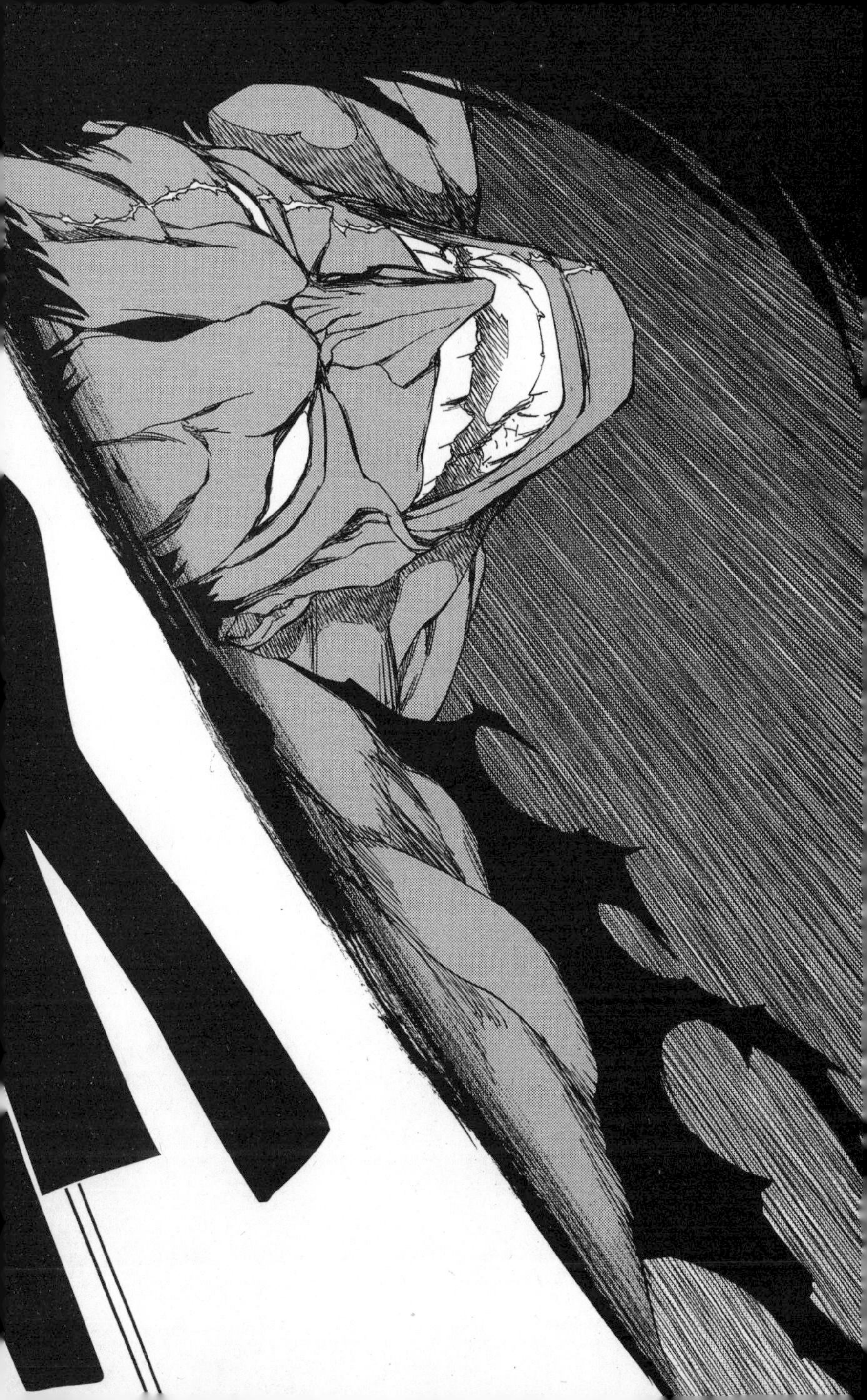

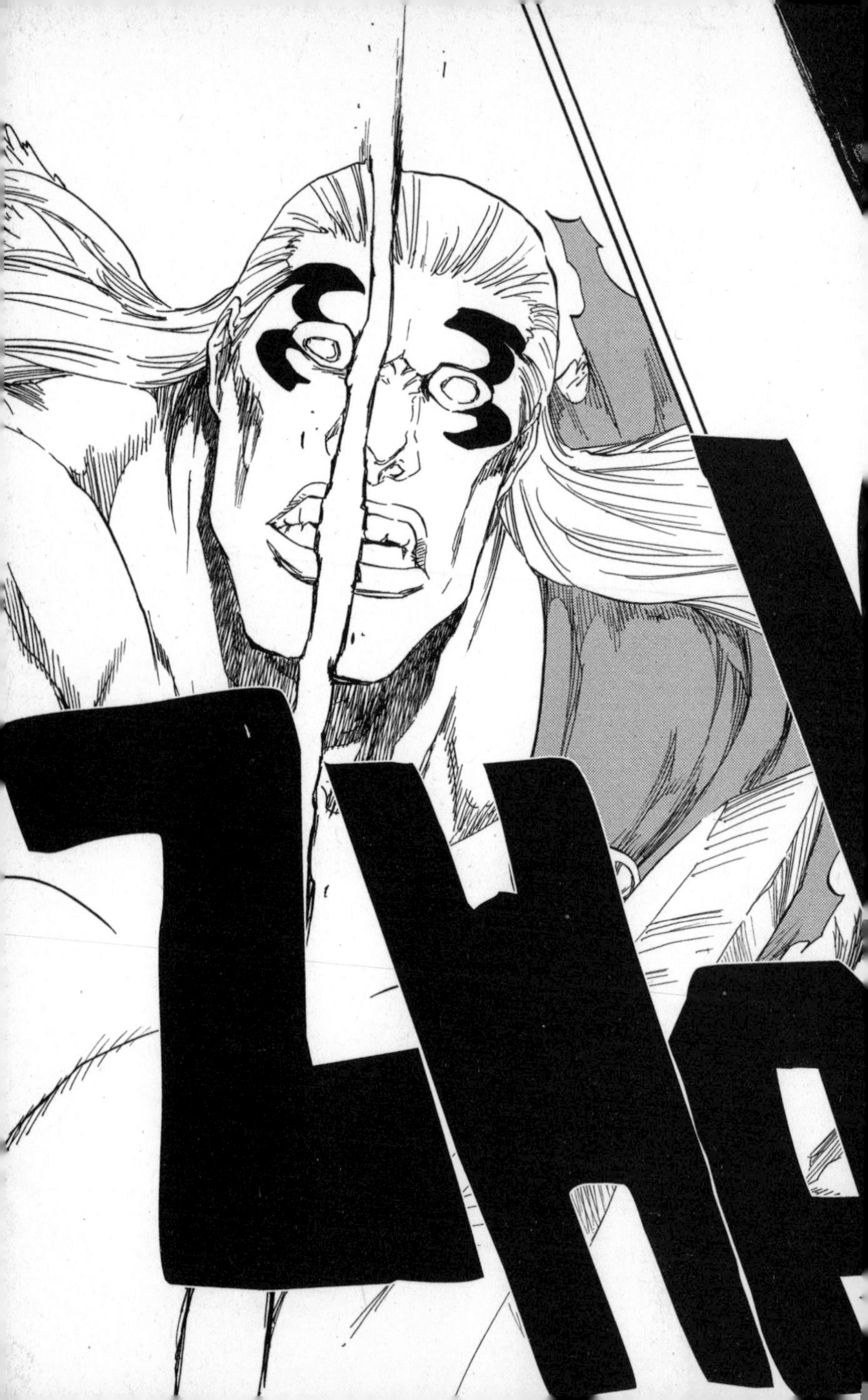

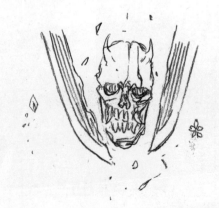

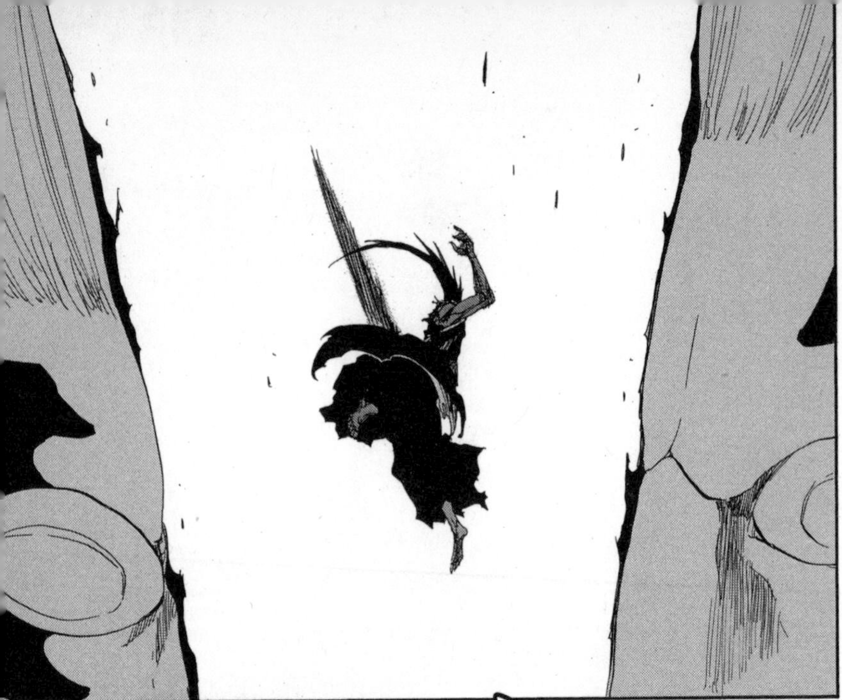

670. THE PERFECT CRIMSON

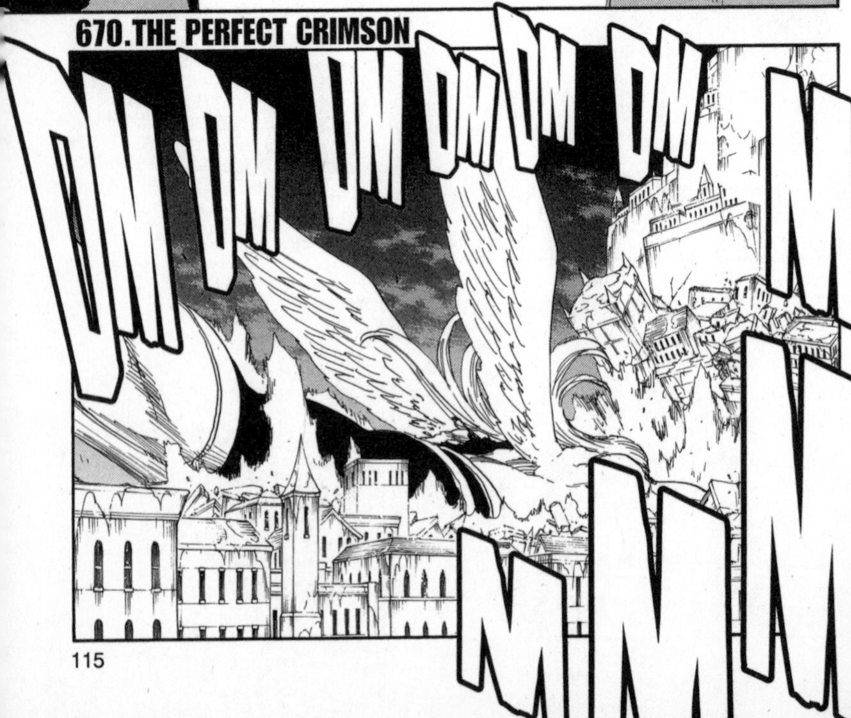
DM-DM DM DM DM DM
MMMMM

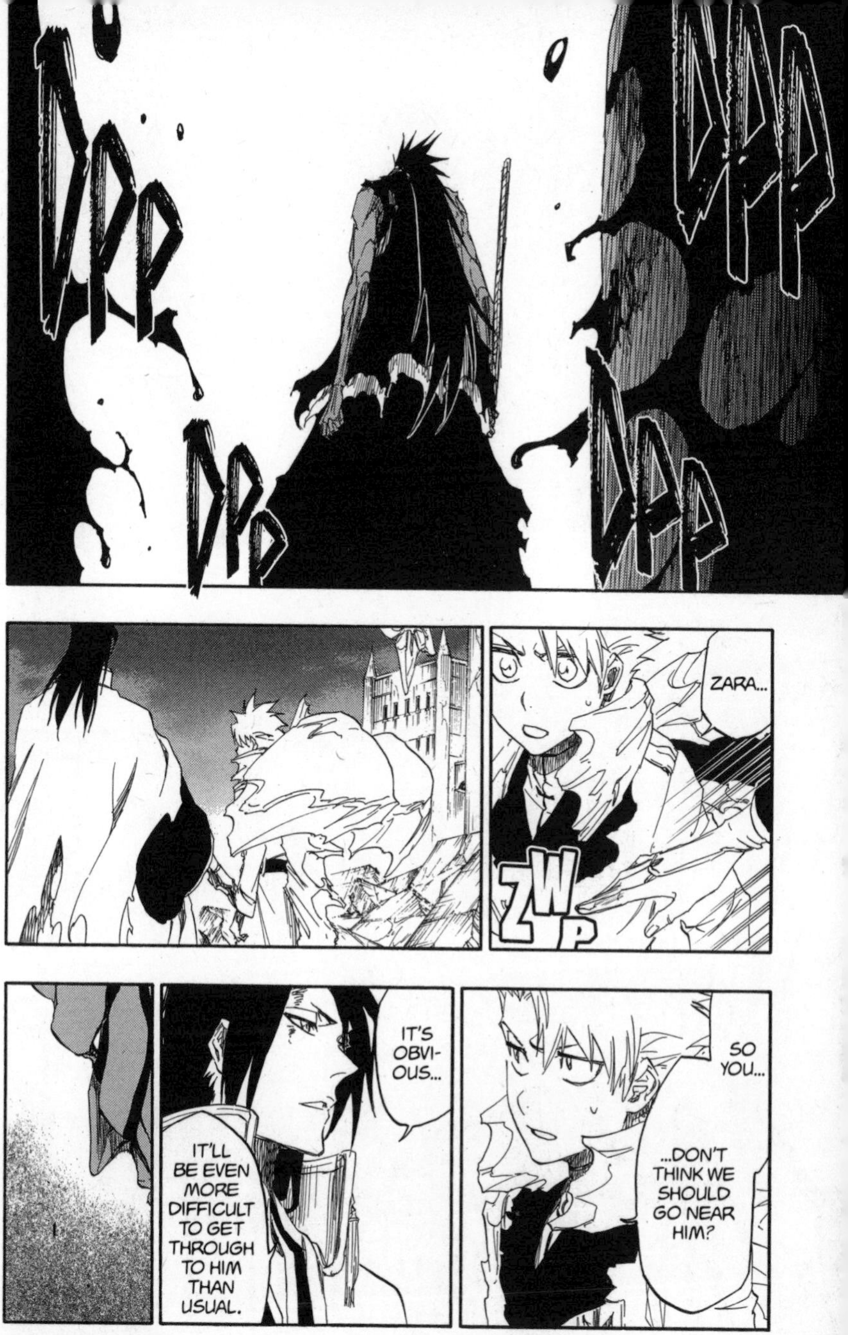
DPP
DPP
DPP
DPP
ZARA...
ZWP
SO YOU...
...DON'T THINK WE SHOULD GO NEAR HIM?
IT'S OBVI-OUS...
IT'LL BE EVEN MORE DIFFICULT TO GET THROUGH TO HIM THAN USUAL.

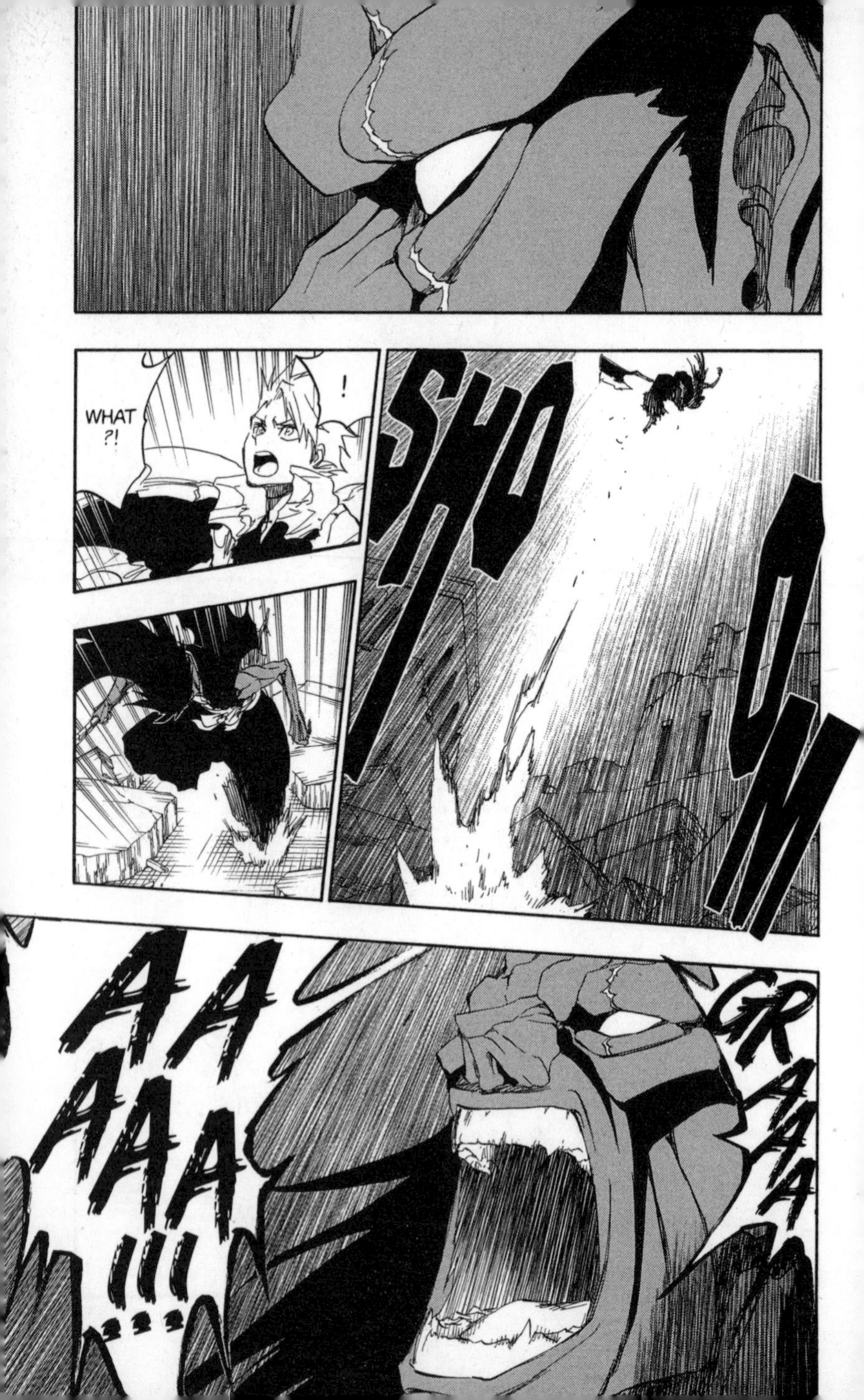
SHOOM
!
WHAT ?!
GRAAAAA
AAAAA!!!

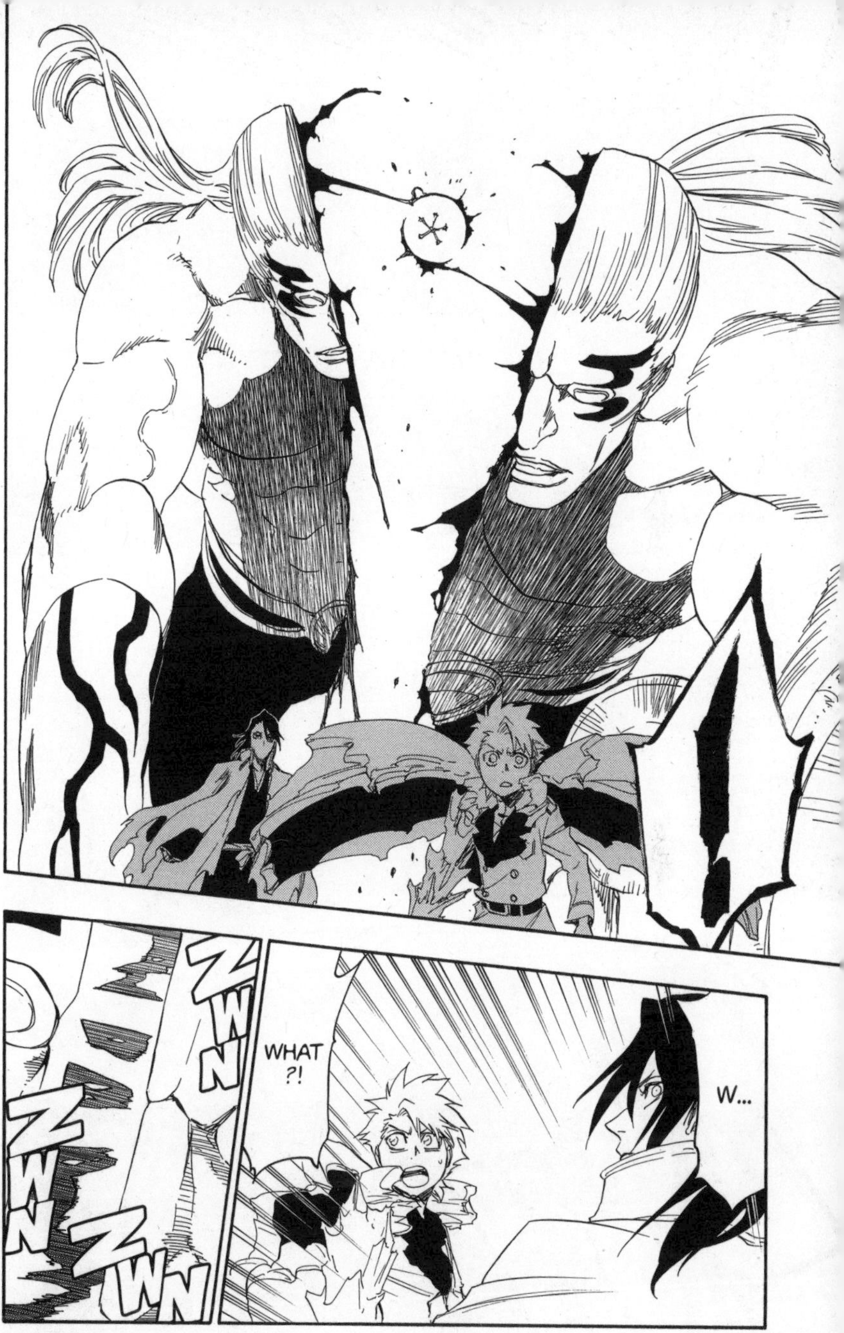
W...
WHAT ?!
ZWN
ZWN
ZWN

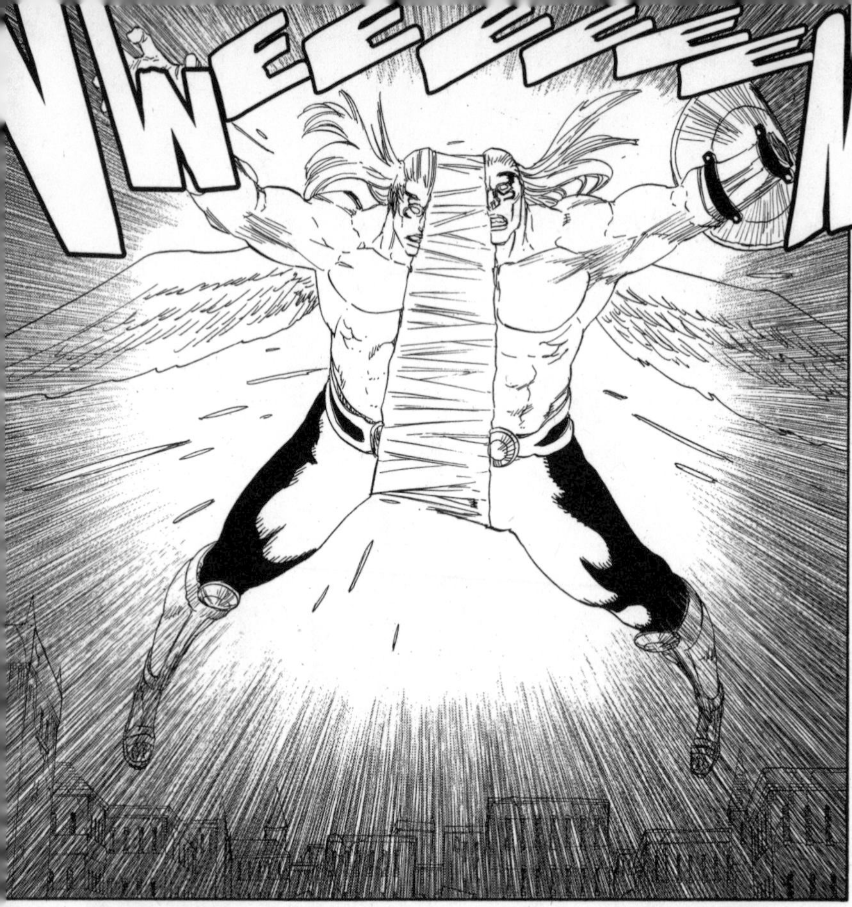
VWEEEEEEN

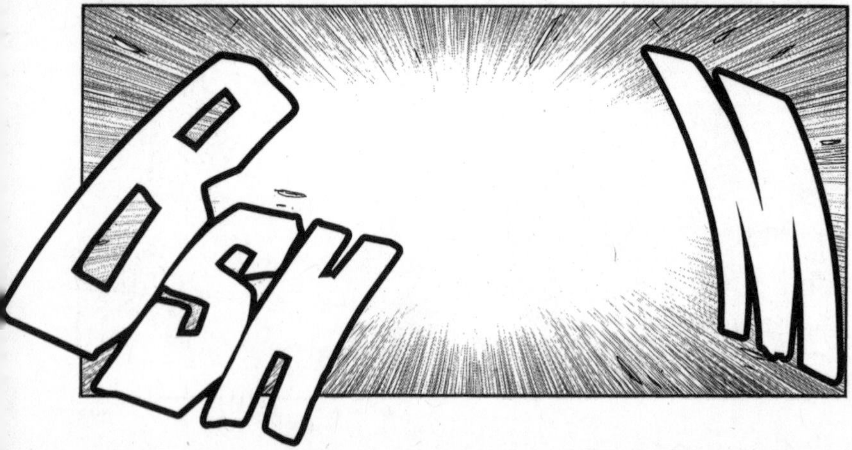
BOSH
M

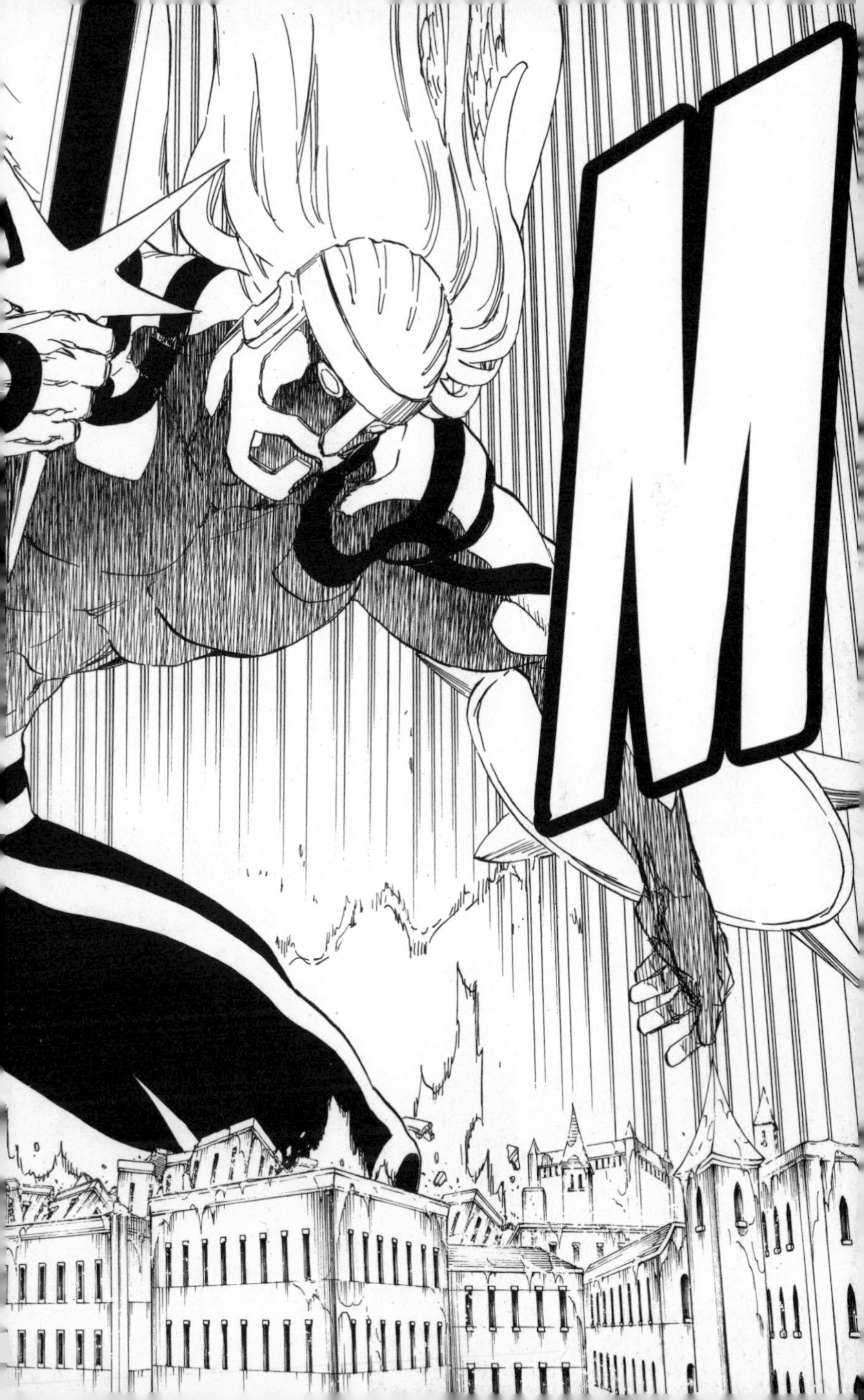
M

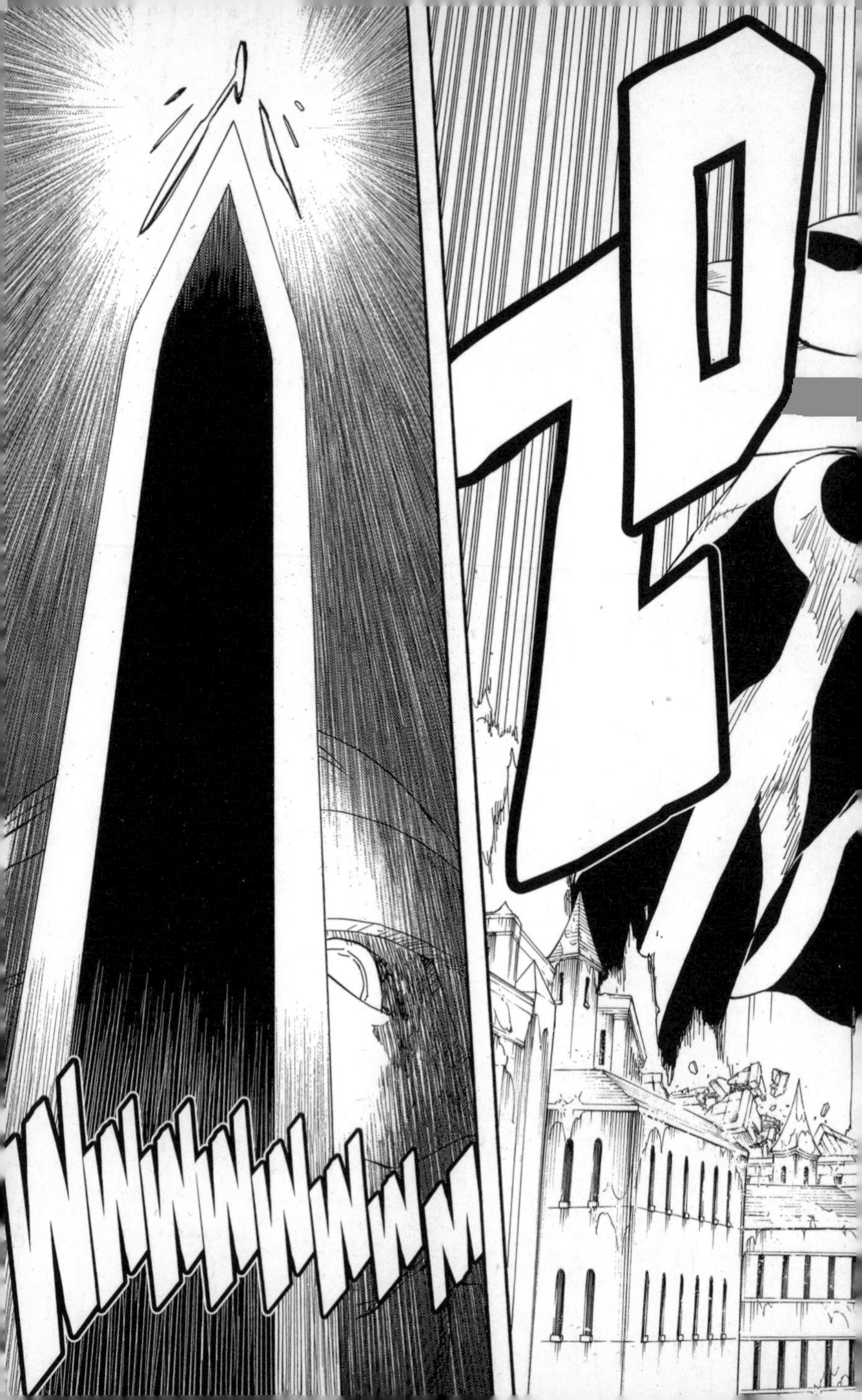
ZO

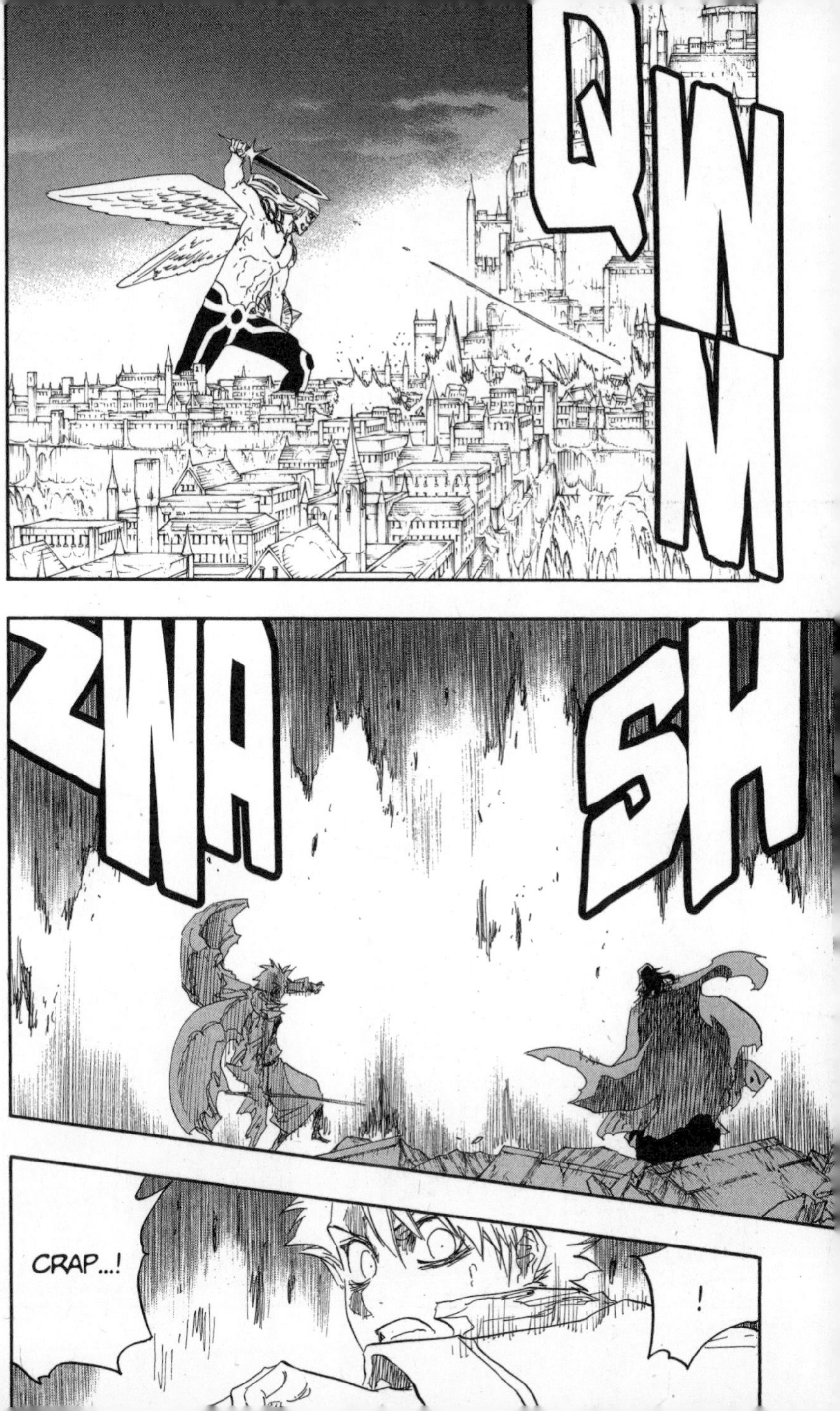
GWM
ZWA
SH
!
CRAP...!

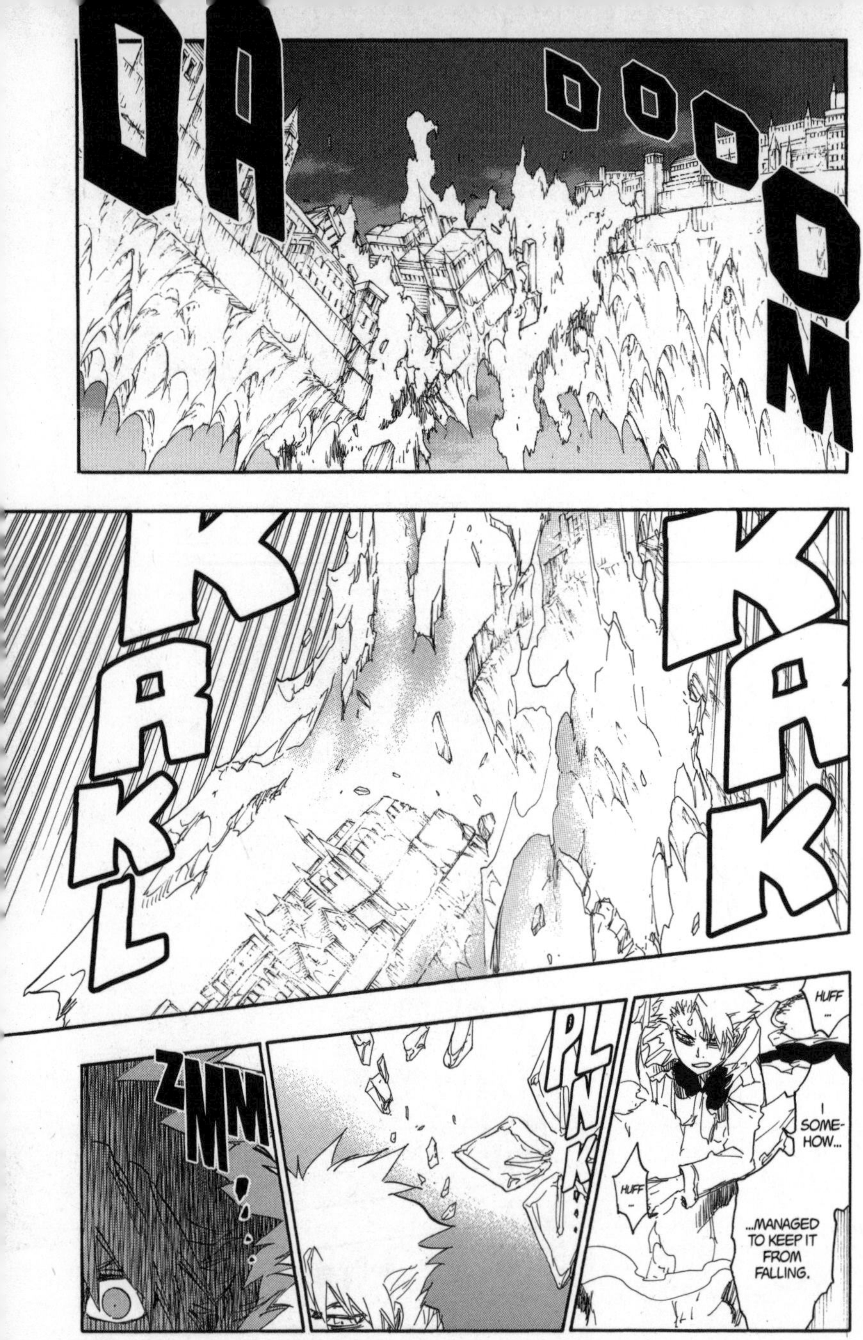
DAOOOOM
KRAK
KRAKL
HUFF...
I SOMEHOW...
HUFF...
...MANAGED TO KEEP IT FROM FALLING.
PLINK...
ZMM!...

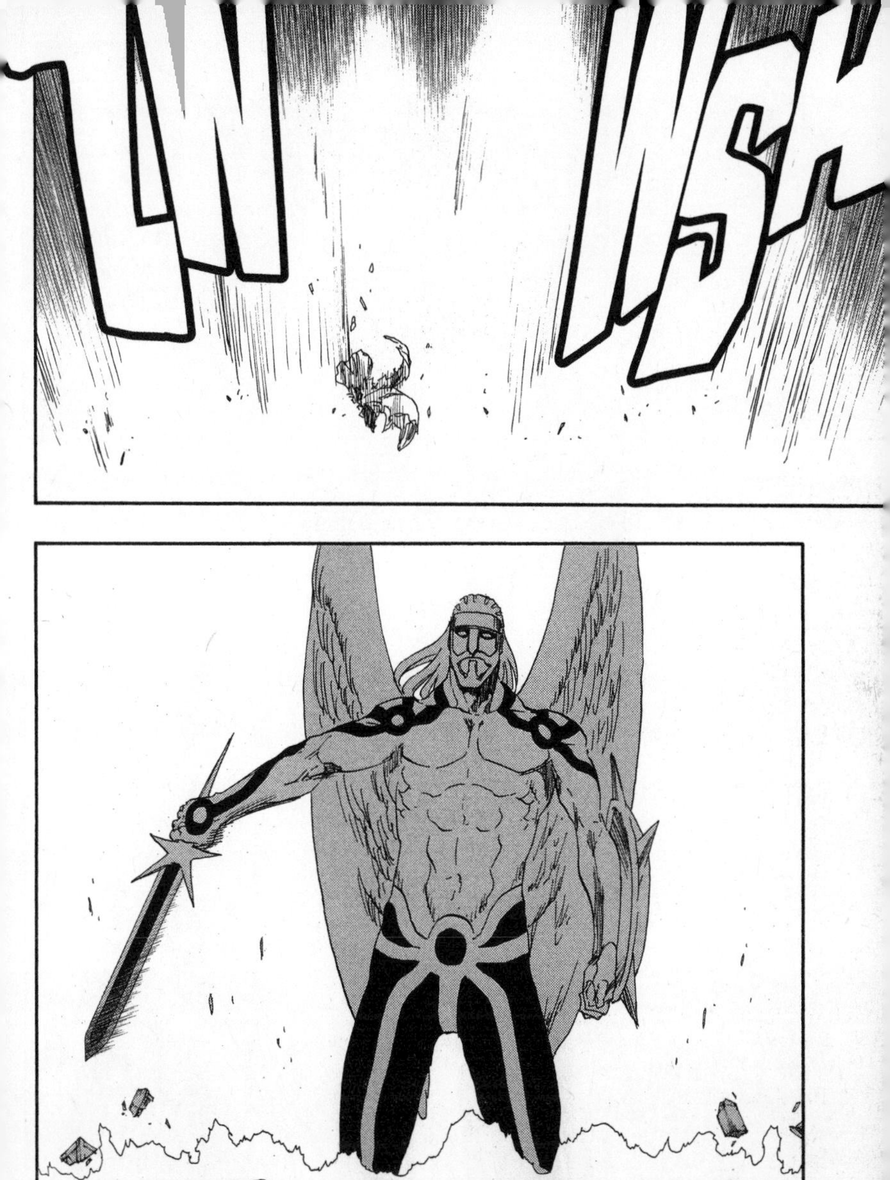

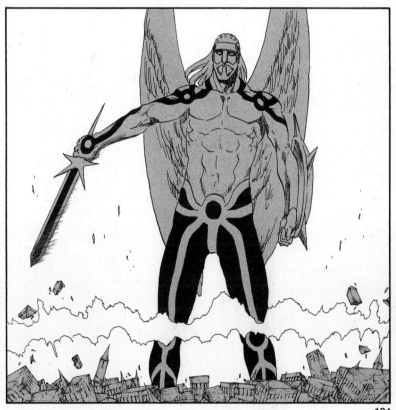

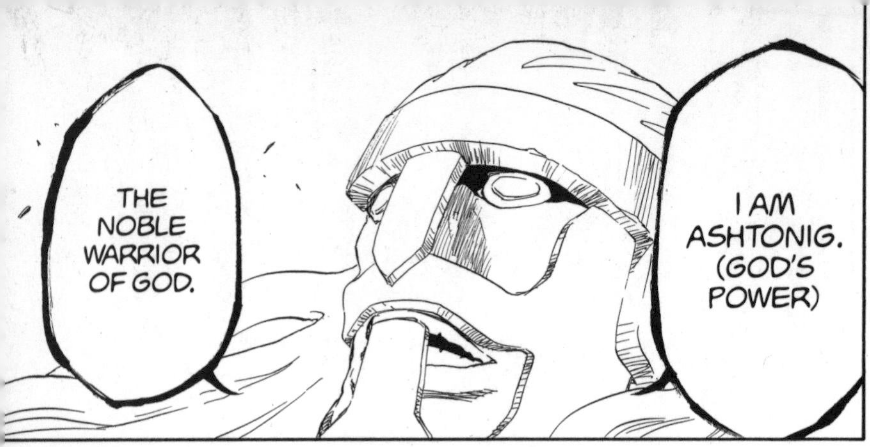
I AM ASHTONIG. (GOD'S POWER)
THE NOBLE WARRIOR OF GOD.
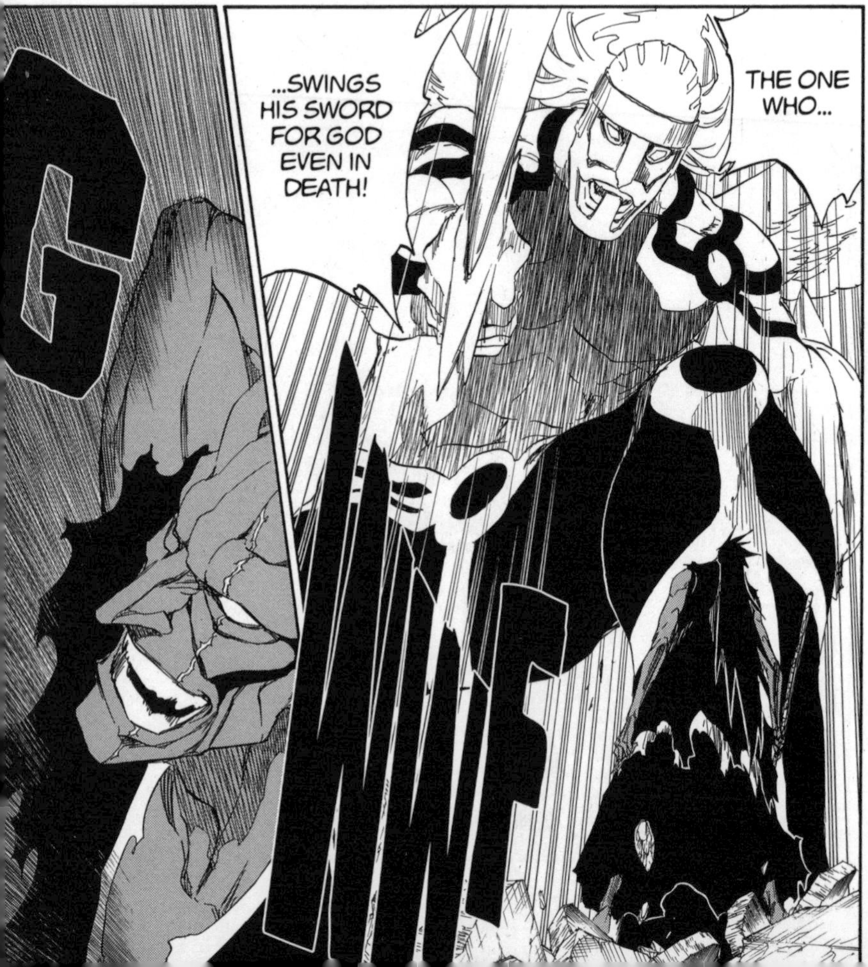
THE ONE WHO...
...SWINGS HIS SWORD FOR GOD EVEN IN DEATH!

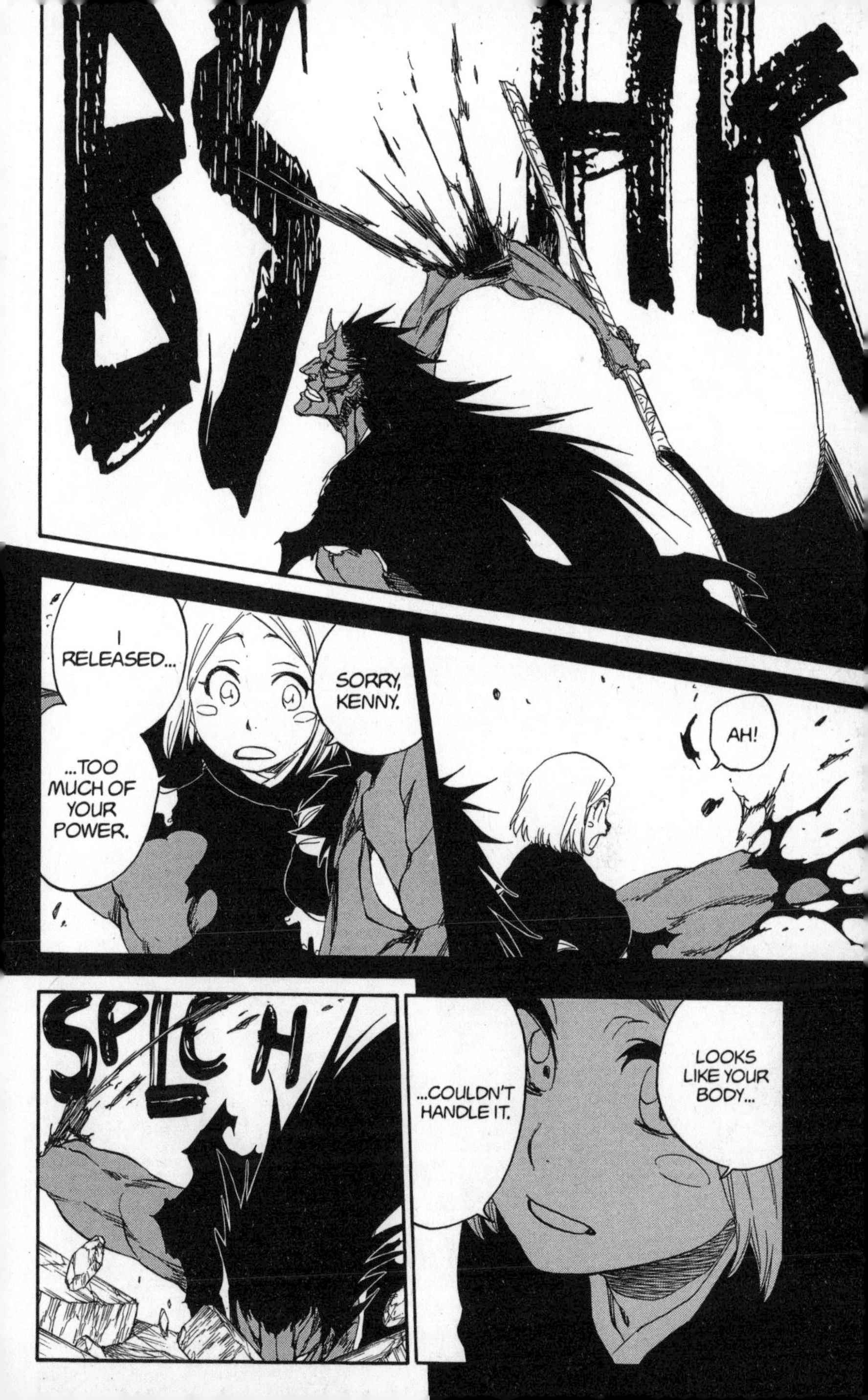
AH!
SORRY, KENNY.
I RELEASED...
...TOO MUCH OF YOUR POWER.
LOOKS LIKE YOUR BODY...
...COULDN'T HANDLE IT.
SPLCH

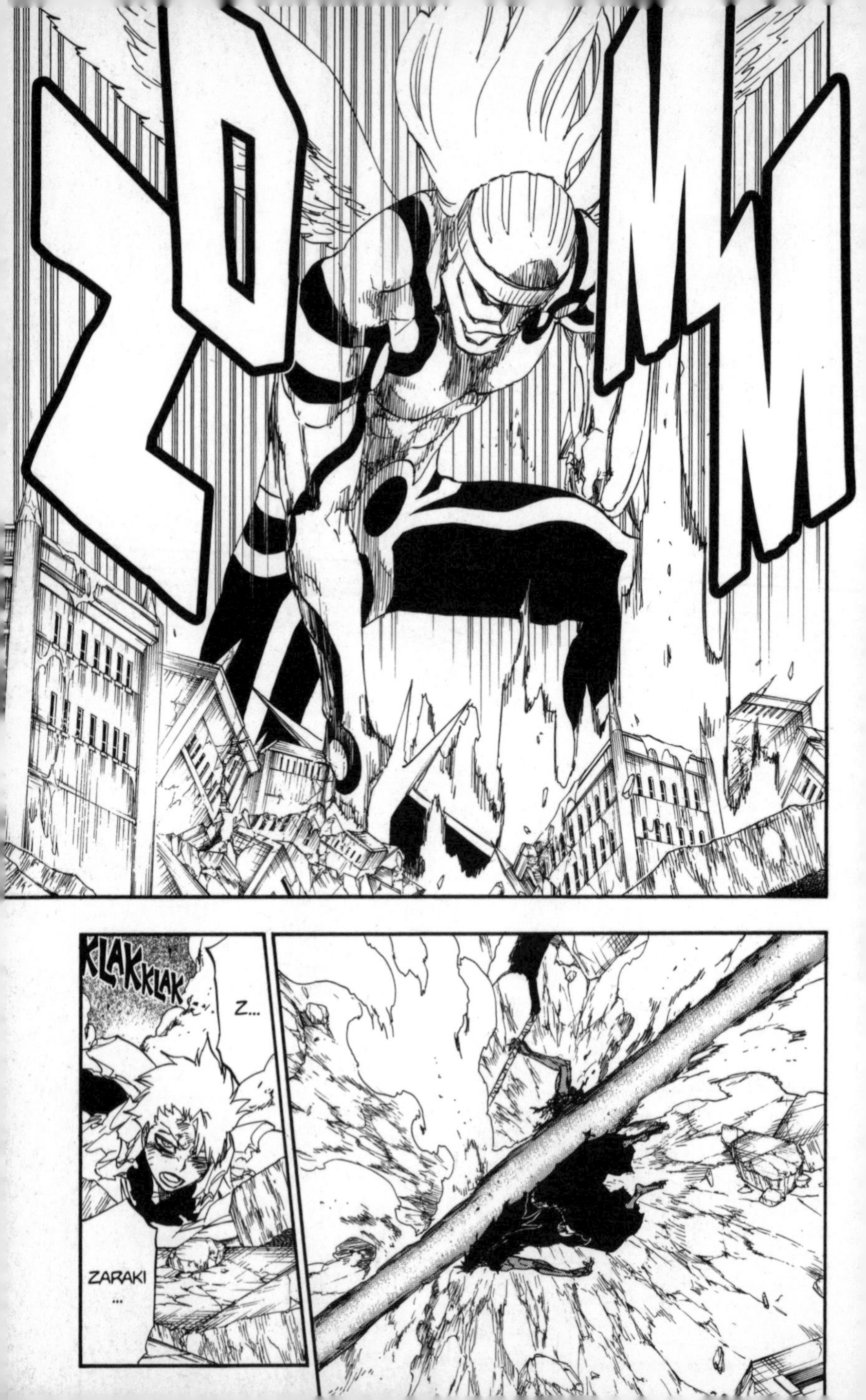
ZOMM
KLAK KLAK
Z...
ZARAKI ...

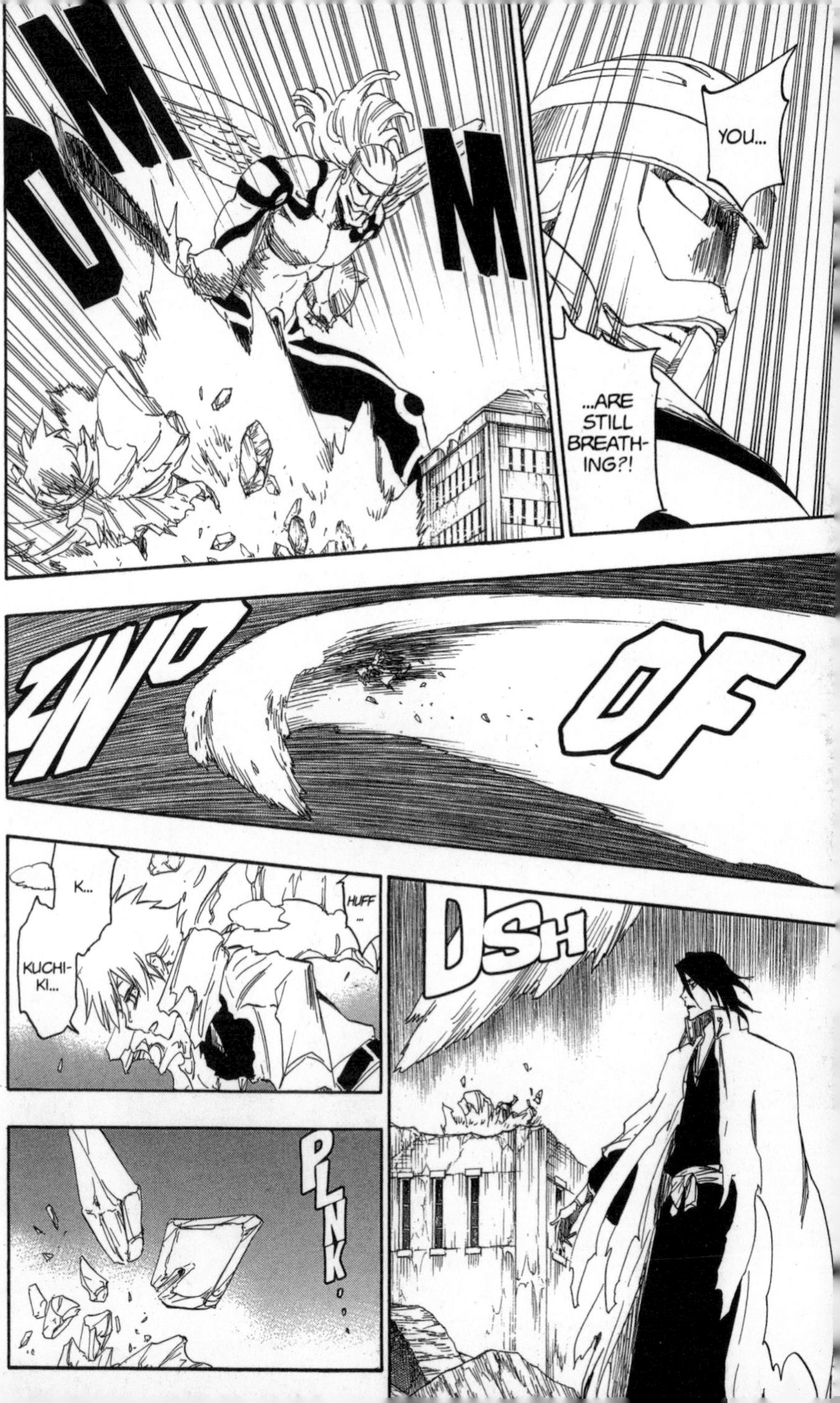
YOU...
...ARE STILL BREATHING?!
DMM
ZNOOF
DSH
HUFF...
K...
KUCHIKI...
PLNK

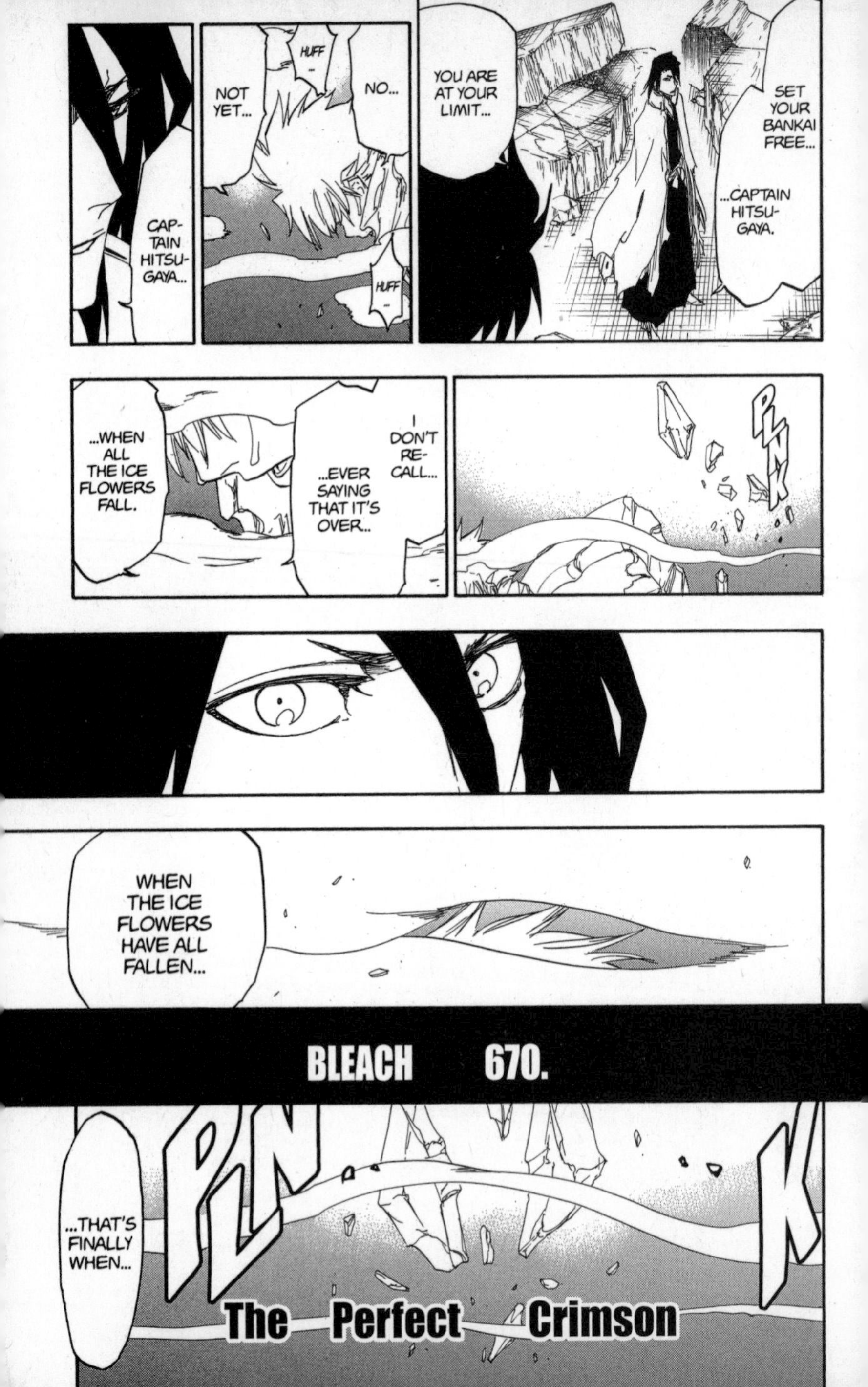
YOU ARE AT YOUR LIMIT...
SET YOUR BANKAI FREE...
...CAPTAIN HITSUGAYA.
HUFF
NO...
NOT YET...
HUFF
CAPTAIN HITSUGAYA...
PLINK
I DON'T RECALL...
...EVER SAYING THAT IT'S OVER...
...WHEN ALL THE ICE FLOWERS FALL.
WHEN THE ICE FLOWERS HAVE ALL FALLEN...
BLEACH 670.
PLINK
...THAT'S FINALLY WHEN...
The Perfect Crimson

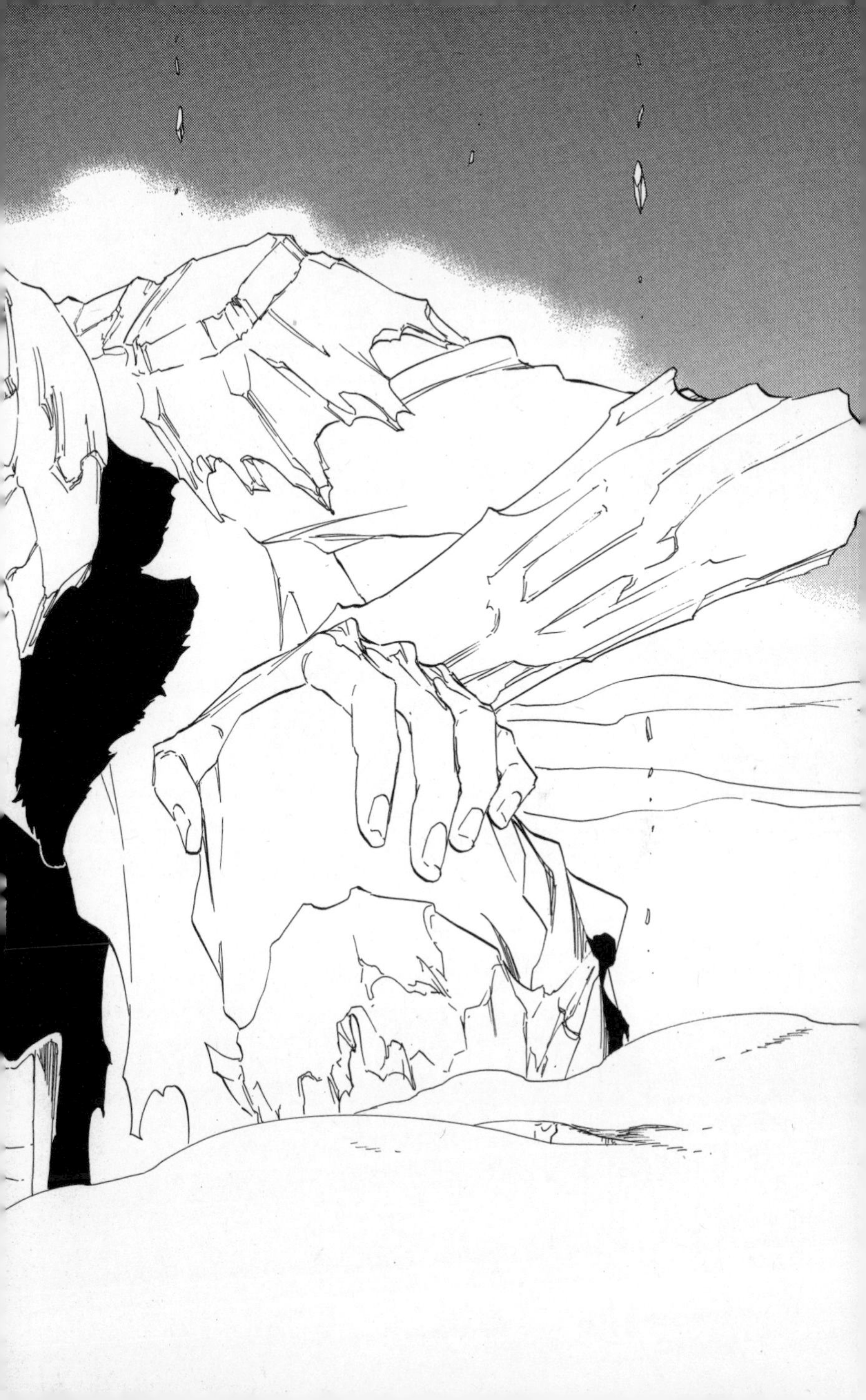

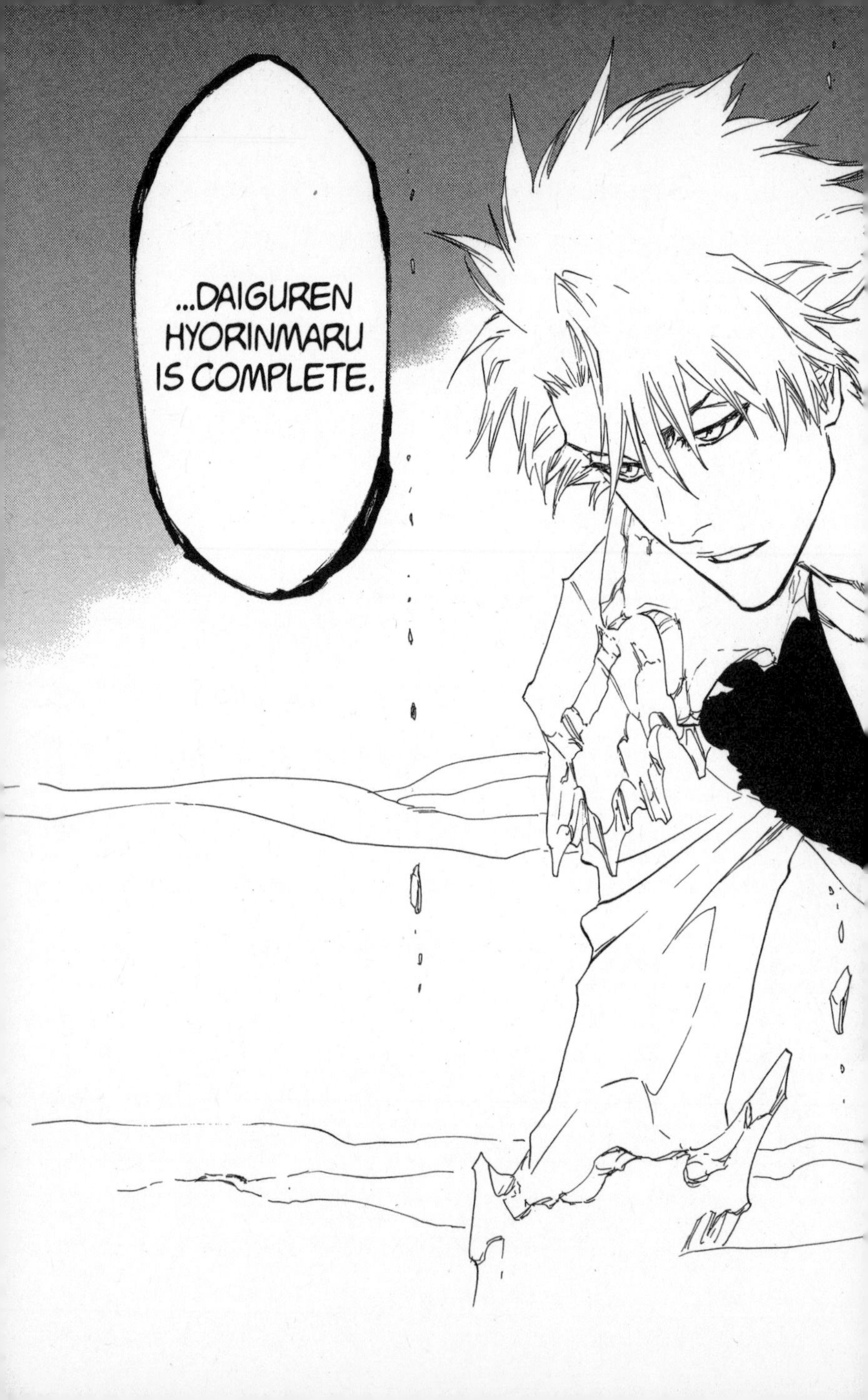
...DAIGUREN HYORINMARU IS COMPLETE.

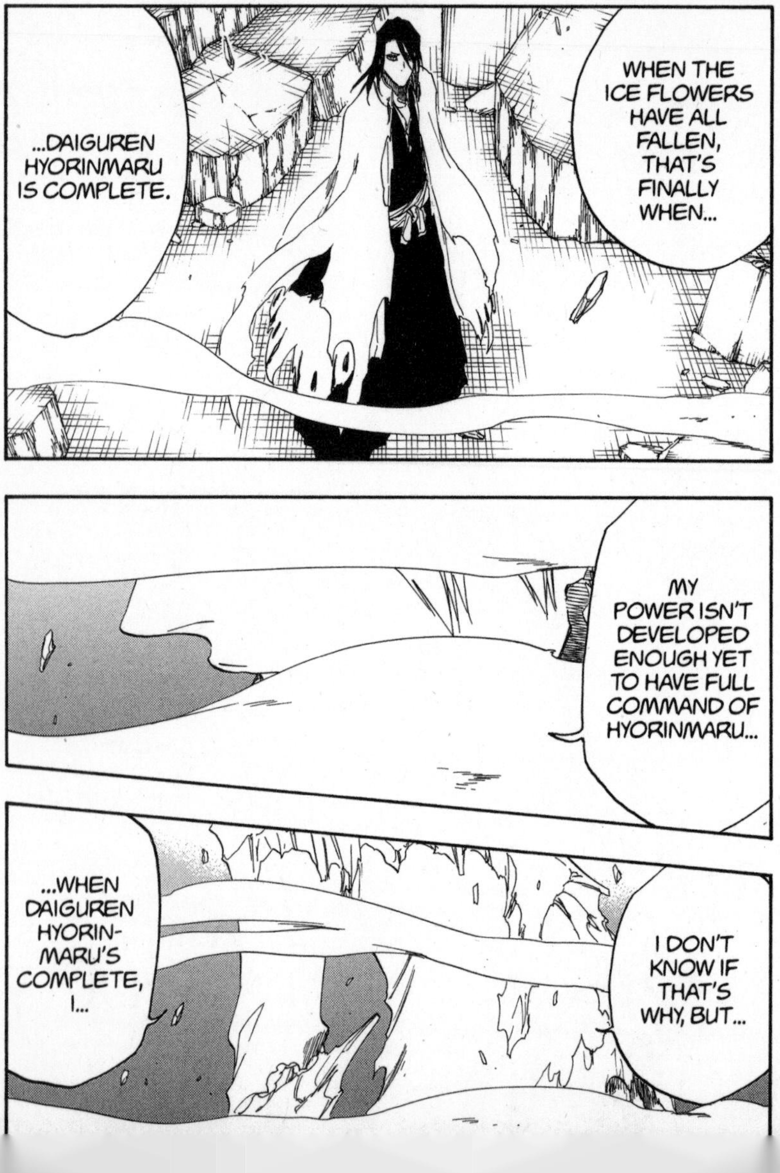
WHEN THE ICE FLOWERS HAVE ALL FALLEN, THAT'S FINALLY WHEN...
...DAIGUREN HYORINMARU IS COMPLETE.
MY POWER ISN'T DEVELOPED ENOUGH YET TO HAVE FULL COMMAND OF HYORINMARU...
I DON'T KNOW IF THAT'S WHY, BUT...
...WHEN DAIGUREN HYORIN-MARU'S COMPLETE, I...

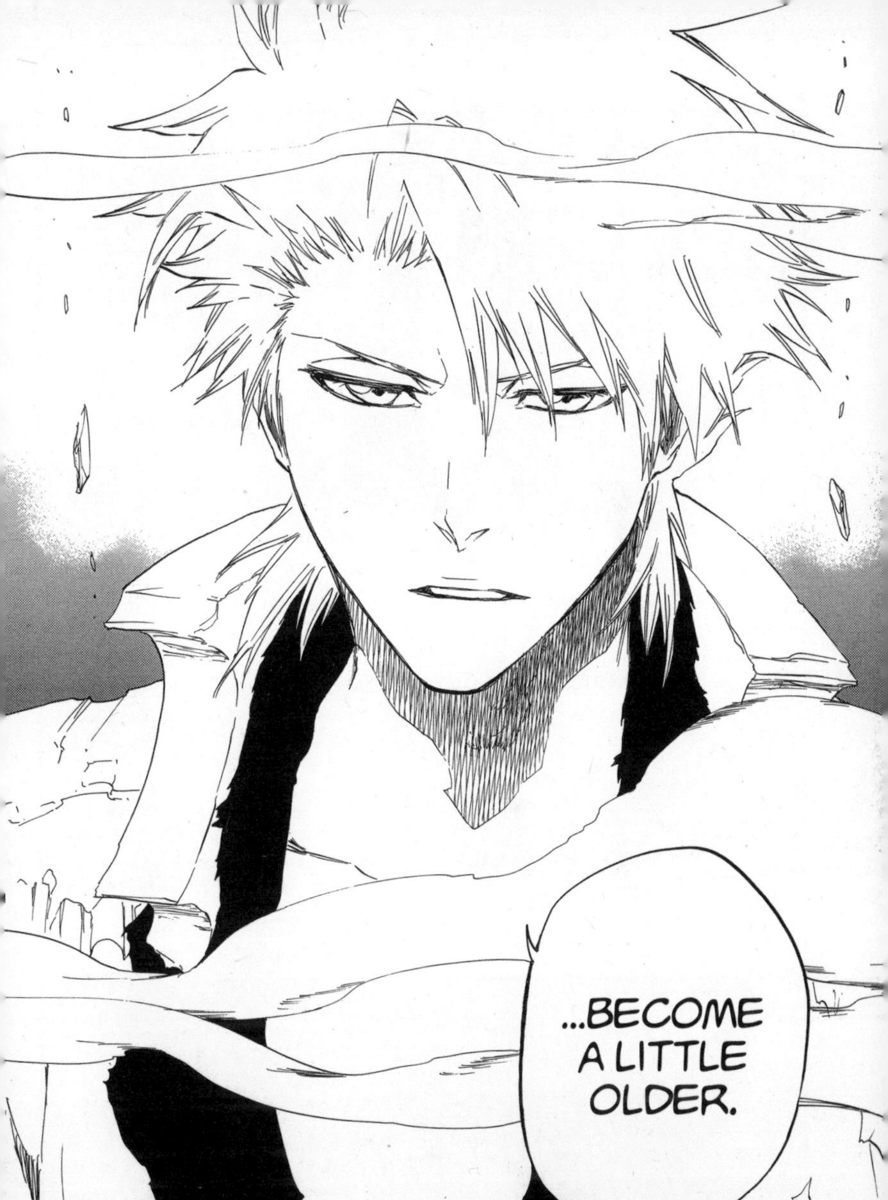
...BECOME A LITTLE OLDER.

The Perfect Crimson 2

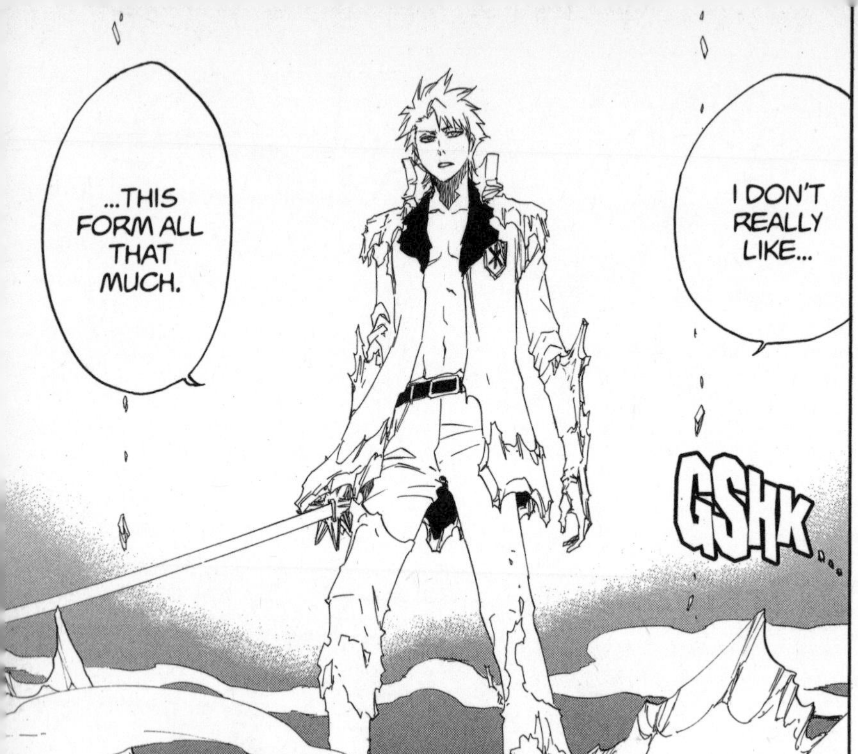
I DON'T REALLY LIKE...
...THIS FORM ALL THAT MUCH.
GSHK...

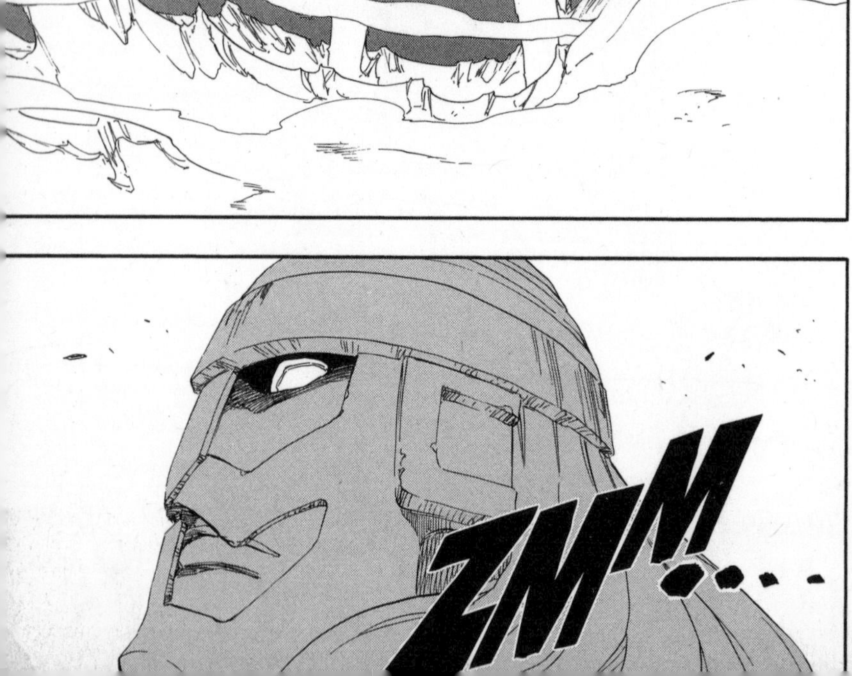
ZMM!....

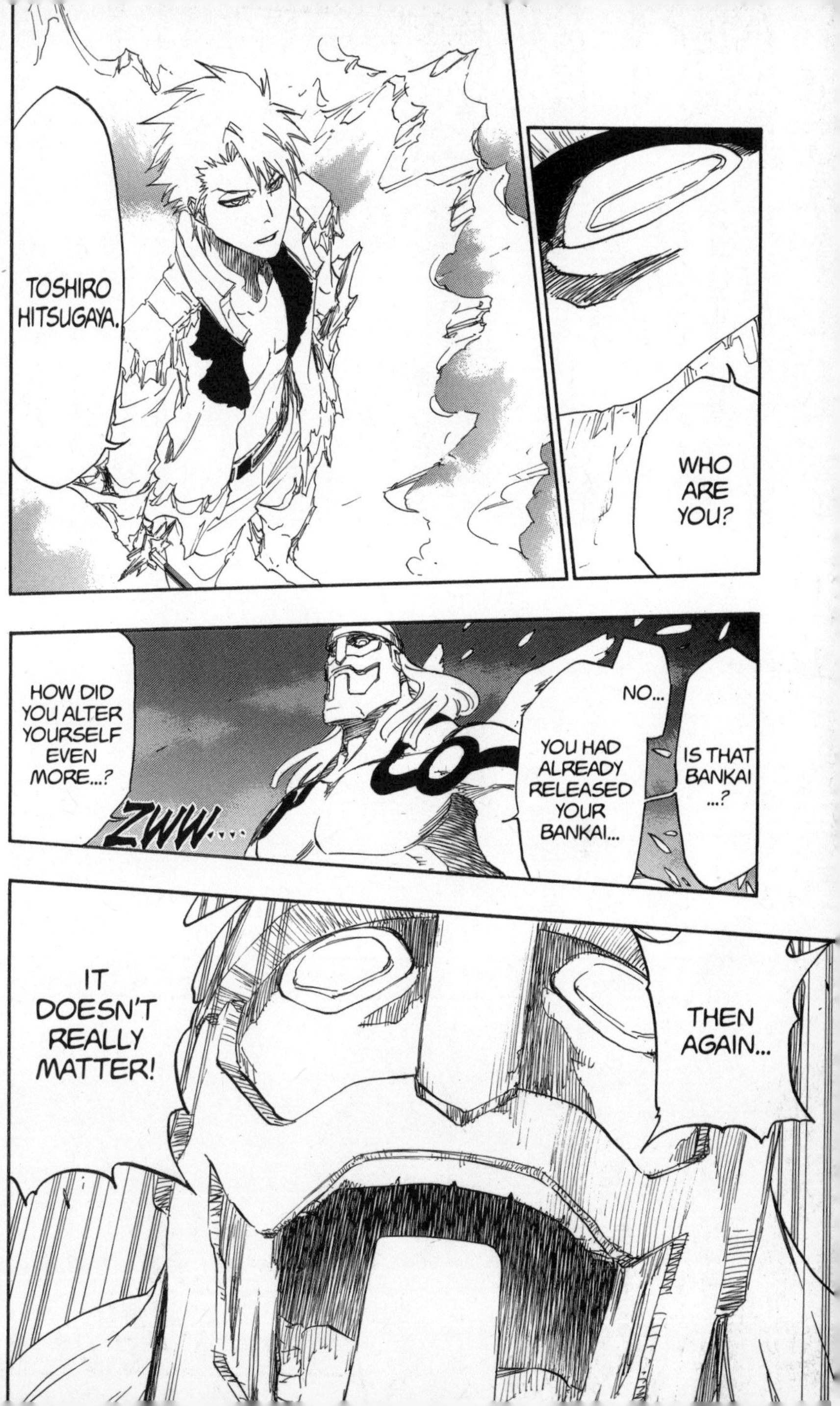
WHO ARE YOU?
TOSHIRO HITSUGAYA.
IS THAT BANKAI ...?
NO...
YOU HAD ALREADY RELEASED YOUR BANKAI...
HOW DID YOU ALTER YOURSELF EVEN MORE...?
ZWW...
THEN AGAIN...
IT DOESN'T REALLY MATTER!

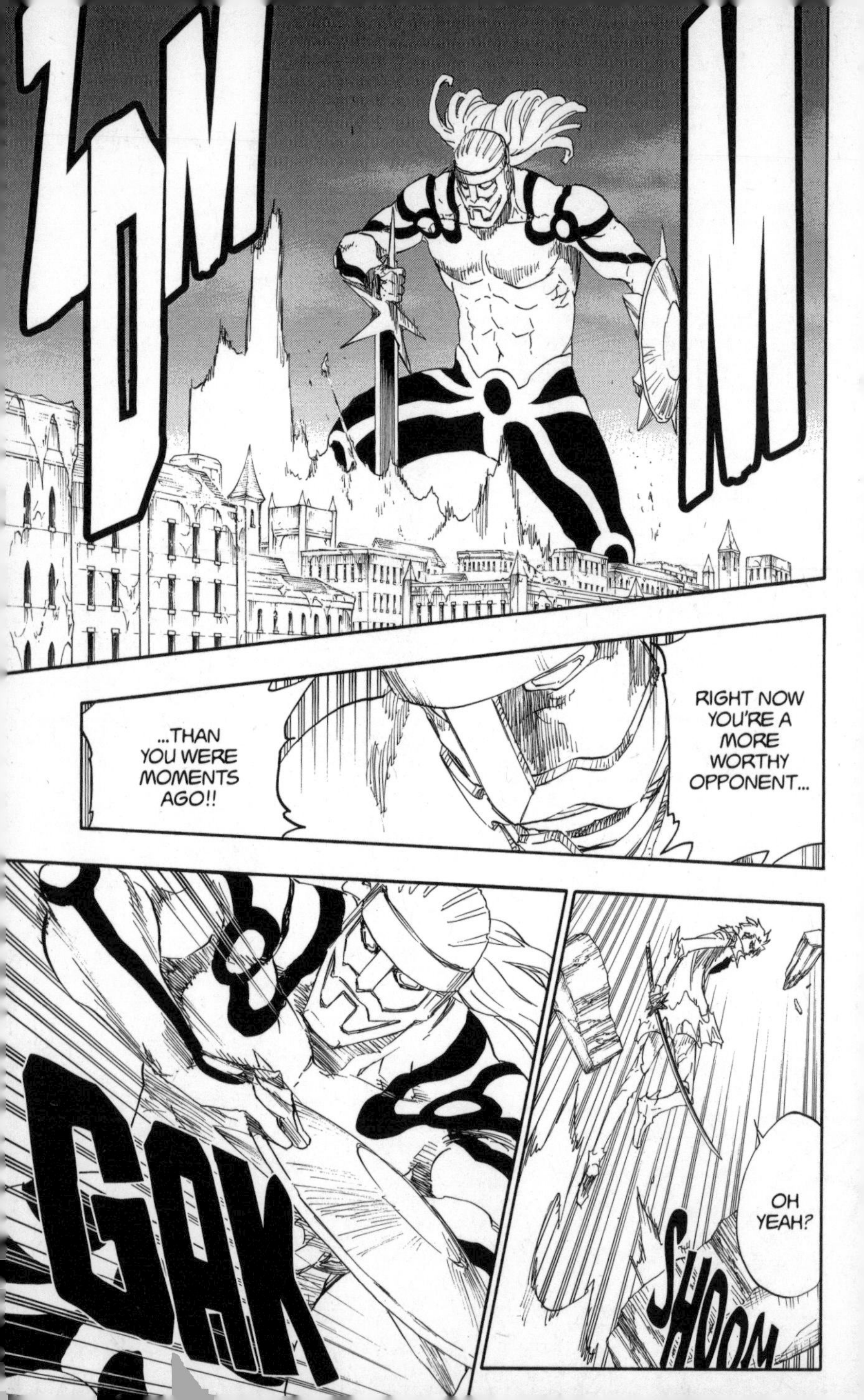
ZOM M
RIGHT NOW YOU'RE A MORE WORTHY OPPONENT...
...THAN YOU WERE MOMENTS AGO!!
OH YEAH?
SHOOM
GAK

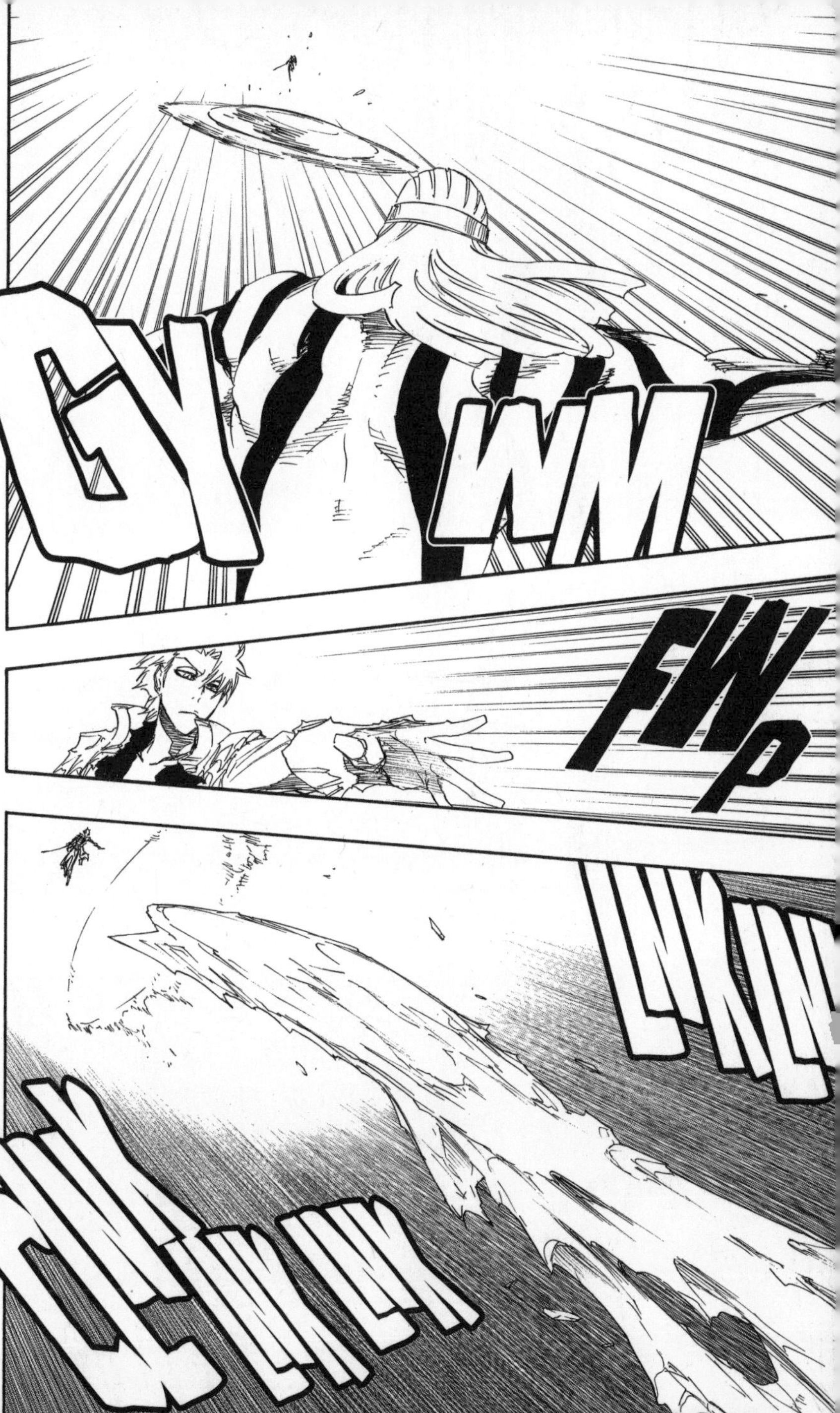
FWP

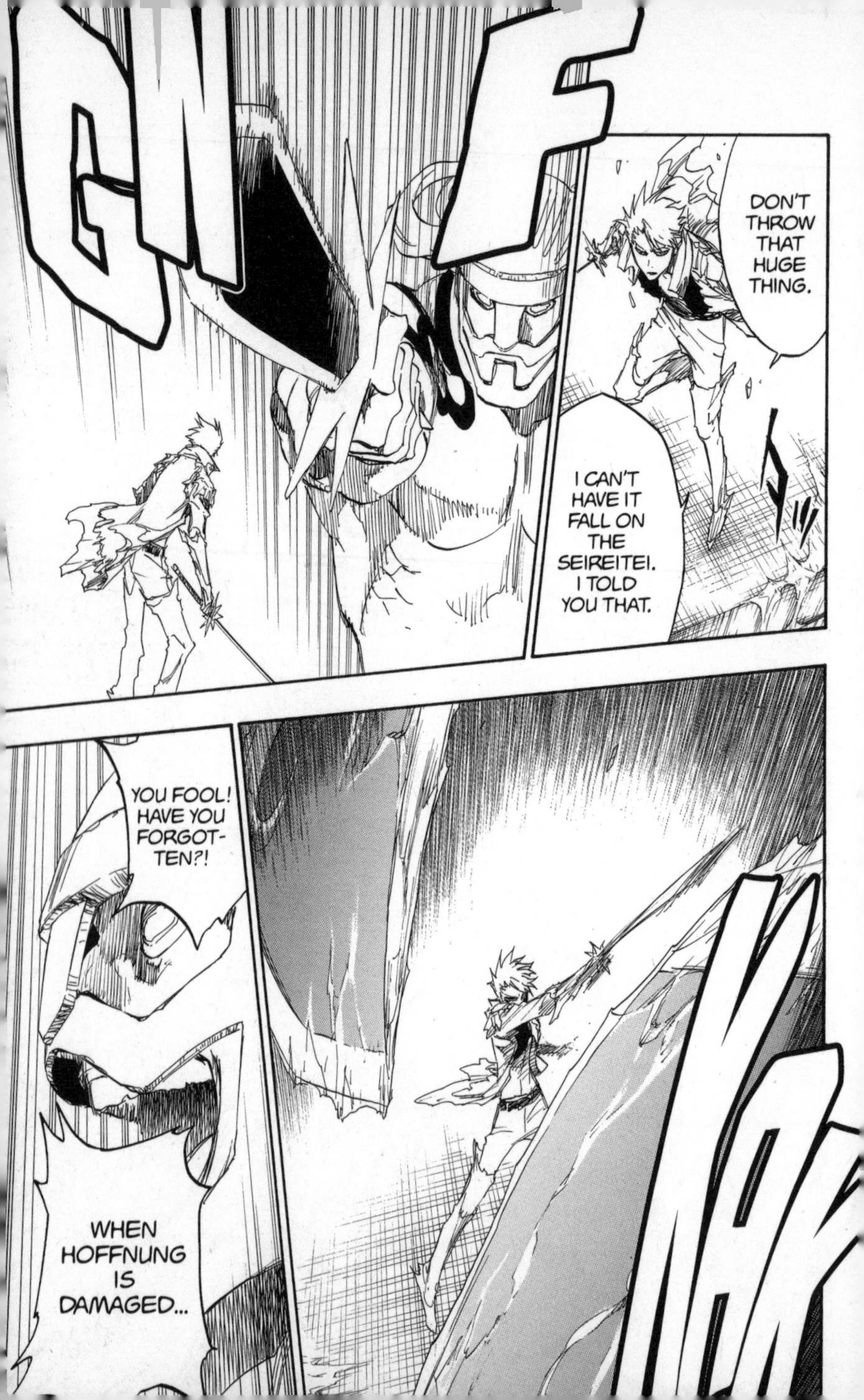
DON'T THROW THAT HUGE THING.
I CAN'T HAVE IT FALL ON THE SEIREITEI. I TOLD YOU THAT.
YOU FOOL! HAVE YOU FORGOT-TEN?!
WHEN HOFFNUNG IS DAMAGED...

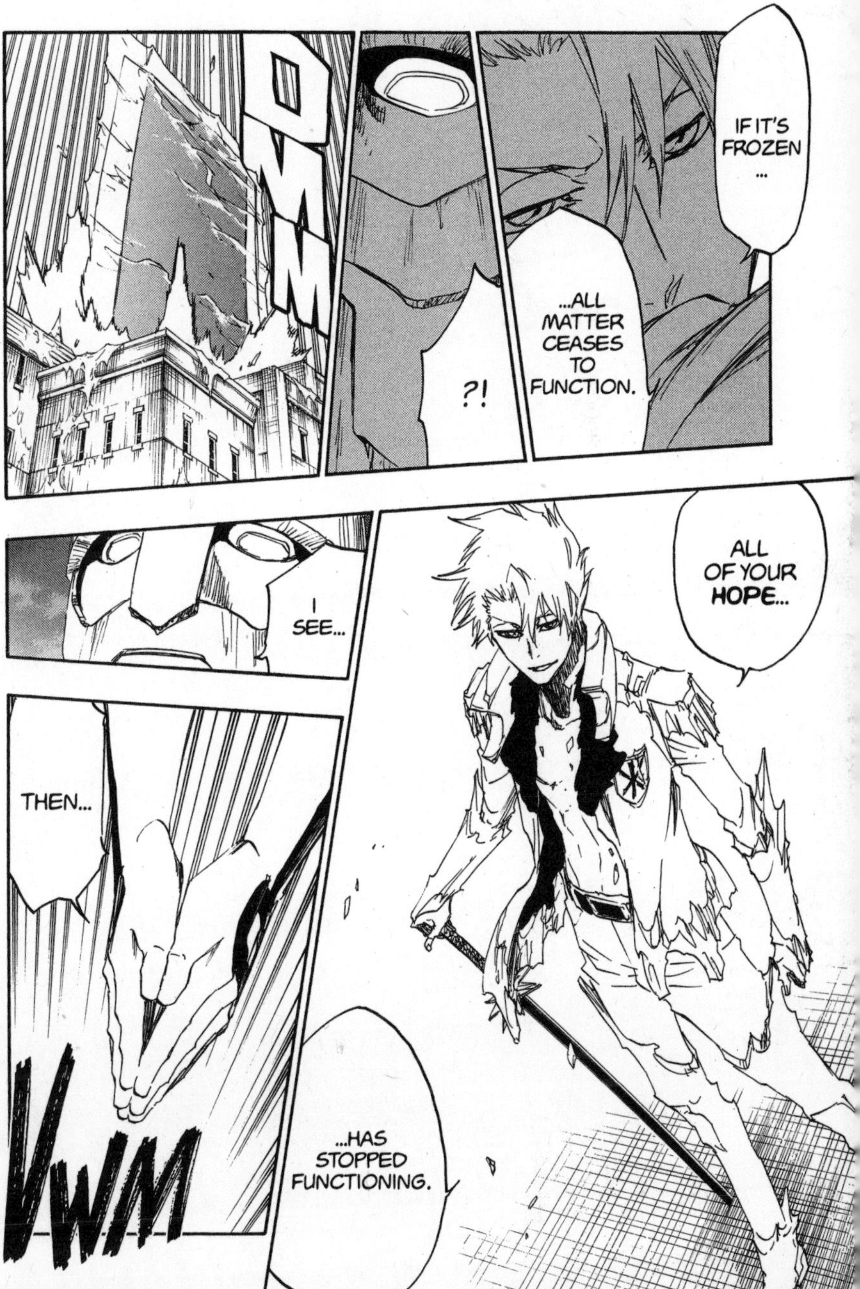
IF IT'S FROZEN...
...ALL MATTER CEASES TO FUNCTION.
?!
DMM
ALL OF YOUR HOPE...
...HAS STOPPED FUNCTIONING.
I SEE...
THEN...
VWM

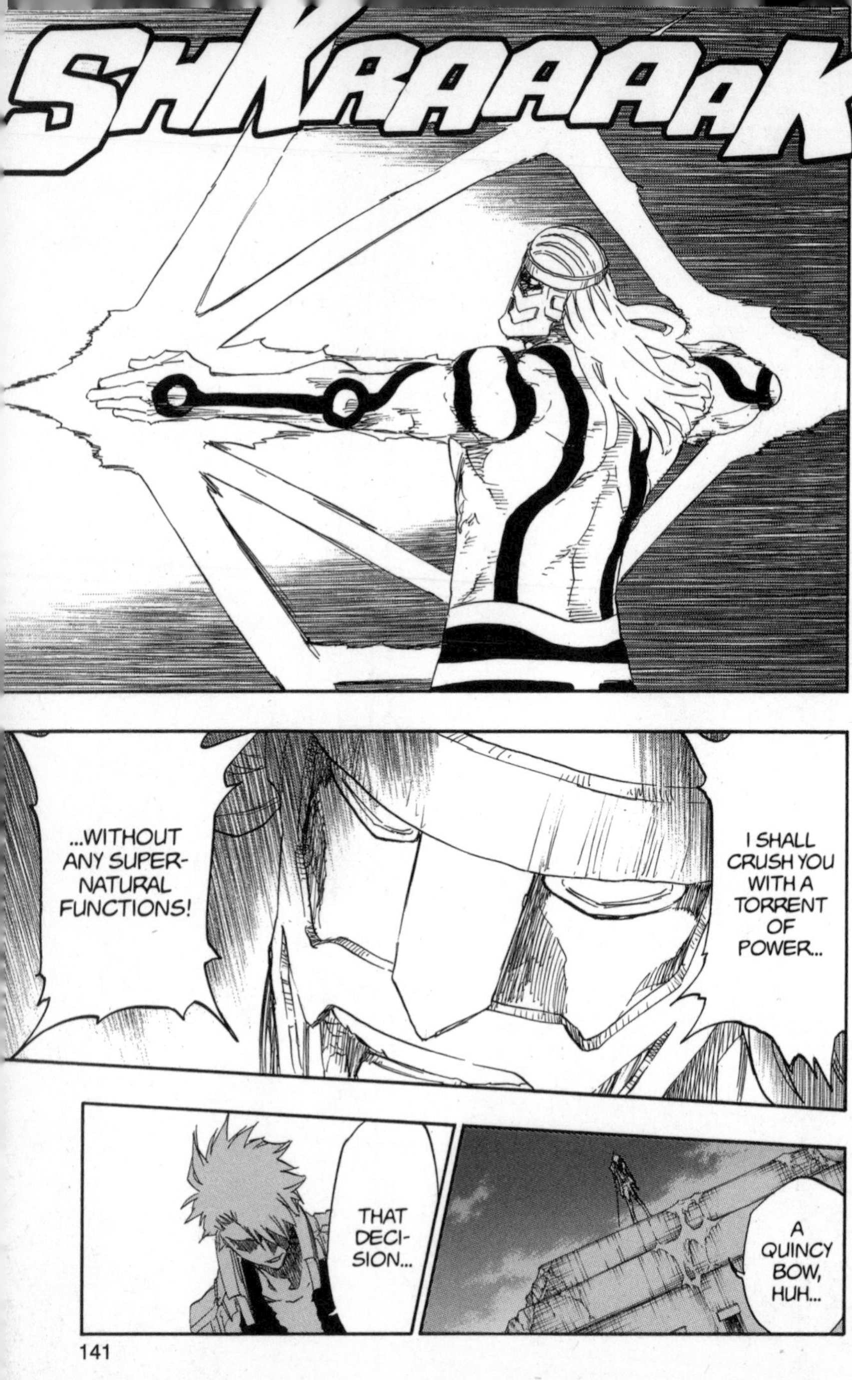
SHKRAAAAAK
I SHALL CRUSH YOU WITH A TORRENT OF POWER...
...WITHOUT ANY SUPER-NATURAL FUNCTIONS!
A QUINCY BOW, HUH...
THAT DECI-SION...

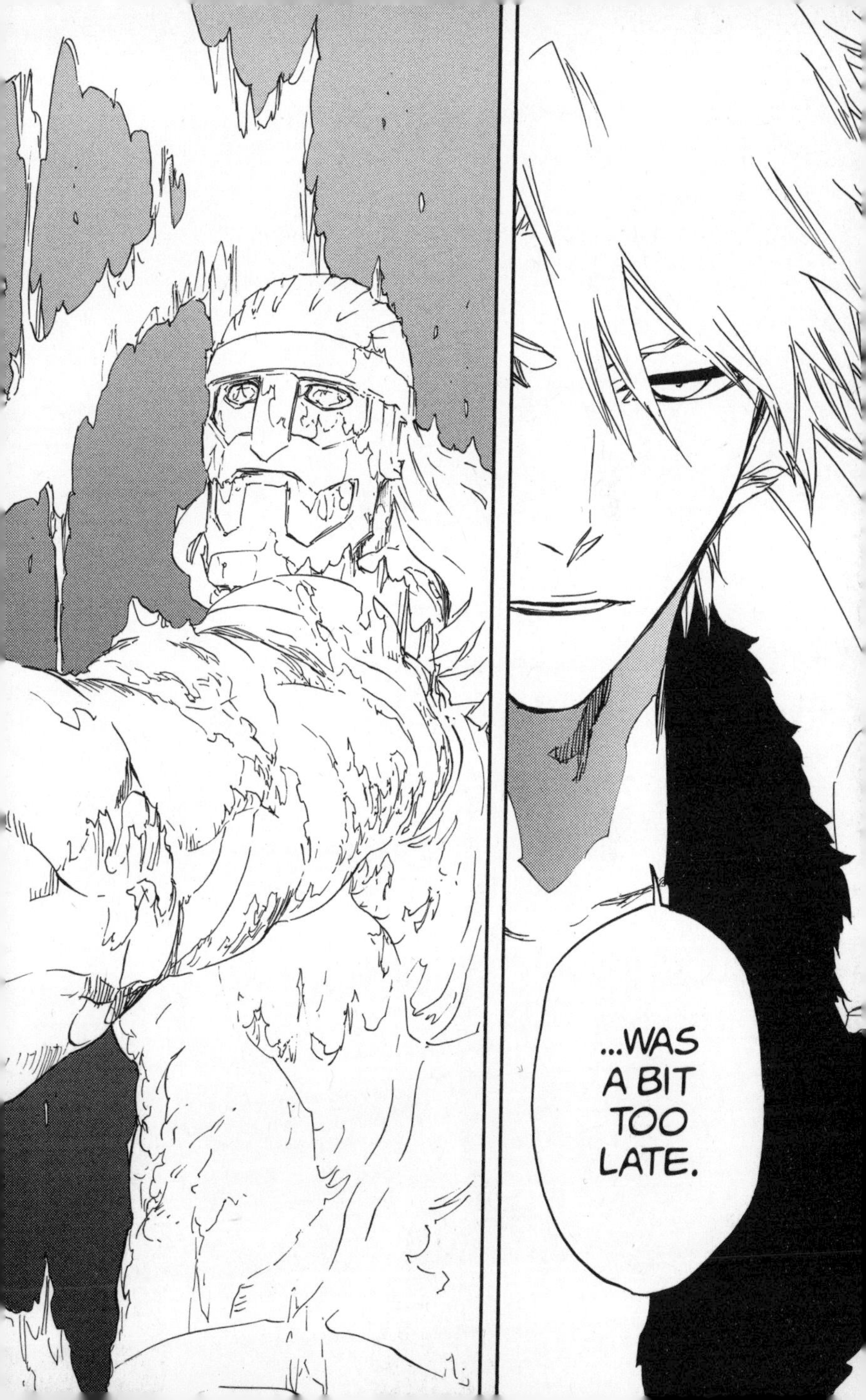
...WAS A BIT TOO LATE.

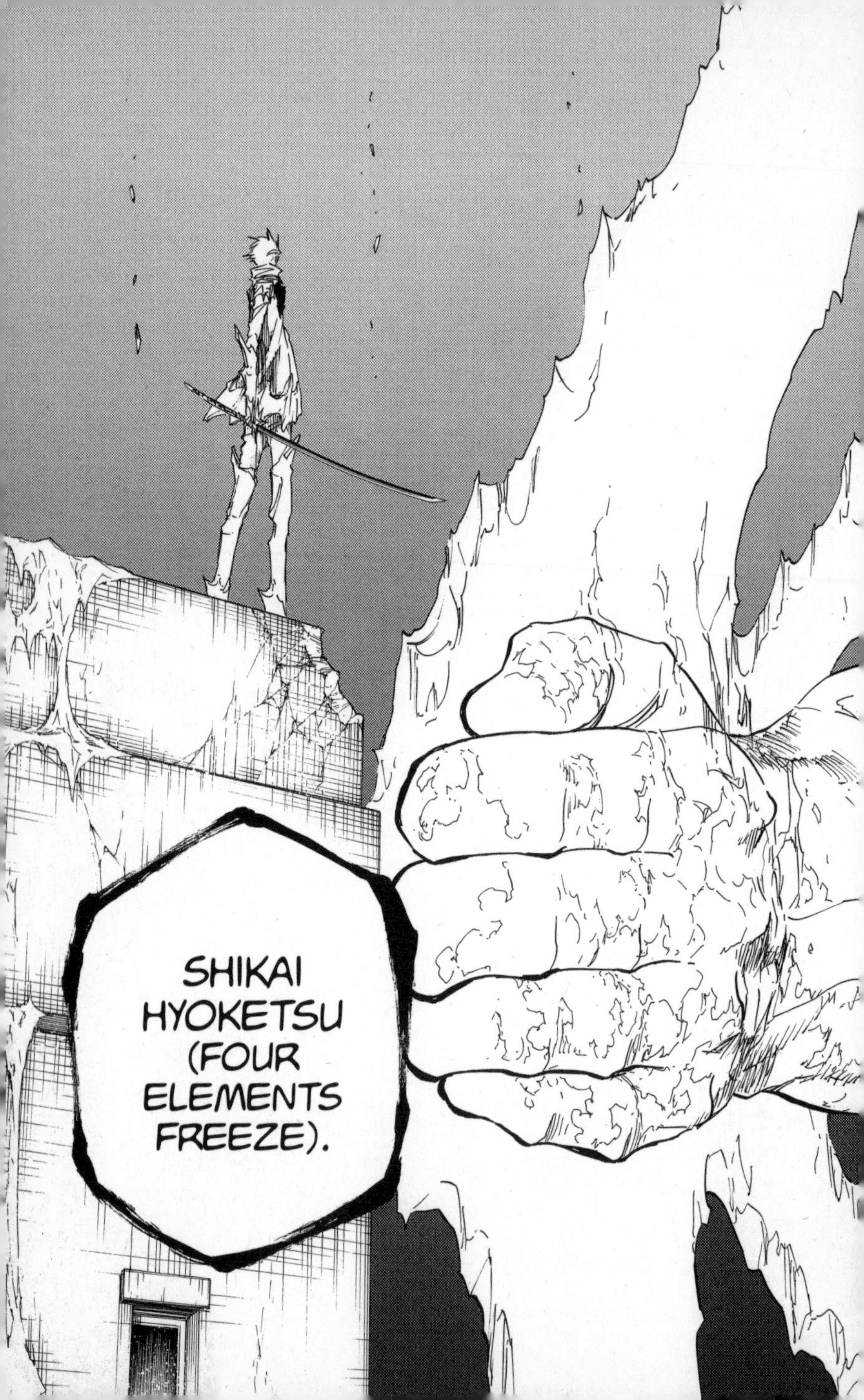
SHIKAI HYOKETSU (FOUR ELEMENTS FREEZE).

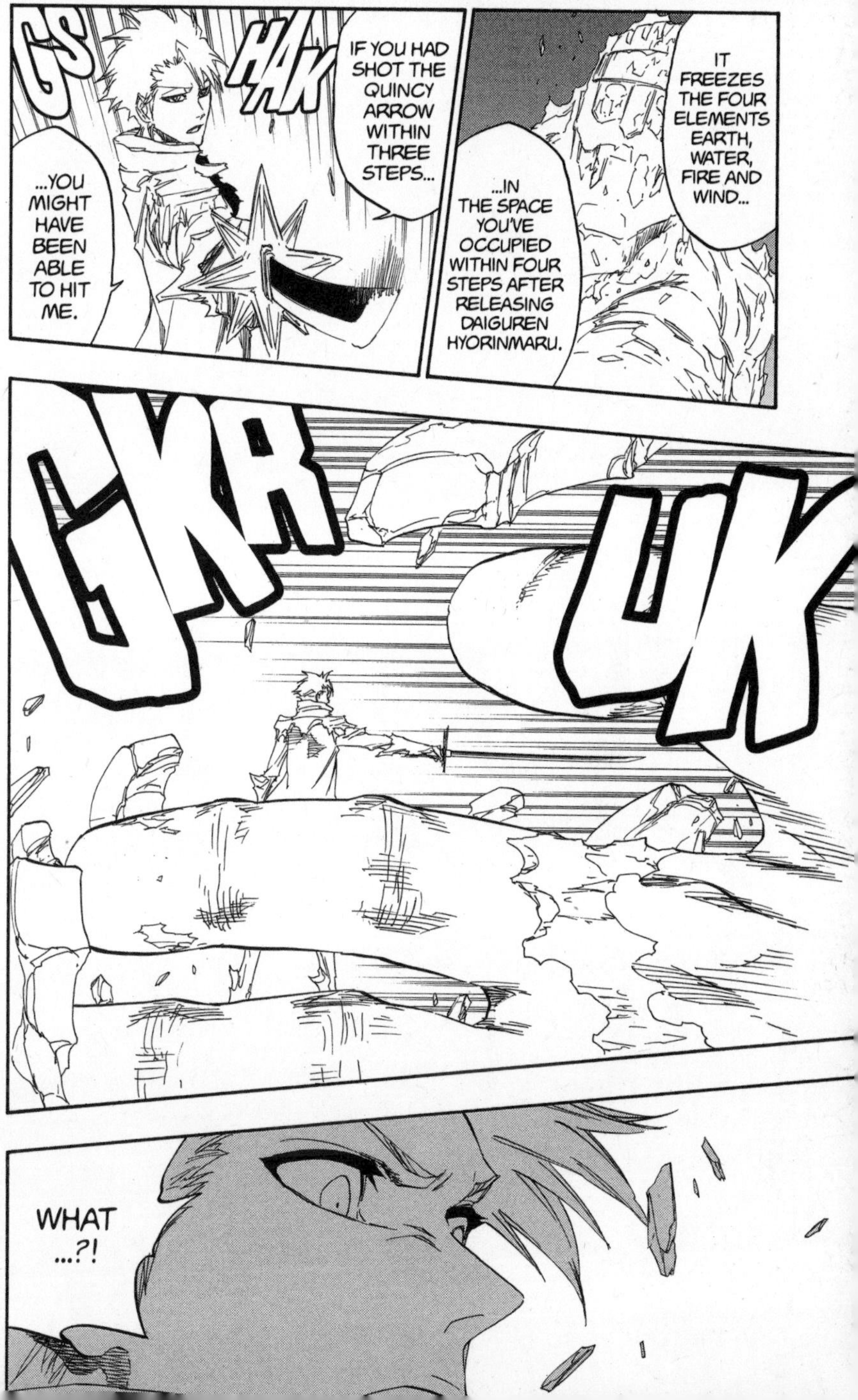
IT FREEZES THE FOUR ELEMENTS EARTH, WATER, FIRE AND WIND...
...IN THE SPACE YOU'VE OCCUPIED WITHIN FOUR STEPS AFTER RELEASING DAIGUREN HYORINMARU.
HAK
IF YOU HAD SHOT THE QUINCY ARROW WITHIN THREE STEPS...
GS
...YOU MIGHT HAVE BEEN ABLE TO HIT ME.
GKRA
UK
WHAT ...?!

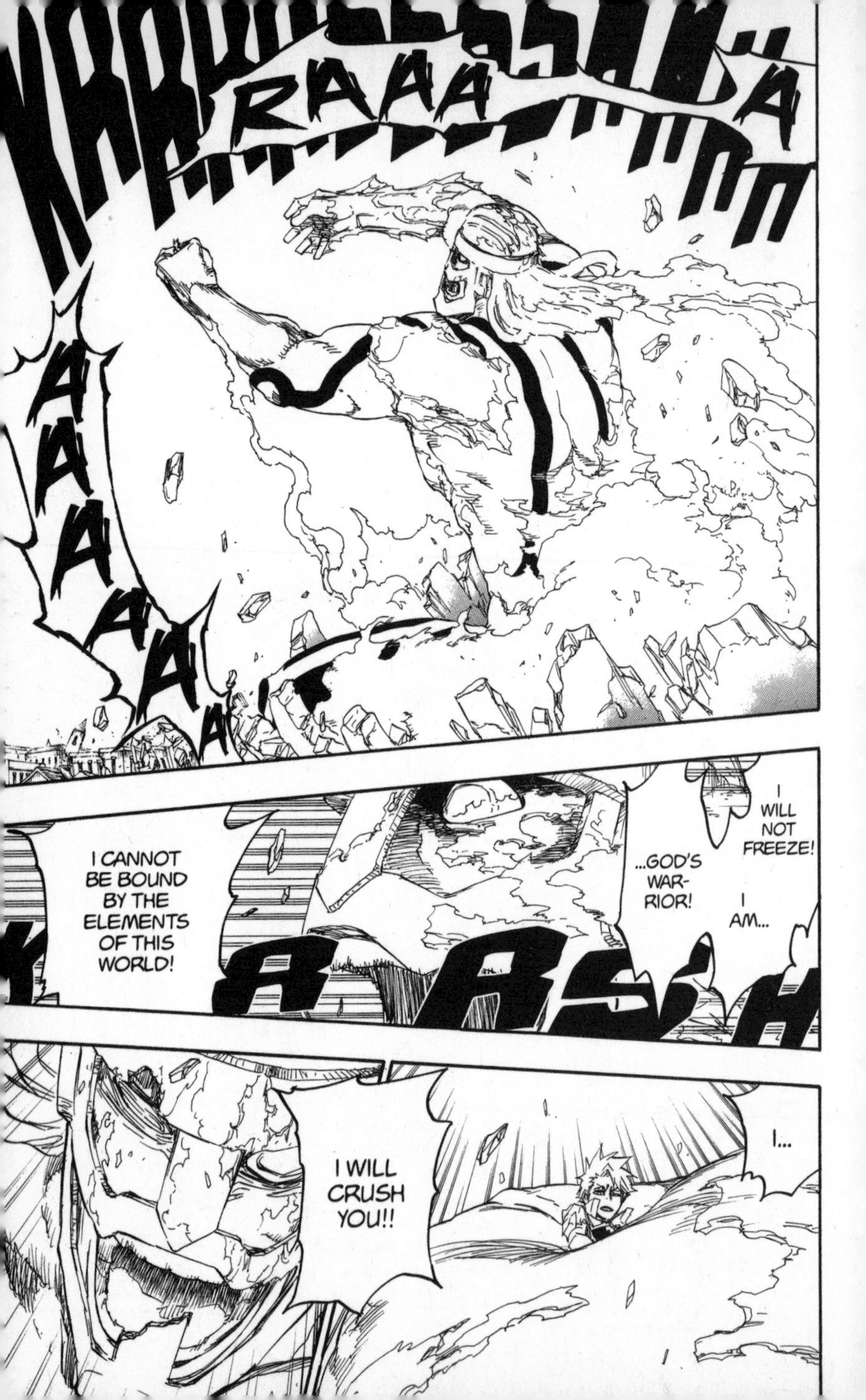
RAAAA
I WILL NOT FREEZE!
I AM...
...GOD'S WARRIOR!
I CANNOT BE BOUND BY THE ELEMENTS OF THIS WORLD!
I...
I WILL CRUSH YOU!!

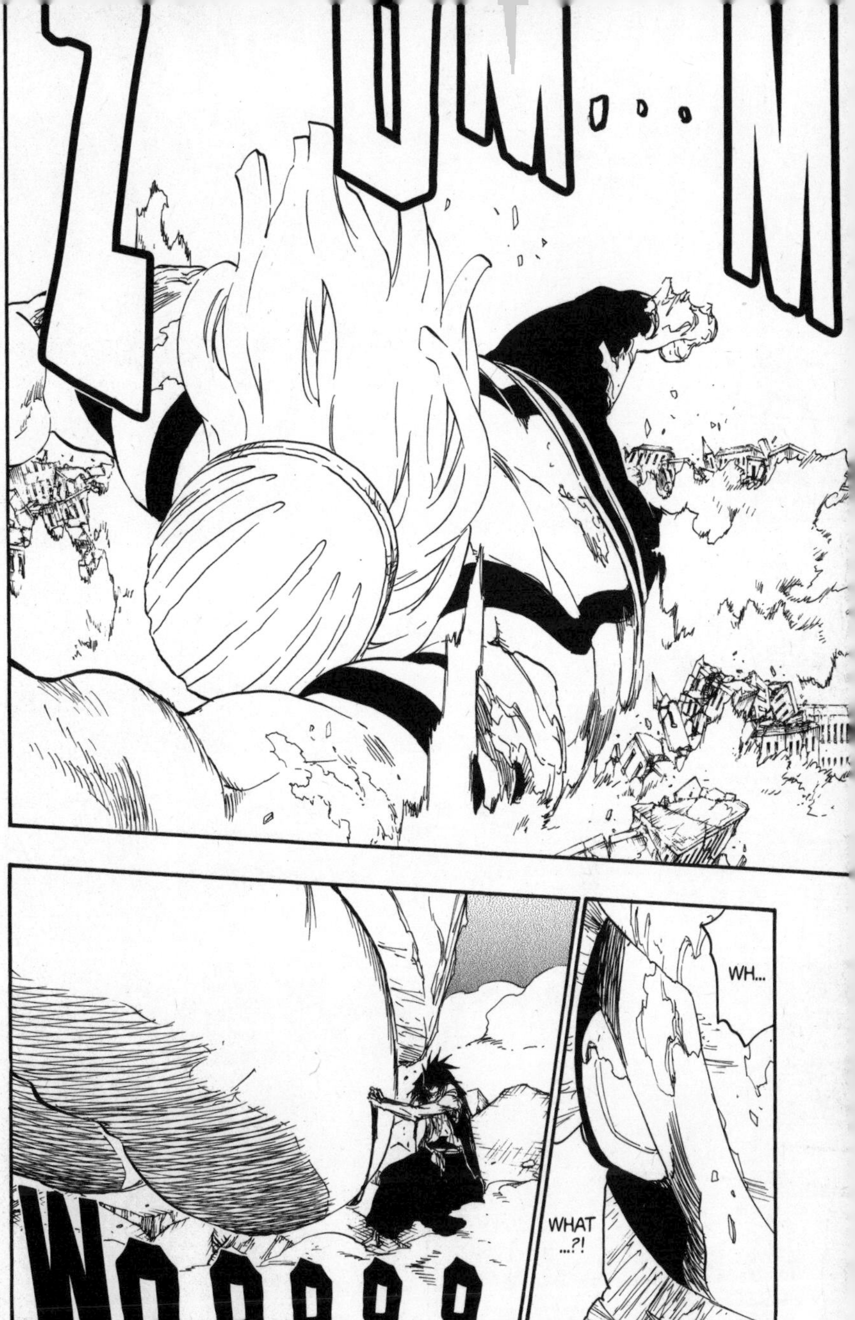
WH...
WHAT ...?!
WOOOOO

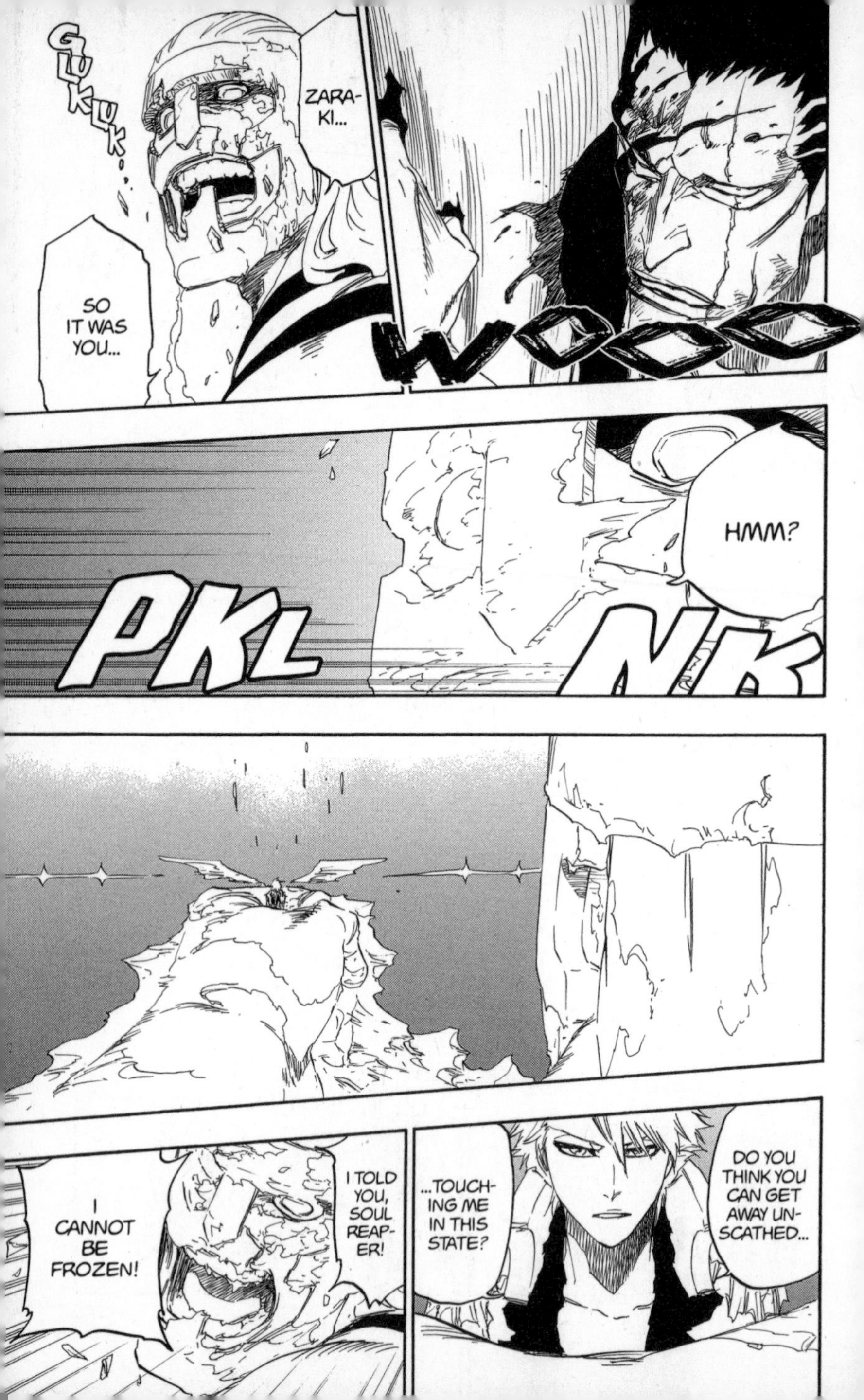
WOOOOO
GLUKLUK
ZARA-KI...
SO IT WAS YOU...
HMM?
PKLNK
DO YOU THINK YOU CAN GET AWAY UN-SCATHED...
...TOUCH-ING ME IN THIS STATE?
I TOLD YOU, SOUL REAP-ER!
I CANNOT BE FROZEN!

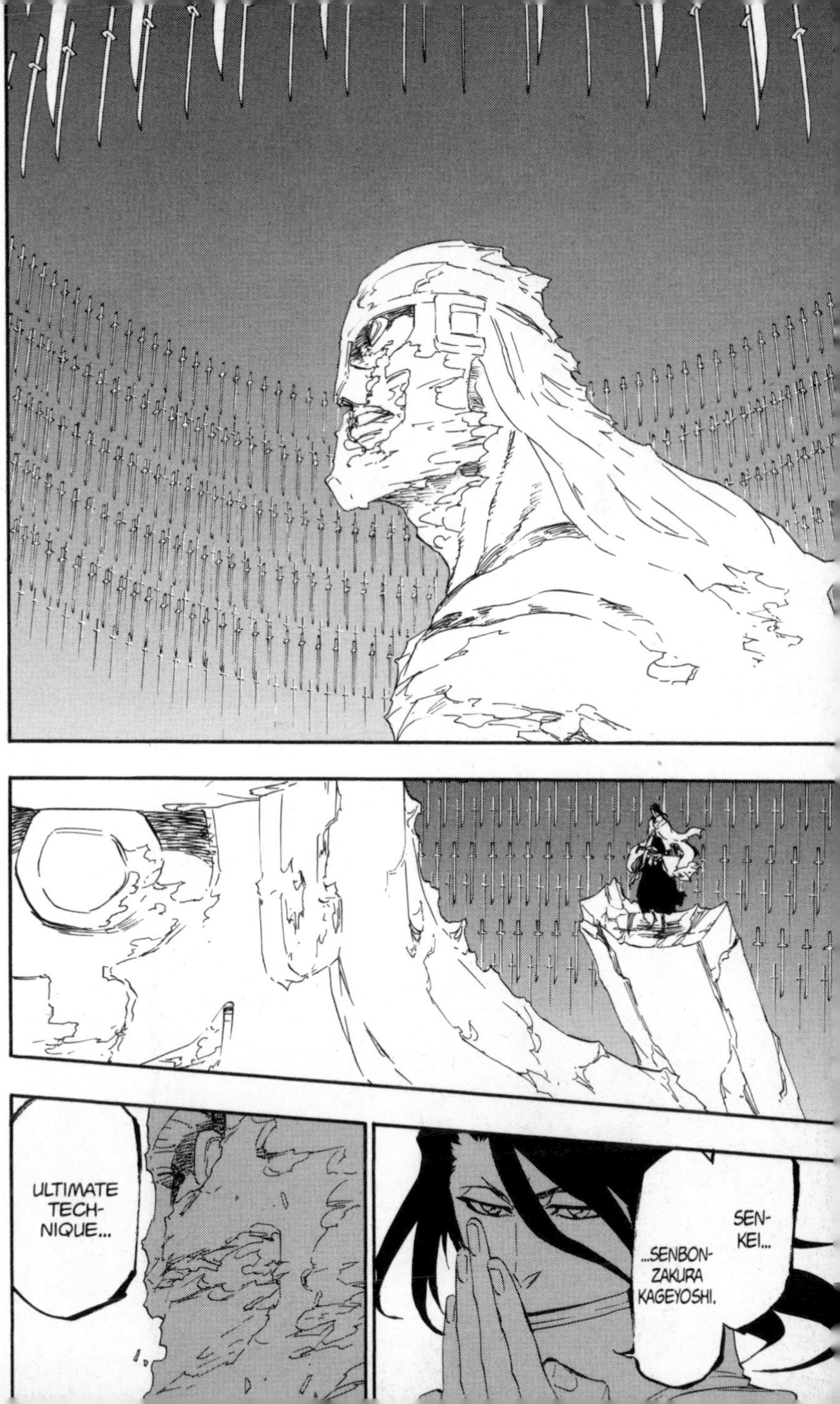
SEN-KEI...
...SENBON-ZAKURA KAGEYOSHI.
ULTIMATE TECH-NIQUE...

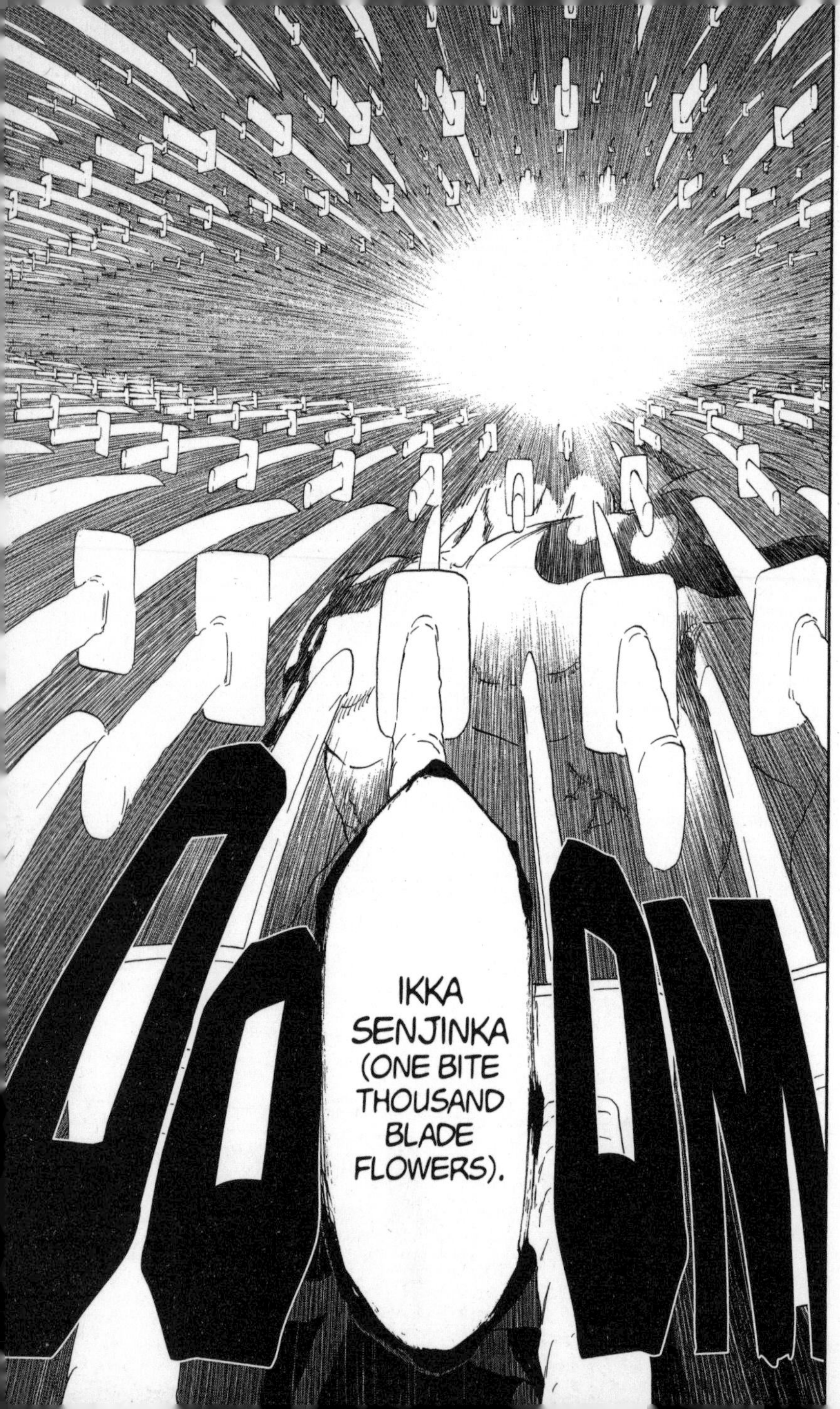
IKKA SENJINKA (ONE BITE THOUSAND BLADE FLOWERS).

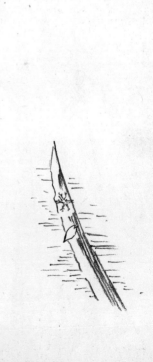

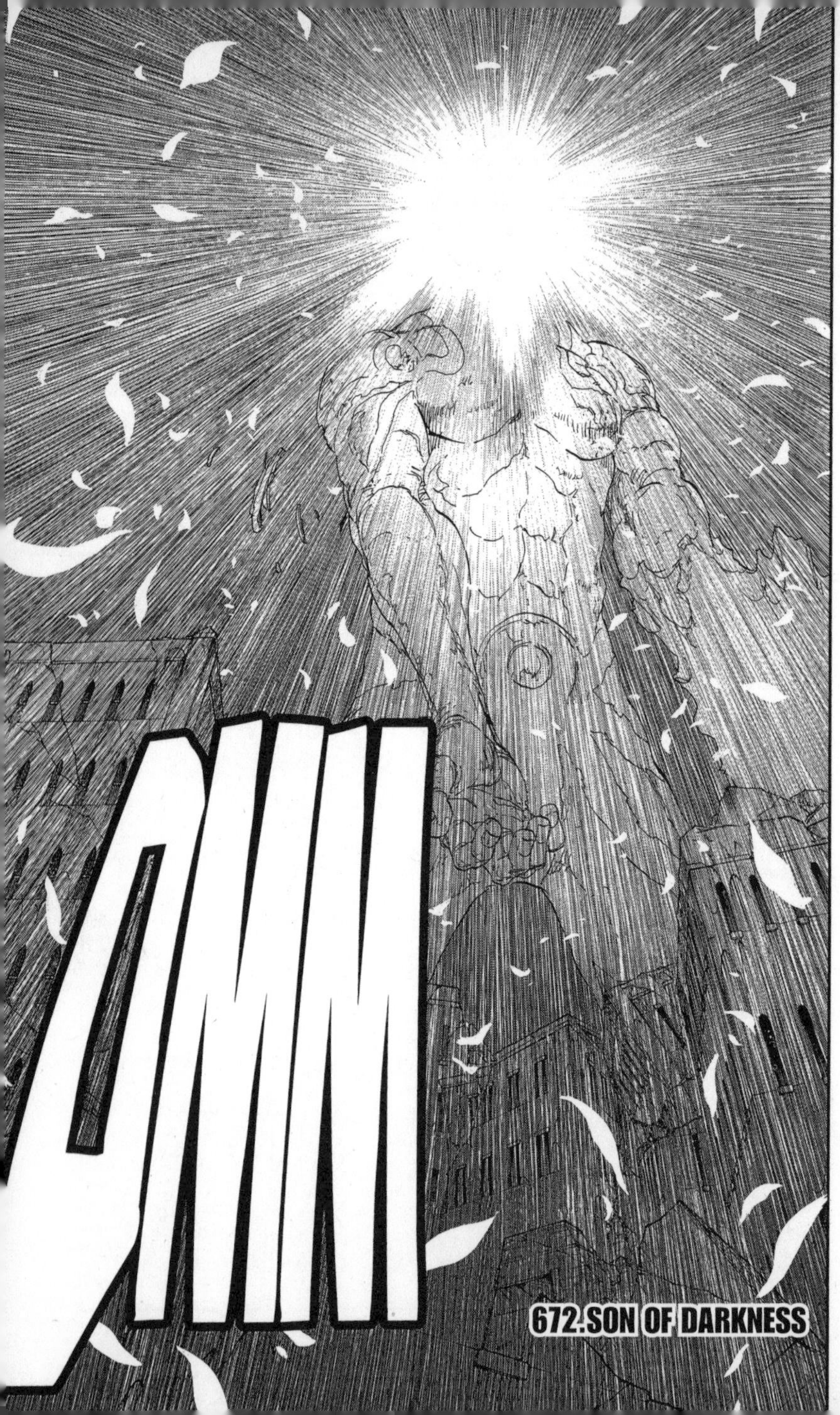
672. SON OF DARKNESS

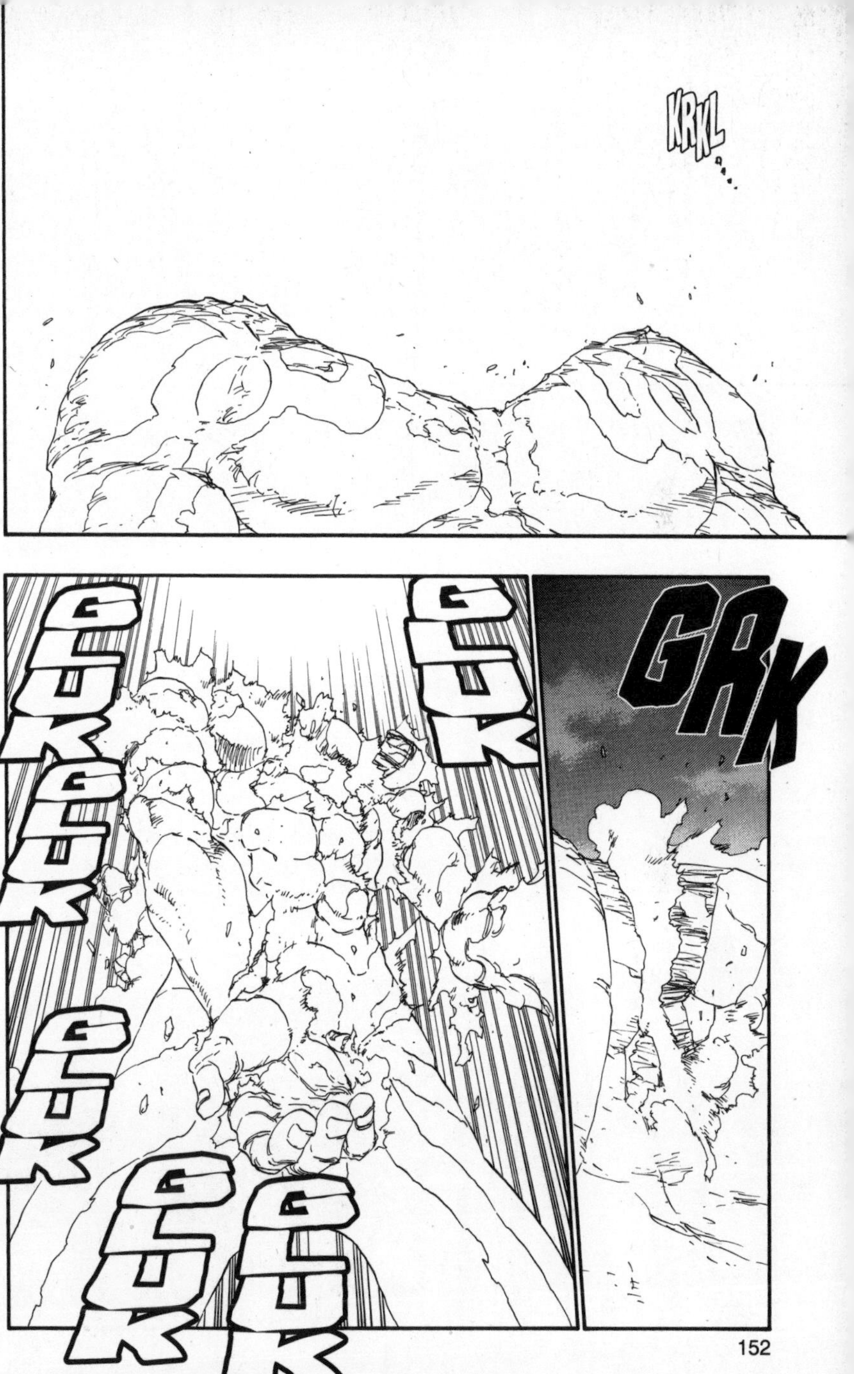
KRKL
GRK
GLUK
GLUK
GLUK
GLUK
GLUK
GLUK

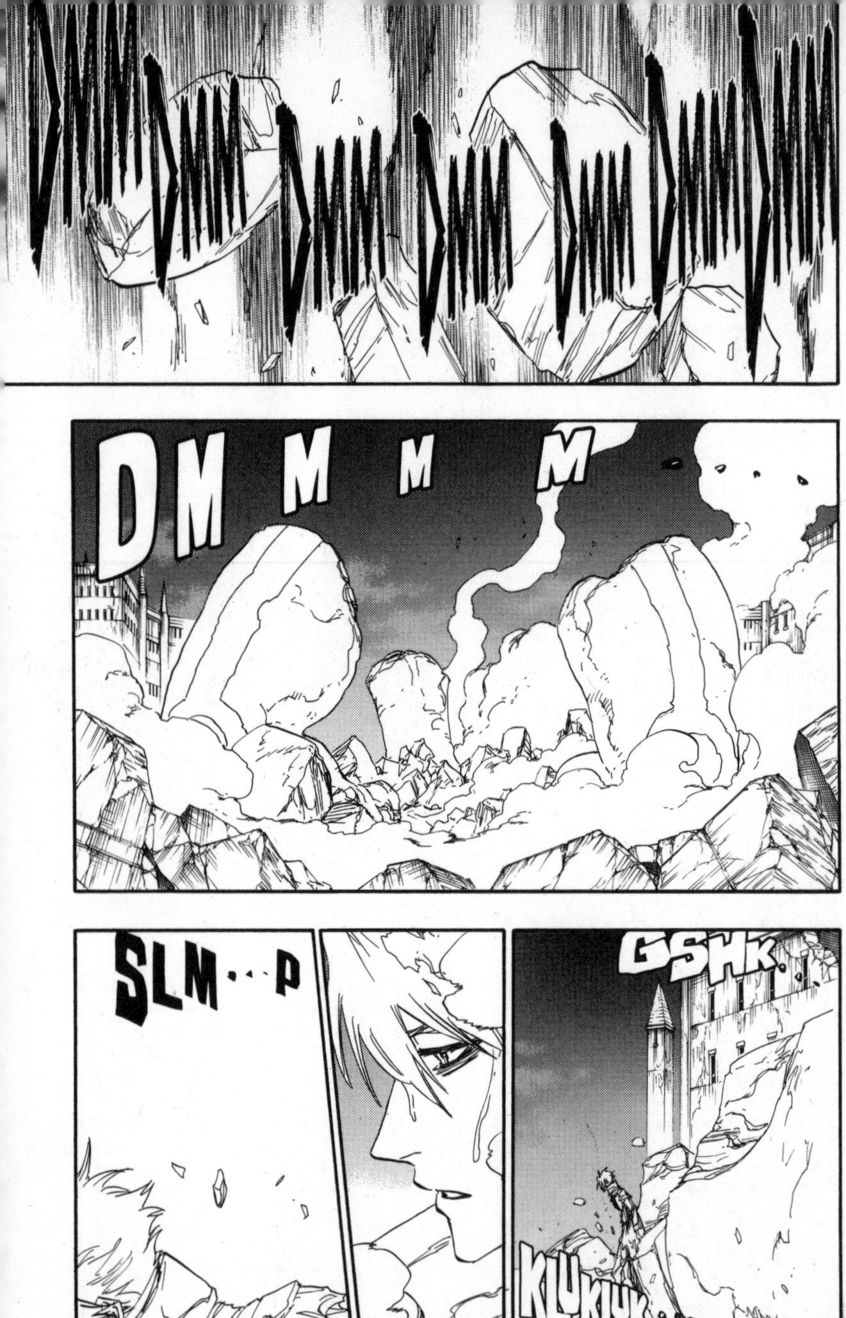
DMMMM
GSHK
KLUKLUK
SLM...P

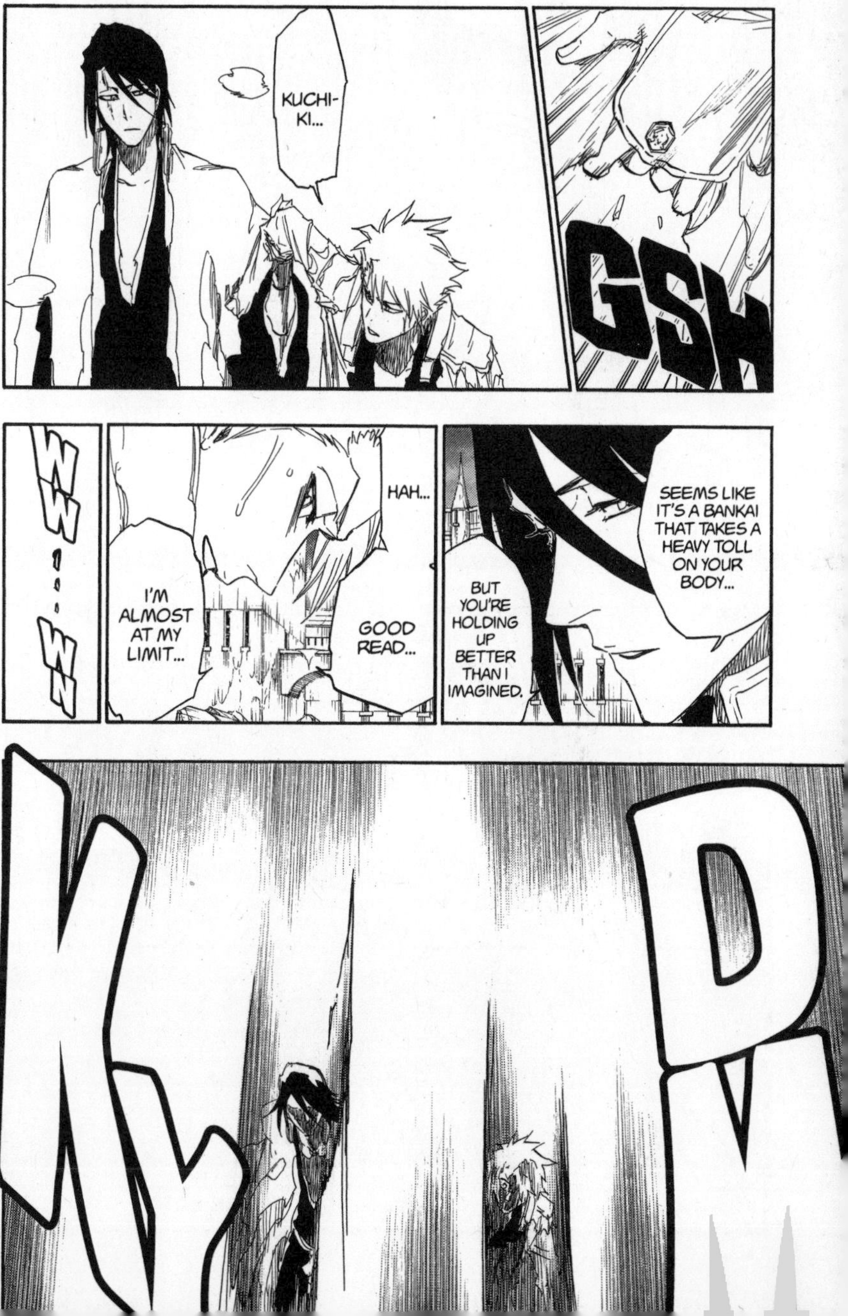
GSH
KUCHI-KI...
SEEMS LIKE IT'S A BANKAI THAT TAKES A HEAVY TOLL ON YOUR BODY...
BUT YOU'RE HOLDING UP BETTER THAN I IMAGINED.
HAH...
GOOD READ...
I'M ALMOST AT MY LIMIT...
WWW...WN

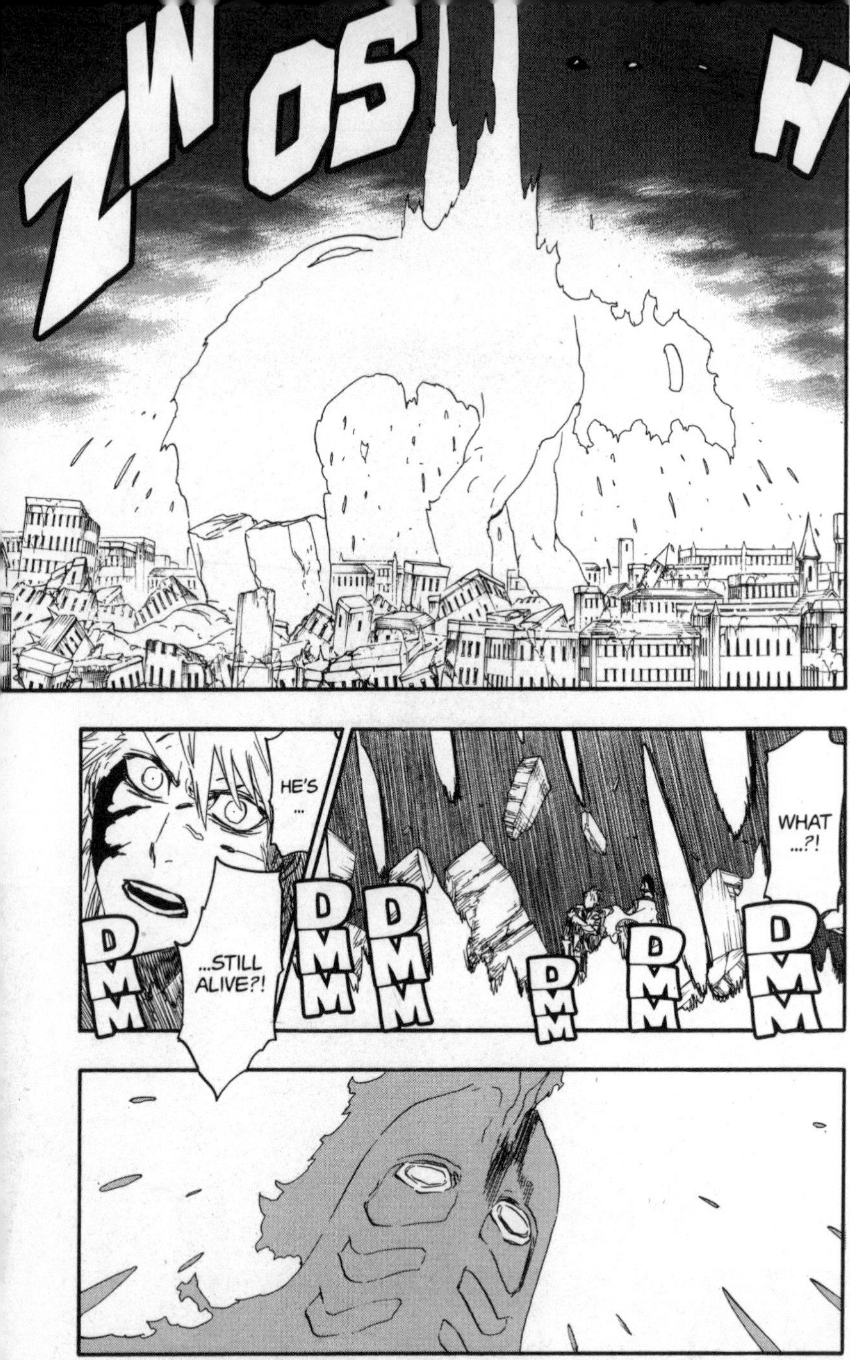
ZWOSH
WHAT ...?!
DMM
DMM
DMM
DMM
DMM
DMM
HE'S ...
...STILL ALIVE?!

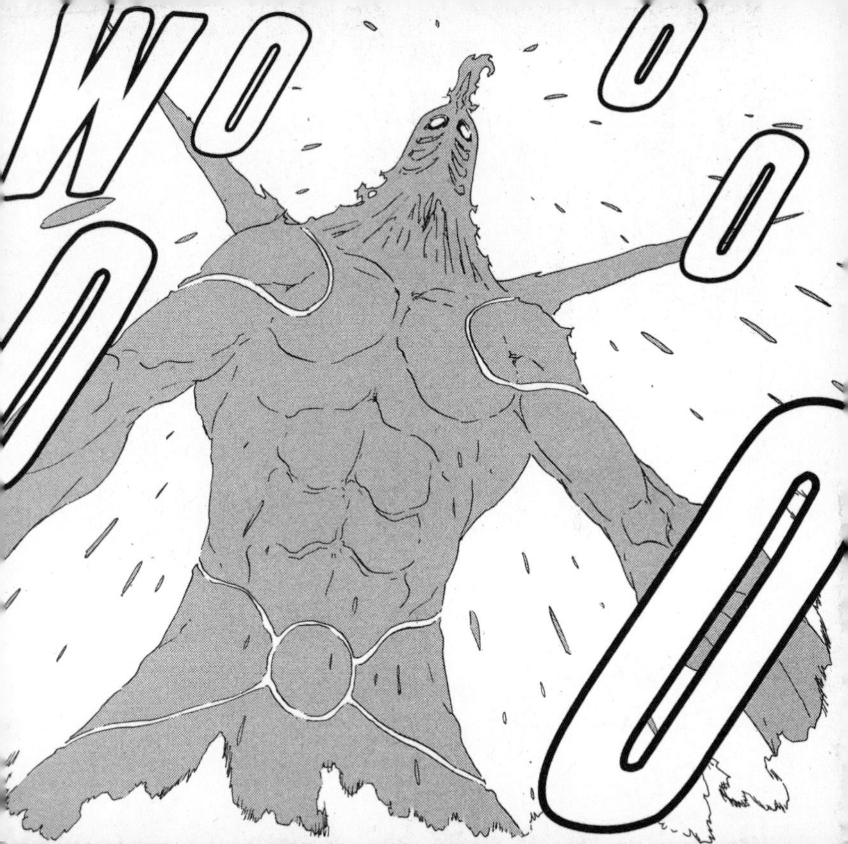
WOOOOO

Son of Darkness

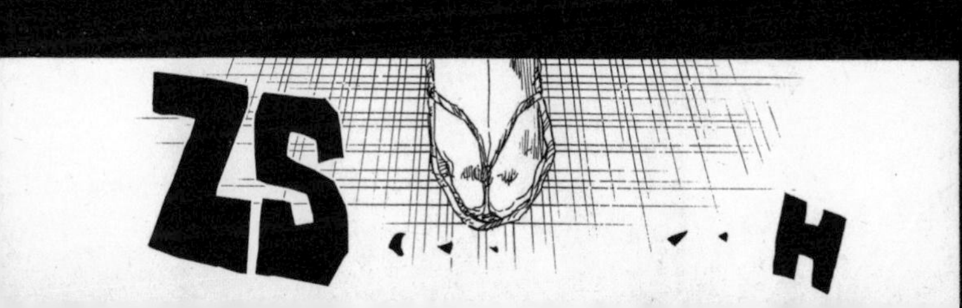
ZS...H

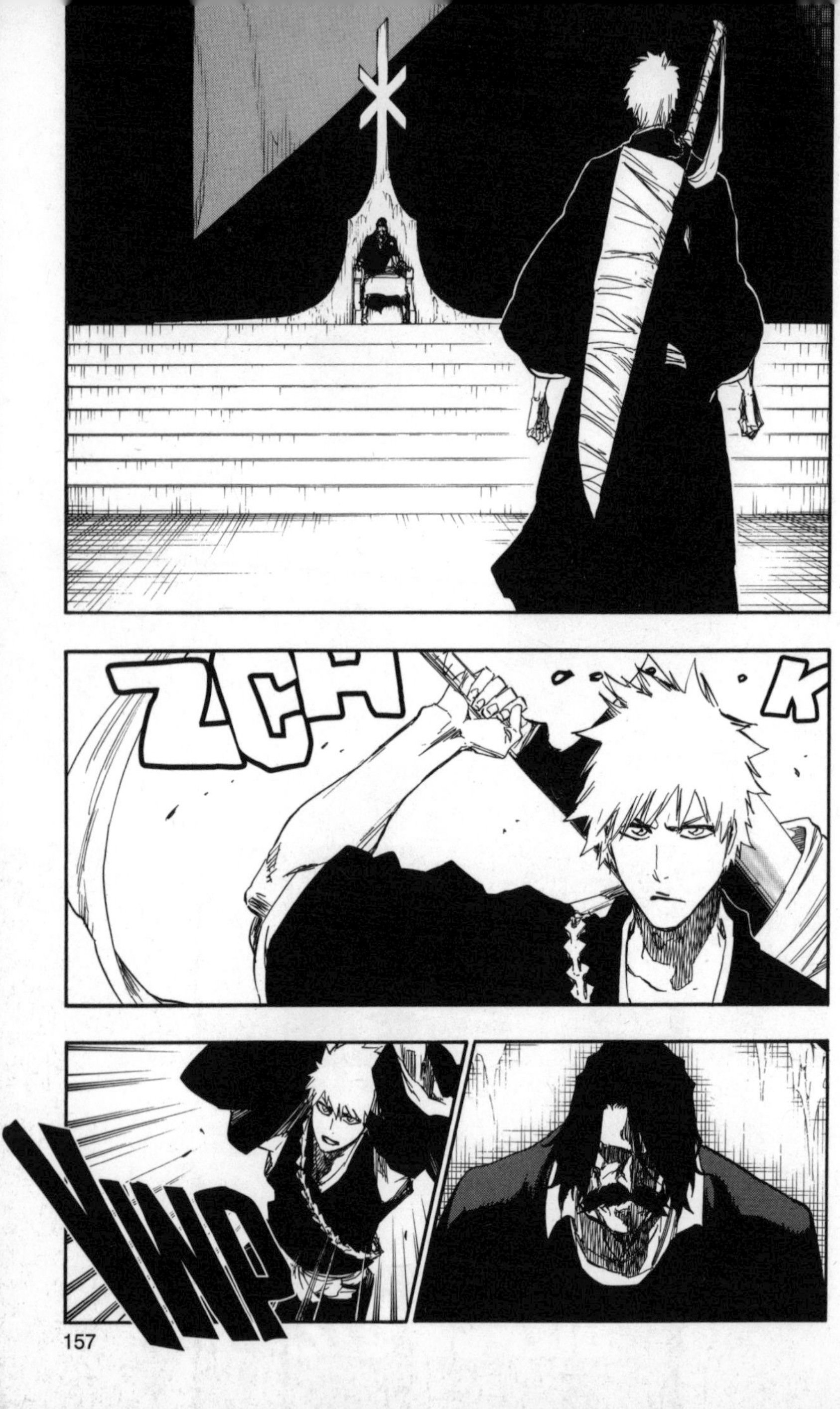
ZCH....K

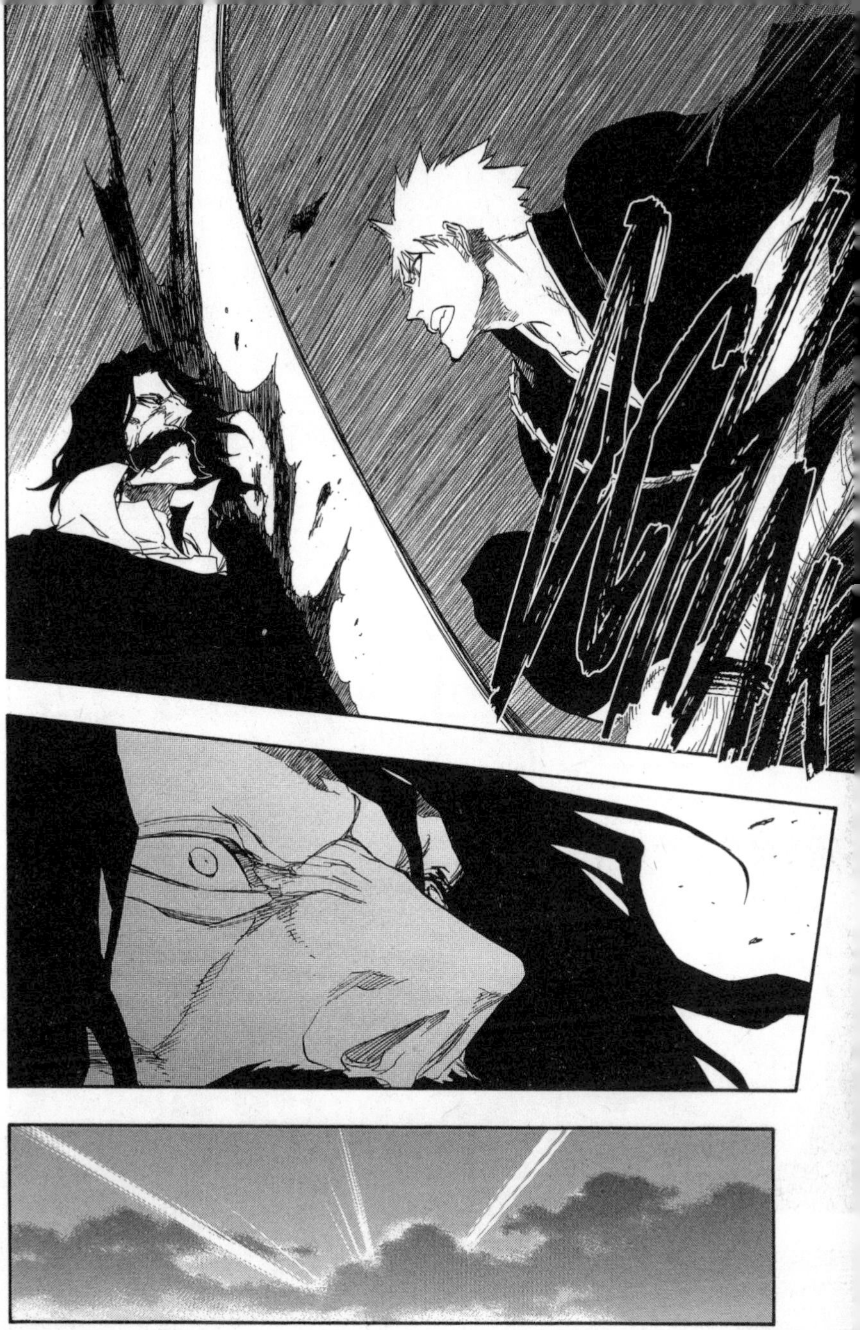

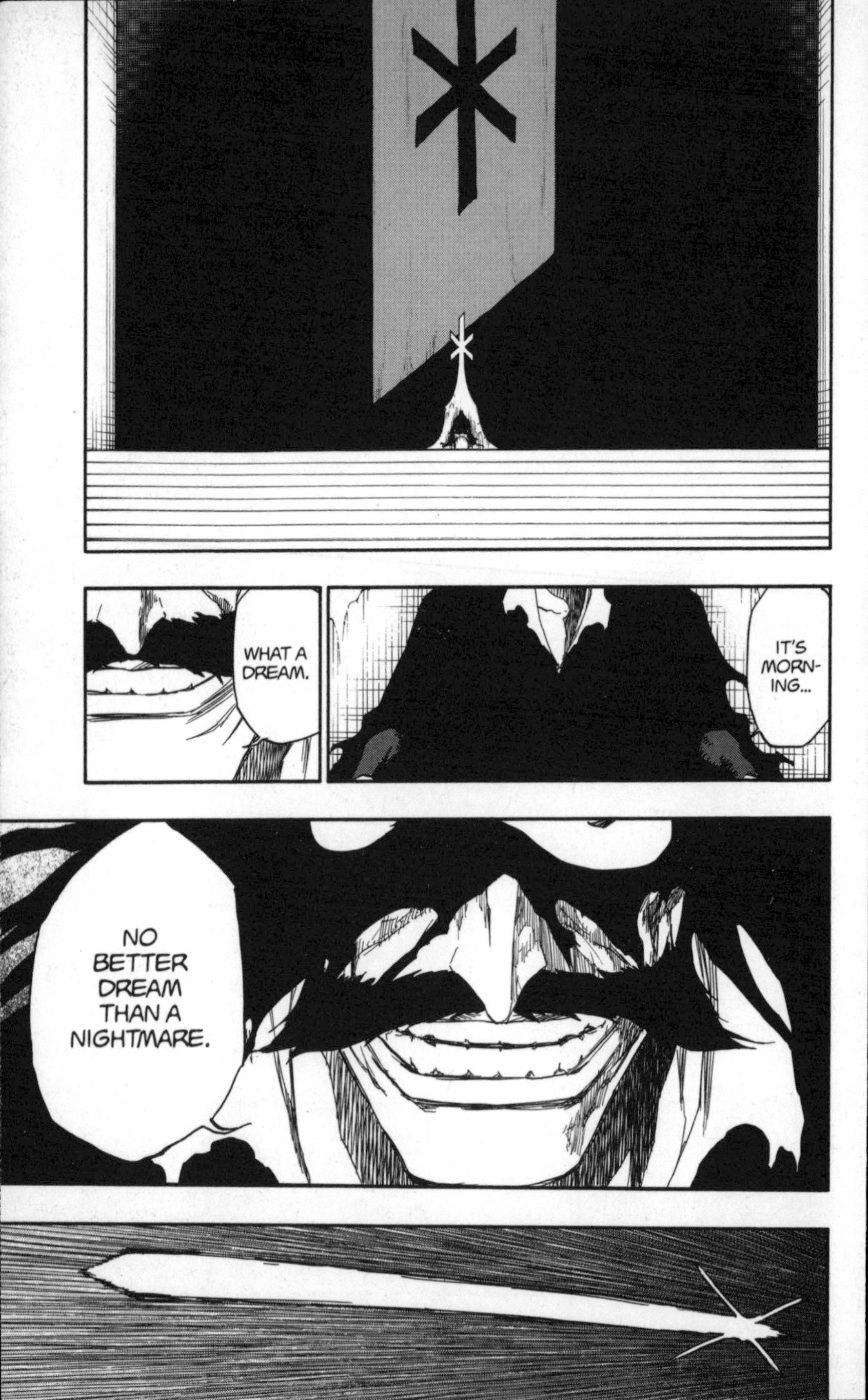
IT'S MORNING...
WHAT A DREAM.
NO BETTER DREAM THAN A NIGHTMARE.

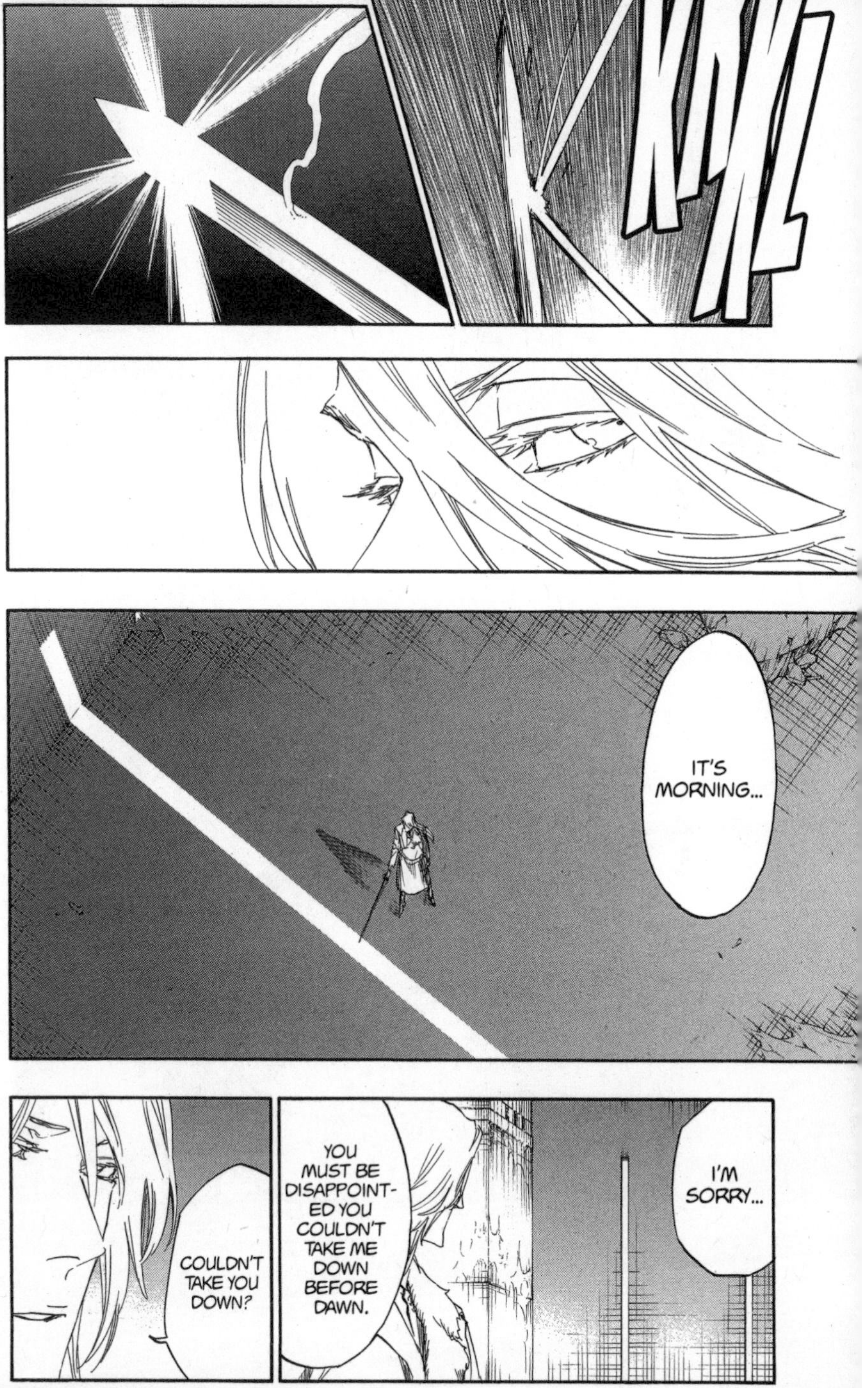
IT'S MORNING...
I'M SORRY...
YOU MUST BE DISAPPOINTED YOU COULDN'T TAKE ME DOWN BEFORE DAWN.
COULDN'T TAKE YOU DOWN?

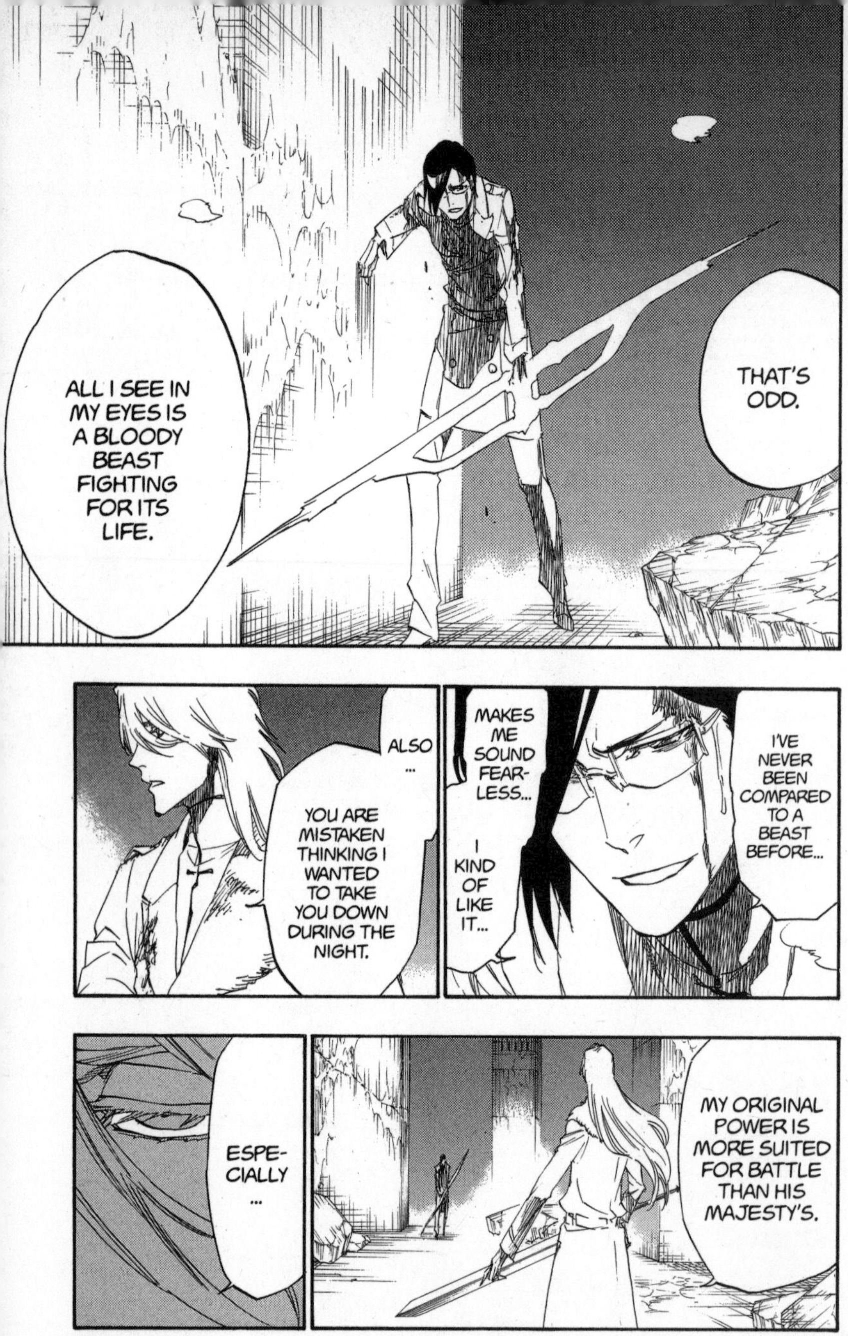
THAT'S ODD.
ALL I SEE IN MY EYES IS A BLOODY BEAST FIGHTING FOR ITS LIFE.
I'VE NEVER BEEN COMPARED TO A BEAST BEFORE...
MAKES ME SOUND FEAR-LESS...
I KIND OF LIKE IT...
ALSO ...
YOU ARE MISTAKEN THINKING I WANTED TO TAKE YOU DOWN DURING THE NIGHT.
MY ORIGINAL POWER IS MORE SUITED FOR BATTLE THAN HIS MAJESTY'S.
ESPE-CIALLY ...

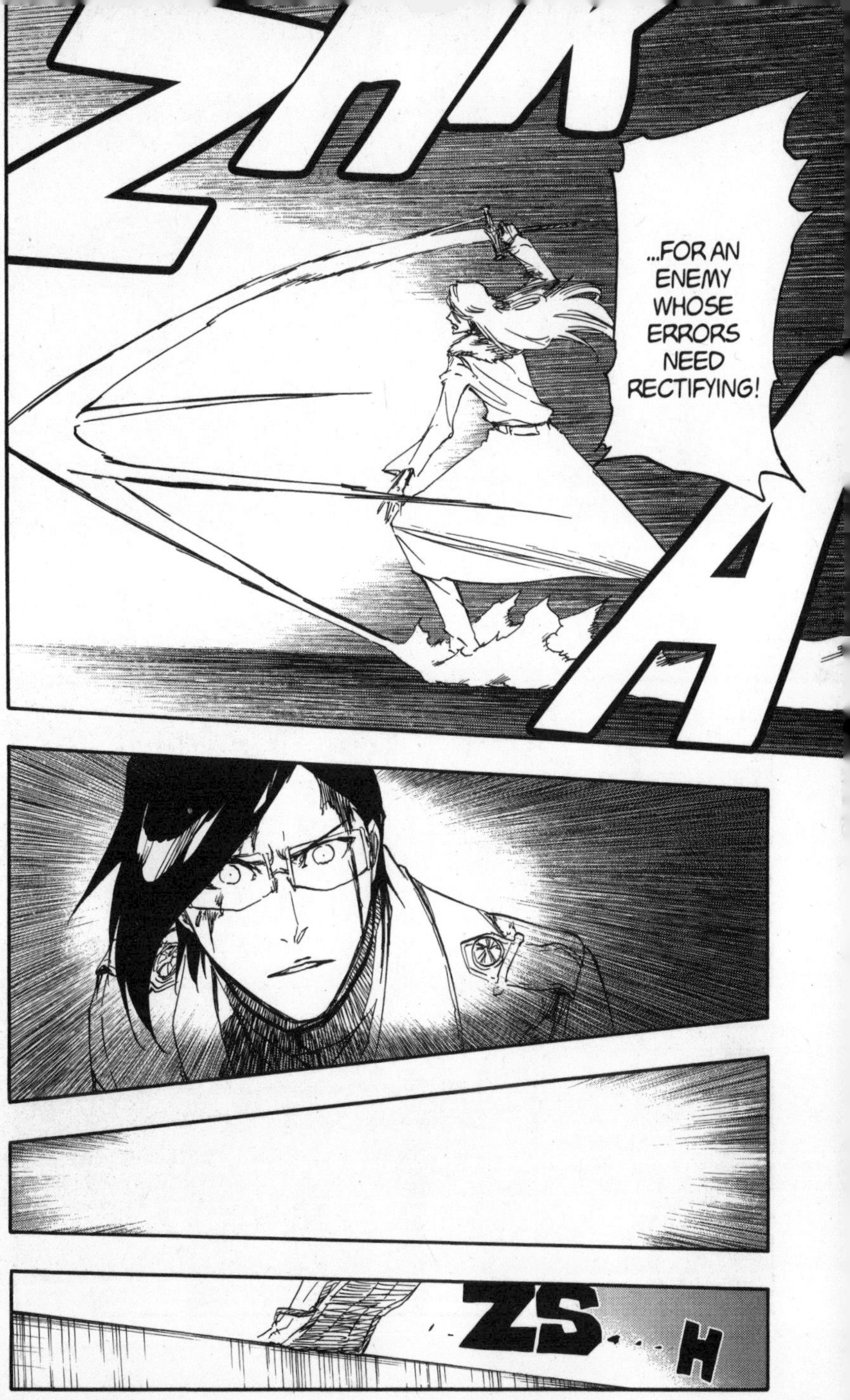
...FOR AN ENEMY WHOSE ERRORS NEED RECTIFYING!
ZS...H

I DO...

YOU FEEL THAT...

...INOUE?

YEAH...

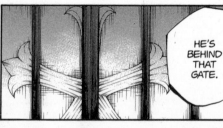

HE'S BEHIND THAT GATE.

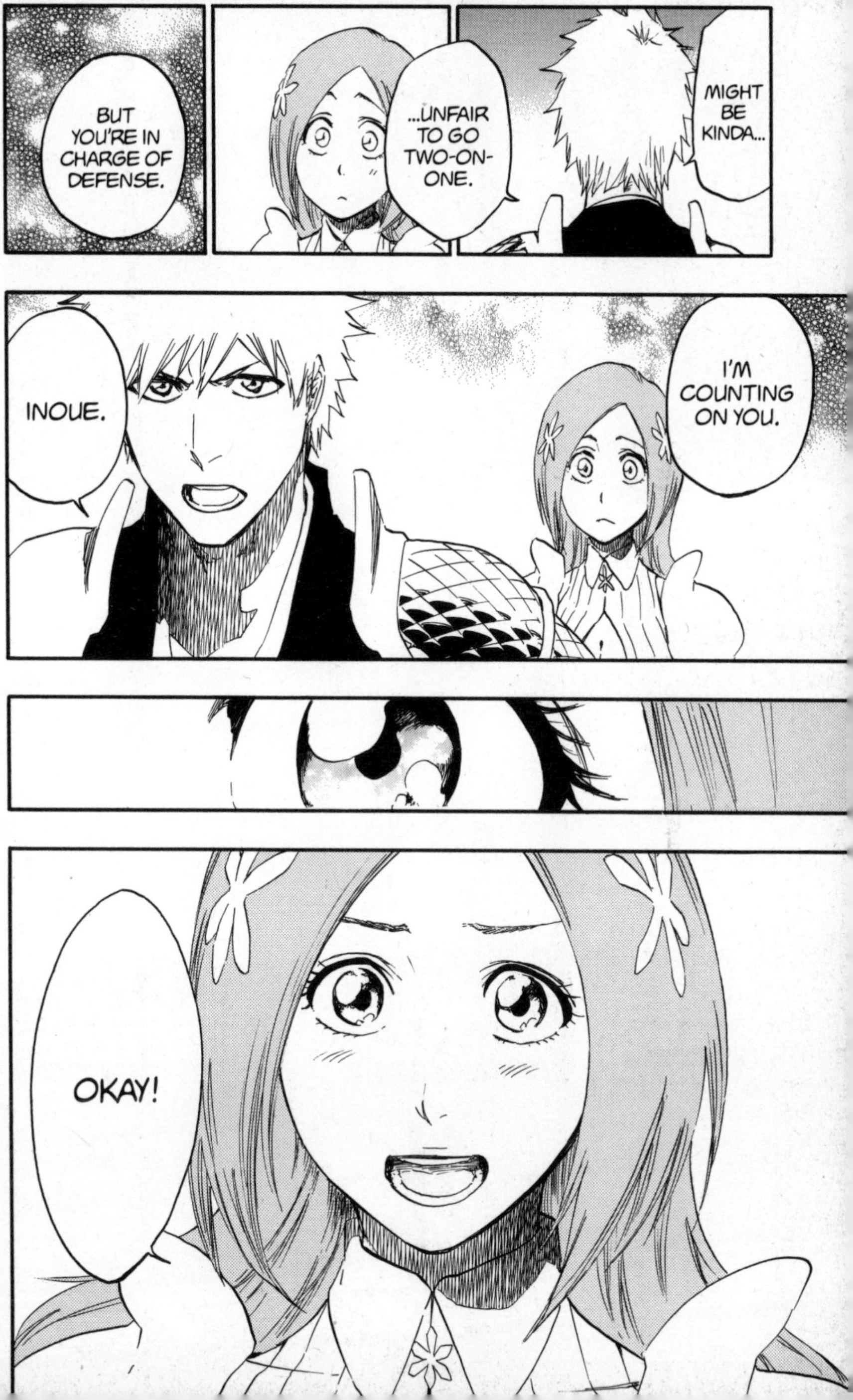
MIGHT BE KINDA...
...UNFAIR TO GO TWO-ON-ONE.
BUT YOU'RE IN CHARGE OF DEFENSE.
I'M COUNTING ON YOU.
INOUE.
OKAY!

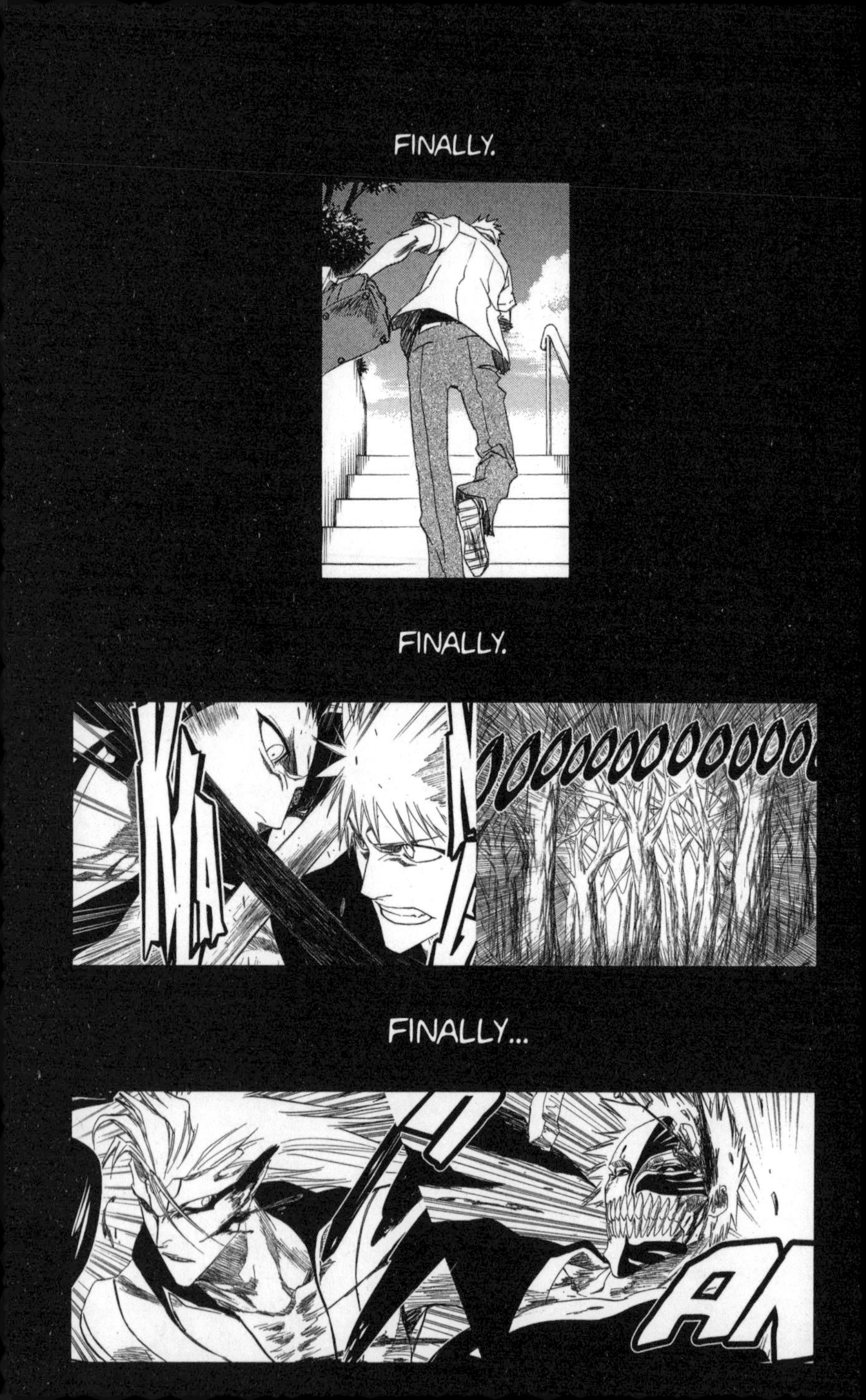
FINALLY.
FINALLY.
FINALLY...

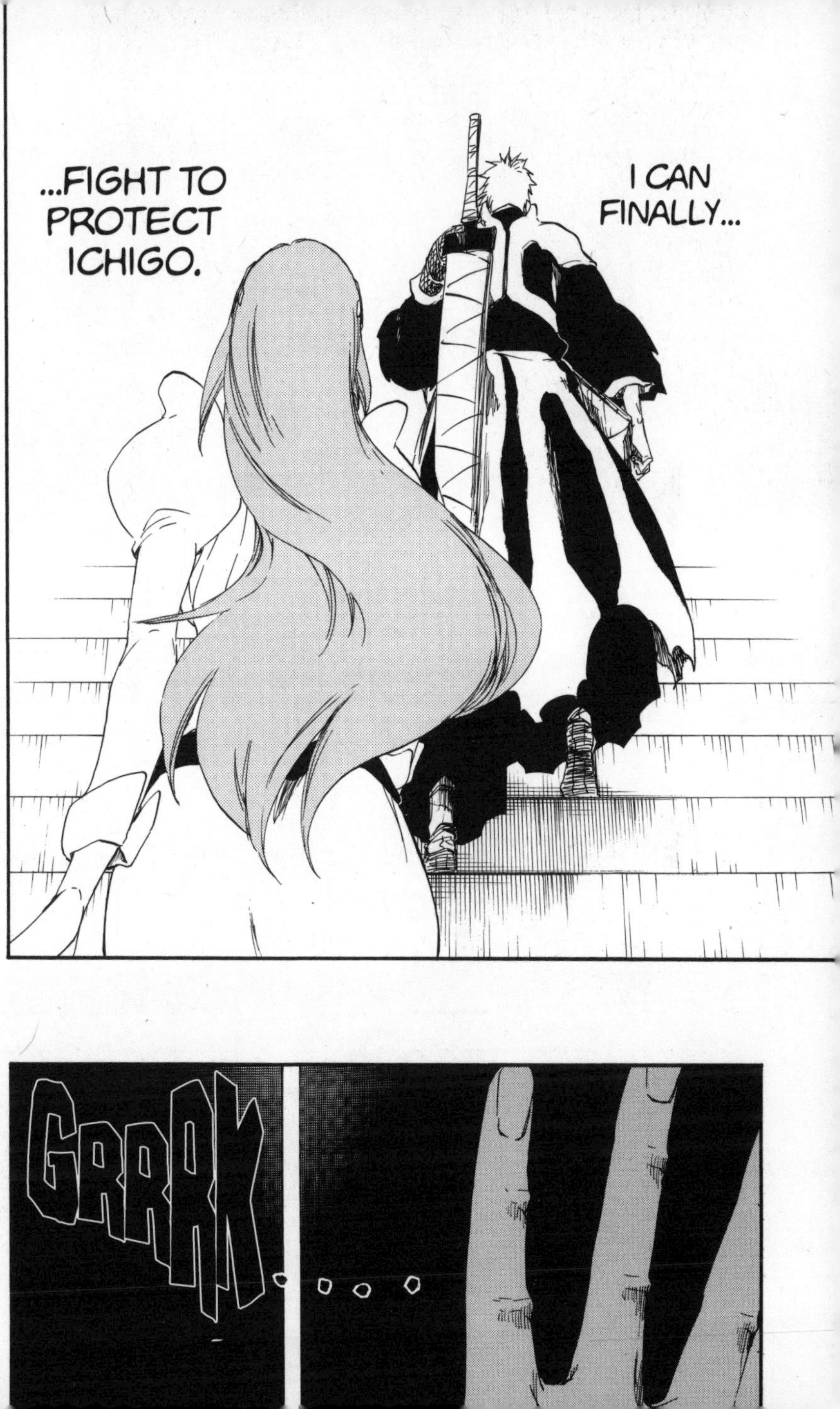
I CAN FINALLY...
...FIGHT TO PROTECT ICHIGO.
GRRRK

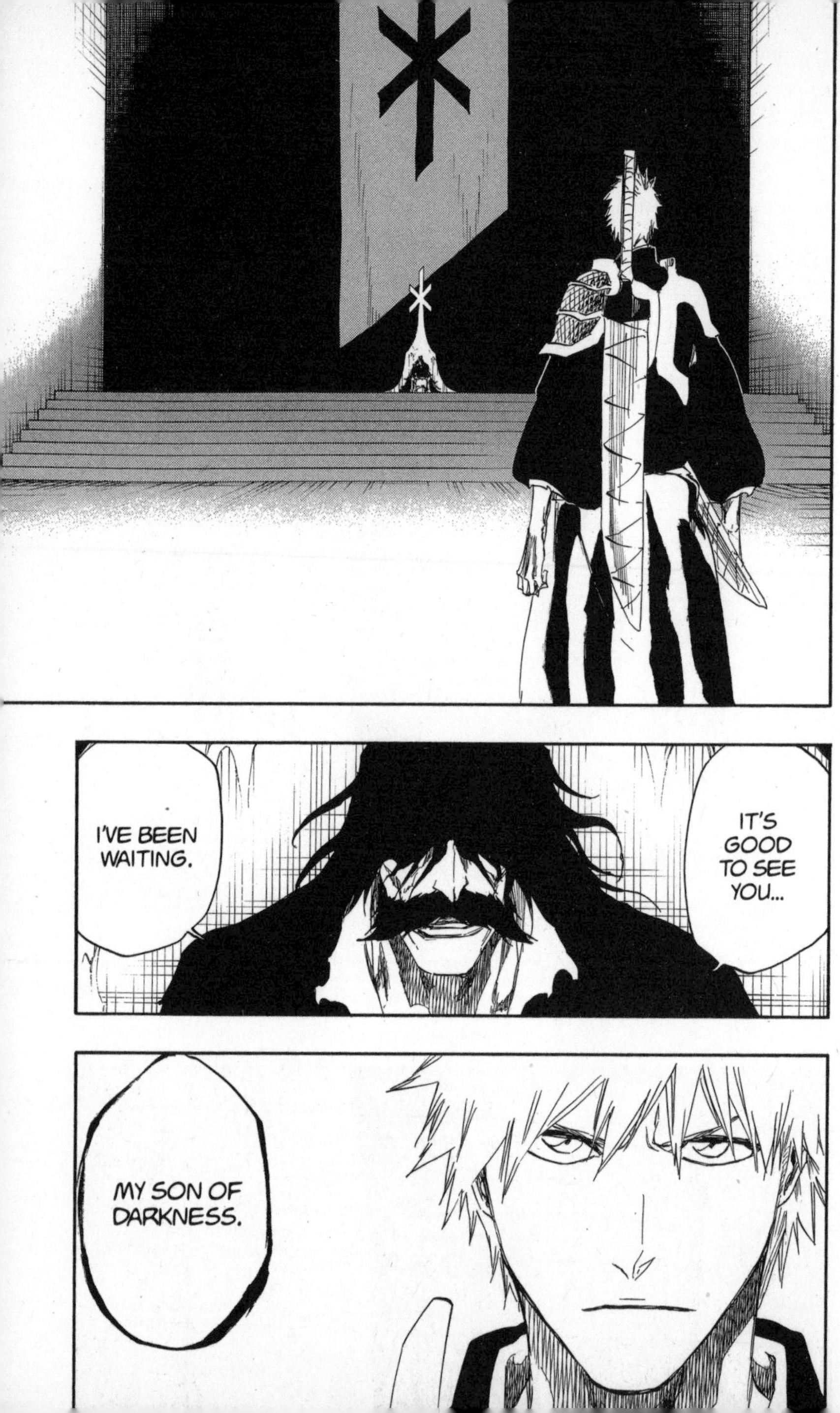
IT'S GOOD TO SEE YOU...
I'VE BEEN WAITING.
MY SON OF DARKNESS.

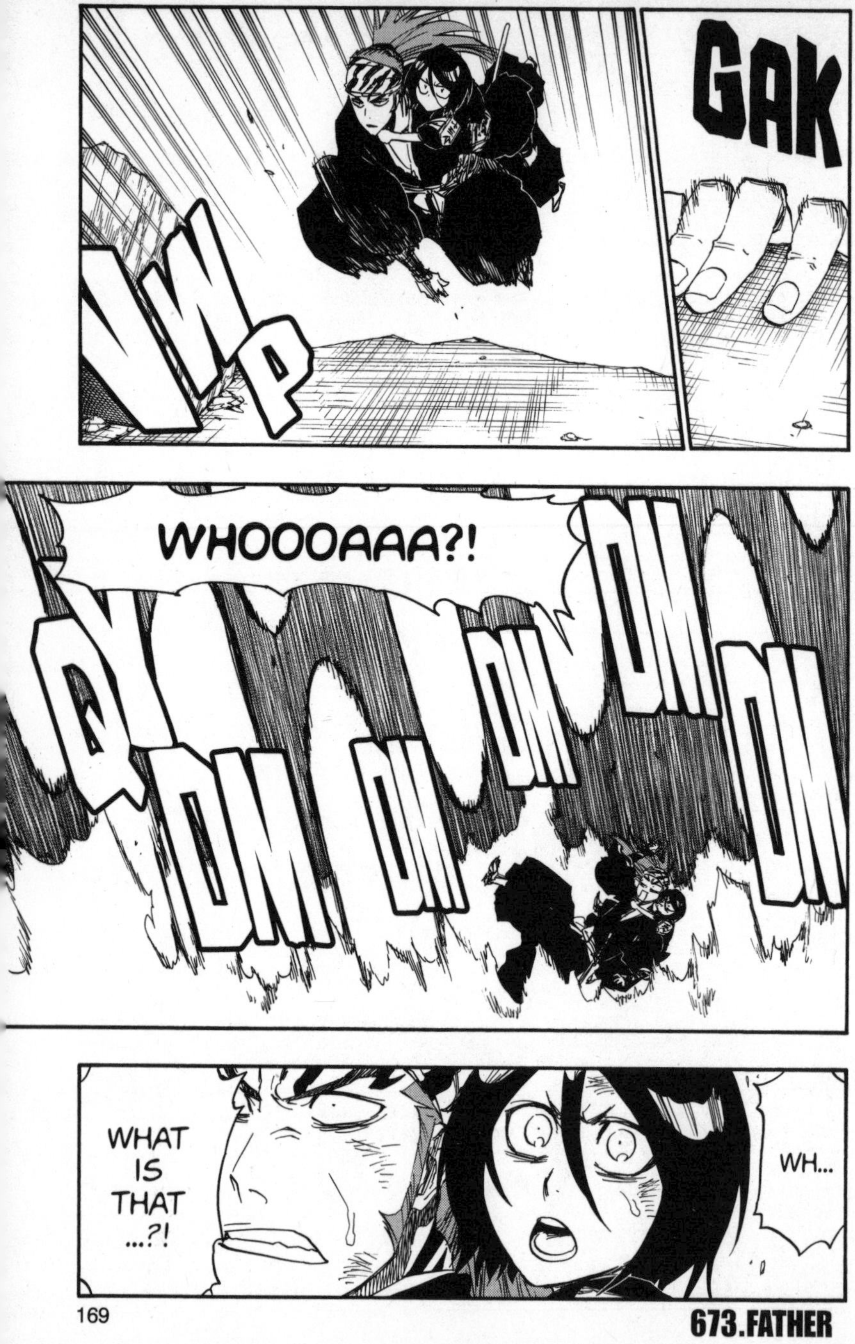
GAK
VWP
WHOOOAAA?!
WH...
WHAT IS THAT ...?!

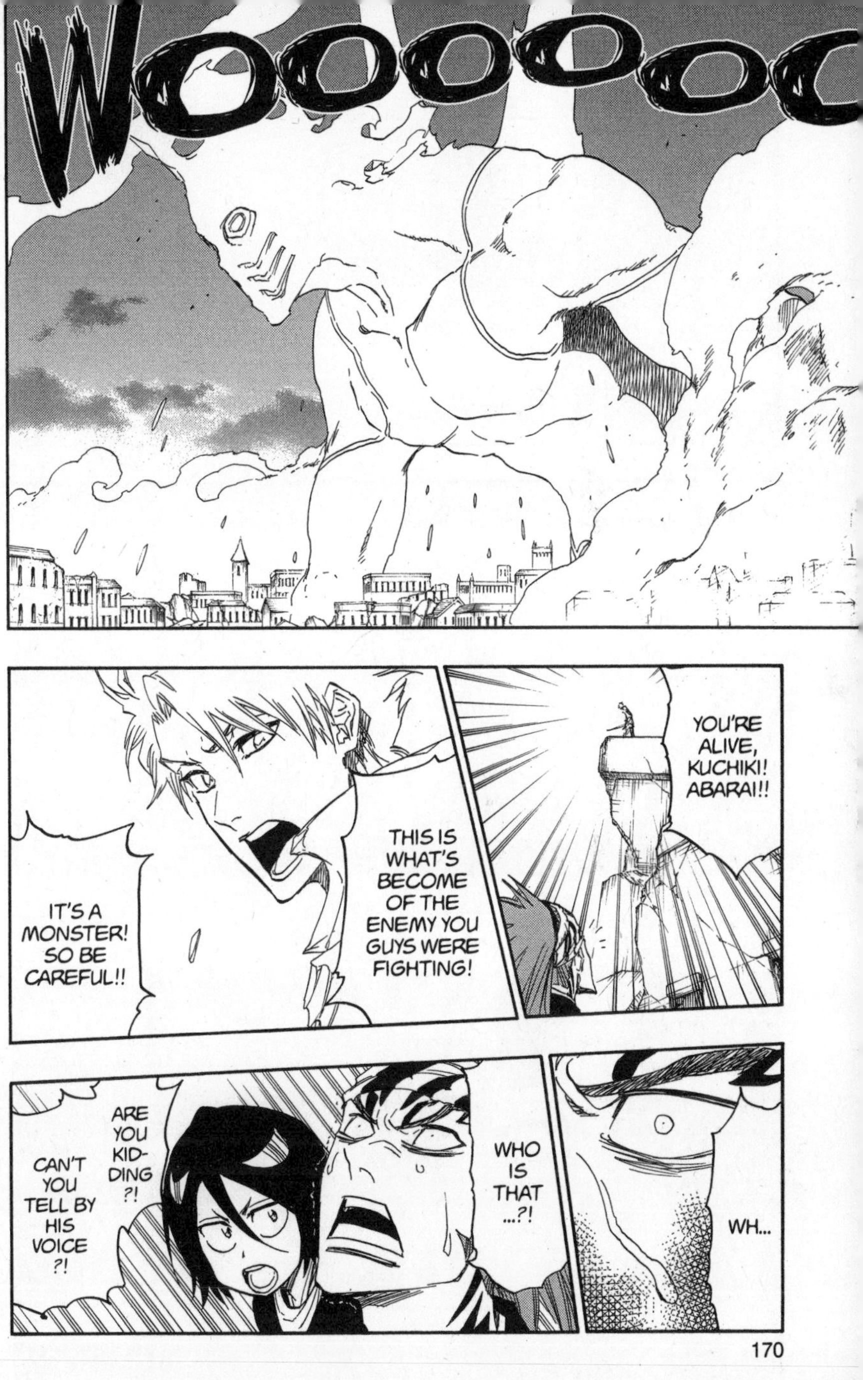
WOOOOOO
YOU'RE ALIVE, KUCHIKI! ABARAI!!
THIS IS WHAT'S BECOME OF THE ENEMY YOU GUYS WERE FIGHTING!
IT'S A MONSTER! SO BE CAREFUL!!
WH...
WHO IS THAT ...?!
ARE YOU KIDDING?!
CAN'T YOU TELL BY HIS VOICE?!

READ THIS WAY

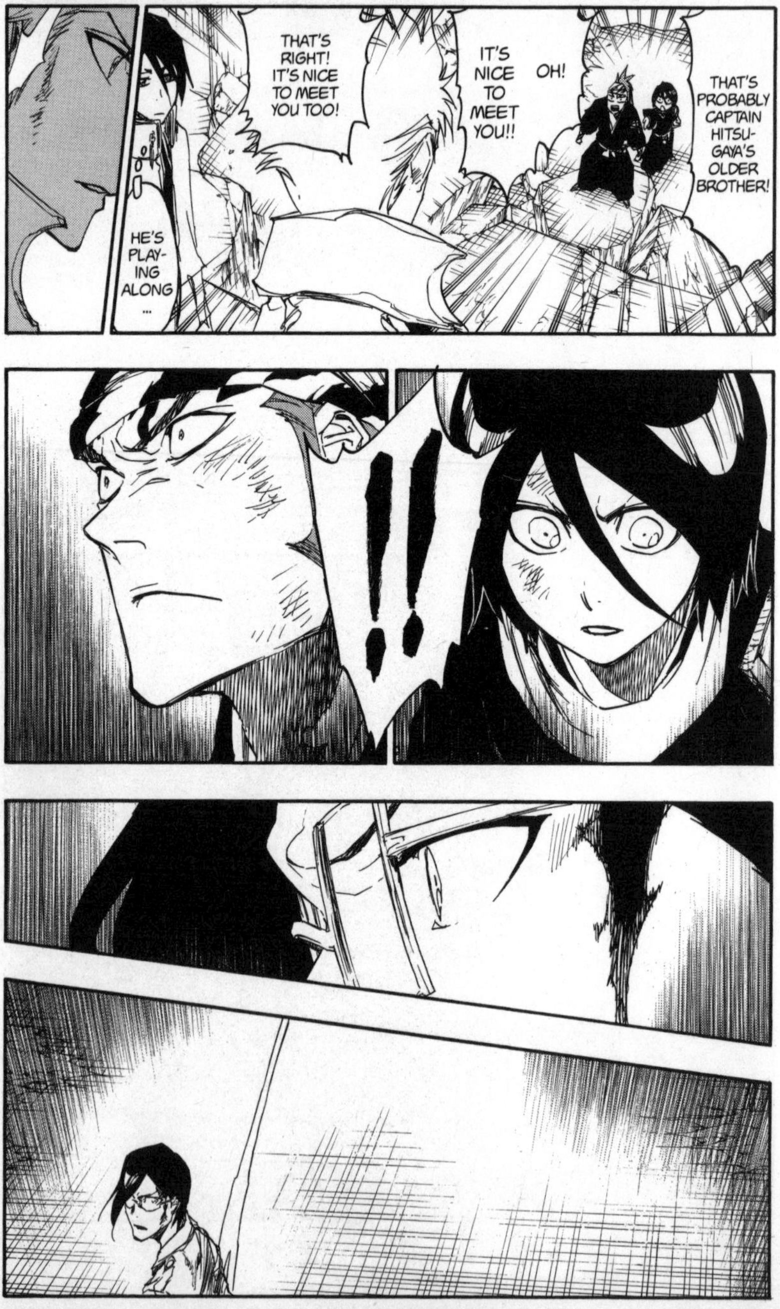
THAT'S PROBABLY CAPTAIN HITSU-GAYA'S OLDER BROTHER!
OH!
IT'S NICE TO MEET YOU!!
THAT'S RIGHT! IT'S NICE TO MEET YOU TOO!
HE'S PLAY-ING ALONG ...
!!

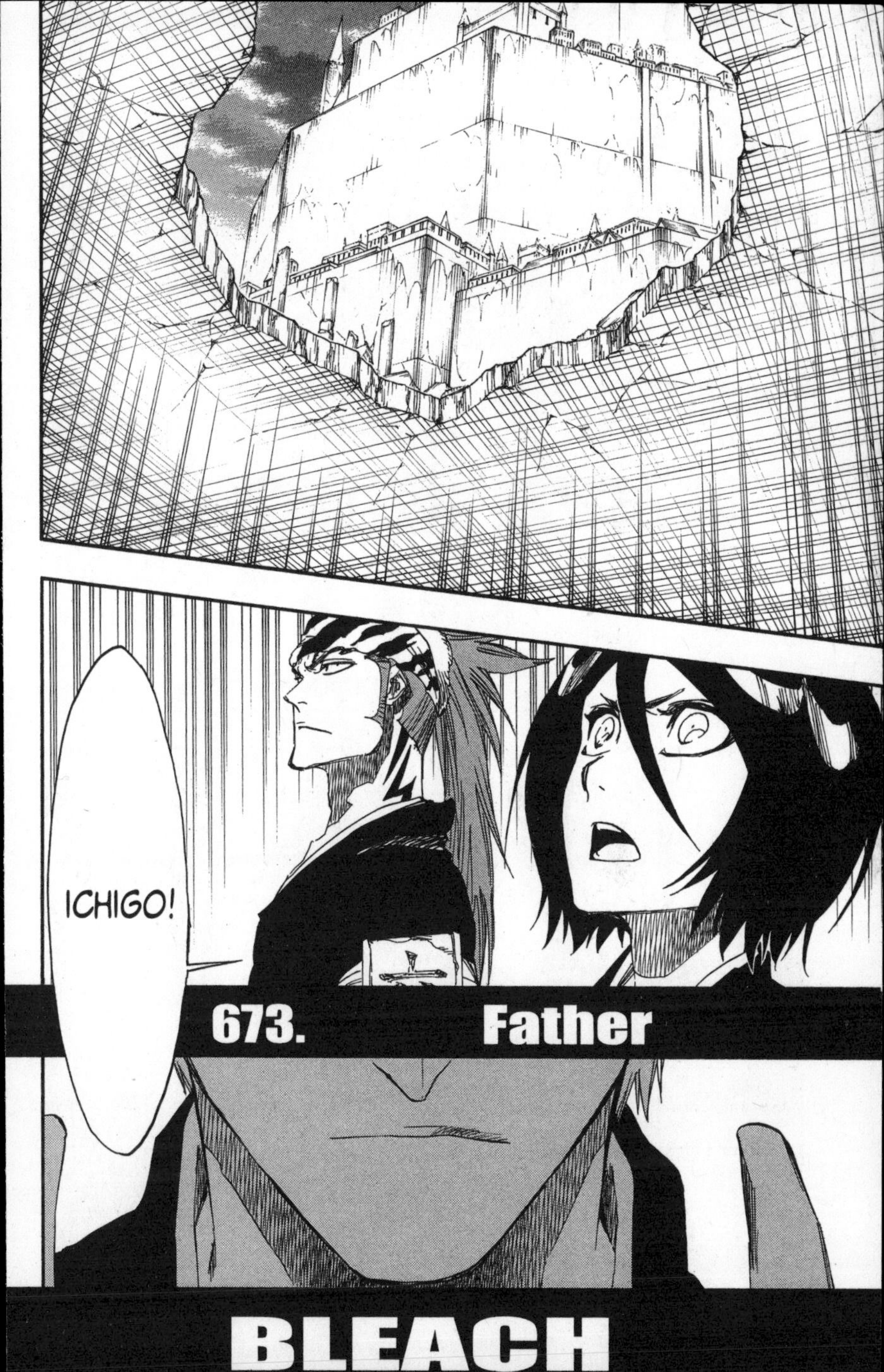
ICHIGO!
673. Father
BLEACH

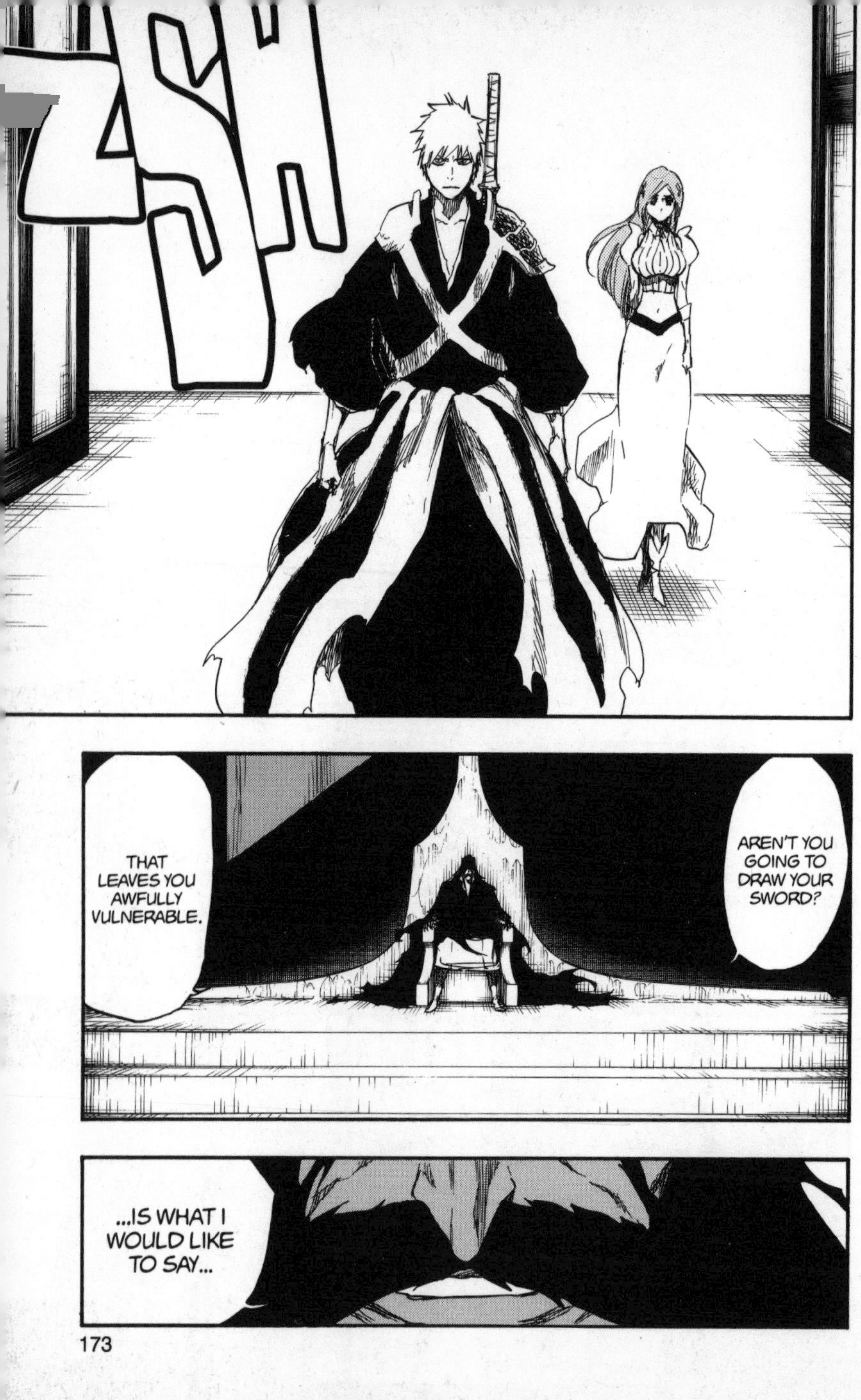
ZSH
AREN'T YOU GOING TO DRAW YOUR SWORD?
THAT LEAVES YOU AWFULLY VULNERABLE.
...IS WHAT I WOULD LIKE TO SAY...

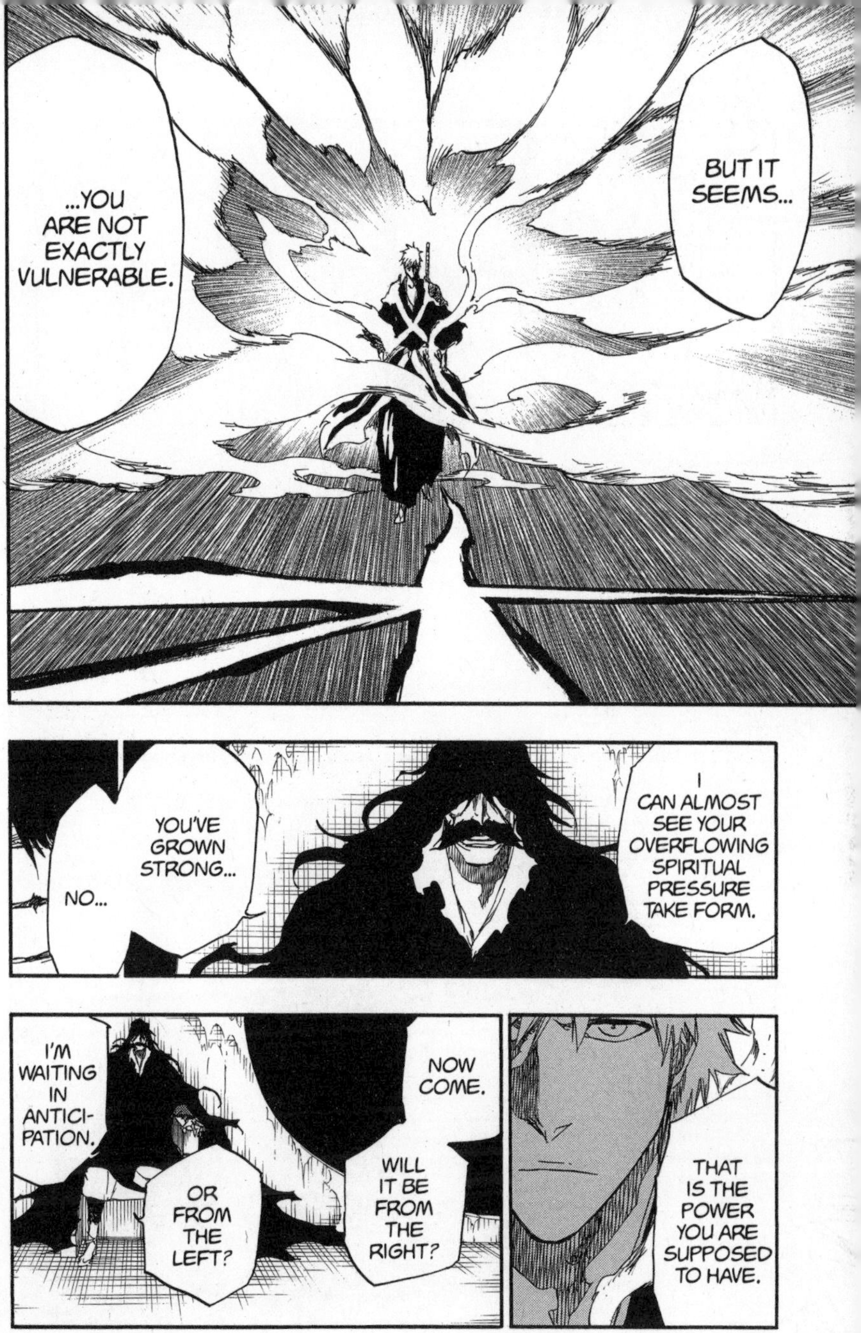
BUT IT SEEMS...
...YOU ARE NOT EXACTLY VULNERABLE.
I CAN ALMOST SEE YOUR OVERFLOWING SPIRITUAL PRESSURE TAKE FORM.
YOU'VE GROWN STRONG...
NO...
THAT IS THE POWER YOU ARE SUPPOSED TO HAVE.
NOW COME.
I'M WAITING IN ANTICI-PATION.
WILL IT BE FROM THE RIGHT?
OR FROM THE LEFT?

READ THIS WAY

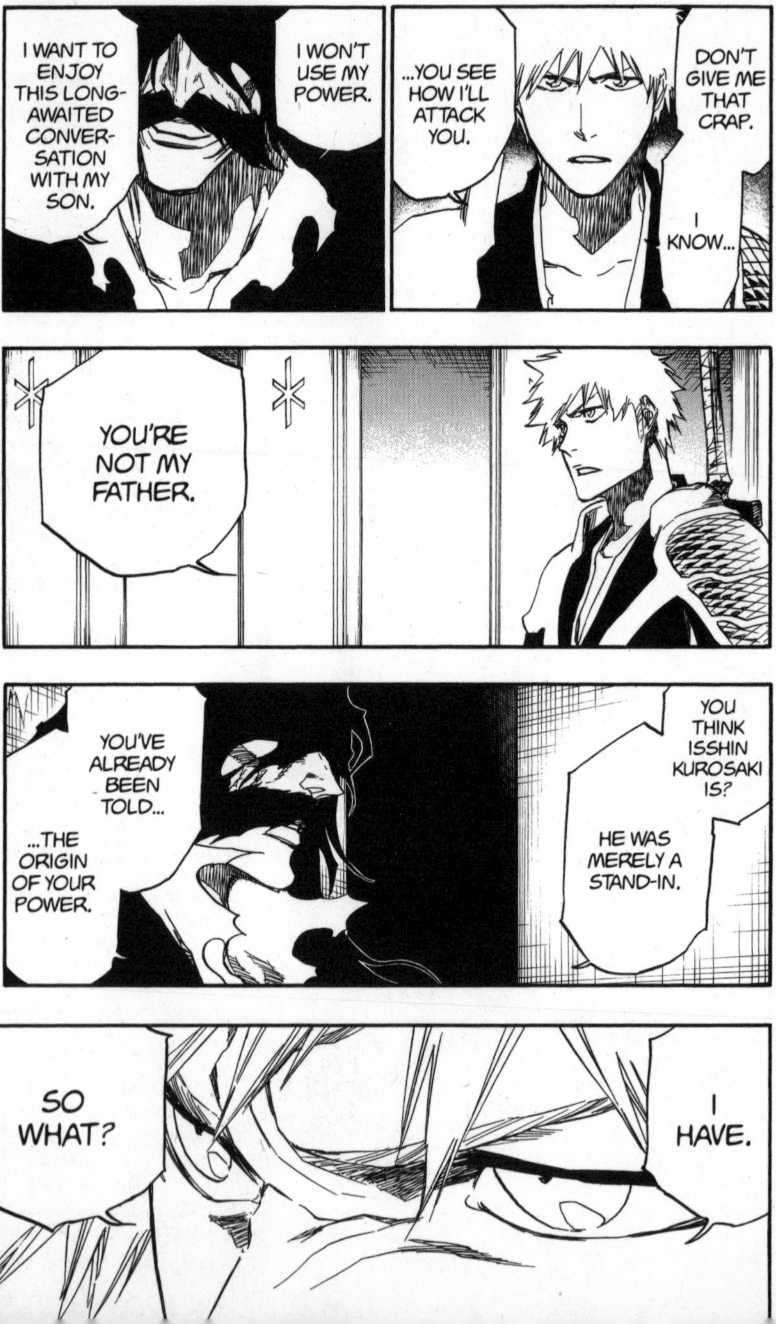
DON'T GIVE ME THAT CRAP.
I KNOW...
...YOU SEE HOW I'LL ATTACK YOU.
I WON'T USE MY POWER.
I WANT TO ENJOY THIS LONG-AWAITED CONVERSATION WITH MY SON.
YOU'RE NOT MY FATHER.
YOU THINK ISSHIN KUROSAKI IS?
HE WAS MERELY A STAND-IN.
YOU'VE ALREADY BEEN TOLD...
...THE ORIGIN OF YOUR POWER.
I HAVE.
SO WHAT?

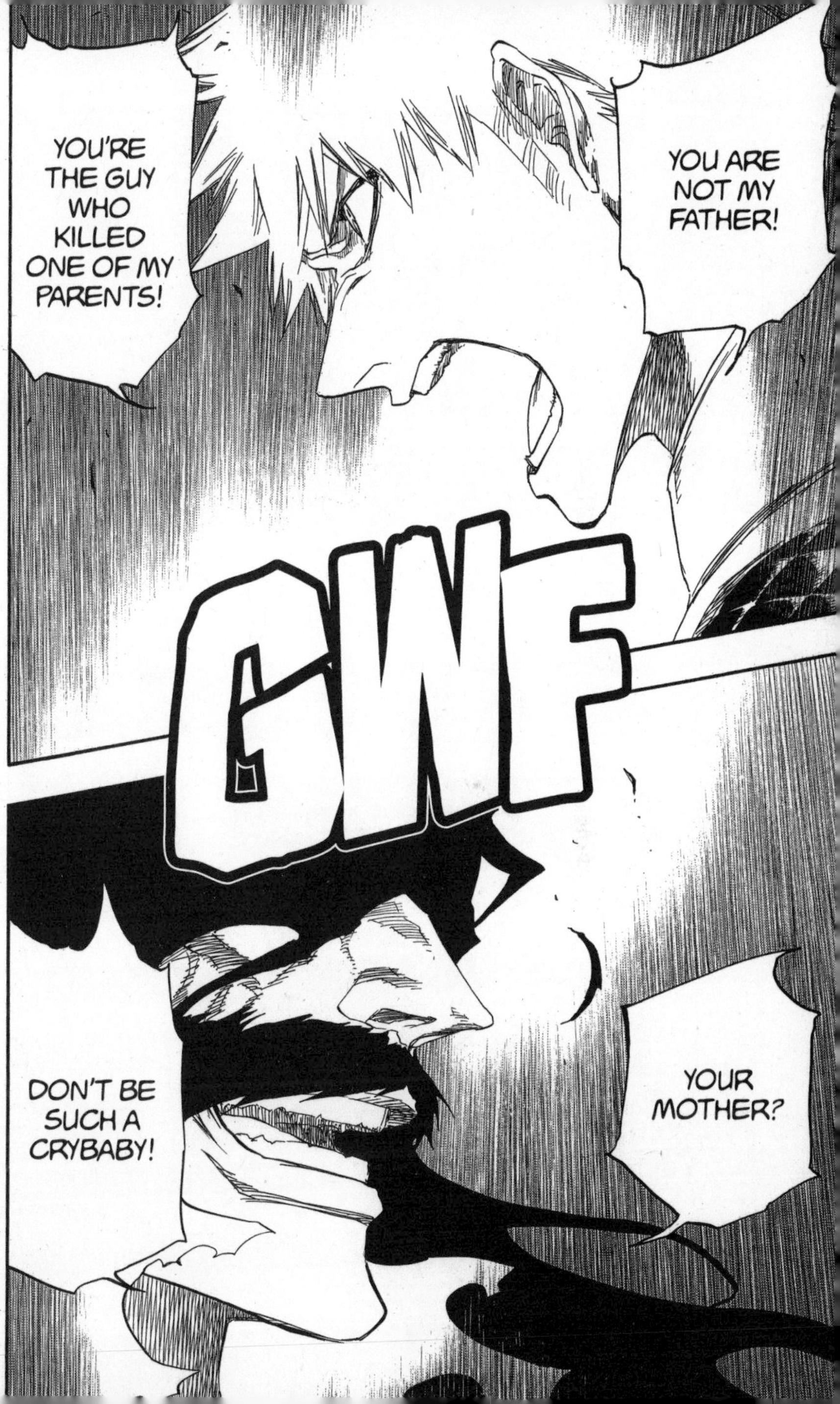
YOU ARE NOT MY FATHER!
YOU'RE THE GUY WHO KILLED ONE OF MY PARENTS!
GWF
YOUR MOTHER?
DON'T BE SUCH A CRYBABY!

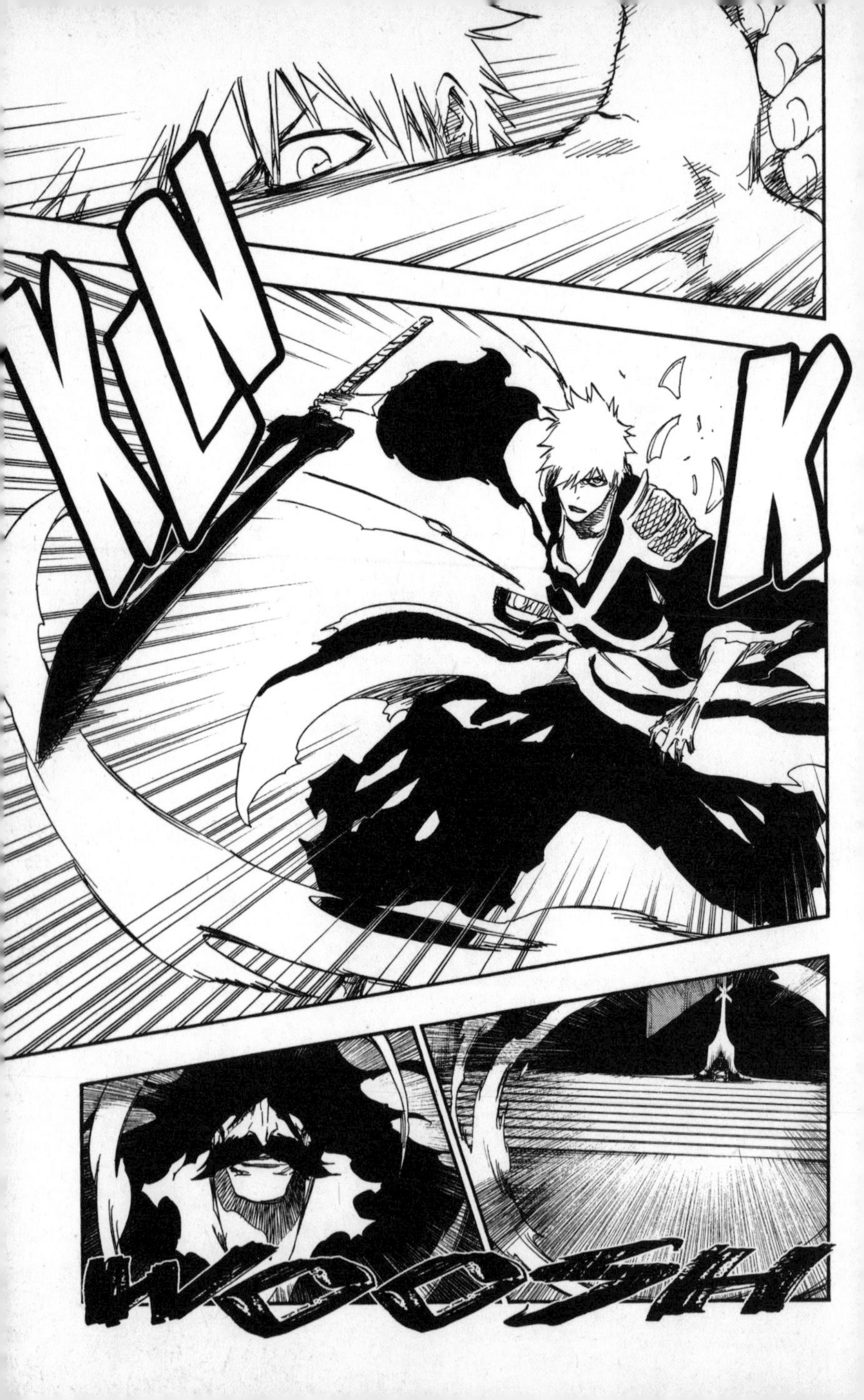

KIN
K
WOOOSH

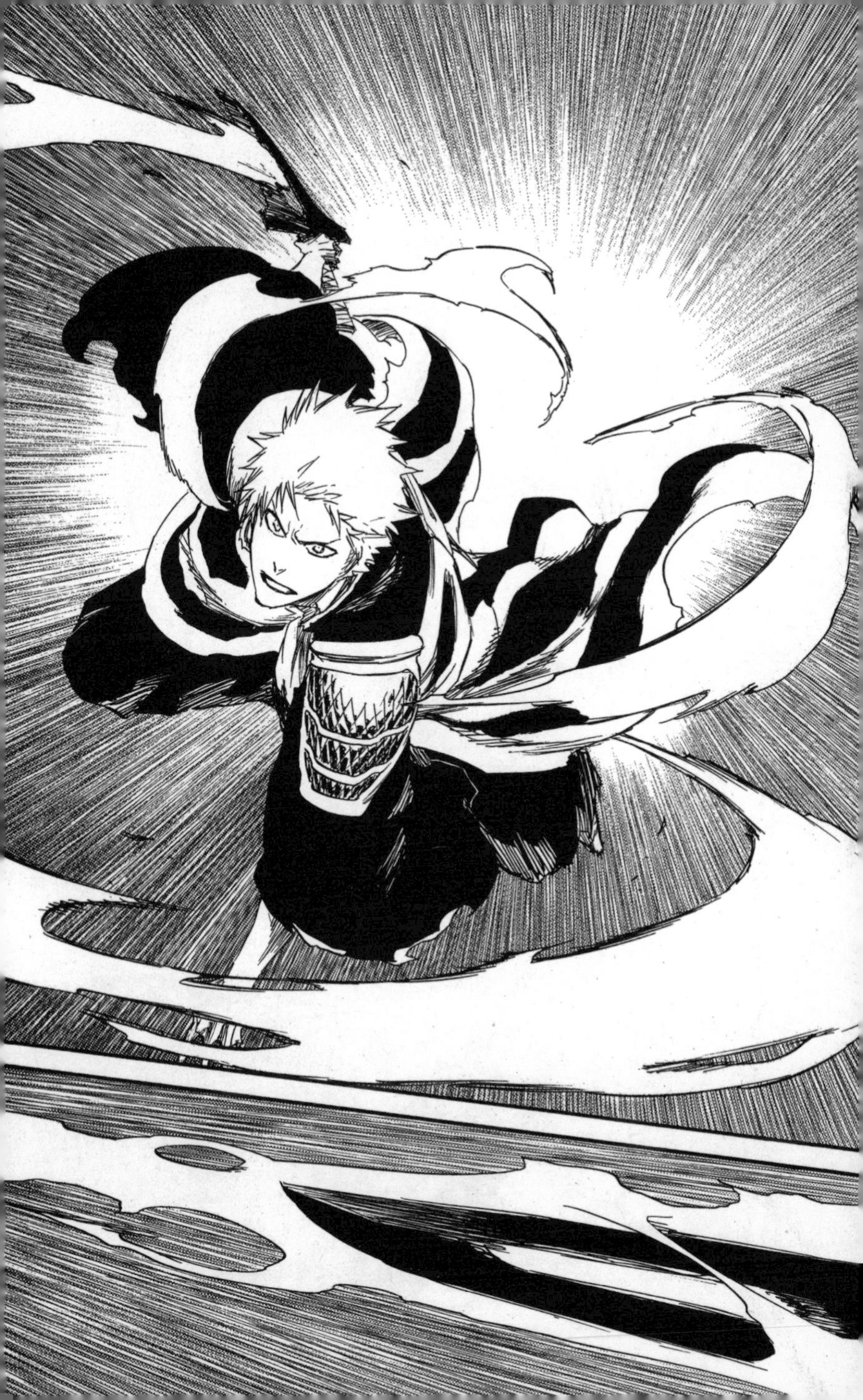

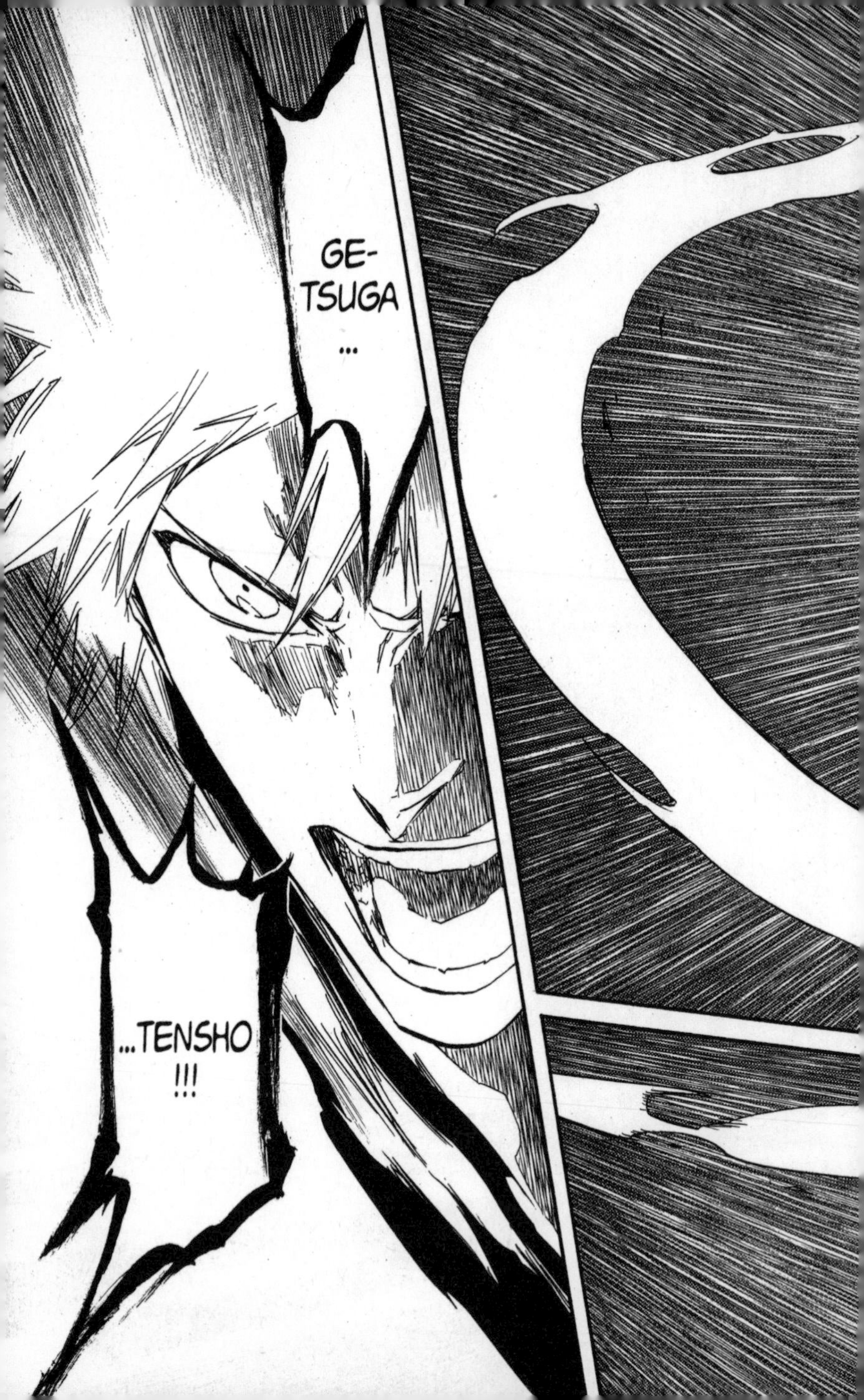
GE-
TSUGA
...
...TENSHO
!!!

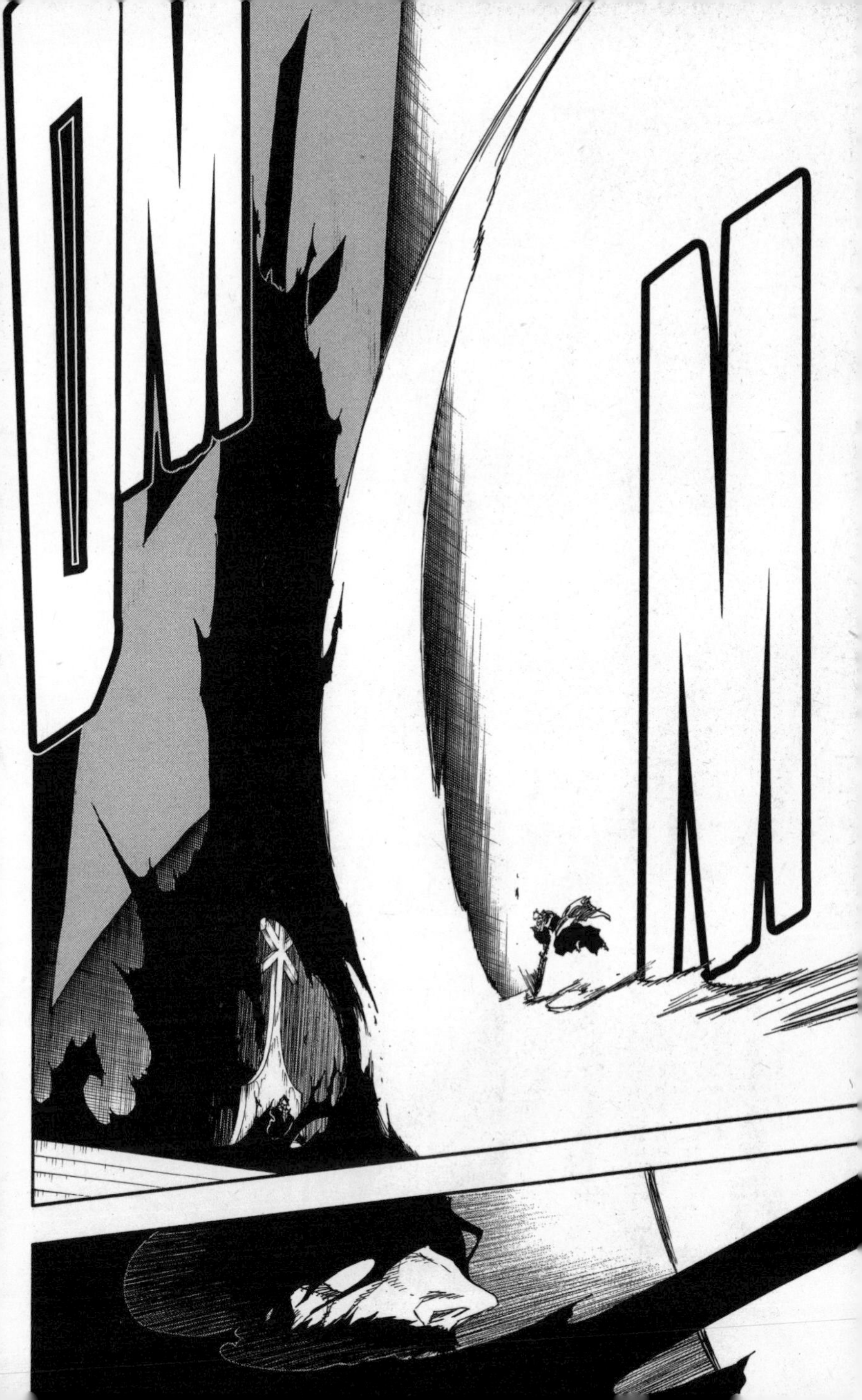
DOOM

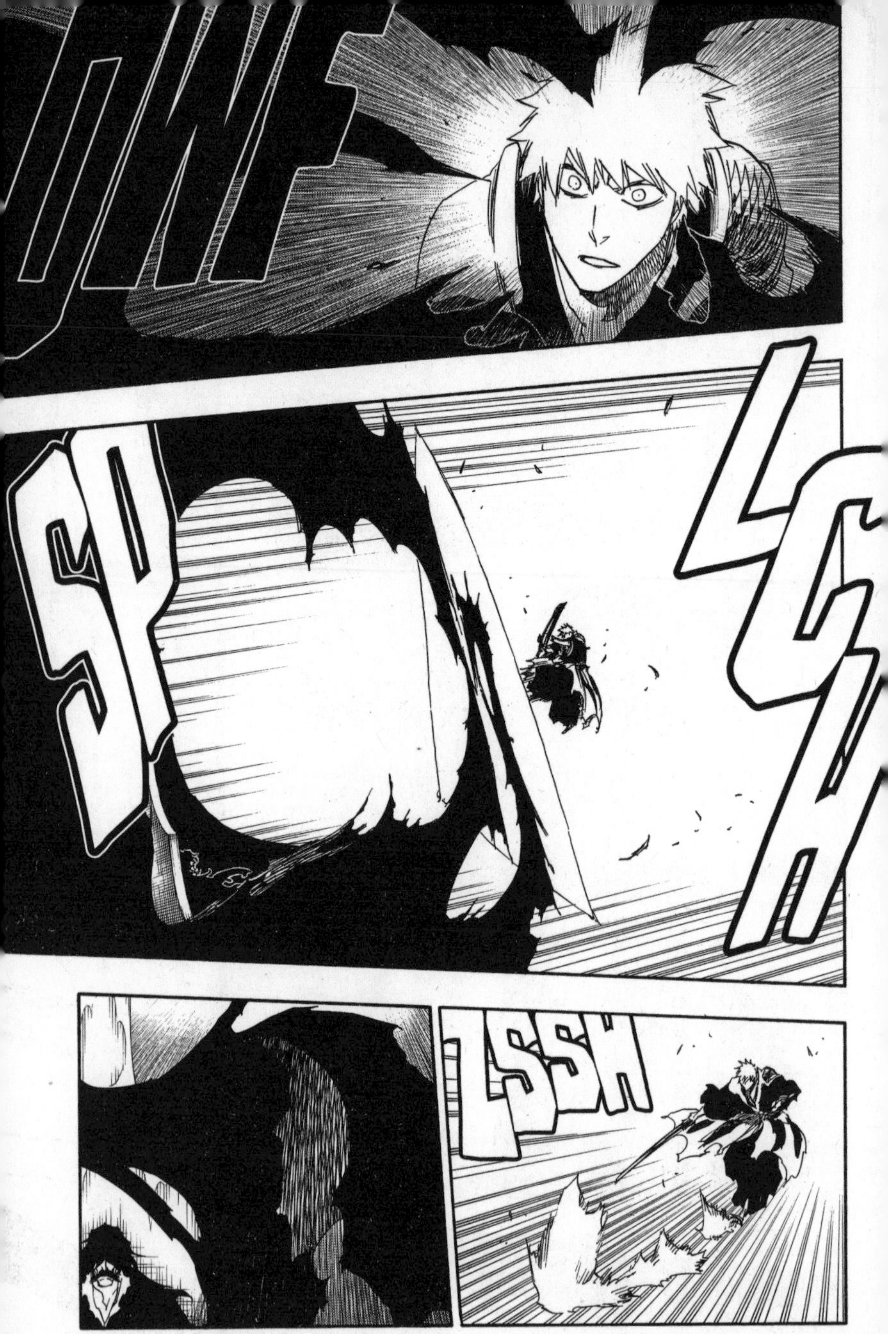
LSSH

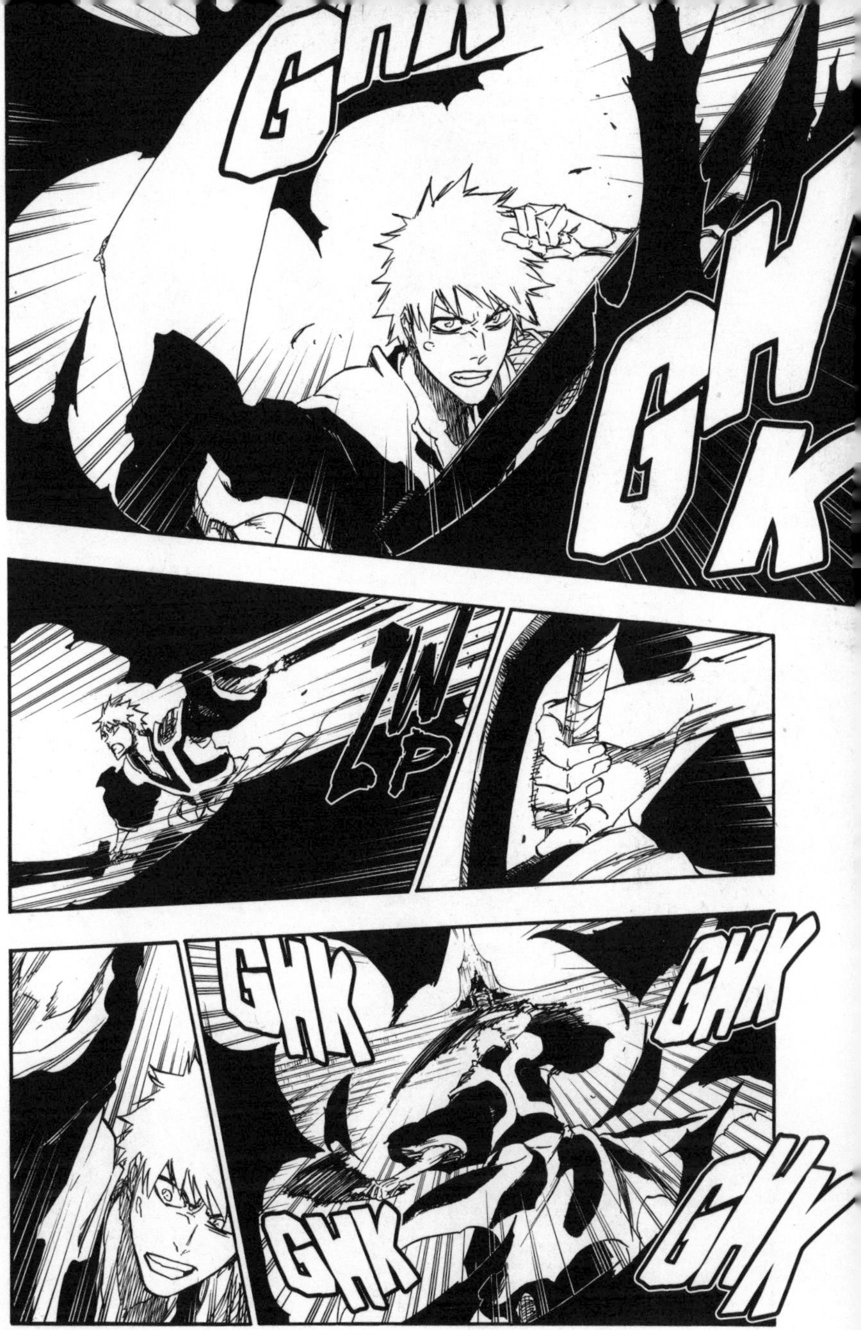
GHK
GHK
GHK
GHK

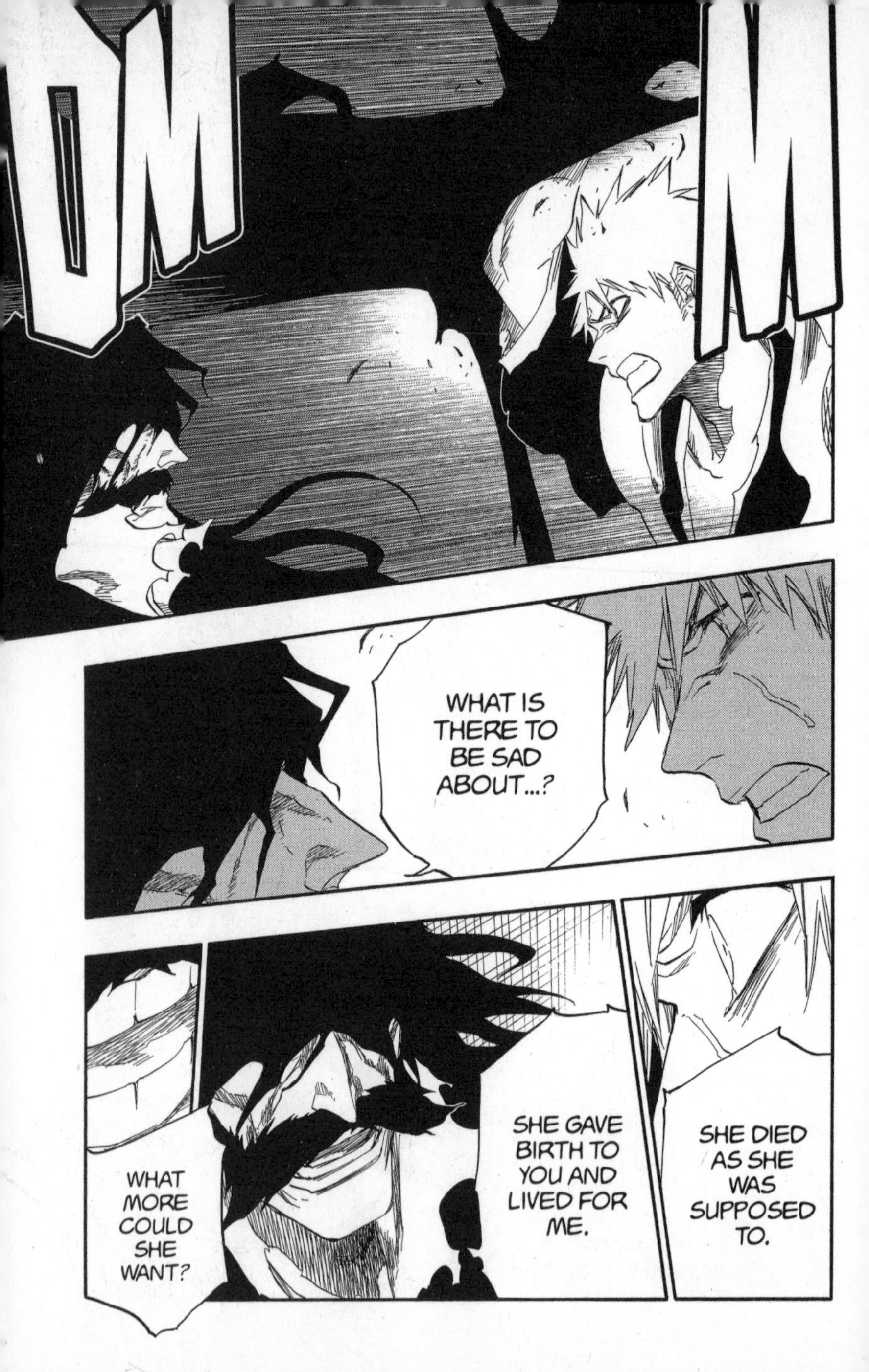
WHAT IS THERE TO BE SAD ABOUT...?
SHE DIED AS SHE WAS SUPPOSED TO.
SHE GAVE BIRTH TO YOU AND LIVED FOR ME.
WHAT MORE COULD SHE WANT?

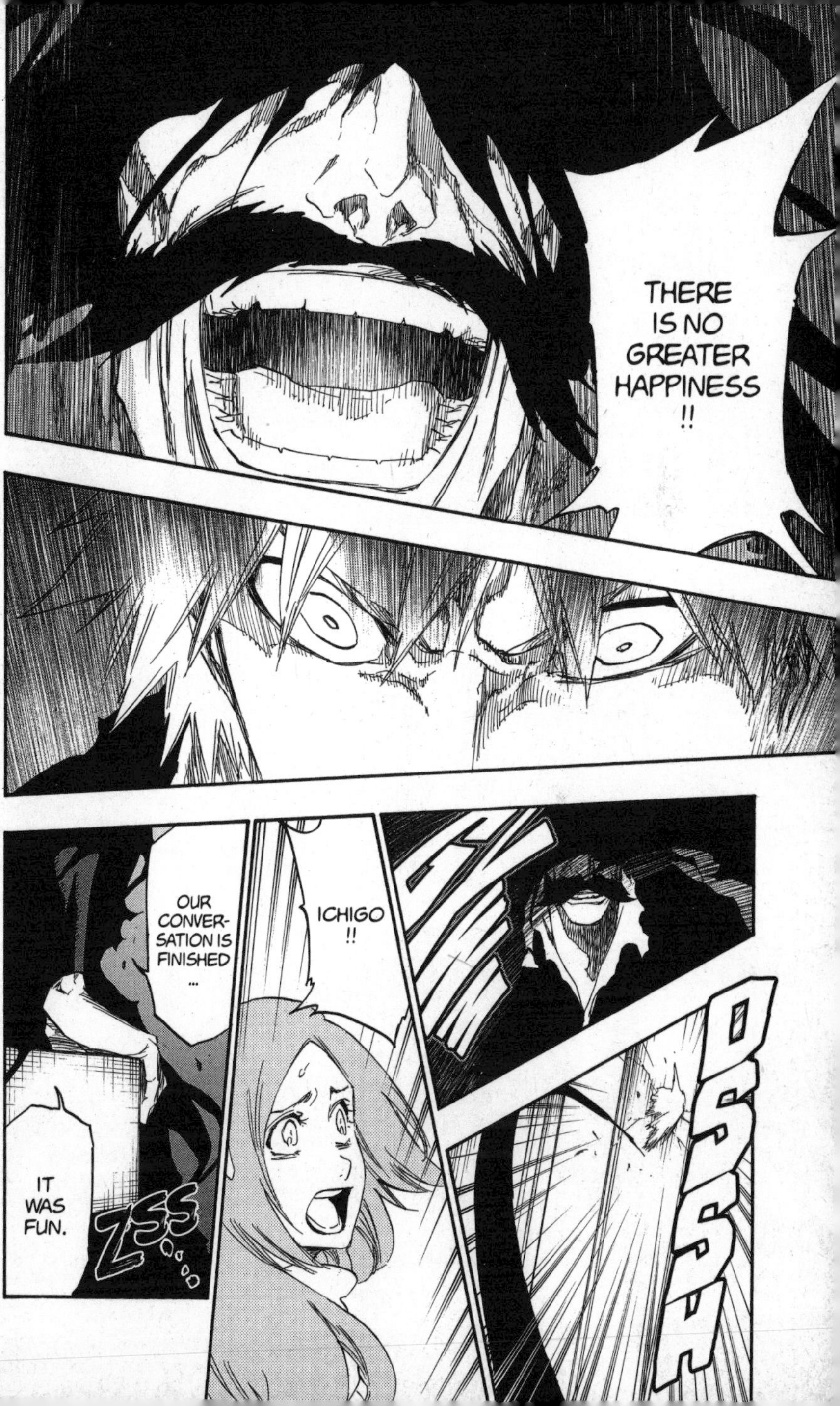
THERE IS NO GREATER HAPPINESS !!
DSSH
ICHIGO !!
OUR CONVER-SATION IS FINISHED ...
IT WAS FUN.
ZSS

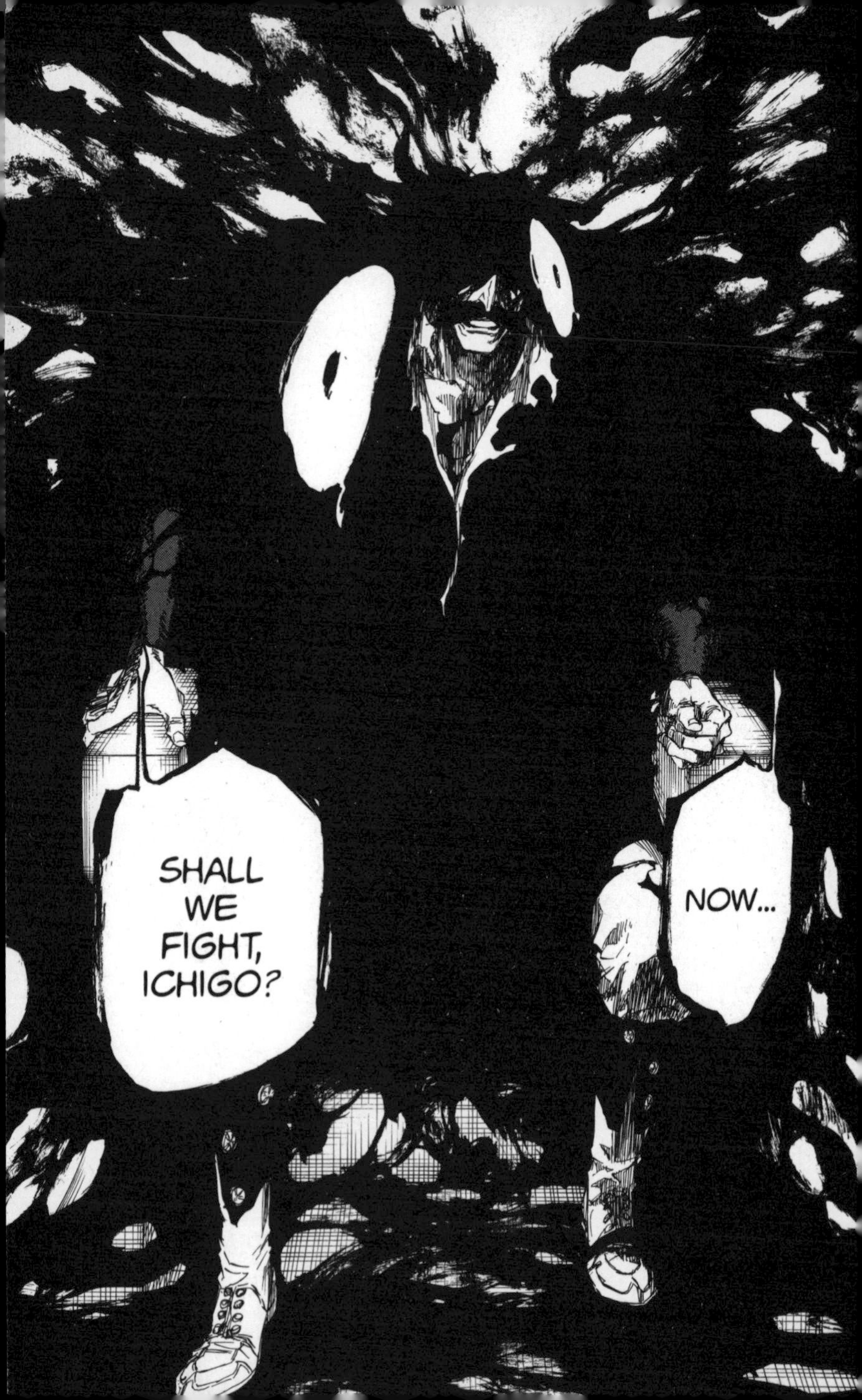
NOW...
SHALL WE FIGHT, ICHIGO?

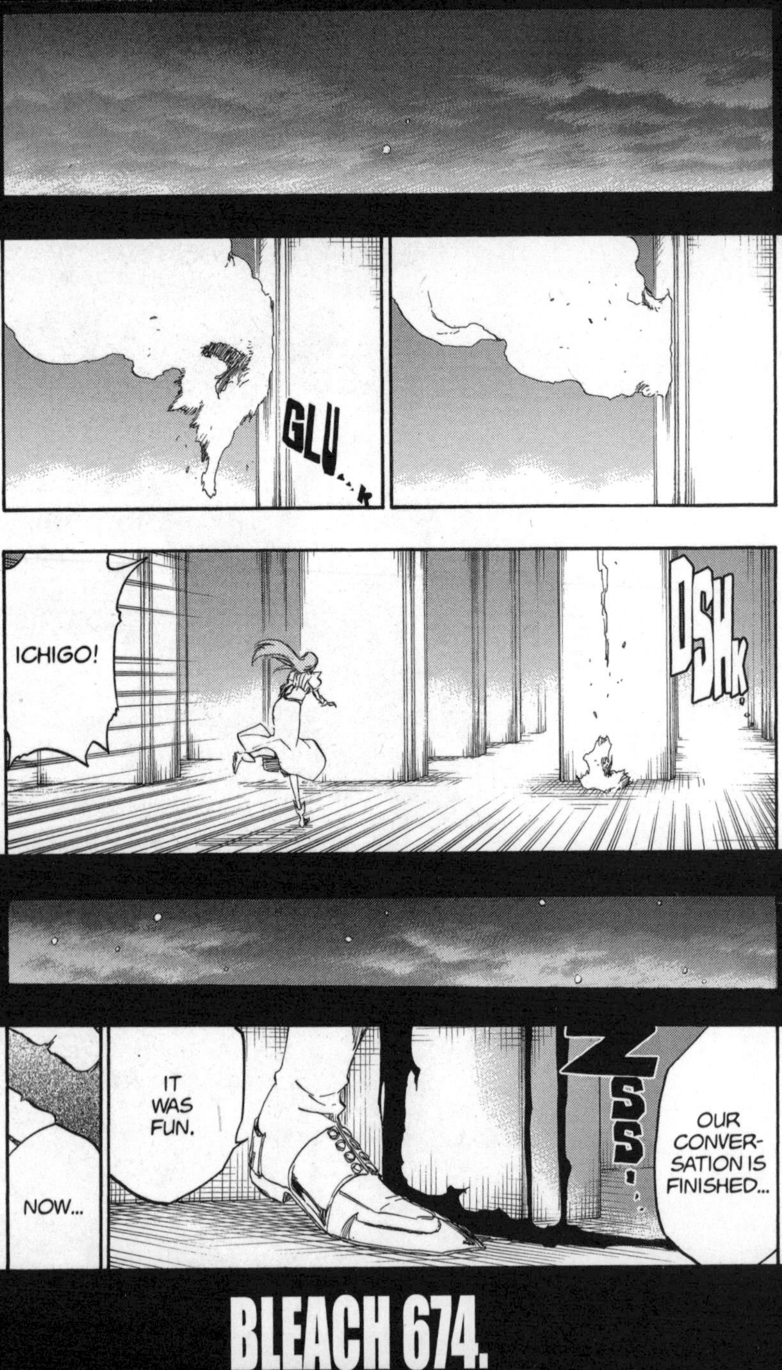
GLU...K
DSHK
ICHIGO!
OUR CONVERSATION IS FINISHED...
ZSS...
IT WAS FUN.
NOW...

BLEACH 674.

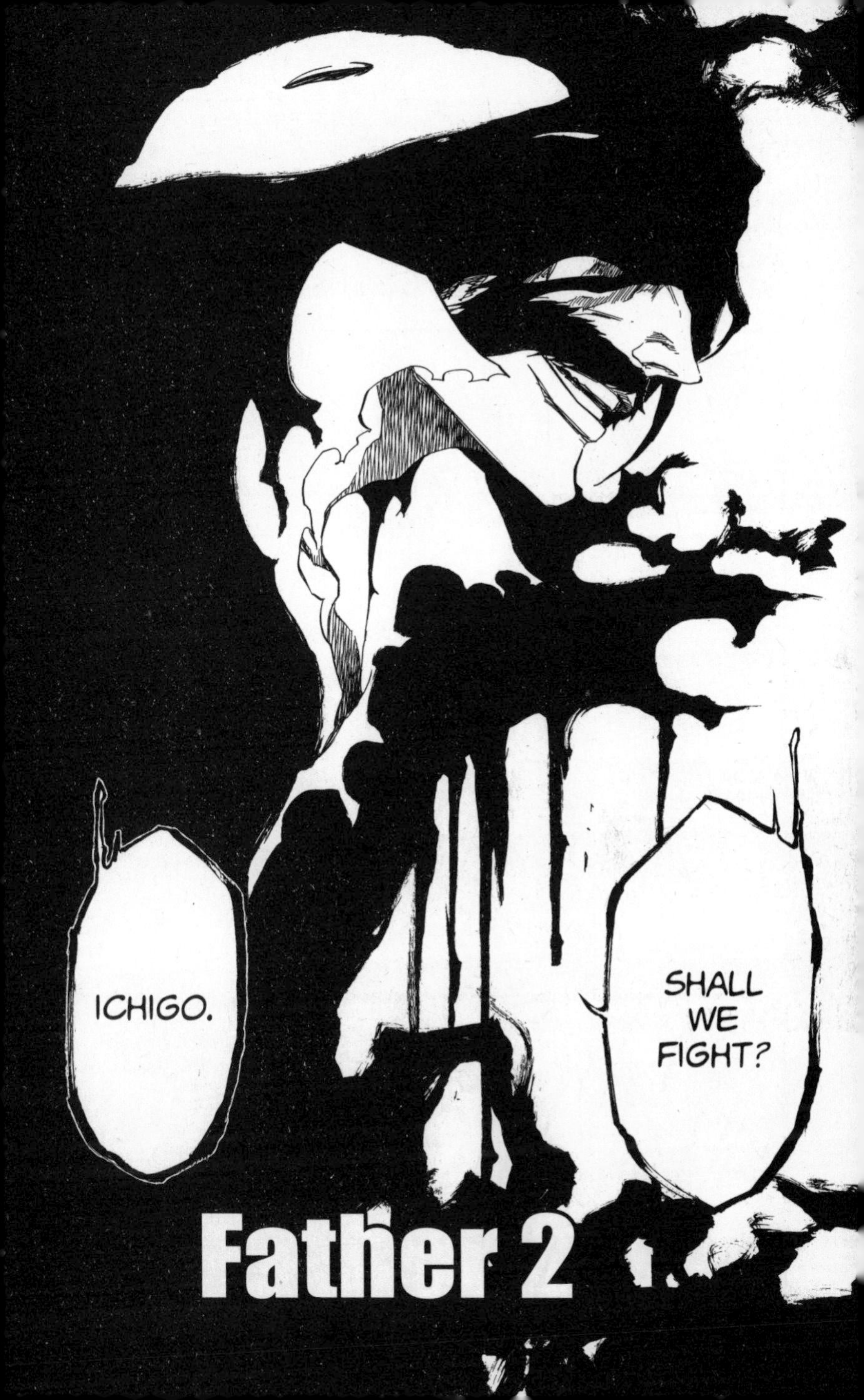
SHALL WE FIGHT?
ICHIGO.
Father 2

READ THIS WAY

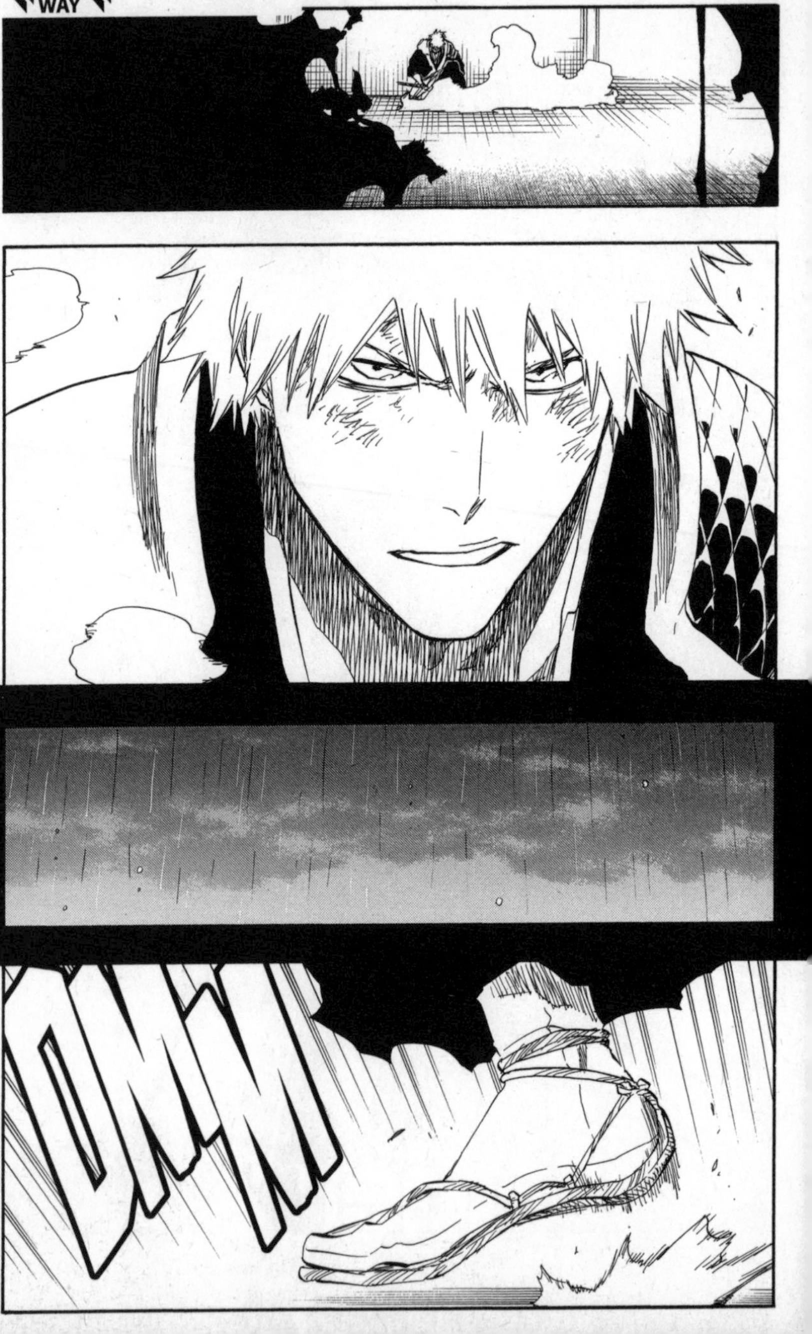
DMM

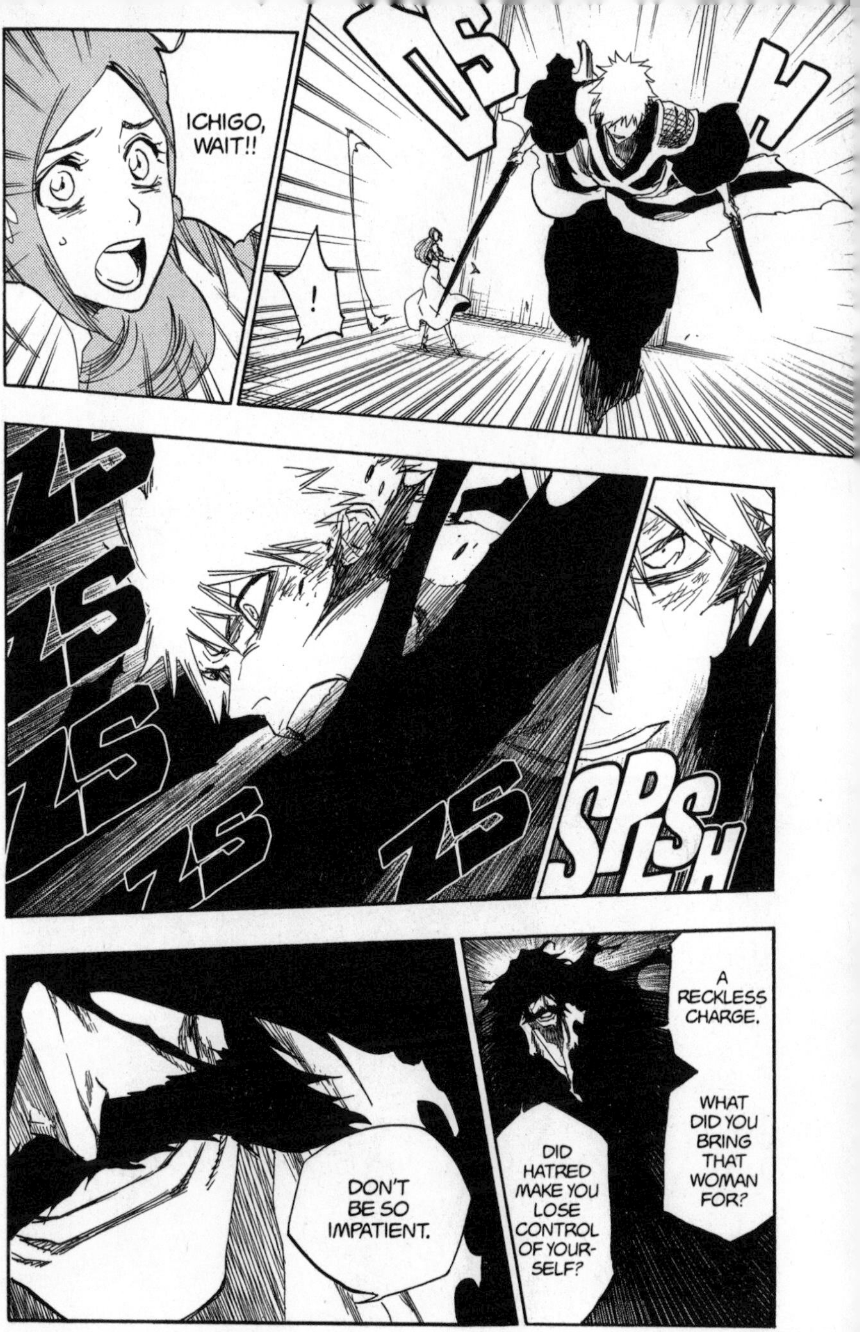
!
ICHIGO, WAIT!!
A RECKLESS CHARGE.
WHAT DID YOU BRING THAT WOMAN FOR?
DID HATRED MAKE YOU LOSE CONTROL OF YOUR-SELF?
DON'T BE SO IMPATIENT.

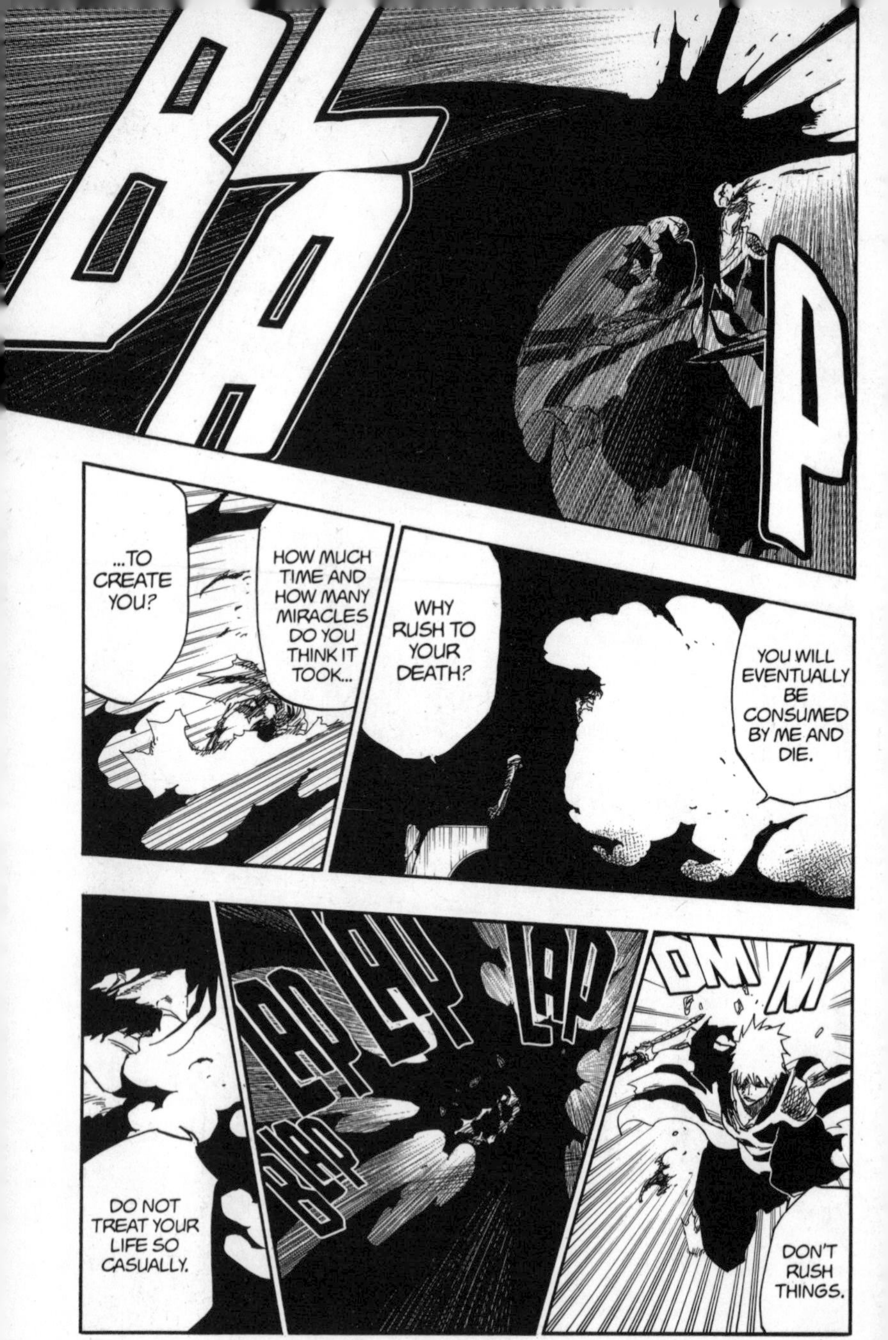
BLAP
YOU WILL EVENTUALLY BE CONSUMED BY ME AND DIE.
WHY RUSH TO YOUR DEATH?
HOW MUCH TIME AND HOW MANY MIRACLES DO YOU THINK IT TOOK...
...TO CREATE YOU?
DON'T RUSH THINGS.
DO NOT TREAT YOUR LIFE SO CASUALLY.

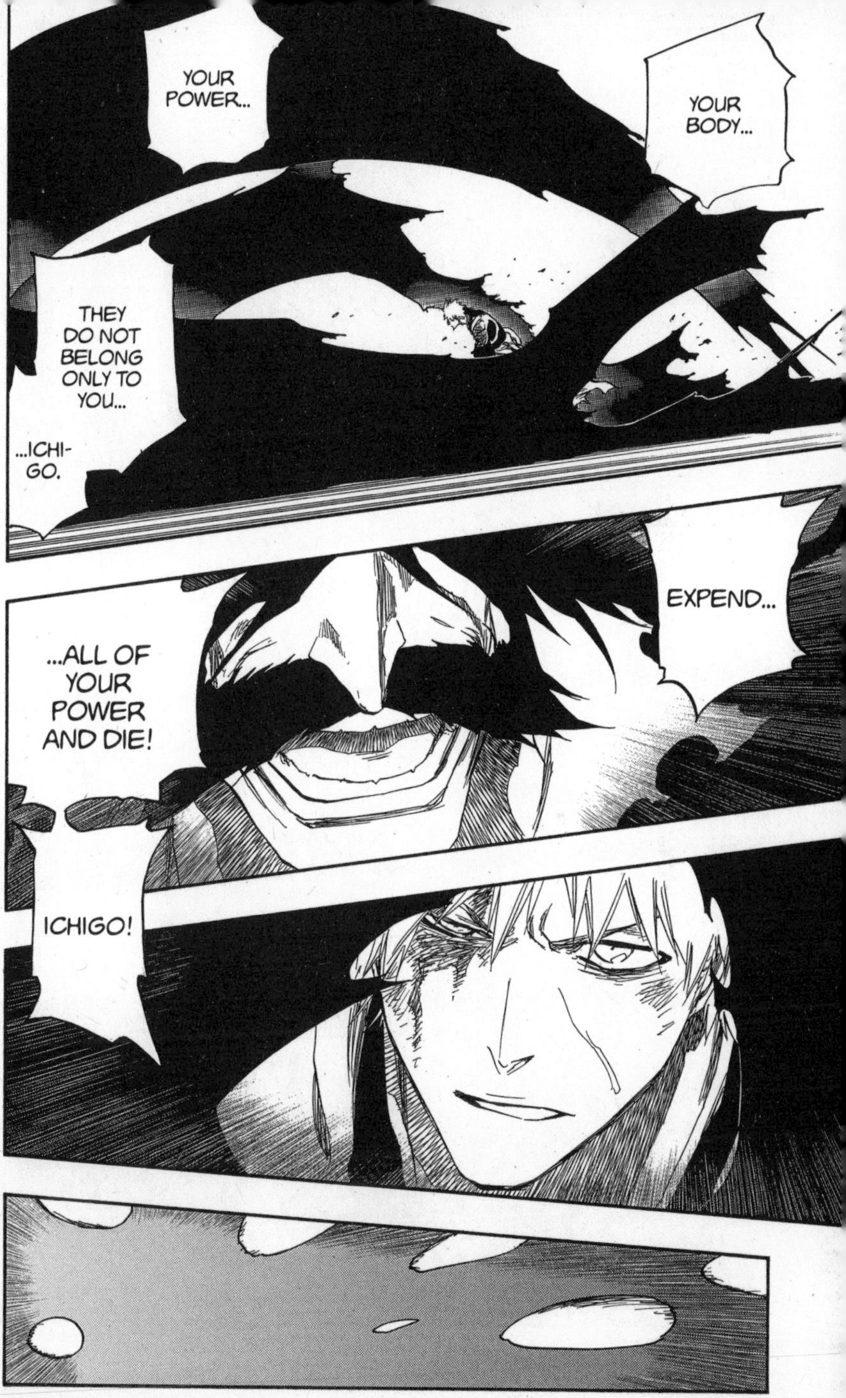
YOUR BODY...
YOUR POWER...
THEY DO NOT BELONG ONLY TO YOU...
...ICHIGO.
EXPEND...
...ALL OF YOUR POWER AND DIE!
ICHIGO!

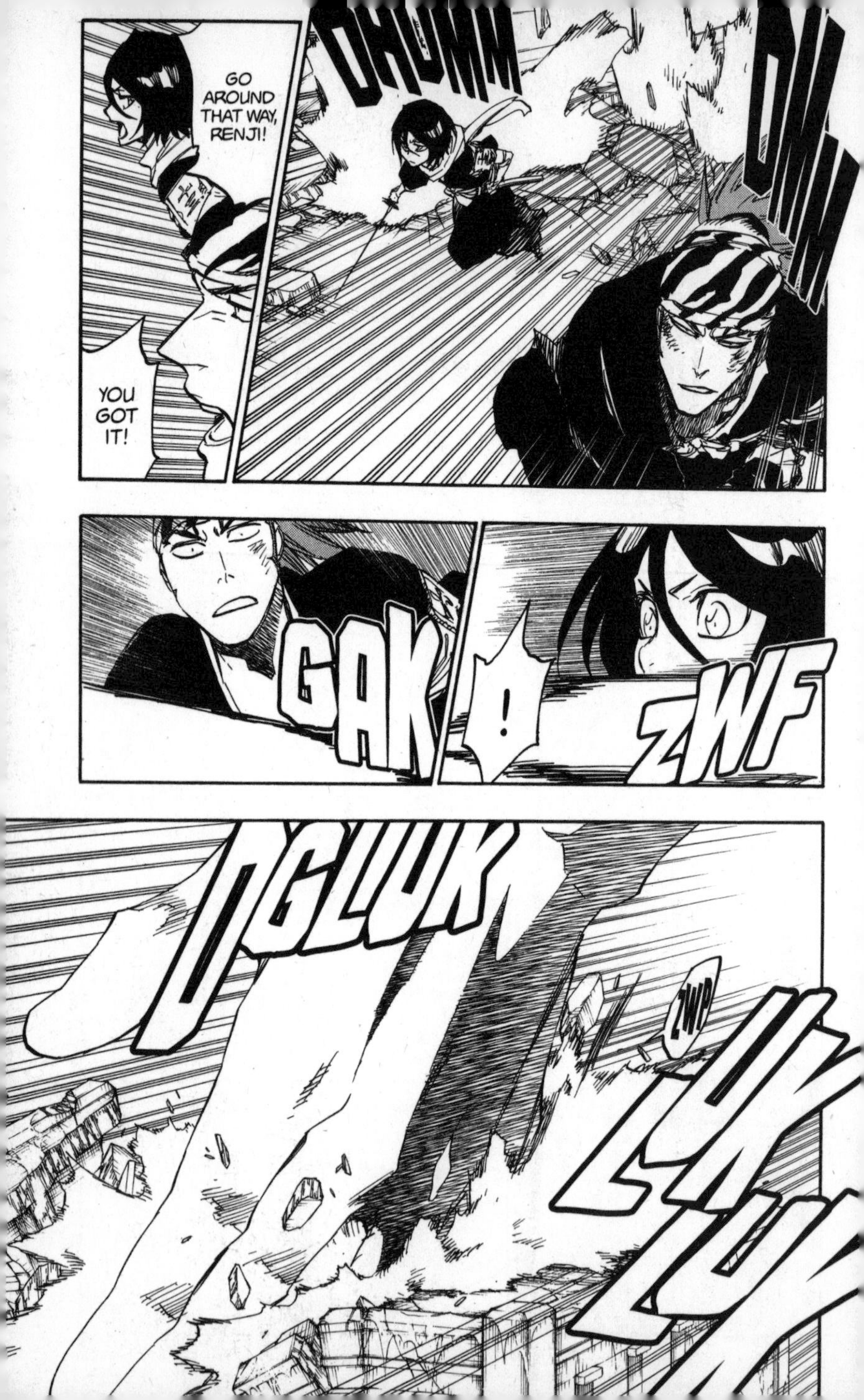
DMM
DHUMM
GO AROUND THAT WAY, RENJI!
YOU GOT IT!
ZWF
!
GAK
ZWP

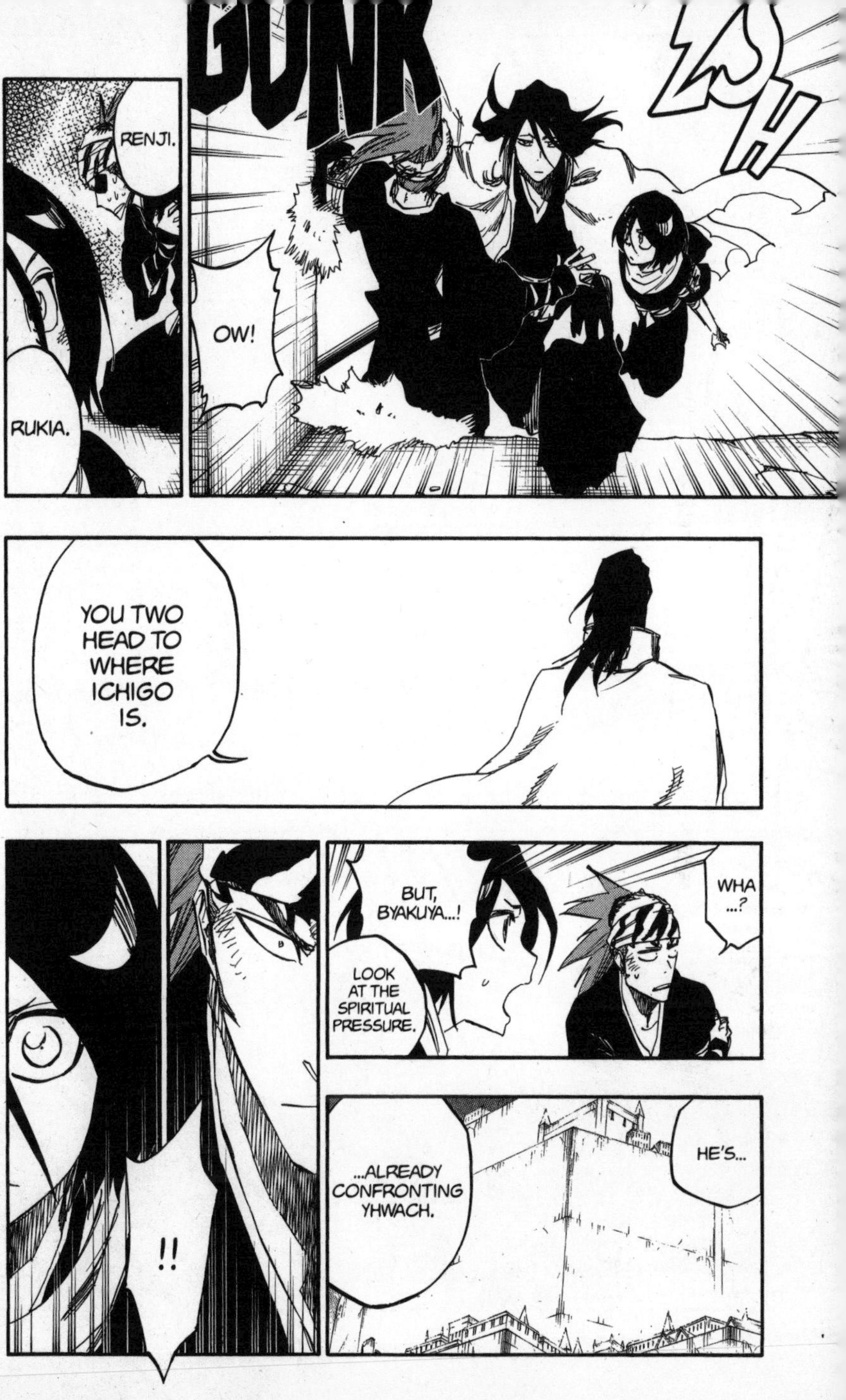
ZASH
GUNK
OW!
RENJI.
RUKIA.
YOU TWO HEAD TO WHERE ICHIGO IS.
WHA ...?
BUT, BYAKUYA...!
LOOK AT THE SPIRITUAL PRESSURE.
HE'S...
...ALREADY CONFRONTING YHWACH.
!!

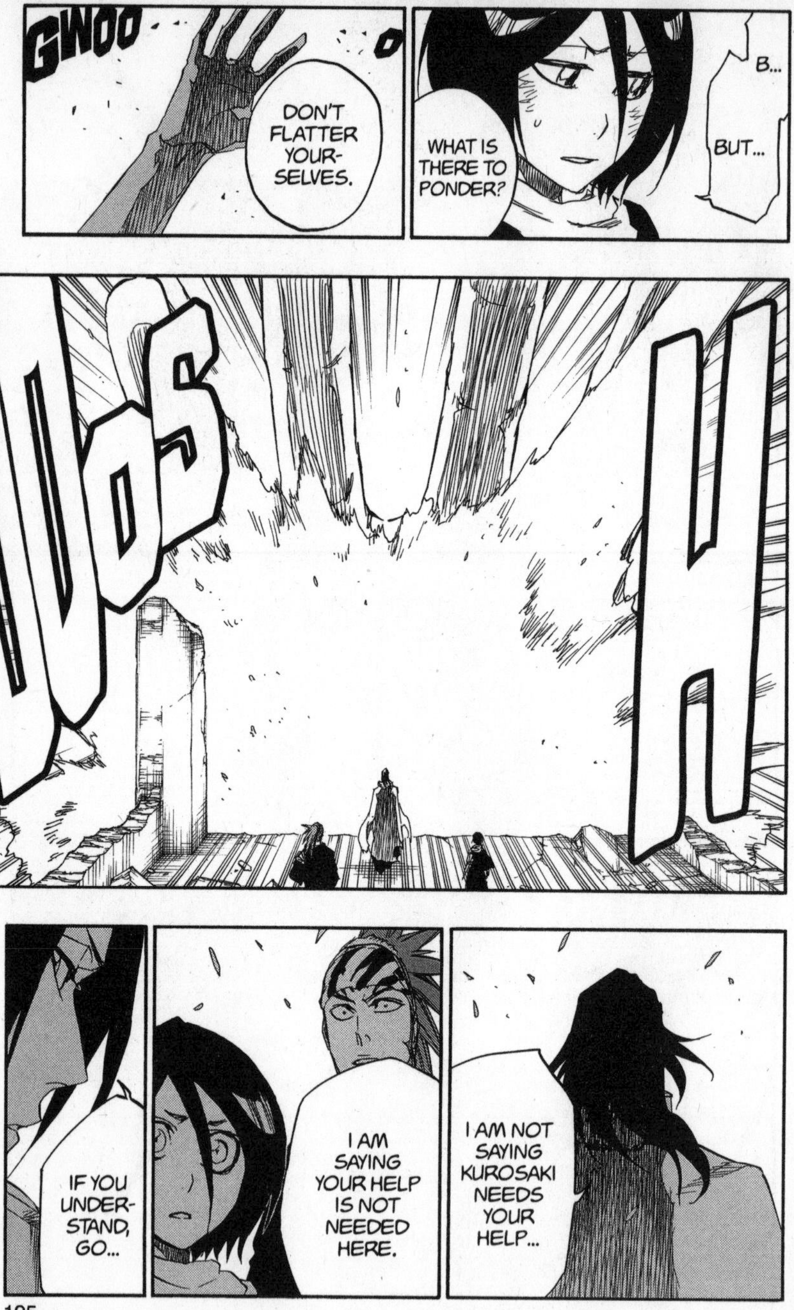
B...
BUT...
WHAT IS THERE TO PONDER?
GWOO
DON'T FLATTER YOUR-SELVES.
DOSH
I AM NOT SAYING KUROSAKI NEEDS YOUR HELP...
I AM SAYING YOUR HELP IS NOT NEEDED HERE.
IF YOU UNDER-STAND, GO...

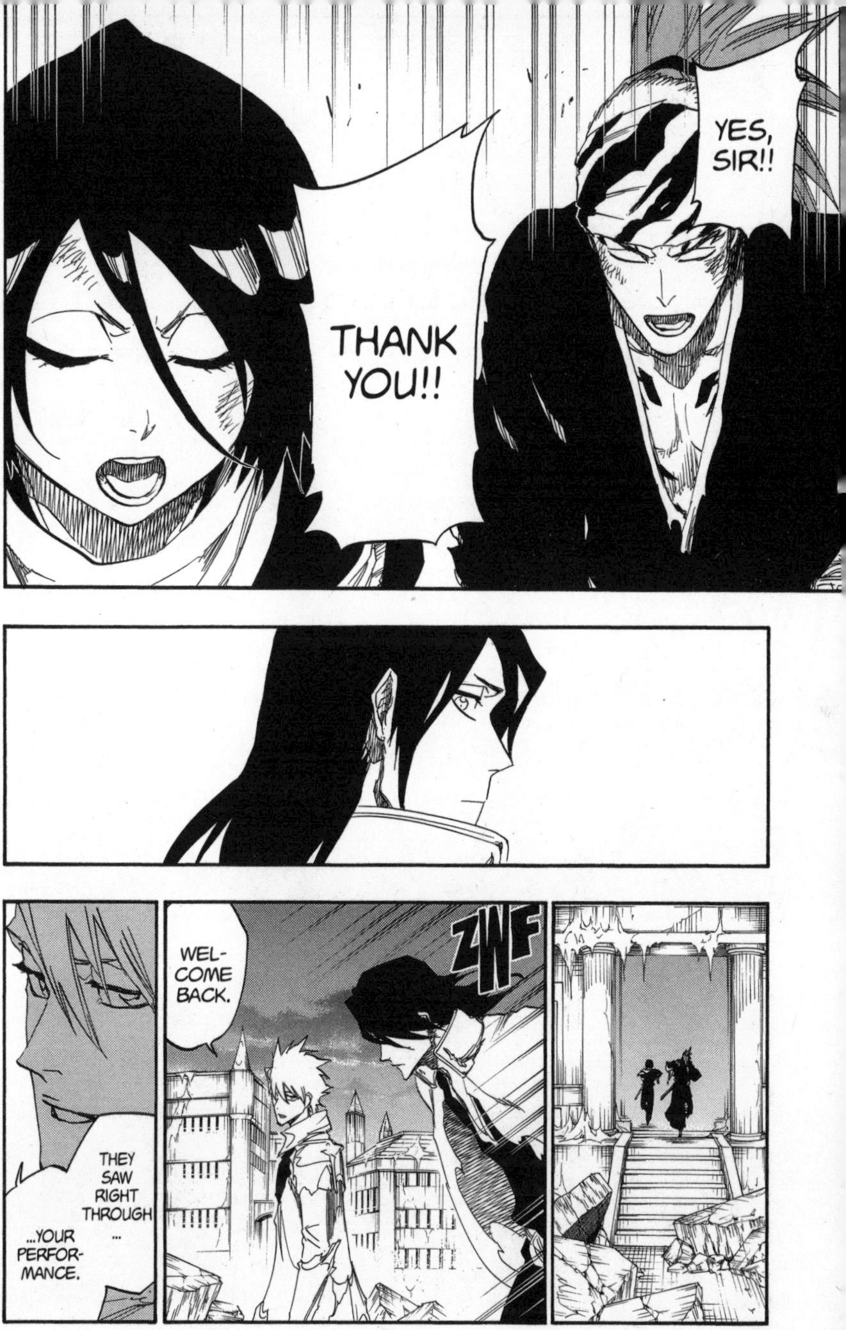
YES, SIR!!
THANK YOU!!
ZWF
WEL-COME BACK.
THEY SAW RIGHT THROUGH...
...YOUR PERFOR-MANCE.

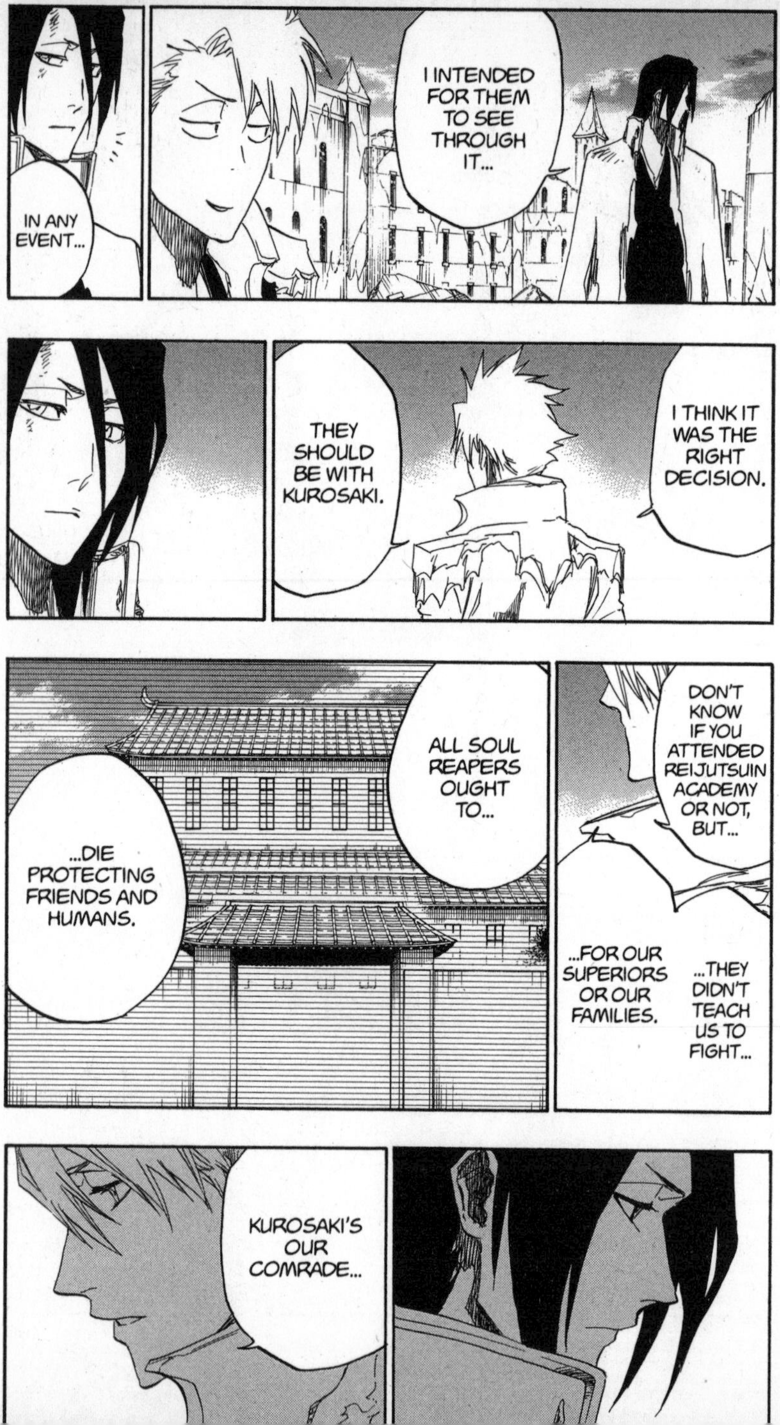
I INTENDED FOR THEM TO SEE THROUGH IT...
IN ANY EVENT...
I THINK IT WAS THE RIGHT DECISION.
THEY SHOULD BE WITH KUROSAKI.
DON'T KNOW IF YOU ATTENDED REIJUTSUIN ACADEMY OR NOT, BUT...
...THEY DIDN'T TEACH US TO FIGHT...
...FOR OUR SUPERIORS OR OUR FAMILIES.
ALL SOUL REAPERS OUGHT TO...
...DIE PROTECTING FRIENDS AND HUMANS.
KUROSAKI'S OUR COMRADE...

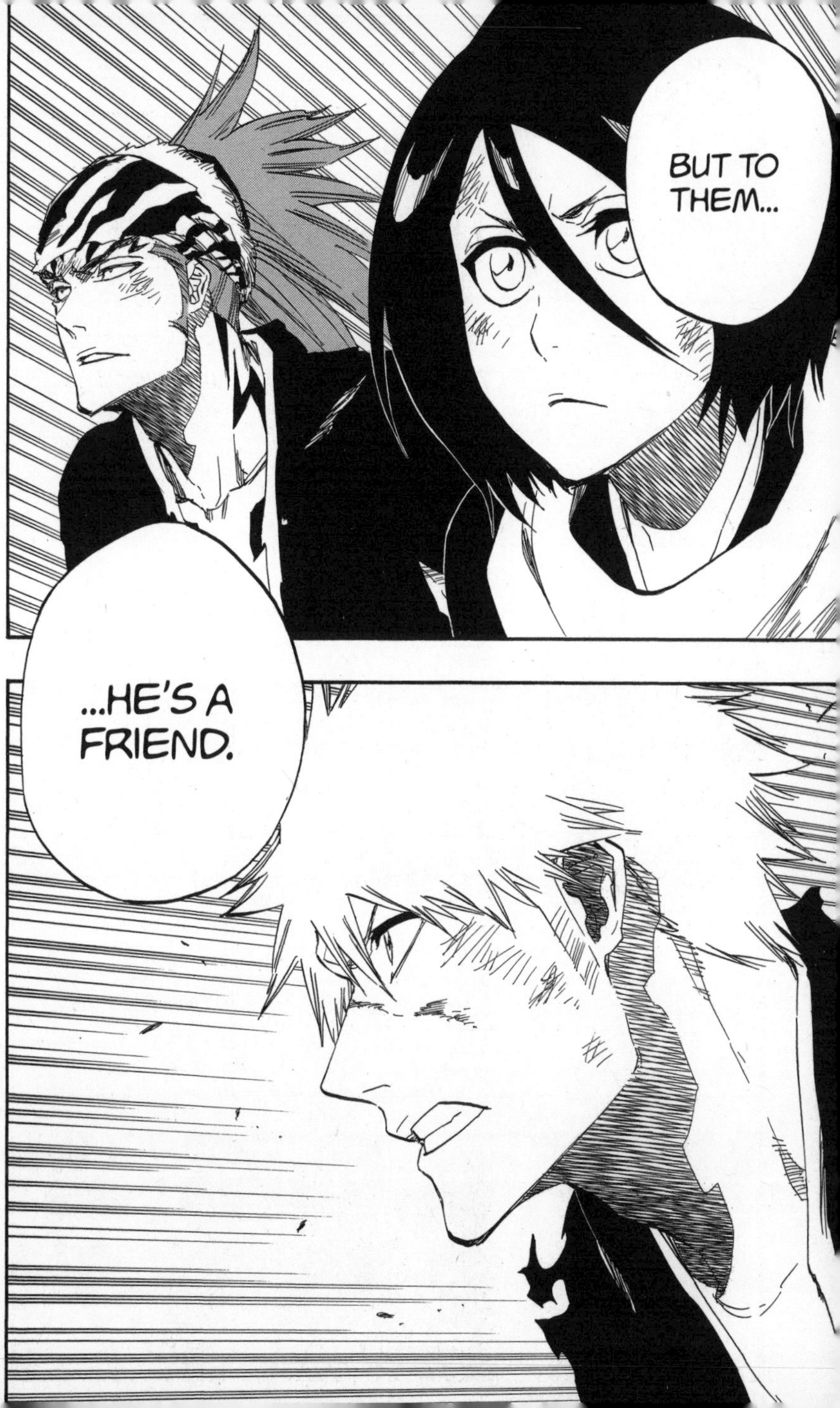
BUT TO THEM...
...HE'S A FRIEND.

READ THIS WAY

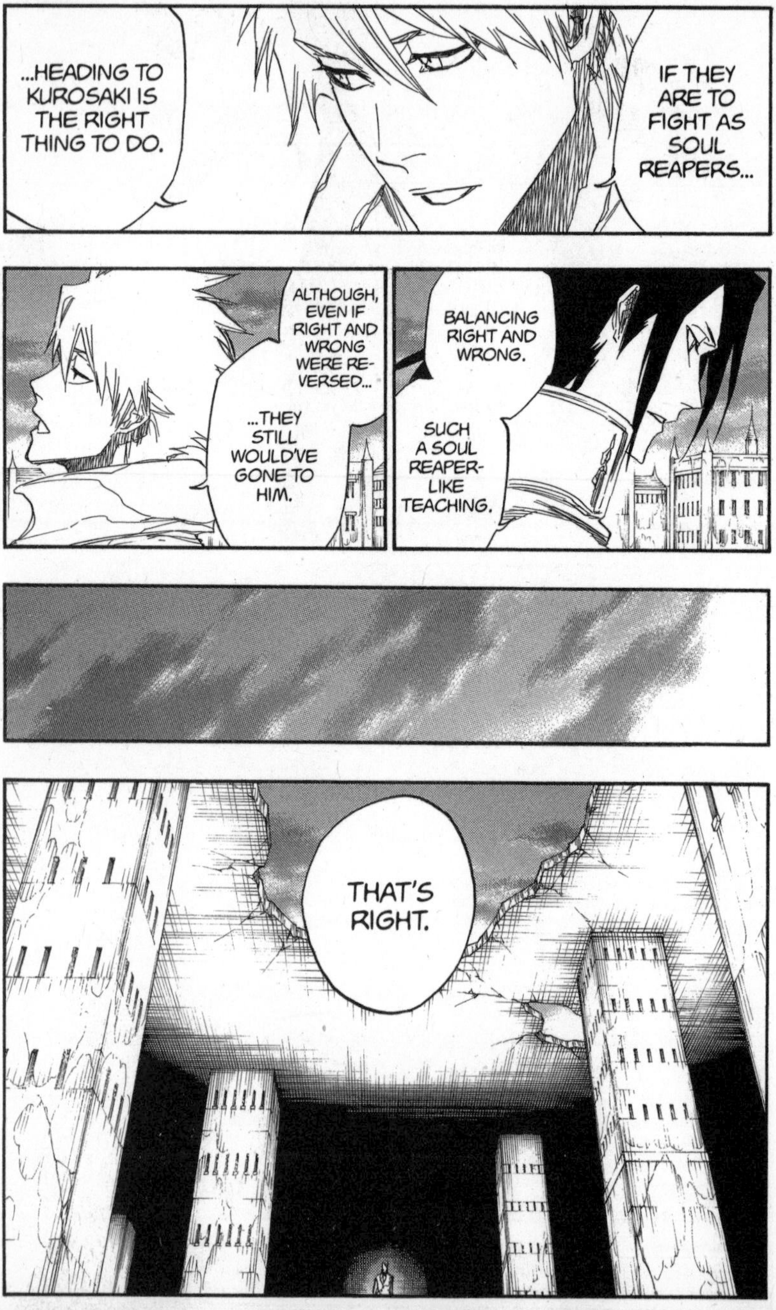
IF THEY ARE TO FIGHT AS SOUL REAPERS...
...HEADING TO KUROSAKI IS THE RIGHT THING TO DO.
BALANCING RIGHT AND WRONG.
SUCH A SOUL REAPER-LIKE TEACHING.
ALTHOUGH, EVEN IF RIGHT AND WRONG WERE RE-VERSED...
...THEY STILL WOULD'VE GONE TO HIM.
THAT'S RIGHT.

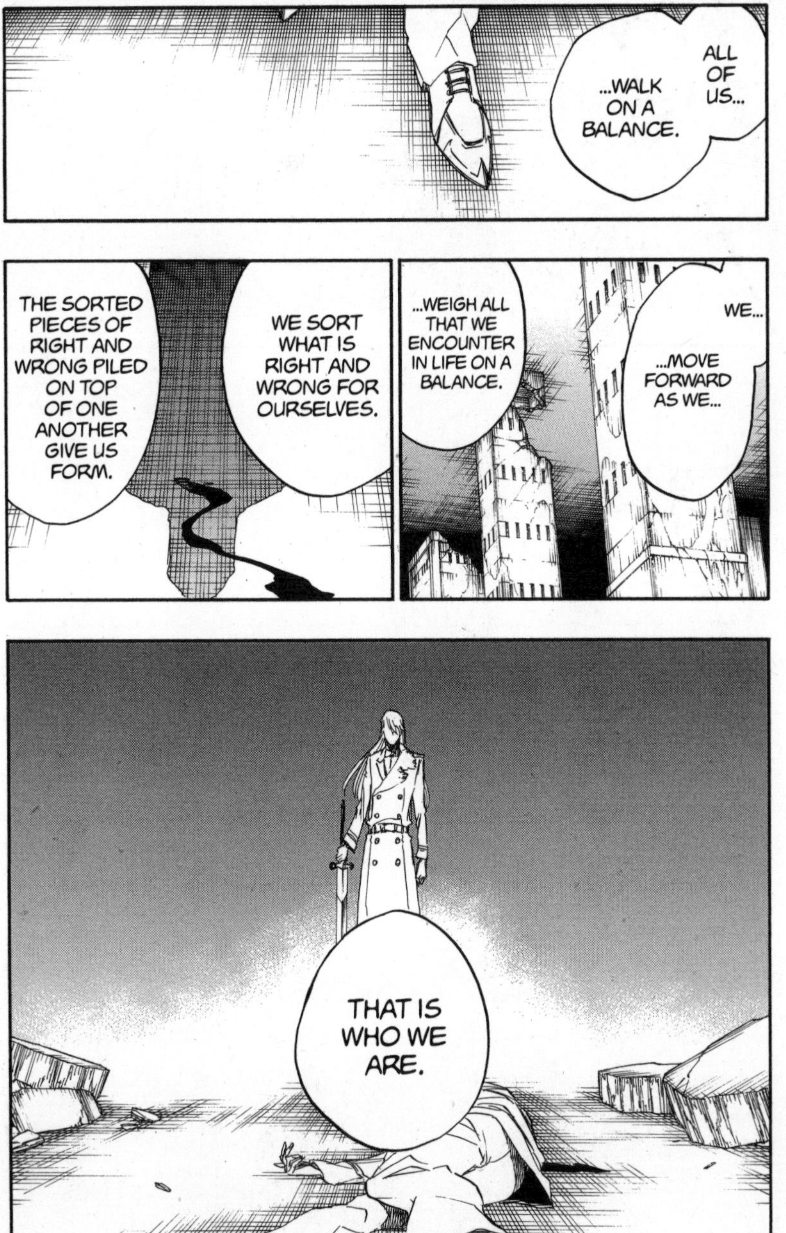
ALL OF US...
...WALK ON A BALANCE.
WE...
...MOVE FORWARD AS WE...
...WEIGH ALL THAT WE ENCOUNTER IN LIFE ON A BALANCE.
WE SORT WHAT IS RIGHT AND WRONG FOR OURSELVES.
THE SORTED PIECES OF RIGHT AND WRONG PILED ON TOP OF ONE ANOTHER GIVE US FORM.
THAT IS WHO WE ARE.

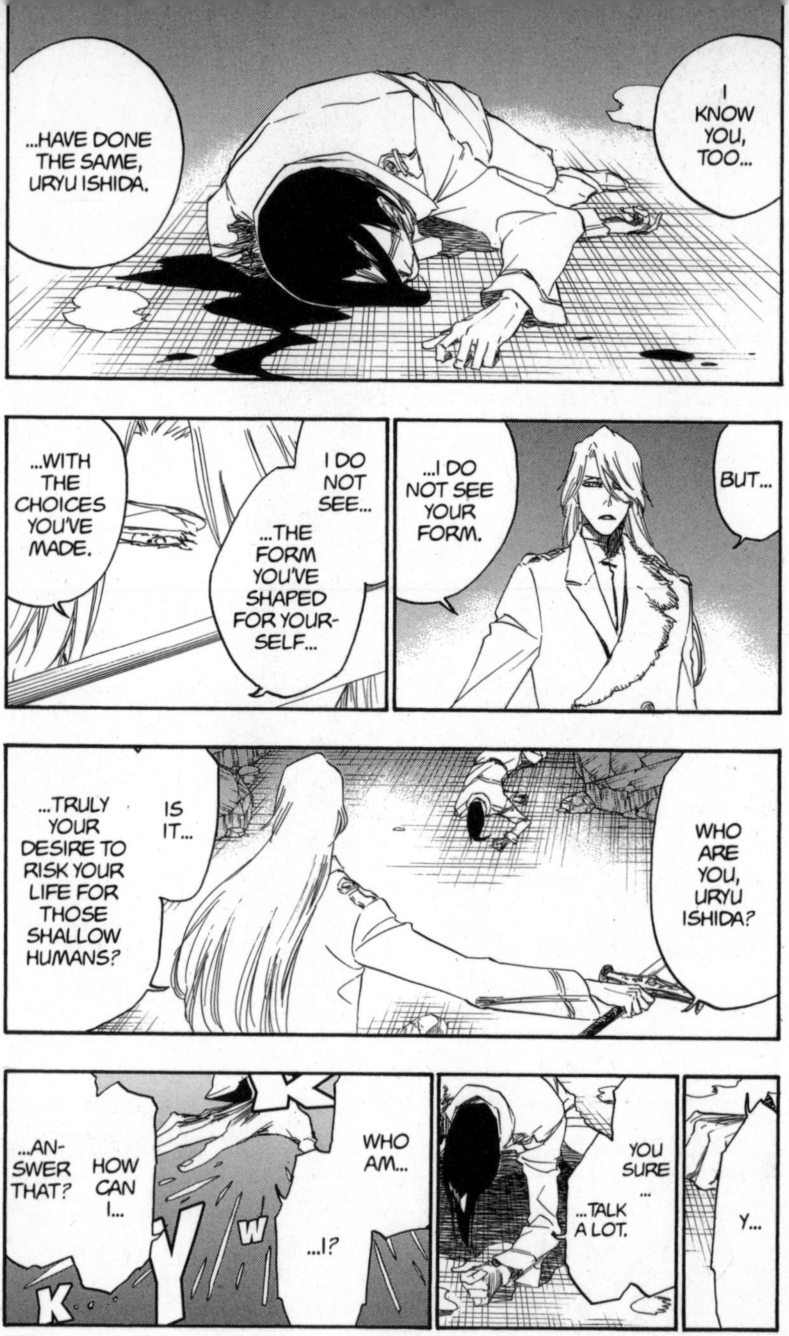
I KNOW YOU, TOO...
...HAVE DONE THE SAME, URYU ISHIDA.
BUT...
...I DO NOT SEE YOUR FORM.
I DO NOT SEE...
...THE FORM YOU'VE SHAPED FOR YOUR-SELF...
...WITH THE CHOICES YOU'VE MADE.
WHO ARE YOU, URYU ISHIDA?
IS IT...
...TRULY YOUR DESIRE TO RISK YOUR LIFE FOR THOSE SHALLOW HUMANS?
Y...
YOU SURE...
...TALK A LOT.
WHO AM...
...I?
HOW CAN I...
...AN-SWER THAT?
K
W
Y
K

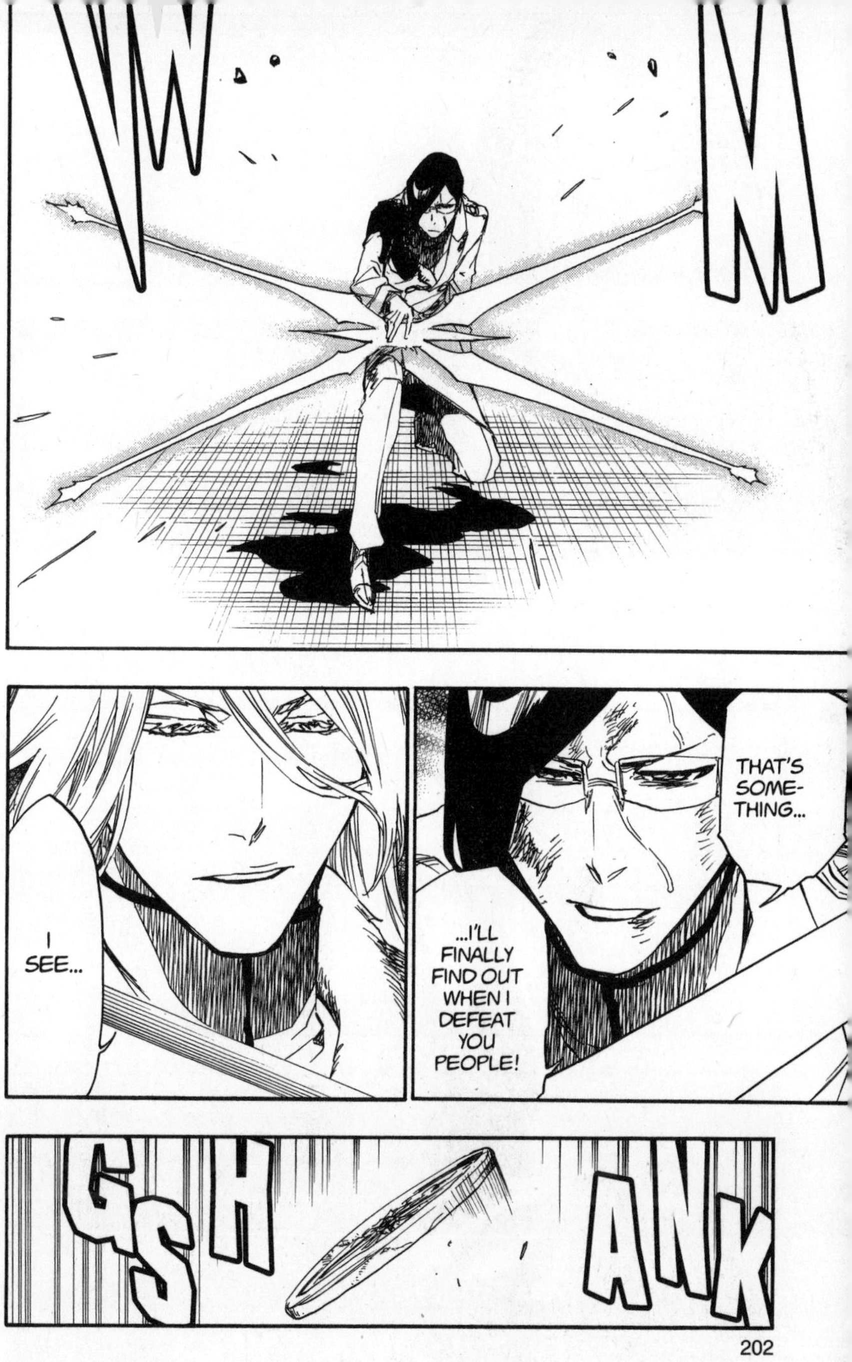
VWM
THAT'S SOMETHING...
...I'LL FINALLY FIND OUT WHEN I DEFEAT YOU PEOPLE!
I SEE...
GSHANK

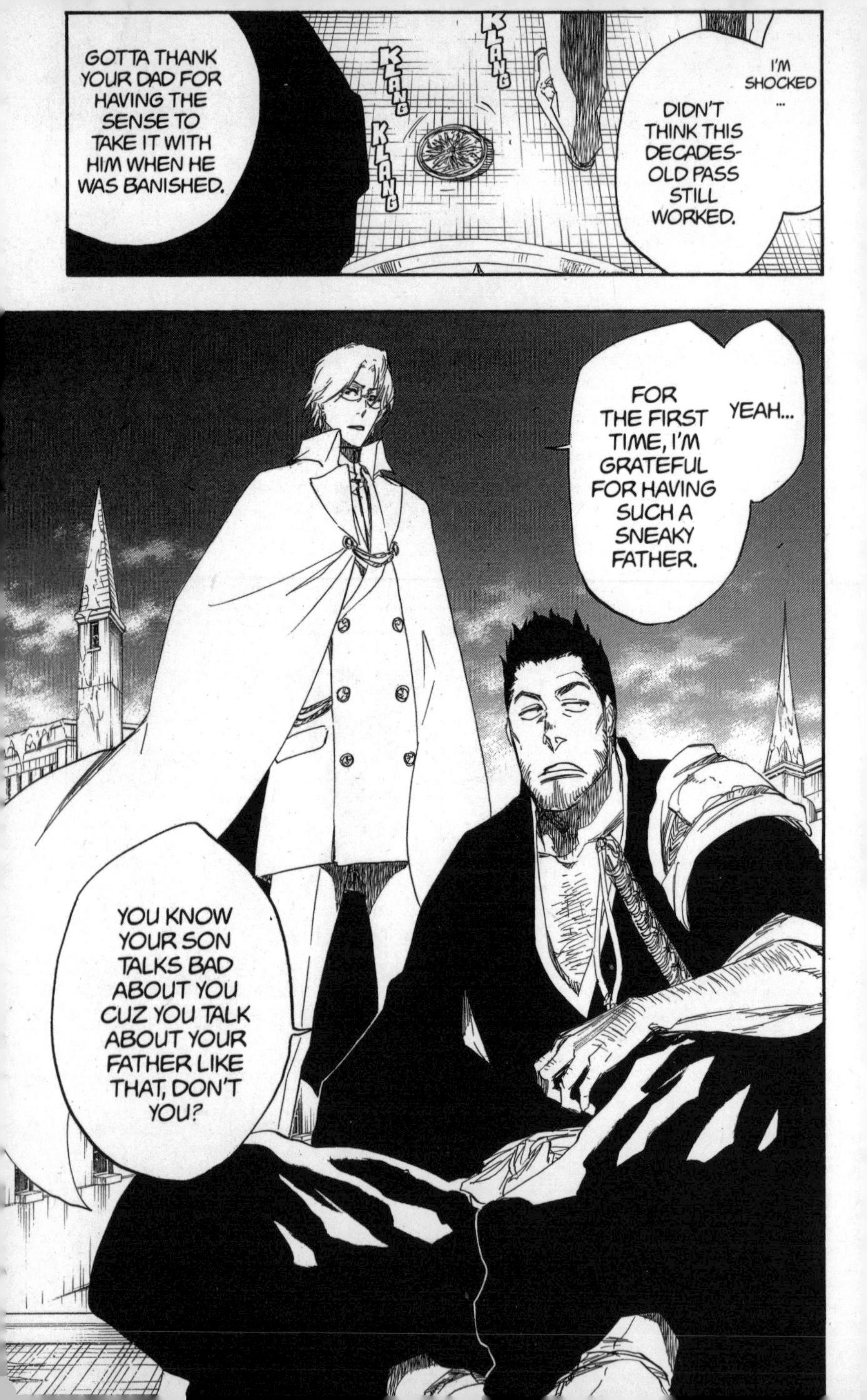
I'M SHOCKED...
DIDN'T THINK THIS DECADES-OLD PASS STILL WORKED.
KLANG
KLANG
KLANG
GOTTA THANK YOUR DAD FOR HAVING THE SENSE TO TAKE IT WITH HIM WHEN HE WAS BANISHED.
YEAH...
FOR THE FIRST TIME, I'M GRATEFUL FOR HAVING SUCH A SNEAKY FATHER.
YOU KNOW YOUR SON TALKS BAD ABOUT YOU CUZ YOU TALK ABOUT YOUR FATHER LIKE THAT, DON'T YOU?

CONTI
NUED
IN
BLEACH
74

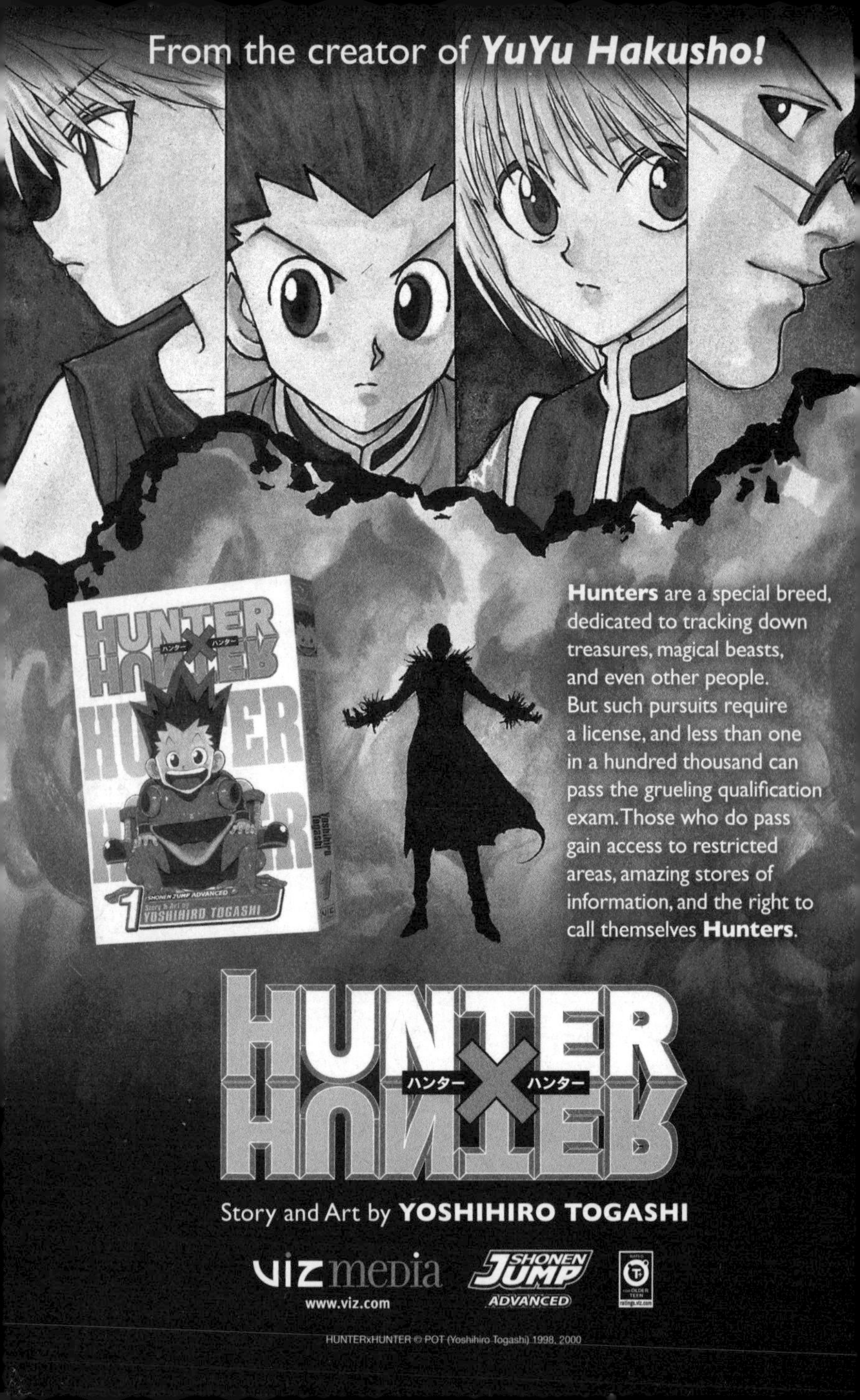
From the creator of ***YuYu Hakusho!***
Hunters are a special breed, dedicated to tracking down treasures, magical beasts, and even other people. But such pursuits require a license, and less than one in a hundred thousand can pass the grueling qualification exam. Those who do pass gain access to restricted areas, amazing stores of information, and the right to call themselves **Hunters**.
HUNTER ハンター × ハンター HUNTER
Story and Art by **YOSHIHIRO TOGASHI**
viz media
www.viz.com
SHONEN JUMP ADVANCED
HUNTERxHUNTER © POT (Yoshihiro Togashi) 1998, 2000

You're Reading ... the Wrong Way!!

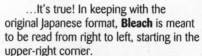

...It's true! In keeping with the original Japanese format, **Bleach** is meant to be read from right to left, starting in the upper-right corner.

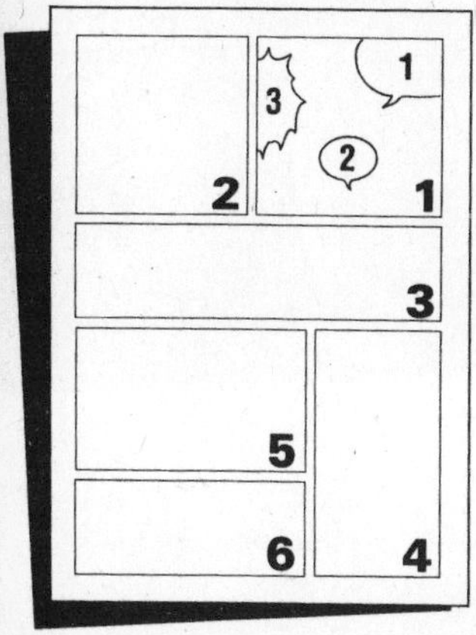

Unlike English, which is read from left to right, Japanese is read from right to left, meaning that action, sound effects and word-balloon order are completely reversed... something which can make readers unfamiliar with Japanese feel pretty backwards themselves. For this reason, manga or Japanese comics published in the U.S. in English have sometimes been published "flopped"—that is, printed in exact reverse order, as though seen from the other side of a mirror.

By flopping pages, U.S. publishers can avoid confusing readers, but the compromise is not without its downside. For one thing, a character in a flopped manga series who once wore in the original Japanese version a T-shirt emblazoned with "M A Y" (as in "the merry month of") now wears one which reads "Y A M"! Additionally, many manga creators in Japan are themselves unhappy with the process, as some feel the mirror-imaging of their art skews their original intentions.

We are proud to bring you Tite Kubo's **Bleach** in the original unflopped format. For now, though, turn to the other side of the book and let the adventure begin...!

—Editor